LYGIA PAPE

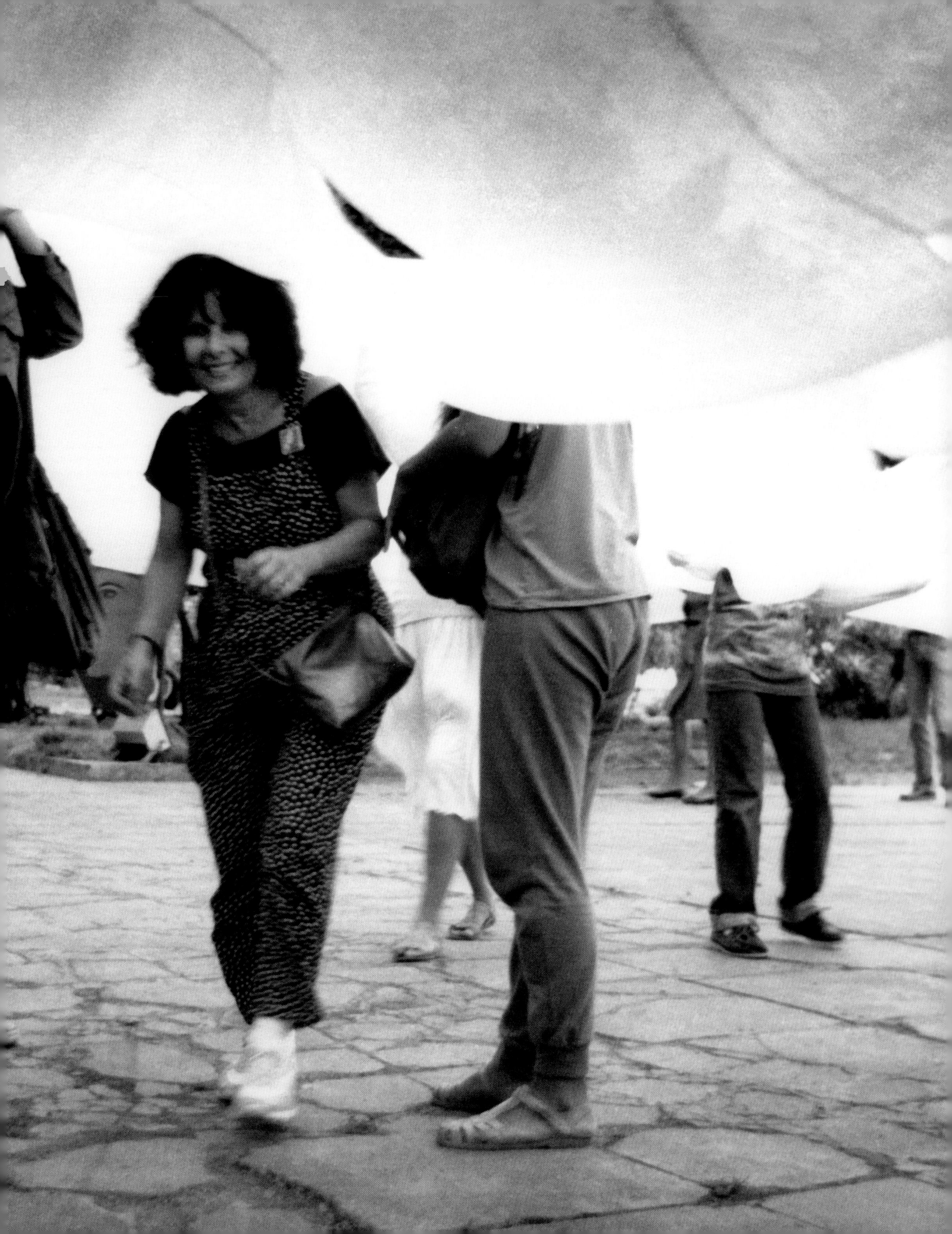

IRIA CANDELA

GLÓRIA FERREIRA

SÉRGIO B. MARTINS

JOHN RAJCHMAN

Lygia Pape

a multitude of forms

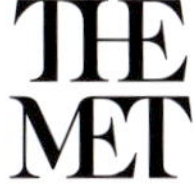

THE METROPOLITAN MUSEUM OF ART, NEW YORK

DISTRIBUTED BY YALE UNIVERSITY PRESS, NEW HAVEN AND LONDON

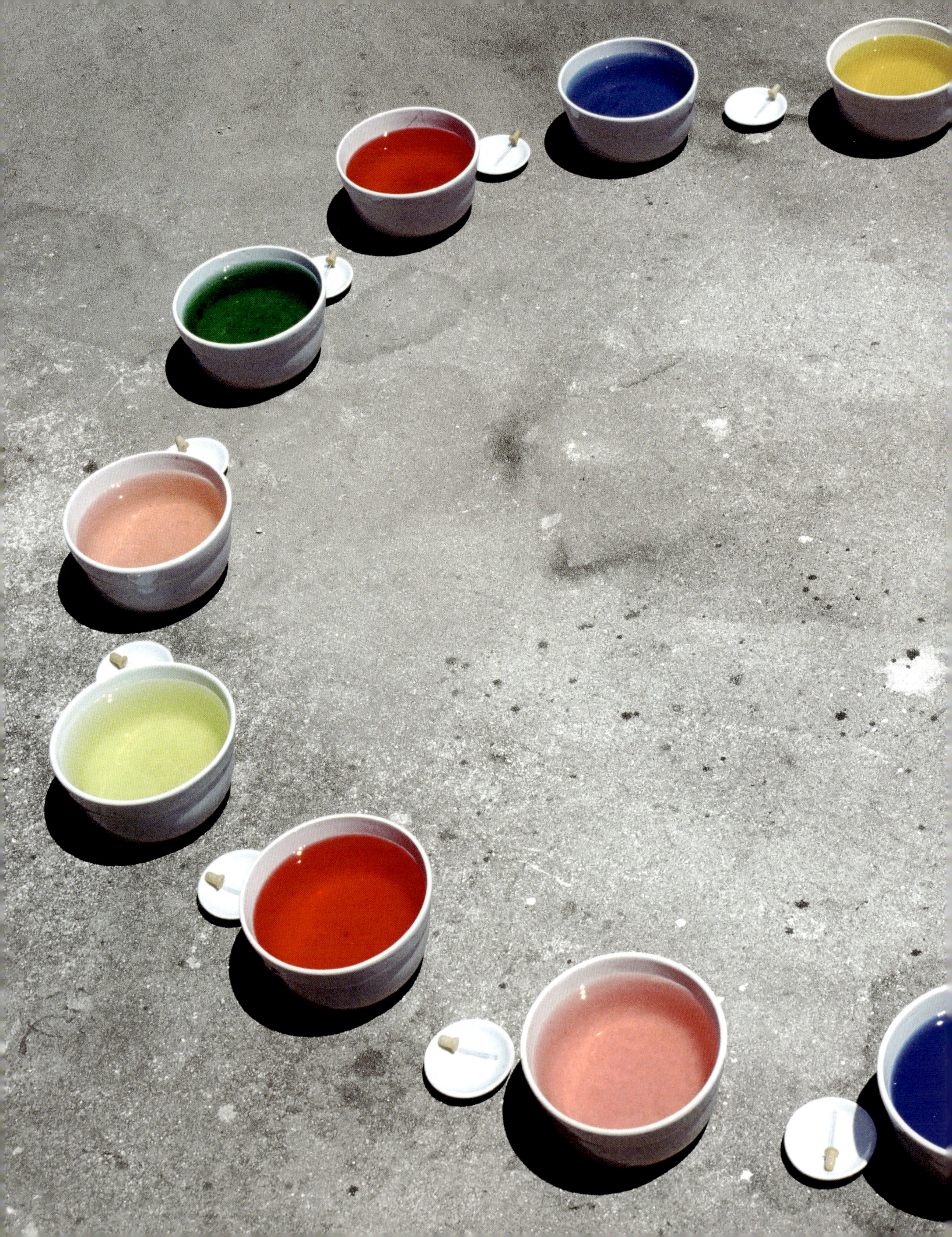

Director's Foreword

This exhibition offers the first major opportunity in the United States to experience the remarkable work of Lygia Pape, a key participant in the effervescent artistic and cultural milieu of postwar Brazil. This period of intense industrialization and progressive national development was epitomized by the inauguration in 1960 of Brasília, one of the few political capitals in the past century constructed entirely following an urban master plan. A generation of artists, architects, and designers enthusiastically embraced the optimistic and constructive spirit of the time, reworking the legacies of the European avant-garde by applying the language of abstraction to a new cultural context and social purpose. Neoconcretism, the experimental art movement founded in Rio de Janeiro in 1959 by Pape and her peers Hélio Oiticica, Lygia Clark, and others, became her most recognized legacy.

Although Pape is best known for her role in that breakthrough moment in twentieth-century art, throughout her career she explored media as varied as print, performance, sculpture, and film in a quest to expand and invigorate the normative principles of geometric abstraction. She aimed to imbue her work with a sense of time and place and what she called *vivência*, or lived experience. After a coup d'etat in 1964, when the establishment of an authoritarian regime shattered all dreams of shared prosperity in Brazil, she continued to pursue her art against the odds. Her oeuvre is testament to both her vitality and her resilience. Despite the violent events in her country, Pape envisioned Brazil as a blueprint for the multicultural society of a not-too-distant future.

As a multidisciplinary artist working outside the mainstream of Western art, Pape has not been granted the place in art history that she deserves. This long overdue presentation of her work in the United States is also the first exhibition at The Met Breuer devoted to a Latin American artist. The show is part of a broader program at The Met focusing on the extraordinary art produced in the southern part of the Western Hemisphere, much of which remains unknown to the broader public.

This exhibition was curated by Iria Candela, the first Estrellita B. Brodsky Curator of Latin American Art. The organization of the project benefited from the collaboration of the Projeto Lygia Pape in Rio de Janeiro, led by Paula Pape, to whom we are deeply grateful.

We appreciate the tremendous generosity extended by Daniel and Estrellita Brodsky in support of the exhibition. Our thanks also go to Renata and Claudio Garcia, Tanae and Claudio Ferro, Amalia and Roberto Thompson Motta, and Juliana and Francisco Sá for their dedicated commitment to the project.

THOMAS P. CAMPBELL
Director, The Metropolitan Museum of Art

Preface

When we talk about Lygia Pape, we are astonished by the complexity and extent of her oeuvre as well as the diverse materials and freedom of expression she both championed and put to use. The need to ensure a collection's physical survival is ever present. Such an act must mesh with the artist's conceptual and artistic legacy, and it is between these two points that I seek to position myself.

I grew up when the principal events of the history of contemporary Brazilian art took place, and although, at the time, I did not quite understand it all, I have armed myself with that parallel reality, which has become part of me since then. There was an aesthetic, sensorial, conceptual, and political certainty about all the artistic manifestations Lygia created in the gardens of the Museu de Arte Moderna, in the Aterro do Flamengo, in the homes of her friends and fellow artists, and in car journeys around the city. These experiences would shape me forever and determine my current relationship to Lygia Pape's archive. She was never fond of repeating herself, nor was she obsessed with formulas for success. The exploration of the creative act—the experimental exercise of freedom that critic Mário Pedrosa championed—was always the prominent and vital quest of her work.

Lygia wanted her work to be physically and conceptually cared for. In 2003, I helped her compile a list of works for a future catalogue raisonné, and in the following year, we created the Projeto Lygia Pape. Establishing the PLP was the first step; the second and more difficult task was creating the necessary conditions for maintaining the archive's integrity. There were several stages in the PLP's existence as we quickly outgrew our original location, incorporating the building next door and completing a storage facility in 2007. Since then, the PLP has become a "magnetized space" of sorts from which Lygia's concepts radiate in all directions. Recently, we had the pleasure of finding descriptive material for the unrealized exhibition "Alegria de viver, alegria de criar" ("Joy of Living, Joy of Creating"), a project developed by Mário Pedrosa and Lygia Pape. Such discoveries are particularly rewarding and reassure us that the job of retrieving the artist's lost (or little known) projects, ideas, and thoughts is extremely important.

I would like to acknowledge the unconditional support of the members of the Projeto Lygia Pape throughout all these years: Ricardo Henrique Souto Fortes, Pedro Pape Fortes, Luíza Pape Fortes, Günther Pape (deceased in 2005), and our friends and collaborators Maria Clara Amado Martins, José Mario Brandão, Antonio Leal, Astrid Suzano, Viviane Negreiros, Fernando Correa, the gallery Hauser & Wirth, and Galeria Luisa Strina.

Special thanks to Thomas P. Campbell, Sheena Wagstaff, and Iria Candela for the honor of realizing this magnificent retrospective exhibition of Lygia Pape's work at The Metropolitan Museum of Art.

PAULA PAPE
President, Projeto Lygia Pape

Acknowledgments

Lygia Pape: A Multitude of Forms traces the artistic path of one of the most remarkable artists working in Brazil in the last half century. For her seminal Neoconcrete work *Livro do tempo* (*Book of Time*), Pape designed 365 different relief pieces out of the basic geometric shape of the square, a defiant experiment conveying the capacity to invent a new form each day of the year and an affirmation that form was dependent on time. The numerous forms in varied media created during her five-decade-long career are as much a testament to her pioneering approach as to her irreverent personality and constant experimentation—as her friend Hélio Oiticica said, she was a "permanently open seed." Her interdisciplinary practice conveys her disdain for hierarchies in art as well as her belief in the creative potential of every individual.

I have been fortunate to organize this exhibition with a multitude of creative and talented individuals. First and foremost, I am indebted to the generosity and continual support of Paula Pape. Her living knowledge of her mother's work was crucial for deciphering lesser-known aspects of Lygia Pape's oeuvre. I am ever grateful to her and to Ricardo Henrique Souto Fortes and Pedro Pape Fortes for opening their home and Projeto Lygia Pape in Rio de Janeiro and for kindly giving access to the artworks and archive. At the PLP, I am also thankful to António Leal for the attention and diligence he dedicated to the successful presentation of this exhibition as well as to Astrid Suzano, Viviane Negreiros, and Fernando Correa.

Among the many individuals who encouraged or helped me with their knowledge and advice in the course of my research and exhibition development, I would like to mention Guy Brett, Estrellita B. Brodsky, Claudia Calirman, Paulo Herkenhoff, Aleca Le Blanc, Luiz Camillo Osorio, Gabriel Pérez-Barreiro, John Rajchman, and Vicente Todolí. José Mário Brandão of Galeria Graça Brandão in Lisbon and Marli Matsumoto of Galeria Luisa Strina in São Paulo kindly liaised with the PLP and with a number of lenders to this exhibition, as did Ana Sokoloff during early conversations about the show. Thanks are also due to Olivier Renaud-Clément for his advice.

This exhibition reassesses the extraordinary trajectory of a female Brazilian artist whose work remains underrepresented within Western museum collections. Lygia Pape has never had a major show in the United States, and Director Thomas P. Campbell embraced this historic opportunity from the outset with sheer conviction. I am indebted to him and to the vision of Sheena Wagstaff, Leonard A. Lauder Chairman of Modern and Contemporary Art, who enthusiastically championed this project. Their advocacy has been instrumental to presenting this exhibition at The Met Breuer. In the Director's Office I would also like to acknowledge Jennifer Russell, former Associate Director for Exhibitions, and Quincy Houghton, current Associate Director for Exhibitions, whose wise counsel was essential. I am grateful to Martha Deese and Linda Sylling for their time and diplomacy regarding many logistical and organizational matters. Amy Desmond Lamberti and Nicole Sussmane in the Counsel's Office oversaw all legal aspects concerning our collaboration with the PLP and the negotiation of major international loans.

Every exhibition is the result of a team effort, and at The Met this seems particularly true. I am privileged to have worked with many exceptional colleagues who have inspired me with their dedication and professionalism. In the Department of Modern and Contemporary Art, Pari Stave offered much appreciated help and advice on practical matters. I am particularly grateful to Tina Rivers Ryan, who expediently supported every aspect of this complex exhibition. Sally McBride, Rebecca R. Kusovitsky, Cynthia Iavarone, Anthony Askin, Jeff Elliott, Brooks Shaver, and Sandie Peters also provided vital administrative assistance. Fellows and interns have contributed their time over the course of my research, and my sincere thanks go to Sara Garzón, Nicholas Fitch, and Maria Castro. Lygia Pape would have been pleased to see her work displayed in the galleries of Marcel Breuer's building, and I would like to thank Katy Uravitch for her diligent oversight of the planning and installation of the project at The Met Breuer. Allison E. Barone expertly managed the loans, and Patrick John Paine and Ellium Roberts led the installation with skill and care.

This volume exemplifies the extraordinary quality of scholarly catalogues published by The Met's Publications and Editorial Department headed by Mark Polizzotti, Publisher and Editor in Chief, alongside Gwen Roginsky, Associate Publisher and General Manager, Peter Antony, Chief Production Manager, and Michael Sittenfeld, Senior Managing Editor. I am particularly grateful to Anne Rebecca Blood for her precise editing and thoughtful suggestions, which benefited the catalogue as a whole. Jayne Kuchna was a meticulous bibliographer and Elizabeth De Mase and Crystal A. Dombrow ensured the highest-quality photographs were acquired. Peter Antony and Lauren Knighton efficiently oversaw the production and printing of the book. Thanks are also due to Frances Malcolm, who assisted with the editing, and Briana Parker, who provided logistical support throughout the project. Stephen Anthony Berg and Philip Sutton contributed fine translations, and the catalogue's beautiful design is due to Catherine Mills, who felt inspired by the world of Pape.

I would like to thank Glória Ferreira, Sérgio B. Martins, and John Rajchman for their fresh and scholarly contributions to the catalogue and Vivian A. Crockett for compiling the most complete chronology of Lygia Pape's life and work yet published. Lúcia Carneiro, Ileana Pradilla, and Angélica de Moraes graciously allowed us to translate and reproduce their interviews with the artist, giving us the opportunity to read the artist's own voice in the English language.

An exhibition presenting work in almost all media requires the collective expertise of many conservators. Shawn Digney-Peer oversaw paintings; Kendra Roth, sculpture; and Rebecca Capua, works on paper. Nora Kennedy, Sherman Fairchild Conservator in Charge, Photograph Conservation, and Lisa Barro handled the photographs, while Paul Caro, Robin Schwalb, and Kate Farrell cared for time-based media. Margo Delidow and Eric Meier at Whryta Contemporary Art Conservation, New York, made a facsimile of the *Livro da criação* (*Book of Creation*) for visitors to handle and manipulate. Well-deserved credit is due to the team in the Design Department, led by Emile Molin, Interim Head of Design, including Brian Oliver Butterfield, Aubrey L. Knox, and Ria Roberts. Special thanks also go to Michael Langley and Yen-Wei Liu for creating an inspiring museum experience with their design for the exhibition and graphics, respectively.

Colleagues across other departments at The Met gave their invaluable time and effort to the exhibition. In Education, Sandra Jackson-Dumont, Frederick P. and Sandra P. Rose Chairman of Education, has been an effective advocate for Latin American art in the Museum. Jennifer Mock coordinated a symposium on the art and times of Lygia Pape with international experts presenting insightful responses to the ideas in the exhibition. In Concerts and Lectures, Limor Tomer, General Manager, organized the restaging of Pape's historic performance *Divisor* (*Divider*) in the streets of New York, aided by Prentiss Kwabena Slaughter, Erin Flannery, and Elysia Dawn. Alexandra Kozlakowski, Senior Press Officer, Marketing and External Relations, worked tirelessly on the communications front. In Development I would like to mention especially Jason Herrick

and Marilyn B. Hernandez for their support, ably complemented by Elizabeth A. Burke, Sarah Higby, Jessica M. Sewell, and Hillary S. Bliss. Lastly, I wish to acknowledge Barbara J. Bridgers, Juan Trujillo, and Katherine Dahab in the Imaging Department, and Elizabeth Stoneman, Chiara Ponticelli, and Lauren Gallagher in Merchandising and Retail.

An exhibition such as this is an ambitious endeavor, which was realized through the vital contribution of a committed group of donors. I am particularly grateful to Daniel and Estrellita Brodsky for their extraordinary support. My sincere thanks are also extended to Renata and Claudio Garcia, Tanae and Claudio Ferro, Amalia and Roberto Thompson Motta, Juliana and Francisco Sá, and the Projeto Lygia Pape. This exhibition would have not been possible without the generosity of many lenders, and we warmly thank our colleagues in lending institutions: Glenn Lowry, Ann Temkin, Luis Pérez-Oramas, Marissa Klein-Kundrath, Kathy Curry, Emily Cushman, and Jennifer Tobias at the Museum of Modern Art, New York; Maria de Lourdes Egydio Villela and Cecília Zuchi Vezzoni at the Museu de Arte Moderna, São Paulo; Manuel Borja-Villel, Teresa Velázquez Cortés, Victoria Fernández-Layos Moro, and Carmen Cabrera Lucio-Villegas at the Museo Nacional Centro de Arte Reina Sofía, Madrid; Miguel Lobo Antunes, José Miguel Caissotti, and Isabel Corte-Real at the Coleção Caixa Geral de Depósitos, Lisbon, Portugal; and Suzanne Cotter and Helena Abreu at the Fundação de Serralves—Museu de Arte Contemporânea, Porto, Portugal. I am also extremely grateful to private lenders: Andréa and José Olympio Pereira, Harald Orneberg Collection, Luisa Malzoni Strina, B.A.F. Collection, Estrellita and Daniel Brodsky Collection, Colección Patricia Phelps de Cisneros, Ella Fontanals-Cisneros Collection, Diane and Bruce Halle, Clarissa and Edgar Bronfman, Jr., and those who wish to remain anonymous.

IRIA CANDELA
Estrellita B. Brodsky Curator of Latin American Art
Department of Modern and Contemporary Art
The Metropolitan Museum of Art

Lenders to the Exhibition

PUBLIC COLLECTIONS
Coleção Caixa Geral de Depósitos, Lisbon, Portugal
Fundação de Serralves—Museu de Arte Contemporânea, Porto, Portugal
Museo Nacional Centro de Arte Reina Sofía, Madrid
Museu de Arte Moderna, São Paulo
Museum of Modern Art, New York

PRIVATE COLLECTIONS
B.A.F. Collection
Estrellita and Daniel Brodsky Collection
Clarissa and Edgar Bronfman, Jr.
Colección Patricia Phelps de Cisneros
Ella Fontanals-Cisneros Collection
Diane and Bruce Halle
Harald Orneberg Collection
Andréa and José Olympio Pereira
Projeto Lygia Pape
Luisa Malzoni Strina

And those who wish to remain anonymous

Contributors

IRIA CANDELA is Estrellita B. Brodsky Curator of Latin American
Art in the Department of Modern and Contemporary Art at
The Metropolitan Museum of Art, New York.

GLÓRIA FERREIRA is a professor at Escola de Belas Artes,
Universidade Federal do Rio de Janeiro.

SÉRGIO B. MARTINS is a professor in the History Department
at Pontifícia Universidade Católica do Rio de Janeiro.

JOHN RAJCHMAN is a philosopher who teaches in the Department of Art History and Archaeology at Columbia University,
New York.

LYGIA PAPE

IRIA CANDELA

the risk of invention

A crucial figure in modern and contemporary Brazilian art, Lygia Pape is commonly associated with Hélio Oiticica and Lygia Clark as the central protagonists of the Neoconcrete movement, which developed in Rio de Janeiro between 1959 and 1963 and proposed the fusion of the artistic object with life experience.[1] Yet Pape's artistic venture spans more than five decades and extends both before and after that key moment in the history of Brazilian art. Throughout her prolific career, she engaged with a wide range of media, including not only drawing, painting, poetry, film, ballet, graphic design, and sculpture, but also installation, photography, and performance. This breadth makes her a transmedia artist *avant la lettre*, unclassifiable and on occasion even elusive.

Through her work, Pape absorbed and reoriented early twentieth-century European modernism in accordance with the cultural and historical conditions of postwar Brazil, seeking the consummation of the avant-garde's primary quest of integrating art into everyday life and achieving a synthesis of the arts. In particular, she reclaimed the universal vocabulary of abstract geometric art from artists such as Kazimir Malevich (1878–1935) and Theo van Doesburg (1883–1931), among others, and adapted it into the contingent spaces of the city of Rio de Janeiro, where she lived and worked all her life. She was one of the first artists to consider the merging of the artwork with the viewer's space, a paradigm shift in twentieth-century art that manifested internationally in happenings and performance art in the 1960s. Whether making art, writing poetry, or teaching classes, Pape was always experimenting with something new, finding an original way to confront the canonical under the motivation, as she put it, of the "risk of invention."[2] Her career is less a progressive evolution of a specific style than an internal development in fits and starts, a process of continuous reinvention in which past works may also be cyclically revisited. Crucial to her remarkable contribution is the fact that Pape pursued her radical aesthetic position of fulfilling the ideals of the avant-garde while living under the military repression of a dictatorial regime that ruled Brazil from 1964 to 1985. This means that between the ages of thirty-seven and fifty-eight, during her years of personal maturity, Pape worked in a dual context of artistic and political challenge.

ORGANIZING THE EYE: THE CONCRETE PERIOD OF GRUPO FRENTE

Lygia Carvalho was born on April 7, 1927, in Nova Friburgo, in the state of Rio de Janeiro, to a middle-class family with musical sensibilities. Her father also had a fondness for birds, and Pape recalled that throughout her childhood and adolescence, dozens of parrots, toucans, and herons were loose in the house.[3] In 1949, at the age of twenty-two, she married Günther Pape, a chemist of German descent, and the two lived together in Arraial do Cabo and Petrópolis (where Pape first met artist Décio Vieira) until settling permanently in Rio de Janeiro in 1952. Pape had no classical academic training in fine art. Nevertheless, she frequented gatherings of artists in Rio, including those organized by Ivan Serpa, who by that time had started giving classes at the Museu de Arte Moderna (MAM-RJ), then housed in the Ministry of Education and Health (later the Ministry of Education, MEC).[4]

After the Second World War, Pape witnessed Brazil's intense industrialization and modernization, which produced profound social and cultural changes, including transformations in the country's main cities and even the creation of a new nation's capital, Brasília (fig. 1). The construction of the city of Brasília between 1956 and 1960 epitomized the reimagining of Brazil and President Juscelino Kubitschek's promise of "fifty years of progress in five." Yet the promise was short lived, and the risk of the invention of history materialized in the country's regression after the coup d'etat of 1964.

During this period after the war, Pape took part in a moment of artistic effervescence that sought to invigorate Brazilian art, which clung to figuration and lacked any tradition of abstraction. The nonfigurative artistic tendency that had begun in the 1910s with Neoplasticism in the Netherlands and Suprematism in Russia spread through Europe in the 1930s and 1940s, becoming redefined by Van Doesburg as Concrete art.[5] As they did in other countries in Latin America, Concrete art and Constructivism took root in Brazil between 1947 and 1951 owing to a combination of factors. New galleries opened and there emerged a generation of Brazilian art critics with an internationalist aspiration, Mário Pedrosa among them. Yet what really facilitated artistic exchange was the opening of three museums: the Museu de Arte de São Paulo in 1947, which held an exhibition on Max Bill in 1950; the Museu de Arte Moderna, São Paulo (MAM-SP), in 1948, which hosted a show the following year entitled "Do figurativismo ao abstracionismo" ("From Figurativism to Abstractionism"); and the Museu de Arte Moderna, Rio de Janeiro, in 1948. The inauguration of the Bienal de São Paulo in 1951 also allowed for a profound revision of aesthetic values.

In 1952 the Concrete art movement Grupo Ruptura was founded in São Paulo, and in 1954 Grupo Frente was formed in Rio de Janeiro by Aluísio Carvão, Lygia Clark, Lygia Pape, Ivan Serpa, and Décio Vieira, among others, who were joined the following year by Hélio Oiticica, Abraham Palatnik, Franz Weissmann, and others.[6] In jubilant protest the Grupo Ruptura manifesto vehemently proclaimed, "There is no more continuity!"[7] Writing in 1955, Pedrosa summed up the principles of Grupo Frente on the occasion of their second exhibition, the 2a Mostra do Grupo Frente, held at the MAM-RJ.

> They are all men and women of faith, convinced of the revolutionary, regenerating mission of art. . . . Such a stance does not mean they endorse the ridiculous Parnassian principle of so-called art for art's sake. To them, art is not an activity of parasites, nor is it at the service of the lazy rich or political

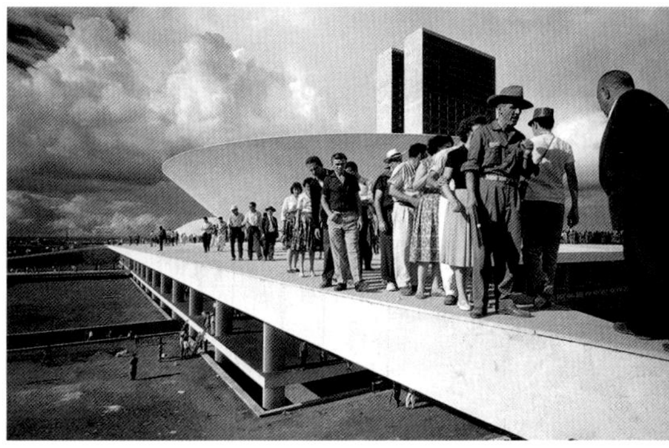

FIG. 1. Thomaz Farkas (Brazilian, 1924–2011). People on the roof of the National Congress on the day of the inauguration of Brasília, April 21, 1960. Photograph. Instituto Moreira Salles, Brazil

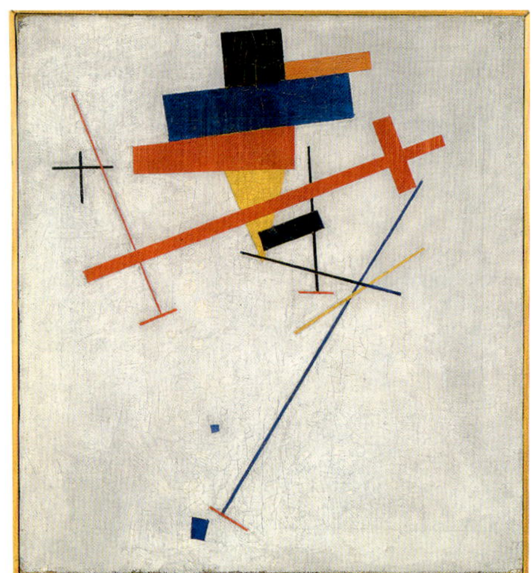

causes of the paternalistic state. An autonomous and vital activity, it aspires to an exalted social mission, namely to give the age style and to transform men, teaching them to fully exercise their senses and to shape their own emotions.[8]

Working with an abstract vocabulary based on simple geometric shapes and primary colors, artists in both groups sought a symbolic and practical way to create new forms from new principles. In addition, the artists' identification with mathematical languages and machine aesthetics was aligned with the phenomenon of developmentalism, an impulse in which art and design, like architecture, were meant to play an active role in the modernization of Brazil.

Pape demonstrated her rigorous adherence to the ideals of Grupo Frente with the paintings and reliefs she produced between 1954 and 1956. Executed on thin panels of fiberboard, the paintings are a standard size of 15¾ by 15¾ inches (40 by 40 centimeters). On a neutral white background, she painted combinations of lines, stripes, and squares, mainly in primary colors (red, blue, and yellow) or black. These compositions are reminiscent of Suprematist paintings by Malevich, such as *Suprematist Composition* (fig. 2), in which the Russian artist used pure forms and colors to represent the dynamics of organisms and planets by way of a new realism in painting, freed from imitative art.[9] Pape also sought a pure universal vocabulary that would relate to reality beyond its objective surface. She made optical games out of dynamic compositions of geometric forms, presenting her works as tools for training the eye and organizing the gaze according to the expanded parameters of sight offered by modern technology.

In her reliefs of this period—the *Relevos* and *Tarugos*—Pape also pursued a geometric aesthetic, creating formations of abstract motifs under a more rigid and structured order in which repetition stemmed from a firm affinity with industrial patterns. Technically, in fact, the reliefs looked machine-made, with hardly any intervention by the artist's hand except to arrange the small wood cutout squares, triangles, or filaments on the square fiberboards mounted on wood frames with a thickness of approximately 2 inches (5 centimeters).[10] On *Relevo* from 1955 (pl. 21), the sides are painted bright blue to contrast with the white on the front, heightening the autonomy of the work, which optically looks like a protuberance on the wall. The front-versus-side dynamic reflects Pape's desire to question the two-dimensional convention of the picture plane, something her Argentinian neighbors of the Arte Madí movement had started to explore the previous decade with their use of relief elements, the discarded frame, and the shaped canvas.[11]

TECELARES OR THE BREAKTHROUGH OF NEOCONCRETISM

It was not until 1979 that Pape used the term *Tecelares* in reference to the prints, mainly woodcuts, she had produced between 1955 and 1960.[12] In 1950s Brazil, woodcut printing was a popular practice seen as more of a craft than an art, and it was linked to folk representations with an expressionist aesthetic. Inverting the hierarchy, Pape made the woodcut the principal medium for channeling the constructive preoccupations of Concrete artists. As Adele Nelson explains, Pape considered herself not a printmaker but an avant-garde artist, and although she took part in print exhibitions in the course of that decade, she criticized the concepts of the medium that prevailed among her contemporaries and reconceived the print as a "contingent original rather than the finite product of a reproducible technical process."[13]

A 1958 photograph shows a young Pape working in her studio in the Jardim Botânico district of Rio de Janeiro (fig. 3). Sitting on the floor, she is testing the configuration of a variety of cutout shapes that were blueprints of a sort for the different woodblocks. At the forefront of her earliest prints is the visual confrontation between figure and background, which is a basic tenet of the Gestalt theory espoused by Grupo Frente. *Tecelar* from 1956 (pl. 28), for example, presents a composition based on black stripes and triangles on a white background in which the use of the mirror effect suggests a certain fluctuation between what is figure and what is background.

By 1957 Pape had relinquished the figure/ground dialectic in her prints to focus on a spatial investigation about the ambivalence of perception as part of the larger search for what was to become a crucial postulate of Neoconcretism: the design of a space that could virtually, then physically, activate the viewer. That moment coincided with a trip she took with her husband to Europe, where she visited the Ulm School of Design in Germany and studied Renaissance painting in Italy. Dating from that time are the *Tecelares* with black backgrounds and designs based on geometric sequences formed by fine white parallel lines, as seen in *Tecelar* from 1957 (pl. 38). Here the multiplication and profusion of white lines blur the distinctness of the black plane, causing the visual narrative of opposing planes to dismantle.[14] In these *Tecelares* black is "printed colour—surface—virtual space," while white is "no colour—light—real space."[15] This dramatic use of black and white in the Neoconcrete *Tecelares* recalls the style of Oswaldo Goeldi, a Brazilian printmaker and illustrator whom Pape and her husband much admired. In Goeldi's *O ladrão* (*The Thief*; fig. 4), white is envisaged as light and represents space within the plane. From Goeldi's prints Pape also learned to appreciate the organic textures resulting from the veins and pores of the wood, as is evident in *Tecelar* from 1960 (pl. 51), in which different qualities and effects were obtained by sanding the surface of the blocks before making the print.[16]

When she wrote about these works two decades later, Pape explained that her choice of medium had less to do with the traditional techniques used by engravers and printers than with the true sense of her work at that time, which was oriented toward spatial investigation: "Space being warped; yarn weaving space; the principle of ambiguity, no privileged position for a base or bottom . . . , surface pared down to black as colour, and the wood's pores acting as vibration to the point of reaching total white."[17] In this way, the later *Tecelares* were the fundamental vehicle for the consolidation of Pape's theoretical and visual transition between

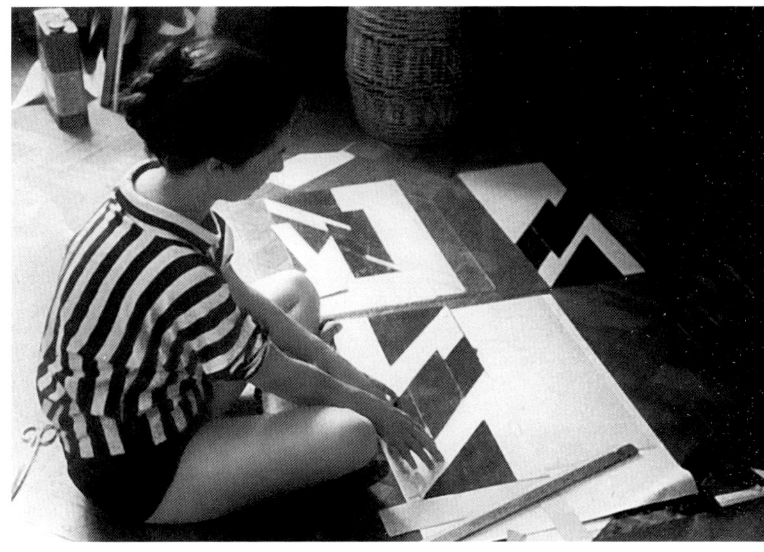

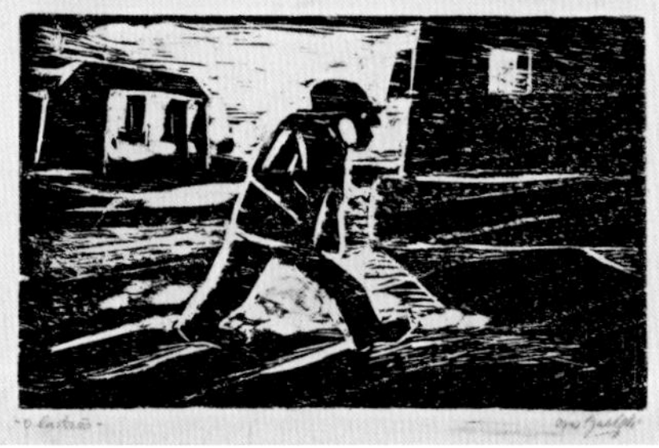

FIG. 3. Lygia Pape working on a *Tecelar* in her studio, Jardim Botânico, Rio de Janeiro, 1958. Projeto Lygia Pape

FIG. 4. Oswaldo Goeldi (Brazilian, 1895–1961). *O ladrão* (*The Thief*), ca. 1930. Woodcut, 6½ × 9¾ in. (16.6 × 24.9 cm). Projeto Goeldi, Taubaté, Brazil

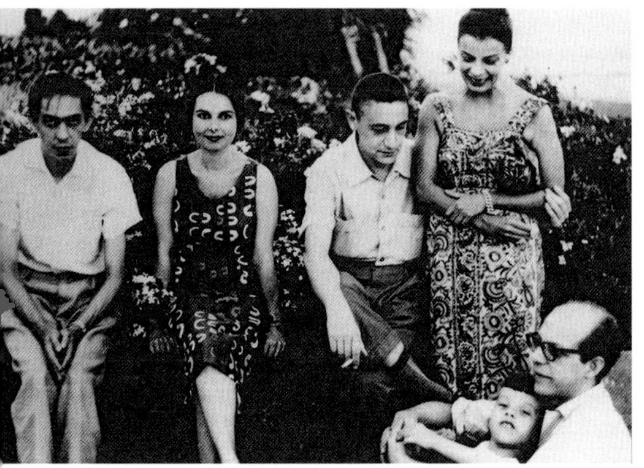

FIG. 5. Ferreira Gullar, Lygia Pape, Theon Spanúdis, Lygia Clark, and Reynaldo Jardim, Museu de Arte Moderna, Rio de Janeiro, 1959

Concretism and Neoconcretism, taking her from "the traditional organization of the category 'printmaking' to real space—a phenomenological transition."[18]

In 1957 there were signs of tension between Grupo Frente and Grupo Ruptura as a result of the 1a Exposição de Arte Concreta, held at the MAM-SP in December 1956 and at the MAM-RJ in February the following year. The disagreement was over the practical application of the Constructivist-Concrete vocabulary: while the *Paulistas* of São Paulo were orthodox in their adherence to its theoretical and scientific precepts, the *Cariocas* of Rio de Janeiro were less strict, more empirical, "almost romantics."[19]

This friction lead to the formation of the Neoconcrete movement, marked by the opening of the 1a Exposição Neoconcreta at the MAM-RJ in March 1959 and the publication of the "Manifesto neoconcreto" in the *Suplemento dominical* of the *Jornal do Brasil*. Between 1956 and 1961, this supplement, edited by the poet Reynaldo Jardim, provided an active platform for the dissemination of European avant-garde and Brazilian Neoconcrete essays. Penned by the poet and writer Ferreira Gullar, the "Manifesto neoconcreto" was underwritten by artists and poets Amilcar de Castro, Lygia Clark, Reynaldo Jardim, Lygia Pape, Theon Spanúdis, and Franz Weissmann (fig. 5).[20] The manifesto assailed the "dangerously rationalist exacerbation" of the Ruptura artists, calling for a reinterpretation of the expressive achievements of geometric art that would prioritize the artwork over theory and seek above all "the total integration of art into everyday life."[21] In a statement that echoes the complex theoretical legacy of the European avant-garde, the Neoconcrete artists declared:

> The Concrete rationalists continue to view the individual as a machine among other machines. . . . We do not envision an artwork either as a "machine," or as an "object" but as a *quasi-corpus*, i.e. a being whose reality is not limited to the exterior relations of its elements. . . . Notions of time, space, form, color—that did not preexist as notions for the work—are so intensely integrated that it would be impossible to speak of them in decomposable terms. Neo-Concrete art asserts the absolute integration of these elements and believes that the "geometric" vocabulary it utilizes can render the expression of complex human realities.[22]

In that same edition of the *Suplemento dominical*, Pape published her article "Ballet: Experiência visual" ("Ballet: A Visual Experience"), a reflection on her own *Ballet neoconcreto I*, which was staged at the Teatro Copacabana Palace in Rio de Janeiro on the evening of August 18, 1958. The ballet is based on a poem by Jardim in which the words *olho* (eye) and *alvo* (target) are arranged in different variations, like the dance steps of a choreographic score. For the ballet, Pape built four white cylindrical structures, each two meters tall and eighty centimeters in diameter, to represent the word *olho*, and four orange parallelepiped volumes of similar dimensions for *alvo* (fig. 6). Eight dancers remained hidden inside the geometric volumes throughout the performance, using small airholes to breathe, while dramatic lighting and the piano music of Gabriel Artusi enlivened the austere choreography on the bare stage. As the artist recalled, "it was magnificent suddenly to see a cylinder advance across the middle of the stage, the other shapes stationary beside them, and a red light make that white cylinder incandescent, set it ablaze. There was an exclamation of dazzled surprise from the stalls. It was a magical, grandiose spectacle."[23]

The performance in a way recalled the experimental ballets of the European avant-garde, from Kazimir Malevich's *Victory over the Sun* (1913) to Oskar Schlemmer's *Triadic Ballet* (1922), in which geometricized choreographies and Cubo-Futurist costumes were a metaphor for man mechanized by modern technology. Fernand Léger even theorized the notion of a ballet without dancers, the result of what he saw as the preponderance of the object in contemporary life. According to him, the realist ballet had reached its zenith, and it was necessary to pass on "to a different plane where the star is absorbed into the plastic ranks, where a mechanical choreography closely connected to its own scenery and music attains a whole, planned unity; . . . where the spectacle's charm encompasses the entire stage."[24] This idea was taken up again in the kinetic experiments of Alexander Calder's series of "ballet-objects" (1930s) and in Nicolas Schöffer's autonomous cybernetic sculpture *CYSP 1* (fig. 7). In "Ballet: Experiência visual," Pape criticizes Schöffer's automaton for not constituting an independent dancing subject that is expressive in its own right, since it merely illustrated the stage while the dancers performed a conventional ballet.[25] As a reconceptualization of the ballet space vis-à-vis the Neoconcretist postulates, *Ballet neoconcreto I* denied the presence of the dancers on the stage, trapped as they were inside abstract volumes that moved on wheels. "The Neo-Concrete experiment of energizing space, conveying equal values to positive-negative," wrote the artist, "gives us an organic integration: space between solids becomes form in a continuing logical development, lending it new meaning, poetic meaning even."[26]

THE BODY AND THE *LIVRO DA CRIAÇÃO*

Despite the goal of a plastic synthesis, the reference to the human body in *Ballet neoconcreto I* is obvious. Indeed, its presence is inevitable given that "there was only the motor of the body to move things along."[27] While *Ballet neoconcreto I* presented a ballet without dancers, the *Livro da criação* (*Book of Creation*), begun the following year, was a book without words. Central to both is the body's interaction with the abstract work, which was the culmination of the Neoconcretists' emphasis on life experience.

The *Livro da criação* is a dossier of sixteen loose leaves of cardboard painted with gouache that illustrates the history of creation in sixteen phases, such as "Man Began to Measure Time" and "Man Invented the Wheel," using basic abstract or symbolic forms. Each leaf is cut and folded, rather like a piece of origami or a page from a pop-up book, and the various flaps and folds can be manipulated to emerge from the plane into three-dimensional space. For example, the episode of "The Water Later Went Down, Down, Down" has three blue flaps superimposed at different heights that enact the withdrawal of the sea when the reader opens them. No single "page" of the book has a privileged orientation, and some were designed to be counterposed to a background. "Light," for instance, has a square orifice to let in

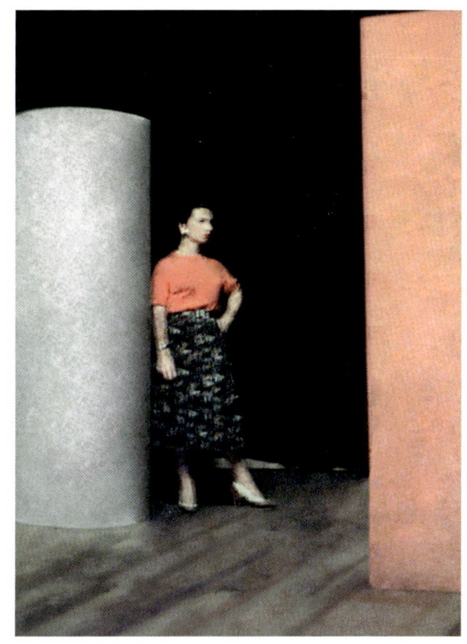

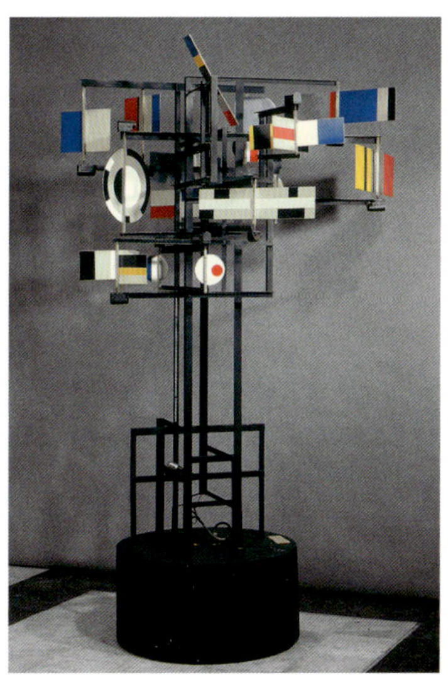

FIG. 6. Lygia Pape with set of *Ballet neoconcreto I*, Teatro Copacabana Palace, Rio de Janeiro, August 1958. Projeto Lygia Pape

FIG. 7. Nicolas Schöffer (Hungarian, 1912–1992). *CYSP 1*, 1956. Mixed media. Private collection

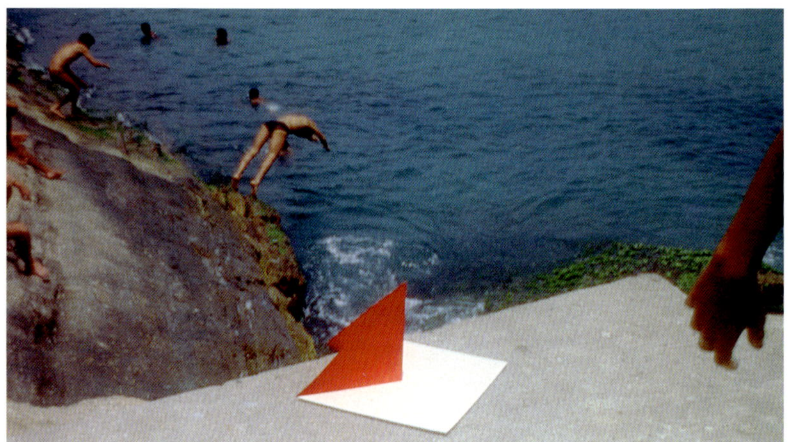

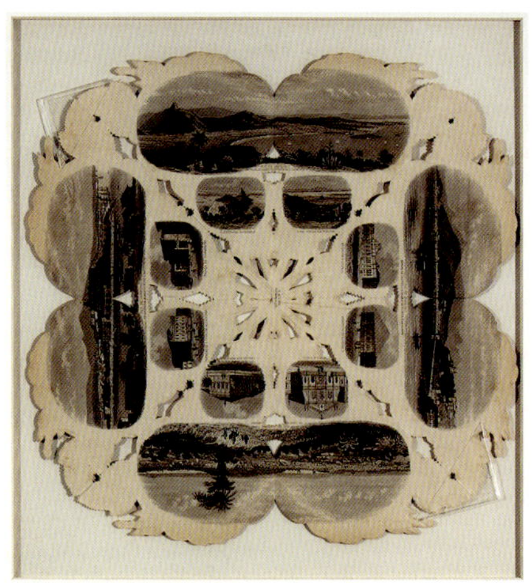

the sunlight. Years later, Pape developed this idea through a series of photographs of the *Livro da criação* contextualized in different vernacular spaces in Rio de Janeiro, such as on a newspaper kiosk or at the seashore (fig. 8). Besides interpolating the spectator's physical action, this variation activated the reader within his or her real spatial coordinates while forming in turn a compendium of views of Rio.

These city views find a local precedent in the pictorial genre of cartographic views (*vedute*), namely the curious nineteenth-century "topographic roses" of Rio de Janeiro.[28] These small pieces of cutout, punched, and folded paper take the shape of a rose when closed and show small printed views of Rio on their four quadrants when opened. Only a few examples of these curiosities remain, such as the *Rosa de Rio de Janeiro*, also known as *Rosa de Adler* (fig. 9), printed in Hamburg with minutely detailed lithographs by the French artists Eugène Cicéri and Philippe Benoist. The rarity of these works is comparable to that of the *Livro da criação* itself. Like the *Rosa de Rio de Janeiro*, the *Livro da criação* invites readers to interact with the object in an intimate way while at the same time encouraging them to apprehend the world around them.

As Pape explained, her book starts in a "passive state," but by means of the viewer's gesture, which "conveys expressive tempo" to each unit, a new and unique meaning emerges for each person.[29] In a way, the *Livro da criação* was a forerunner of Gullar's formulation of the artwork as *não-objeto* (non-object), which was first published in the *Suplemento dominical* in December 1959, and his expanded theory appeared in the brochure printed for the 2a Exposição Neoconcreta, held at the Ministry of Education from November to December 1960.[30] Pape and Gullar were artistically very close to each other during the emergence of Neoconcretism, especially in the formulation of Neoconcrete poetry, from which Pape developed the *Livro da criação*. According to Gullar, the non-object was not an antiobject but a special object that brought about a synthesis of sensory and mental experiences. Liberated from both the pedestal and the frame, the non-object was inserted directly into real space.

> The viewer is asked to *use* the non-object. Mere contemplation is not enough to reveal the sense of the work—and the viewer passes from contemplation to action. But what his or her action produces is the work itself, since that *use*, foreseen in the structure of the work, is absorbed by it, reveals it, and is incorporated into its meaning. . . . The non-object hails the viewer . . . , not as a

passive testimony to its existence but as a very condition of its *making*. Without the viewer, the work barely exists in potential, awaiting the human gesture that will actualize it.[31]

The *Livro da criação* is paradigmatic of the transition from contemplation to action so crucial to understanding Pape's work during the 1960s, much of which requires the viewer's interaction. "Just as color freed itself from painting," Gullar affirmed, "the word freed itself from poetry."[32]

LIVING THINGS AND THE QUESTION OF PUBLIC SPACE

In 1963, the Neoconcrete group disbanded owing to theoretical differences, although some of its members continued to see one another frequently. At that point, Pape's career took another disciplinary and conceptual leap. She was not to return to the visual arts until 1967, working instead with the filmmakers of the Cinema Novo on the design of title credits and posters for their films.[33] In 1960, she also started to work as a graphic designer on the visual branding and product packaging for Piraquê foods.

The second half of the 1960s in Brazil was shaped by the dictatorship that was established following the coup d'etat against President João Goulart on March 31, 1964. The fusion of art and life as initiated by Neoconcretism intensified during these years in artworks that embody the yearning for freedom of a generation confronted with such a dramatic inversion of history. Key moments in the arts during this period include the collective exhibition "Nova objetividade brasileira" ("New Brazilian Objectivity"), organized by Hélio Oiticica and others in 1967, and Pedrosa's call for an international boycott of the X Bienal de São Paulo in 1969 in response to the heightened repression after the implementation of the anticonstitutional Institutional Act Number Five in 1968.

"Nova objetividade brasileira" was on view from April 6 to 30 at the MAM-RJ. Intended as an overview of contemporary visual arts in Brazil, it included work by more than thirty artists of various artistic affiliations and different generations, from Ivan Serpa (1923–1973) to Antonio Dias (born 1944). In his catalogue essay "Esquema geral da nova objetividade" ("Overall Scheme of New Objectivity"), Oiticica declared that contemporary Brazilian art responded to a state he defined as "new objectivity," made up of many different tendencies beyond any kind of "ism." The principal characteristics of new objectivity were—or were supposed to be—a general constructive aspiration; a tendency toward the object, since easel painting had been surpassed; an interest in viewer participation; a clear position on political, social, and ethical issues; a predilection for collective production; and a focus on the reemergence of the concept of antiart.[34]

Oiticica was a person of crucial importance to Pape. From the 1950s until his death in 1980, when Pape became involved in founding Projeto Hélio Oiticica, they had a very close friendship and even lived on the same street in Jardim Botânico. When Pape was invited to contribute to "Nova objetividade brasileira," she felt encouraged to produce a radical new work that would incorporate what she described as "living things." The artist presented a pair of sculptural works: *Caixa*

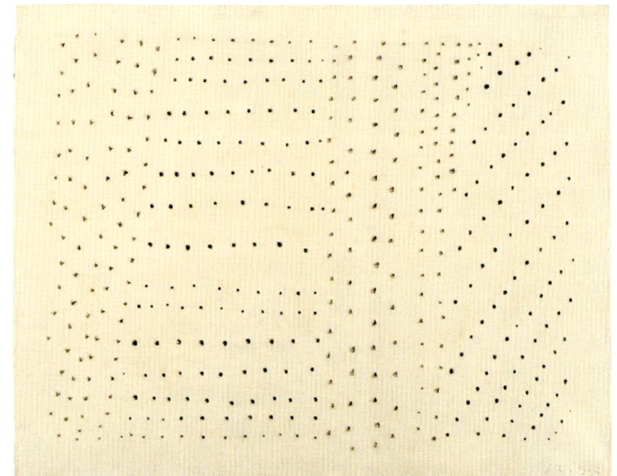

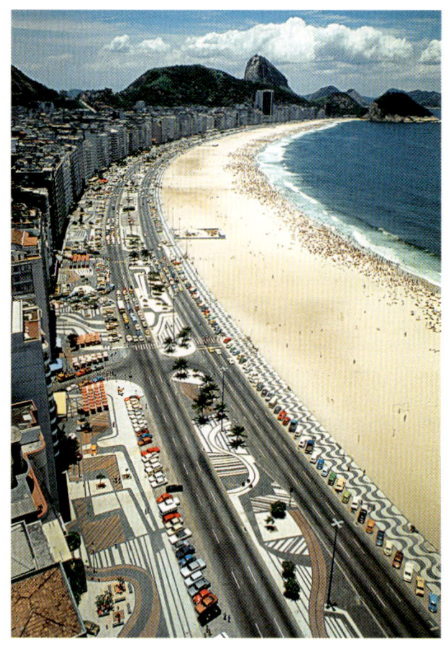

FIG. 10. Lucio Fontana (Argentinian, 1899–1968). *Concetto spaziale* (*Spatial Concept*), 1960. Oil on canvas, 24⅞ × 31⅞ in. (63 × 81 cm). Fondazione Lucio Fontana, Milan

FIG. 11. Roberto Burle Marx (Brazilian, 1909–1994). Design of Avenida Atlântica, Copacabana, Rio de Janeiro, 1970

das formigas (*Box of Ants*), which included live ants circulating around a piece of fresh meat, and *Caixa das baratas* (*Box of Cockroaches*), a methacrylate box containing preserved cockroaches aligned in a grid pattern. In this box the insects are mounted on a mirrored surface, so that when viewers bend over to look at the work, they find their own faces reflected beneath the cockroaches. *Caixa das baratas* poses an implicit critique of the role of museums in the deactivation of the ethical and aesthetic content of the work of art, for which Pape found an effective metaphor in the insect collections of entomology. In the context of a museum dedicated to modern art, the embalmed cockroaches, more readily associated with a natural history museum, functioned as anti-art, a Dadaist joke. Especially significant is the change in Pape's attitude toward the artistic institution, now subsumed under a military regime. In this respect, the dead insects not only serve as a metaphor for the dead art in museums but also for the embalmed subjectivity in the public sphere.[35]

The *Caixas* and other works from the late 1960s, such as *Divisor* (*Divider*) and *Roda dos prazeres* (*Wheel of Pleasures*), reflect social tension, and their ethos contrasts with the sense of confidence and positivism found in her work from the previous decade. Yet Pape's incorporation of "living things" continued her project of overcoming the barrier dividing Constructivist-Concrete art and everyday life in that her new works sought to reconcile the universal mathematical rigor of geometry with the spontaneity of the living and contingent.

Consisting of a piece of monochrome white cloth measuring thirty by thirty meters, *Divisor* has equidistant openings cut into its surface. As torn fabric, it is reminiscent of the perforated canvases (*buchi* and *attese*) produced by Lucio Fontana between 1949 and 1968 in accordance with his theory of spatialism (fig. 10), and in this respect *Divisor* problematizes the two-dimensionality of the picture plane much as Pape's earlier reliefs had done. *Divisor* is nonexistent as an artwork until it is activated by the moving bodies of a human group: it requires the participation of anonymous individuals who put their heads through the slits in the cloth and begin to move, transforming the piece into a kind of living monument, a political work that interacts with and perpetually questions public space. Pape devised this work in 1967 for the interior of a gallery, but finally chose to offer it to a group of children in the favela of Chácara da Cabeça. She then organized various performances of *Divisor* in 1968, including one at the collective event "Apocalipopótese," held in a very different area of the city, the gardens of Aterro do Flamengo, which surround the MAM-RJ. These gardens were designed by Roberto Burle Marx, who was also responsible for the exteriors of Brasília and the Copacabana seafront promenade (fig. 11).

Pape often reminisced about her expeditions with Oiticica to the center and suburbs of Rio de Janeiro.[36] Oiticica's relationships to the samba schools led him to incorporate Brazilian dance and other aspects of vernacular culture into his work. Pape meanwhile documented manifestations of social space in the streets, from the carnival in the film *Carnival in Rio* (1974) to the *camelôs* (street vendors or performers who attract small spontaneous gatherings around them) in the photographic series *Espaços imantados* (*Magnetized Spaces*, 1968–95). In keeping with her engagement with the public sphere, Pape took part in the historic March of the One Hundred Thousand on June 26, 1968, in Rio, when people occupied the streets of the city center in the largest protest yet held against the military dictatorship. Extending from this political involvement, *Divisor* came to function as a metaphor or memorial not only for the "collective body" of a community but also for the subjugated masses affected by Operation Condor, the program of political repression and state terrorism begun in 1968 and officially implemented in 1975 by the dictatorships of the Southern Cone of South America.

LEARNING FROM THE FAVELAS

Although the political situation sent several artists into exile,[37] Pape decided to remain in Brazil owing to the relative stability of her life there with her husband and two daughters. In her correspondence with Oiticica, however, she expressed her difficulty working or doing anything during that time. "I try to live inside myself," she wrote. "The slightest breath denounces the danger of what may come, not the physical danger but a more profound one, more terrible and immolating."[38] Starting in 1969, she went on a series of short trips around Latin America, including visits to Guatemala, Panama, El Salvador, Nicaragua, Mexico, and Peru, an experience that sparked her study of the architecture of indigenous cultures. Her career then took another leap, and she threw herself into researching, writing, and teaching. From 1969 to 1971, she taught at the MAM-RJ (fig. 12) while studying for her bachelor's degree in philosophy at the Universidade Federal do Rio de Janeiro. After graduating in 1972, she started teaching at the Centro de Arquitetura e Artes, Universidade Santa Úrsula, where she regularly taught courses to architecture students on form and space, including lectures on visual methodology and the semiotics of space.

Despite the apparent calm of her life in Brazil, Pape was imprisoned for three months and tortured in 1973. As she related publicly at the end of her life, she had been sanctioned for helping people persecuted by the government when one day she was snatched by three men with machine guns as she was leaving her home. "Little bird in the cage," she remembered them saying over the radio as they took her away. She spent a month in solitary confinement in a cell at the Center for Internal Defense Operations (DOI-CODI) in Maracanã, and was then transferred to the jail for political prisoners in Vila Militar before being tried at the Ministry of Aviation and narrowly acquitted by a margin of four votes to three.[39]

After her release, the artist resumed teaching at Santa Úrsula. Her lectures from this time evince a growing interest in vernacular architecture as she implemented a type of experimental pedagogy that involved taking her students out of the lecture room to visit the least-known parts of Rio de Janeiro, including the favelas. Years later, in an interview with her former student Lauro Cavalcanti, Pape elaborated on the purpose of these excursions, demanding, "How could you be a good architect if you didn't even know Rio de Janeiro?"[40] Pape described how on one occasion her students discovered some dwellings amid large rocks on the coastline of Flamengo.

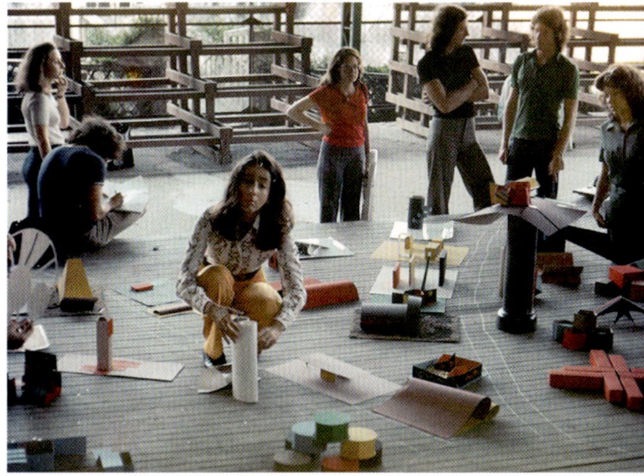

FIG. 12. Students at one of Lygia Pape's free workshops, Museu de Arte Moderna, Rio de Janeiro, 1970s

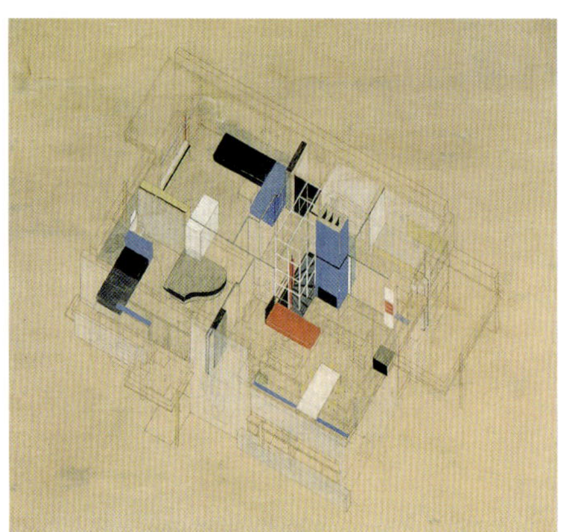

FIG. 13. Gerrit Rietveld (Dutch, 1888–1964). Axonometric projection of the Schröder House, 1924. Collotype with watercolor on cardboard, 33⅛ × 34¼ in. (84 × 87 cm). Rietveld Schröder Archive, Centraal Museum, Utrecht (inv.nr. 004 A 104)

You look at those rocks and then discover people are living there, loving and dying amid those huge boulders. It was a political vision of the world, a political vision of Brazil, because the majority were very alienated and I began questioning how the Indians lived, how a person in a favela lived, how a rich person lived within a mansion, and that started to establish political relations also within the class.[41]

Pape went to nearly all the favelas in Rio, both hillside and lowland, but the one she frequented most was Favela da Maré. Maré was different from other favelas because it was built on stilts over the sea and so appeared to be a "living organism." The reflection of its architecture in the water also reminded her of a photomontage, in which "thousands of images endlessly intertwine in a perpetual motion of infinite plasticity." She was further drawn to the fact that at the same time as she witnessed construction, she also noticed destruction taking place, the two proceeding "side by side."[42]

In 1972, Pape shot and edited *Favela da Maré*, an experimental silent Super 8 film in color. The film records a journey around the favela in two sequences, starting in reverse motion before showing the same journey as it was originally filmed. For Pape, her editing captured "the feeling I had of walking back and forth in the same space."[43] Moving through interiors and exteriors like the continuous flow of an enveloping and labyrinthine space, *Favela da Maré* plays with the spectator's perception through the medium of film and draws attention to the very spatial ambivalence of the favela.

Pape expanded upon her impressions of this urban site in "Favela da Maré ou milagre das palafitas" ("Favela da Maré or Miracle on Stilts"), written that same year, emphasizing the precarious way in which the inhabitants resolve their construction problems.

At Maré, the "inventor-residents" have intuitively devised a fantastic solution that involves the use of internal windows to interconnect their homes. This solution is particularly impressive for spontaneously setting off a chain reaction. . . . Entrances and exits were often modified, nothing lasted very long, and I could not tell where the favela began or ended. Space was constantly being transformed to meet new needs or serve new uses. Like a Moebius strip, paths were intertwined in endless motion. . . . There was no intention of rationalizing space, but of pondering space and its intelligent solutions, some simple, others rather sophisticated.[44]

While studying the favelas, Pape identified parallel examples of their use of flexible unitary space in other cultures, from the original dwellings of the Tupinambá Indians that inhabited the Brazilian coastline to the Neoplasticist house of Gerrit Rietveld (fig. 13), the epitome of modernist architecture, built in 1924 in Utrecht. Oiticica was equally interested in the flexible space of the favelas, as is evident in his installation *Tropicália PN2 and PN3* (1967), first presented at "Nova objetividade brasileira," in which panels subdivide spaces that include plants, plastic objects, curtains, parrots, and even a television set (fig. 14). Visually, the installation transports the architecture of the favela to the realm of the museum, in what Oiticica regarded as the first "conscious attempt at imposing a Brazilian image."[45]

Throughout the 1970s Pape took hundreds of photographs on her visits to the favelas in Rio de Janeiro, pausing to record spatial and architectural details, such as entrances, and more private spaces, such as bedrooms and living rooms (pl. 101). She also portrayed the inhabitants in a series that bears a photojournalistic style, reflecting her active experimentation with a type of research-based artistic practice.

Pape's engagement with popular and marginal cultures is related to a certain crisis of identity felt by Brazilian artists and intellectuals created by the countercultural phenomenon known as Tropicália, exile and repression, and growing awareness of the failure both of Brazil's "economic miracle" and of the emancipatory promise of modernism. Pape's films of the 1970s like *Favela da Maré* (1972), *Carnival in Rio* (1974), and *A mão do povo* (*The Hand of the People*, 1975), and installations like *Eat Me* (1976), reflect the artistic vision of a fragmented city in which social space is transgressed by industrialization, mass consumption, and close military surveillance. Long gone are the utopian aspirations embodied by modern architecture and urbanism as encoded in the 1959 script for her unrealized film *Brasília*, in which she depicted the Palácio da Alvorada as a rising sun on the Brazilian horizon, alluding to the name of the building, which relates to President Juscelino Kubitschek's famous saying: "Que é Brasília, se não a alvorada de um novo dia para o Brasil!" (What is Brasília, if not the dawning of a new day for Brazil!).[46]

JOY OF CREATING

One of Pape's first projects to address the marginal cultures of Brazil was her ten-minute experimental Super 8 film *Our Parents "Fossilis"* (1974), which is composed of shots of postcards of Brazilian Indians that were produced for tourists and sold at street kiosks in the city. The film consists of a visual sequence made with simple frontal shots using only the lens of the camera to zoom closer to or farther away from the postcards. The sequence begins with images that show the Indian as a savage, and then proceeds to subvert this perception with scenes of children playing with animals or women bathing in the river, displaying a more humanized vision of this community. The soundtrack, the film's only sound, is a song in a native language. *Our Parents "Fossilis"* is a simple statement about the lack of knowledge about a culture, which, in an exercise of genealogical archaeology ("fossils"), Pape considers to be "our parents." At the same time, the film criticizes the exploitation of the Indian as an exotic souvenir within Brazilian mass culture.

In 1977, Pape was invited by Pedrosa, who had recently returned from his exile in Paris, to collaborate on the planning of an exhibition. Pedrosa was a constant intellectual influence for Pape (fig. 15), from the days of the meetings of the Grupo Frente until the end of his life, when Pape portrayed Pedrosa eating fruit as part of

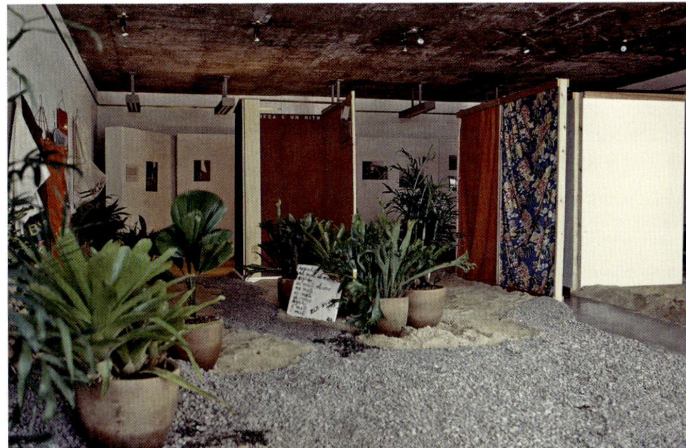

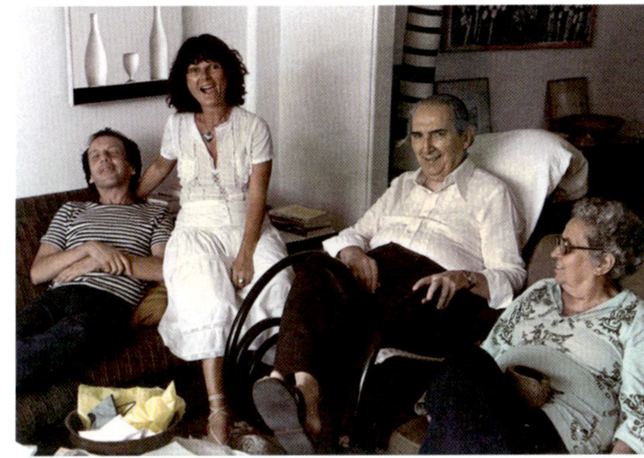

FIG. 14. Hélio Oiticica (Brazilian, 1937–1980). *Tropicália PN2 and PN3*, 1967. Multimedia installation, dimensions variable. Projeto Hélio Oiticica, Rio de Janeiro

FIG. 15. Hélio Oiticica, Lygia Pape, Mário Pedrosa, and Mary Pedrosa at the Pedrosas' home, Rio de Janeiro, 1978

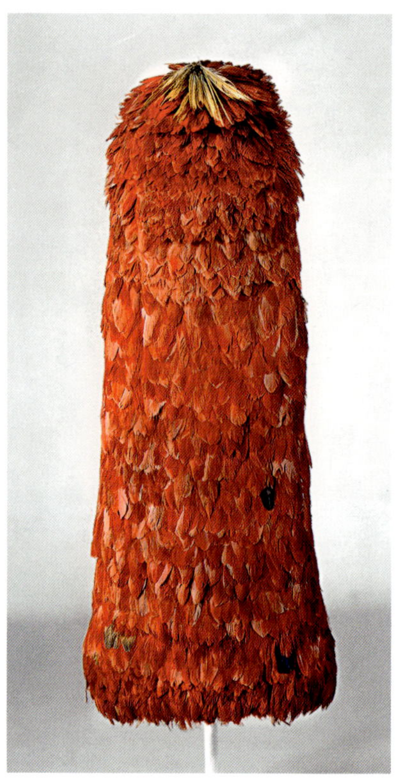

FIG. 16. *Manto dos Tupinambás* (*Mantle of the Tupinambás*). Tupinambá peoples, Brazil. Before 1679. Ibis and parrot feathers, 47¼ in. (120 cm). National Museum of Denmark, Copenhagen

her artistic experiments on gluttony and seduction (pl. 104). To be held at the MAM-RJ and entitled "Alegria de viver, alegria de criar" ("Joy of Living, Joy of Creating"), the exhibition had the following mission.

> Our show . . . must appear in the eyes of the Brazilian public, both the elite and the common people, as a sort of historical, cultural and moral reparation made by the whole population to the Mother Nation of our people, the Indians. . . . This will be the first time in the history of Brazil that indigenous art and culture are represented scientifically, artistically and museographically in their entirety. For the first time we shall have the opportunity of a fair aesthetic and anthropological comparison of the indigenous arts of Brazil with the great pre-Columbian art of the brother peoples of America. We shall be able to assess precisely and objectively what in the art and culture of our Indian people can be regarded as equal and what distinguished as our own vis-à-vis the formidable pre-Columbian cultures.[47]

Pedrosa thought this great exhibition of the art of the indigenous peoples of Brazil was of historical relevance and would represent a "cultural and artistic movement" in its own right.[48] To accomplish it, the cooperation of the ethnology and archaeology departments of the Museu Nacional was of paramount importance, and a large working team was assembled to assist with the project.[49] Moreover, it was vital to borrow crowning monuments of the country's cultural history that had been kept in European collections since the sixteenth century, among them the so-called *Manto dos Tupinambás* (*Mantle of the Tupinambás*; fig. 16).[50] The exhibition was scheduled for the fall of 1978 and many loans had been secured, but the museum was severely damaged by a fire on July 8, 1978, and the project was never resumed.[51]

Supervised by Professor Creusa Capalbo, Pape received her master's in philosophy in 1980.[52] Entitled "Catiti-Catiti, na terra dos Brasis" ("Catiti-Catiti, in the Land of the Brasis"), her thesis articulated the crisis of art in the contemporary world, a matter in Pape's view caused by the decadence of the avant-garde in developed nations. She reclaimed for the inhabitants of the so-called Third-World—those "disinherited of fortune"—the task of taking leadership in the field of creativity and forming a new artistic framework based on the idea of a "Brazilian conscience." In this vein she differentiated between "artist-inventors," who had already begun the task of invention with the project of Brazilian construction, and the "man of the people," who is "plunged in misery," with his anonymous creations. Pape maintained it was not possible to continue to use models "that are not ours," and regarded the study of cultural references not as a search for "Brazilian roots," liable to be confused with folklore, but as an attempt to defend "our anthropophagous hunger" as a single force with an ability to vitalize creative acts.[53] Nor was it a question of systematically rejecting everything occurring abroad: "As good descendants of the first peoples of this land of Brazil, the Tupinambá, we shall devour everything, we will swallow up all the Bishop Sardinha we find, and we will vomit back—or rather, we already started long ago to vomit back—the profound fury of our new creation."[54]

Although the revered *Manto dos Tupinambás* never came to be shown at the MAM-RJ, Pape continued studying the material culture of the Brazilian Indians and collecting their handicrafts, especially those with designs that demonstrated an autochthonous constructive-geometric tradition, such as their painted stools. In her *Tupinambá* series (1997–2003), Pape recalled the history of the colonial period, including the massacre of the tribes that inhabited the coasts of Brazil, by covering abstract spheres or everyday objects with red feathers, an allusion to the Guará rubra (scarlet ibis), whose precious red feathers were treasured by the Tupinambá tribes. The Tupinambá comprise a native Indian nation made up of several communities that live along the Brazilian coastline, share a common language, and were all called Tupi by the Jesuit settlers. The Tupiniquim are one of those communities, and their name is used in popular speech to mean "Brazil" or "Brazilian." In the photomontage *Manto Tupinambá* (*Tupinambá Mantle*, 2000) Pape presents a view of Rio de Janeiro with a red cloud in the sky, alluding both to the bloodiest events in the colonization of the coast and to the persistence of cultural traditions in Brazil.

RECOMMENCE: FROM *AMAZONINOS* TO *TTÉIAS*

The continuum of inside/outside as manifest in the Moebius strip, a figure Pape liked to refer to, has its equivalent in the circular structure, where the end returns to the beginning. In the *Amazoninos* series (1989–92), Pape recovered the exercises in pure geometry of her early works, and in particular the notion of the protuberance, which had characterized the reliefs of the Grupo Frente period. *Amazonino* (pl. 116), for example, is an abstract sculptural piece that hangs from the wall. For this work, the artist tackled the technical challenge of using iron plates as if they were leaves of paper, easy to cut and manipulate, presenting a new confluence of geometric and organic forms, which, as the subtitle *Amazonino* might suggest, seems ever mindful of the natural landscape of Brazil, from the sinuous contours of Rio de Janeiro to the exuberant jungles of the Amazon, either as a starting point or as an afterimage (fig. 17).

The artist also revived aspects of her *Tecelares* in the installations of golden thread entitled *Ttéias*,[55] whose major presentation took place in 2002 at the Paço Imperial in Rio de Janeiro. The threads of the *Ttéias* are woven across the viewer's space from floor to ceiling or from wall to wall (fig. 18), and they evoke the lines of the Neoconcrete *Tecelares*, which had tried to break the convention of the figure/background pairing by imagining the reversed possibility of a pictorial space dissolved in real space. The *Ttéias* exemplify the artist's ideal of dissolving pictorial space, especially in how they recall beams of natural light entering a room.[56]

Through her continued experimentation, which began in the 1950s and concluded upon her death in 2004, Pape embodied the ideal of the transmedia artist-inventor. Resisting a firm adherence to any specific medium or style, she tirelessly pursued a political-poetic image that would run the risk of inventing an art beyond the object, and so lead to a symbiosis of art and living through which the life of her most immediate surroundings would be revealed.

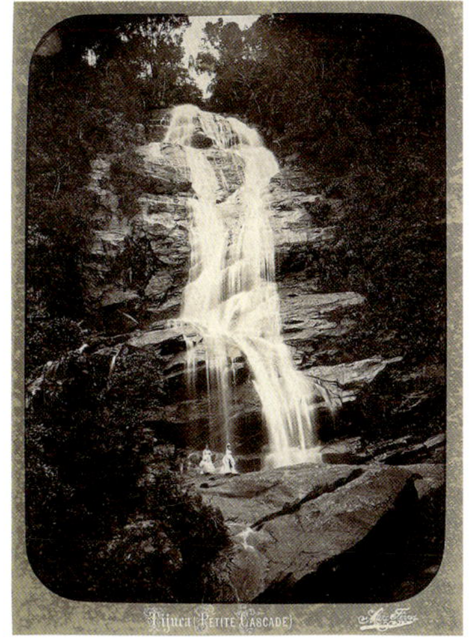

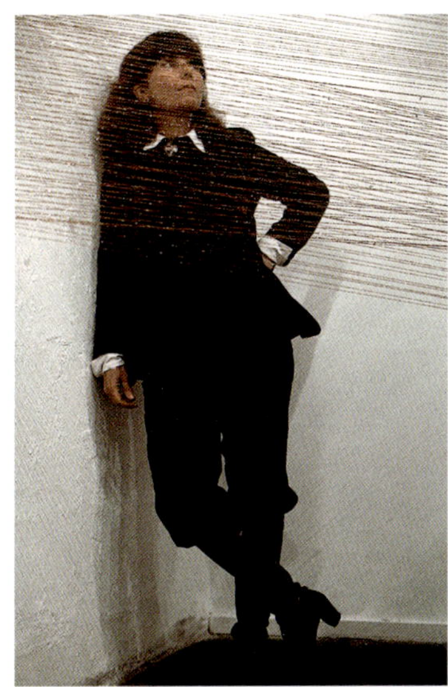

FIG. 17. Marc Ferrez (Brazilian, 1843–1923). *Tijuca Falls*, ca. 1885. Vintage photograph, 15½ × 11 in. (39.4 × 27.9 cm). Colección Patricia Phelps de Cisneros

FIG. 18. Lygia Pape with *Ttéia 1, A*, at Espaço Galpão, São Paulo, 1978

birds of marvelous colors

LYGIA PAPE INTERVIEWED BY LÚCIA CARNEIRO AND ILEANA PRADILLA

This interview was conducted across a number of sessions between March and August 1997 at Lygia Pape's studio in Rio de Janeiro. The translated text is excerpted from a longer, published transcript.[1]

Lúcia Carneiro and Ileana Pradilla: From childhood on, your biography reflects your great kinship with various modes of artistic expression. As a child, you expressed a desire to be a classical singer. Beyond whatever fascination that a singer's life—that the dream of becoming a singer—might hold for a child, was there any specific feature of classical singing that awakened such an interest?

Lygia Pape: My family influenced my interest in classical singing. My father and my uncle loved opera and had beautiful voices. As a child, I sang and listened to a lot of opera. That could explain why I considered becoming an opera singer. I even took lessons, but I was terribly shy. It was there as a student that I discovered my shyness. Whenever I was in class and we had a visitor, I would lose my voice. The teacher would go raging mad. So I decided to put an end to my career right there.

LC/IP: So you grew up in a family environment that stimulated a strong connection with the arts?

LP: There was an artistic sensibility that was especially connected to music as well as to my father's curiosity for collecting Brazilian birds. To him, there was something seductive about the beauty of a bird. So from a very early age I became used to seeing birds of marvelous colors, like cardinals and many others. There was an interest in the arts, yes, but it wasn't something we bragged about, we didn't consider ourselves intellectuals. The taste for music and the curiosity about birds were spontaneous individual expressions within our family. I felt like I was living in an Indian village because we had about thirty toucans and fifty macaws at home. It was over the top. My exposure to the beauty of music and birds was something natural.

LC/IP: This admiration for the beauty of birds was your first contact with the subject of visuality. But how did you arrive at the visual arts?

LP: I went to live in Arraial do Cabo for a while, a place that was proud of having been home to and inspiring artists such as José Pancetti and Yoshiya Takaoka. At that time, it was still possible to come upon traces of them. I stayed there a long time, without much of anything to do. In the afternoons, I would climb white dunes that looked like a painting by Kazimir Malevich. As I plunged into the white masses of the dunes, the sun would appear suddenly from behind them, like a red circle. Visually, that was a wonder. It was there that I began to want to do something in the visual arts. . . .

After Arraial, I went to live in Petrópolis. There I found a group interested in art to which Décio Vieira belonged. We became friends and he took me to the Palácio de Cristal, where some people got together to draw under the instruction of a Czech teacher. The lessons were characterized by a freedom to pursue whatever we wanted. The teacher was a likable person but exerted no influence that might define anyone's destiny. My professional relationship with the plastic arts actually began when the Museu de Arte Moderna, Rio de Janeiro (MAM-RJ), was inaugurated. Ivan Serpa was already teaching classes there, but I didn't study under him. I met Serpa through Décio Vieira, and, little by little, we began to meet people and create a circle of friends with common interests.

LC/IP: At that time, were you trying to understand the interest in geometric forms that preoccupied the group and discussing among yourselves what it was you intended to do?

LP: Not at that moment, no. We were more intuitive. We were just a group that occasionally organized parties or outings. Once, the entire group went down to Suruí, a small town on the Baixada Fluminense, to paint. Those were the kinds of adventures we had—we weren't preoccupied by theoretical concerns then. Artistic activity became more intense in Rio as we grew more conscious of what we wanted and connected with people who had similar interests. It was there that what later became known as the Grupo Frente emerged. At that moment, the discovery of Pre-Socratic philosophy made an impact upon me because I was on the lookout for something like a beginning, something new, a start.

LC/IP: Do you think that the creation of the MAM-RJ and the subsequent institutionalization of modern art in Rio de Janeiro, which stimulated the professionalization of artistic activity, was essential to this awareness of yours and that of the group?

LP: I think the MAM-RJ was very important, but it emerged in 1958.[2] We were already meeting before then, among the columns of the Ministry of Education and Health (later the Ministry of Education, MEC) building, and we also frequented Serpa's home a lot. We were really just starting out and only began to organize more consciously around 1953 or 1954.

LC/IP: Apparently, Ivan Serpa was someone who brought people together; he was a sort of guide to those youths who were just starting out. What was the difference between him and the other participants at the gatherings? The sum of his cultural experiences? His charisma?

LP: Serpa was a more charismatic figure. He had undoubtedly lived an eventful life and had been at work longer than most of us. He was a friend of Almir Mavignier's and Mário Pedrosa's and, together with Abraham Palatnik, they went to the Hospital Psiquiátrico do Engenho de Dentro, where Dr. Nise da Silveira was just starting her research. Almir Mavignier was an instructor there. At the first edition of the Bienal de São Paulo in 1951, Serpa won the Prêmio de Pintura Jovem and Palatnik presented a kinetic work he had made in 1949, which was apparently the first work of that kind made anywhere in the world. Therefore, they already had professional experience when the group began to form.

Lygia Clark was living in Paris then and beginning to paint with André Lhote and Fernand Léger. When she came back, we began to organize a group in Rio along with Décio and others. In São Paulo there was the Grupo Ruptura, which had more or less similar interests. So we continued to develop an awareness of art that was unlike anything else that was being made: something new, uncluttered, and more attuned to the geometric. It was a matter of affinity. All those people wanted to work within a new concept of art.

LC/IP: That group of youths was also linked to the critic Mário Pedrosa, who, in addition to his solid background in philosophy, had an enormous sensibility for and knowledge of modern art. How did he influence the work and discussions of a group that was just starting out?

LP: I think "influencing" may not be the right term. He was a very charismatic person, very well informed and endowed with tremendous intuition, culture, and intelligence—he was ultimately someone you always learned from with each encounter. He had a lot of extremely important information for us, and he was a great friend and an important person within the movement. He brought information, he knew everyone, and he had already participated in a series of international events. I was very close to him. I was always quite interested in the culture and the problems of the Brazilian Indian. But prior to his exile in Paris, Mário referred to the Indian without much interest. He wrote a text there called "Discurso aos Tupiniquins ou Nambás" ("Speech to the Tupiniquim or the Nambá Peoples") in which he focused on the question of the art crisis, stating that, from then on, the world would begin turning to the cultural production of the so-called Third World, of the "earth's dispossessed."[3] . . . When he was granted the writ of habeas corpus and returned to Brazil in 1977, we continued to meet at his home.

At that time, Mário was revisiting his former positions on the subject, and we set off to work on a project together. He was interested in compiling an important exhibition about the Brazilian Indian from an aesthetic perspective, not an anthropological or ethnological one. His project consisted of a large exhibition at the MAM in Rio de Janeiro that would then go to São Paulo in which he would show the Indian as a creative being, a producer of beauty. In that sense, he was connected to my idea of seeing the Indian from that perspective. We were frequent visitors to the Museu Nacional da Quinta da Boa Vista, where, despite the infernal heat, he never opened his mouth to complain. It was pure passion. The proposed exhibition was extremely beautiful and called "Alegria de viver, alegria de criar" ("Joy of Living, Joy of Creating"). Unfortunately, just as we were finishing up our planning work, the MAM-RJ caught fire.[4] It was a shock. The dream burned down. The artworks weren't lost because they hadn't been shipped yet and were still in their original locations. The largest collection of Brazilian feather art, for example, is in Denmark. There aren't any Tupinambá mantles left in Brazil. There's one in Berlin, another in Denmark, and a third in the Musée de l'Homme in Paris. Through letters, we had obtained the loan of the mantle from the Paris museum. Everything was ready for the exhibition, but, unfortunately, it never came about.

Mário also developed the theory of the Museum of Origins, to be composed of five segments on the five sources of creation in Brazilian culture: indigenous culture, black culture, contemporary art, spontaneous art, and the art of images from the unconscious. This idea was proposed to provide a new start for the MAM-RJ after the fire. It was an extremely powerful, beautiful, and moving idea. I was present the day Mário handed over the project to Niomar Muniz Sodré. Niomar didn't understand it.

LC/IP: Could one make an outline of indigenous art based on purely aesthetic terms without taking into consideration the fact that such art was not conceived for contemplation but for practical use? Decontextualized from the society that created them, wouldn't the forms of those objects be treated as mere abstractions?

LP: In making a diamond shape, an Indian wants to speak of something concrete, like the *pacu* fish. That form is a synthesis, not an abstraction. In the exhibition, we were interested in rescuing the painting of the Indians of the Neolithic period as an inventive production of geometric art. Scholars believe that the Neolithic period is the moment in which man learns to conceptualize, given that in the Paleolithic age, painting was figurative. When, at that moment, man began to work with geometric forms, I believe there was a process like that of the Indians that took place; that is, formal syntheses rather than abstractions were being made. For example, Brazilian Indians make sieves with designs on them, and each one of those drawings is related to a concrete element of their world. There are trails of ants, jaguars, alligators, and rheas. It is a synthetic reading of reality.

LC/IP: Do you think that Western man in general and modern art in particular have reduced formal expression to an abstraction?

LP: The Constructivists sought a return to the beginning of things, hence the use of geometric forms. There is another type of abstraction that refers to deformed forms of nature. And today we have the object that is pure presence. I believe that when one speaks of abstraction with respect to the Indian, one speaks from the perspective of Western man, who assumes that geometric form is an abstraction unrelated to reality. But that relationship exists for the Indian because such economy of form is the result of a long process. In a sense, Neolithic man shares the same perspective as the Brazilian Indian, who experiences a specific cultural process. He remains isolated and maintains a structure of perception of his own. The Indians' body painting, for example, is of a mythic nature. He repeats that painting, but perhaps he no longer knows why he does so. Each tribe has its designs. In Guatemala, where each tribe has its own embroidery, tribes maintain a sort of emblematic identity, as if the embroidery were a sign that culturally marks each social group. Haircuts are also a tribal sign.

I have always been a great admirer of Indian culture, and I am extremely concerned about the problems of the destruction of that culture. The Indian has highly developed creative powers, and this should be studied more. However, as soon as he made contact with the white man, he immediately began to destroy himself. I did a study on original and primordial indigenous architecture, and I know that the first thing the white man does when he approaches the Indian is to destroy his home, his original space. Several families of Tupinambá lived in enormous indigenous communal houses. Upon the discovery of Brazil, the priests deemed such arrangements sinful, separated the families, and built individual houses in straight lines, which is not part of Indian culture; the very heart of that culture—its manner of building and experiencing space—was destroyed. Origin myths were undoubtedly splintered.

I'm also interested in the organic quality of indigenous body painting. Its design is sophisticated and follows muscle movement. It is an allegedly primitive, albeit highly sophisticated, culture. If you look at the painting of Frank Stella, you will find relationships to the painting of the Brazilian Indian.

LC/IP: Something else you've shown an interest in is the manifestation of so-called popular culture. And yet your gaze upon it doesn't appear to be the gaze of someone who points to the exotic. How do you relate to these different kinds of work?

LP: I regard them as a part of me. Indigenous culture impregnates so-called Western culture more than we realize. I believe that indigenous, black, and popular cultures are part of my culture. Whenever I visit the interior of Brazil, I am moved by the recycling of material, toys, and objects. This here for example [points to an object in her living room] is an object from Piauí—a can of cooking oil. The person who created it used the bottom of the can as a base, cutting the can down the middle and opening it up into two metal leaves. He then cut the two leaves into thin little twisty strips and, finally, put a wad of plastic-laminated fabric on each tip. Thus, the object became a tree.

That mathematical perception of space, that topological space that makes it possible to use an oil cylinder and give it another meaning, is a poetic moment that moves me. I feel the same emotion when, unexpectedly, an anonymous student in the corner of a classroom produces wonderful work. I don't know whether he'll be able to repeat it or not, or even whether he is conscious of what he has done, but that poetic moment is very gratifying. The emergence of the poetic act is something that happens in that instant. Invention, above all that which is of an anonymous nature, moves me. I believe this creative impulse is inherent to man. It is as if man had a need to create, to bestow new meanings upon forms. You don't have to be creative in the professional sense of the word "art" in order to do that.

LC/IP: You belonged to one of the most important movements in the Brazilian visual arts—Neoconcretism—admired for, among other reasons, its sophisticated reflections on the field of the visual arts. And yet, throughout your discourse, you appear to enjoy presenting yourself as an outsider, as someone who does not belong to elevated intellectual circles and who emphasizes her interest in the popular side of Brazilian culture.

LP: Intellectually speaking, there is nothing more sophisticated than so-called nonerudite culture. My closeness to popular manifestations of culture has something to do with my artist's perception of the world. As regards my personal work, I may be moved by popular inventions, to find them interesting and creative. Everything I observe can nourish me and even serve to subsidize some manifestation or invention

I'm going to make, but not in the idealistic sense of considering art as something vague and simply beautiful. I think it's more incisive. It's a language. It's my way of knowing the world.

Incredible though it might seem, in spite of my apparent independence, I've belonged to many groups throughout my life—to the Grupo Frente, to Concretism, to Neoconcretism. It wasn't until after those that I ceased to participate in groups. I joke about saying that I became a freelancer. Nowadays, I like to feel dissolved in the world.

LC/IP: For many years, since the beginning of your career, you vehemently denied art's commercial aspect, refusing to show your work in galleries and even to sell it. What is your current position on the sale of your work? Are you at all interested in this aspect now?

LP: I am interested, yes. I sell the occasional work, but I don't produce systematically for the market. I think that creating or inventing is taking risks. It is very important to have the courage to take on the risk of invention. And this is something that always involves a sacrifice, an effort, a suffering. I have no interest in creating a piece that "works" and ten more like it to supply the market and make lots of money. It's not that I consider the attitude unethical, but it does bore me somewhat. Sometimes I prefer to just sit and think and meditate, grievously suffering to produce a new invention, something that will really satisfy me.

I've always had an anarchist side; I've constantly refused to belong to the status quo. I enjoy having unrestricted freedom to produce art. Around 1967, I remember the MAM-RJ received a large endowment for purchasing works and asked all the artists to bring theirs along. Everyone brought his or her "conventional" works, all of which were duly acquired for the museum's collection. I took my *Caixa das baratas* (*Box of Cockroaches*, 1967). Obviously it wasn't purchased, but I took it along nonetheless because it was a form of criticism, an anarchic gesture. I felt it was much more important to send in *Caixa* because it was a challenge, an irony, and more in line with my worldview.

I worked outside that circuit for a long time. I wasn't interested in selling any work at all. Whenever I needed to make money, I'd take on some graphic design job or something else, but I had no interest in following the normal flow of an artist's career. I always rejected that. Nowadays, I am accepting of galleries—this is a recent development, less than ten years old—because I feel they've taken on a cultural task of promoting the work.

LC/IP: Could you describe your creative process?

LP: It's not easy. I once talked to Artur Barrio about how we suffer to make our works, for they all possess great "density."

Occasionally, we find works that resemble ours; someone has taken a certain sign from our works and very successfully moved forward with it. Once it's ready, digested, and suffered through, the labor[5] has taken place, and it becomes much easier to move on with. But I have no interest in continuing to make copies of the same thing. I'll do it as long as it's necessary for whatever research and invention I may be involved with. When that runs out, either I stop for breath or go off to study or look at other things.

LC/IP: When you decide to work on a given subject, how do you go about choosing your materials and the medium through which to express yourself?

LP: It's not easy. I always envision the work first before executing it. It's an entirely mental process. Until I settle it, I prepare for several days or months. I experience the work's requirements mentally. I also consider the most appropriate materials for making it. I start a bit, I stop; I make another work. I don't know where this need comes from, but I work on several pieces at once, never on one exclusively. For example, when I was making the *Livro da criação* (*Book of Creation*, 1959–60), it was completely ready—I mean, I already knew what each unit would be like: the form, colors, how to cut. Mentally, it was all ready. After that, it just needed to be technically realized.

LC/IP: Meaning that the execution is rapid, given that it is mental creation that concerns you?

LP: I think that's why I don't enjoy painting. I can't abide the act of painting. To keep mixing colors . . . and, as a color changes, the gestalt of the painting changes. That irritates me. I prefer automotive paint.

LC/IP: What is it that emerges first in the act of creation? Form, color, or material?

LP: It depends on each work. For example, I executed a series of works in metal and iron, the initial problem of which was making works that would hang from a specific height because the gallery where they would be shown had, at that time, a large mezzanine that interested me. I pursued this idea until I arrived at the pieces of a series I called *Amazoninos*. I usually start with certain perceptions that come to me and are later realized as works.

As for *Caixa das baratas* and *Caixa das formigas* (*Box of Ants*, 1967), the starting point is a clear concept: they are criticisms of dead art locked up in museums. I wasn't working toward a merely discursive result; I was looking to create a situation of repugnance, of actual disgust. What could be better than cockroaches for that, right? Instead of presenting a collection of butterflies, all lovely and pinned, which is something that always irritated me a great deal, I made a box with cockroaches. And it really was loathsome.

Next to it, as a sort of counterpoint, I placed a box of live ants that contained a piece of meat, inside of which was written "Gluttony or Lust?" It was the idea of sexual devouring and of hunger. The work was presented for the first time at "Nova objetividade brasileira" ("New Brazilian Objectivity") at the MAM-RJ. It was very satisfying to see those enormous leafcutter ants. I used to leave a tiny opening so they could breathe, and some of them would escape. In the middle of the exhibition, Rubens Gerchman would say: "There's an ant climbing all over my work."

LC/IP: After the work has been structured mentally, you move on to its execution, occasionally through third parties. How do you communicate specifications and details to those producers who aren't always familiar with art?

LP: I draw lines, plans; I explain everything. For instance, the *Amazoninos* were made in a foundry. I selected the sheets, and they were machine cut and folded.

Generally speaking, I do it myself; I pierce, I cut. I know how to do a few things. Of course I don't have enough time or physical strength to execute certain works. Beyond that, I'm allergic to oil paint and automotive paint, which is why I need someone to help. I need to have things painted and stay away at some distance. Despite my lack of interest in manual work, whenever I want to obtain a given color or porousness, then I do it myself.

LC/IP: When you look back on works you did some time ago, how do you feel about them? Do you think they remain fresh?

LP: I think so. I only make a work when I deem it ready to be made. So I'm not usually disappointed. I never do work related to a particular period but rather to a specific form of knowledge that I seek to materialize. For example, I think the *Livro da criação* is as fresh today as it was the day I made it. It hasn't aged. It isn't dated. Why? Because I believe I did a really good job of solving some of the problems I was setting for myself at that moment; these problems were actually conditions for the making of the work. It wouldn't have been worthwhile doing it any other way. The *Livro da criação* needed to leave the plane, move into three-dimensional space, and return to the plane. That was an extremely complicated problem and required a great effort of invention because it had to represent fire, water, the hunter, and the stilt house, and certain elements had to have the ability to be manipulated and rotated. I believe I obtained a maximum level of synthesis and expression there. Whereas to me the *Livro da criação* "narrates" the creation of the world, it could have another meaning for someone else, in keeping with his or her own sensibilities or experience. . . . It is, simultaneously, a poem and an art object. It was the fruit of my fascination with the Pre-Socratic philosophers. Although people are making plenty of art books, no one makes them like mine—books conceived as formal, signifying, wordless language. In addition to the *Livro da criação*, I also made the *Livro da arquitetura* (*Book of Architecture*, 1959–60) and the *Livro do tempo* (*Book of Time*, 1961–63).

The *Livro da arquitetura* "narrates" the creation of architectural styles. It begins with the Paleolithic, moves through the Neolithic and Greek and Baroque styles until it arrives at the contemporary. Also, I included the representation of the desert, which is very beautiful. It is a unit of coarse, yellowish sand, inside of which there is an oasis, the only construction within the desert: a tiny little green cube (all the sheets, or "units," are thirty by thirty centimeters). I think this work is a masterpiece. That book, too, advances into space and moves back to the plane. It's composed of units that might almost be treated as open and independent.

LC/IP: Which artists have influenced your work, and with whom does your work dialogue?

LP: Giorgio Morandi, Alfredo Volpi, and Giotto are my passions, as well as Piet Mondrian and Kazimir Malevich, but I don't know about any dialogue.

Morandi is a wonderful painter. His work is extremely synthetic and clean. It is admirable that he should be able to create a simultaneously rich, simple, uncluttered world from so few elements. I am very fond of his style and always point it out to my drawing students: not limiting form with the use of line. Form and volume are given by surface, by color. It is the area of volume that marks the separation of one object from another. It also equalizes the entire picture. For example, if red is used in a given object on the canvas, he'll use a tiny bit of that red in all the other objects included in the painting, whether they're in the background, at the front of the table, etc. Even white would have a pinch of red in it. I also find his drawings to be incredibly canny. They exemplify a great economy of form. He is truly a great artist. I knew him personally, as I went to Bologna to meet him. He was getting on in years, no longer making prints, and his sight was badly impaired. I remember he used a huge magnifying glass to see. As a gift, he even gave me a print. I also went to Bologna because I wanted to see the work of Giotto, Piero della Francesca, and Paolo Uccello.

In my opinion, Volpi is one of our great colorists. I disagree with the critic Rodrigo Naves when he says in his book *A forma difícil* that, in Volpi's paintings, form is weak and poor and the brushstroke is very primitive.[6] I don't agree. I think Volpi achieves amazing synthesis in the house entrances and the festivals of Saint John. On the contrary, his brushstroke vibrates powerfully. His color was flatter in the early work. But toward the end of his life—when he painted those surfaces with forms that look like flags but are in fact enormous abstractions, in extremely vibrant colors, and changed the direction of the brush in order to obtain a certain vibration—color seems to come alive. I find it so subtle, so rich—it's pure light! . . .

Malevich and Mondrian are more geometric and rigorous, and, additionally, they raise spatial problems that I am particularly interested in. Whereas the other artists' works are pure joy, their art has an affinity with a type of work that I continue to make. In the *Livro da arquitetura*, I paid tribute to Mondrian by making a Japanese house in which the planes moved and whose base is one of his paintings. The architect Gerrit Rietveld made a house with walls that could either be opened or disappear altogether. In terms of inventions, that house is something fantastic. Sliding screens that open up or shut off spaces are powerfully redolent of the Japanese home, which, in turn, greatly identifies with the incredible cubic space of the favela, which I got to know better when I frequented the Favela da Maré and its stilt houses. During the daytime they functioned as totally open cubes with a stove here, a table there, and the occasional bed. Because there are several families sharing these spaces, at night they draw curtains in the form of a cross so as to create various compartments. In each one of those compartments they laid down beds, transforming the compartments into isolated houses—private, demarcated spaces. During the day they opened the curtains—that colored cotton chintz hanging from a wire—and the space reverted to being one marked by common circulation. The same principle is used in the Rietveld and Japanese houses. I enjoy Mondrian's economy, inasmuch as he works on a synthesis of reality until he arrives at his orthogonal solutions. This is a concept of economy that interests me and with which I feel an affinity. In his turn, Malevich develops the sensibility of color, another thing I am deeply interested in. These are my great and fundamental passions.

LC/IP: Curiously, all of the artists you mention are painters. In terms of a dialogue with your work, are there any artists who deal specifically with three-dimensional space?

LP: As a sculptor, Calder is one artist who interests me. His formal repertoire is vast and highly inventive. I saw a gigantic piece of his in a museum in Washington, D.C. The sculpture dips down until it almost grazes people's heads and then suddenly swings back up. It was enough to make you weep—his idea of balancing the pieces, of weighing them, and the way the thing generates movement and rhythm. And the result isn't something kinetic or mechanical. Instead, it belongs to the order of pure sensibility.

LC/IP: You often mention your admiration for the synthesis of Oriental poetry. In what way does that art relate to your work?

LP: I don't know whether it relates to my work, but I am fascinated by Japanese haiku poetry. The Concrete poets were also very interested in it. Haiku is economy itself. In precisely three lines—of five, seven, and five syllables, respectively—you have to say something about the real world. It's like imagist poetry. . . .

I made poems myself during the Neoconcrete period. I have a book of poetry and woodcuts published in the Coleção Espaço.[7] I think the Neoconcrete period was a great experience, a sum of efforts and of discipline, of imposing certain questions and understandings. There was a flowering of subjectivity: new language, new form. It was a very fertile period; it endowed all of us who were part of the movement with a pretty strong set of tools, and I realize how very helpful that was in later inventions. I believe the movement formed a collective consciousness in which artists sought new languages—a paradigm for later generations as well as for ourselves, without a colonized view.

LC/IP: Neoconcretism sought to provide the experience of world-man integration, stimulating public participation in the work of art. Nowadays, do you think it still makes sense to privilege such participation in the work of art, as was emphasized by the Neoconcrete group?

LP: I believe it was important at the time. Many of the group's artists did work in which the spectator's participation was part of the work's expression. That concept is proving hard to assimilate in Europe and in the United States, to judge from the Documenta in Kassel.

I presented a few works that emphasized participation in 1968, but mine were different in nature. When I made *O ovo* (*The Egg*)—a cube covered by a soft surface that a person enters, erupts from, and is "born"—I was interested in the possibility of an authorless work. *Divisor* (*Divider*)—a large, thirty-by-thirty-meter surface, with slits for people to put their heads through—was also a very felicitous work in this regard. At the time, I wanted to make a collective work that people could repeat without my being present. As structures, *O ovo* and *Divisor* are so simple that anyone can repeat them. In ideological terms, this type of proposition would be a very generous thing: public art that people could participate in. They are currently called performances.

Nowadays, I have no work at all in which public participation is important. The facts of invention, of the creation of new languages, of the mixture of categories—all of these were very productive as sources of creative energy for other possible works. They introduce broad and important questions.

I find it quite dangerous to classify artistic production in terms of generations. And yet it is very common to attempt to keep an artist within a certain time frame, as if frozen there. And that's not how things work. One emerges at a particular moment, given that each one of us has a period within which to emerge, yet the process can't really be defined until after the artist has disappeared. This is because processes of identification have to play out across time, as certain issues seem to vanish only to reappear down the line. I find it terribly impoverishing to classify an artist within a generation and to condition a critical view of his work to that world.

LC/IP: What led you to return to the visual arts after your experience with cinema? Were you influenced by cinema in the works you made following your return?

LP: The "Nova objetividade brasileira" exhibition in 1967 led to my return. But when I returned, I did so with new eyes. I showed up with the *Caixa das baratas*, which left everyone perplexed.

There wasn't exactly an influence from cinema. When I returned, I was no longer working with geometric forms. I began to use living objects straight away. And that included doing something that no one was doing, which was using every-day objects: I used hair, ants and cockroaches, and fabric to make *Divisor, Roda dos prazeres* (*Wheel of Pleasures*, 1967), and *O ovo*. I made a vast quantity of works. It was as if they had all been bottled up inside me and needed to stream out. In 1968 I began to incorporate these everyday elements into my work. Later, I made the installation *Eat Me* (1976), in which I used lipstick, bras, panties, hair, teeth and eyelashes, eyebrows and fake hair, peanuts, and apples. This was very different from the Neoconcrete works, in which there was discipline and rigidity. In moving on to other experiences, my work expanded and I was able to use everything I wanted to use, and in every possible way. It was another way of looking at things, another experience.

LC/IP: Once, in an interview with critic Frederico Morais, you declared that you had perceived an "organic path" connecting all of your works.[8] How would you define this thread that runs through your work?

LP: In the Neoconcrete movement there was a certain shared identity and a shared use of consistent content between all the works, characterized by geometric forms and clean colors. When I began making things that were very different from one another, including *Ttéias*, I began to question myself. I felt that—although all very different—those works had a shared identity. In spite of using materials that were very diverse, there was a language and a meaning there in these works that came from me. When I made *Eat Me*, I was satirizing the fact that women transform themselves into objects. For *Ttéias*, I used elements of everyday life to say things that interested me at that time. Obviously, as one lives on, the questions keep changing.

But I believe there is an organic quality that connects the works—a sense of coherence in the materials I've used.

In developing the idea of public art, I believe I arrived at the limit of noncommercial work, a work that anyone can repeat at home. I wanted to give the spectator as many creative elements as I could. I was no longer concerned with the fact of participation, but with the possibility of a person's ability to use or engage elements of the work for herself, in a more personal way. That was the case with *Roda dos prazeres*, a work that could be recreated at home. It was a circle in which I randomly displayed certain flavors in relation to certain colors. I used pepper, salt, vinegar, and some pleasant flavors and some unpleasant ones that were hard to identify. There is a very curious herb in the northern state of Pará called *jambu*, a little green leaf that makes your mouth tremble when it touches your tongue. One imagines one has been poisoned. The recipes for duck *tucupi* and *tacacá* call for this herb. It gives you this delicious, fantastic experience that no one knows about. Of course, the most radical experience in *Roda dos prazeres* would be the use of poison as one of the flavors.

LC/IP: What importance does color have in your work?

LP: For a long time, in the 1950s, the prints I made were always black and white and I called them *Tecelares*. Despite the fact that I was doing other things then, the only work I showed publicly was in black and white. During the Grupo Frente, Concrete, and Neoconcretist periods, I made several works that were rarely shown. They were my color side. I made a very small number of prints in color. Lygia Clark, Ivan Serpa, Aluísio Carvão, Hélio Oiticica, and I made Christmas cards that were a great hit. They were all originals and sold by the MAM-RJ: half paintings, half drawings. I enjoyed working with gouache because of its porousness. I don't like glossy color. Up until the *Livro do tempo* I had an immense color output.

LC/IP: Who are the modern Brazilian artists you admire?

LP: In Brazil, I think Cícero Dias is an important artist. Simultaneously with the Manet show here in Rio, there was an exhibition of Dias's works at the Casa França-Brasil that went almost unnoticed. His paintings and drawings from the 1920s through the 1940s are truly marvelous. He transmits the light of the northeastern state of Pernambuco, the Cubist subdivision of space. Culturally speaking, he is an artist of the utmost importance on both the national and the international levels. He really needs to be reexamined.

Emiliano Di Cavalcanti's work from that period is also extremely powerful. Later on he softened, lost his nerve, and became increasingly conventional until art became a profession to him. It is the rare artist who possesses the drive to go on inventing things until the end of their lives or, at least, to go on being daring. I don't think you can compare Cândido Portinari to early Tarsila do Amaral or early Di Cavalcanti. Tarsila deals with the questions of Brazil in a very pertinent manner. She returned from France with innovative ideas and dealt with the question of Brazilian myths. Her painting *A negra* (1923) and her period of highly dissolved, very surrealistic forms and colors are quite significant.[9] Personally, I prefer the period during which she painted little houses with flat colors. I find Léger's influence on her very productive because it gave her work structure. Tarsila's canvases possess a solid spatial organization.

Insofar as modernity was concerned, Portinari was always mistaken. He doesn't have Tarsila's structural soundness. His painting is authentic when it proposes to be merely academic. But when he attempts to be modern, it's a disaster. But he is a painter for the elites and continues to be Brazil's official artist to this day. He was always in demand, as was Oscar Niemeyer, except Niemeyer was talented whereas Portinari was a great artisan who controlled technique very nicely in academic terms but never had a clear awareness of the modern and cannot be compared to Tarsila or Di Cavalcanti in their time.

LC/IP: This means that, for you, art criticism is unimportant to the artist's creative process.

LP: I think art criticism can have a grasp of art's historical point of view—which is very important—but cannot interfere in the act of creation. Indeed, criticism can remain alert and perceive developments and emergences, and announce them, as Mário Pedrosa did. But the work came from the artist, and Pedrosa would go to the artist to look for his or her elaborations. Obviously, creating a great theory and a historical vision of art is extremely important, because that is what lays the foundation for a culture and a tradition.

LC/IP: Tell us about your relationship with Mário Pedrosa. Did he play the role of the critic, as you noted earlier—that is, one who pointed out questions in your work that had gone unnoticed by you?

LP: No. Our relationship was a posteriori to the emergence of the work. He had no desire to send artists off on any path, even though he was able to understand the emergence of a poetic act from its inception, like an art professor who instantly perceives the emergence of some fantastic revelation made by some student. If the teacher does not possess the ability to perceive the exact moment in which he must show the student the path he is envisioning, all may result in oblivion. It is crucial to theorize about the artist's questions so that this critical moment is not lost, especially nowadays—so that it may be possible to provide theoretical references for a work and for a culture.

LC/IP: In some of your early statements in newspapers, you say that Brazilian art criticism is subservient to international standards. Do you continue to see contemporary Brazilian criticism in the same way?

LP: Journalistic criticism no longer exists in the sense that it once did. There were some critics who always needed an outside model against which to compare (this was not the case with Mário Pedrosa). They lacked the courage to recognize original work born here or to discover it, possibly through an absence of sensibility or conviction. The only people with whom we kept in touch during the Neoconcrete movement were Mário Pedrosa and Ferreira Gullar, who belonged to the group. The others kept trying to knock things down.

LC/IP: You seem to have a demystifying stance toward life. Do you also refuse to accept any form of hierarchy?

LP: I'm intrinsically an anarchist. That doesn't mean I'm disorganized. But I have this terrible inclination not to respect rigid structures. I cannot abide power and hierarchies, so much so that the classes I teach are "anticlasses." Learning is a continuous and individual process of elaboration because every person has his or her own rate of growth. What I attempt to convey to my students is a concept of freedom. This is strongly emphasized. In a drawing class, for instance, I often begin with newspapers. The student starts out by acknowledging a newspaper page as a drawing, perceiving all the shades of gray, the stains, and the interference of the photographic images. This way they recreate the images and begin to have another perspective on things, learning to lose any sense of discriminating between what is art and what is not.

LC/IP: You're one of those few contemporary artists who emphasize a need to take Brazilian cultural roots into account in order to produce art in this country.

LP: I think it's a bit dangerous to talk about Brazilian roots because there is a tendency to look at it as something codified. I once thought of a work, nowadays you would call it an installation, in which I would dig a large hole and stay inside it. Whenever people asked, "What are you doing down there?," I'd answer, "I'm looking for the Brazilian roots." There isn't a nationalist connotation about this preoccupation of mine. It comes from having been born and having lived and suffered these events here. We love *farofa*, which is made using the Brazilian Indian's manioc flour. We love hammocks, another Indian thing. What I want to remind people is that this is where such things come from. There are also African influences in our food that characterize Brazilian cooking. This is something powerful, and it is a part of me. But it has nothing to do with nationalism, the very concept of which horrifies me. We are ashamed to talk about indigenous culture. I remember that the Museu do Índio, near the Maracanã soccer stadium, was struck down under the pretext that it would be taken to Brasília. They succeeded in locating it, rather precariously, in an old mansion on the Rua das Palmeiras in Rio, near the Ministry of the Interior and the police's headquarters. The objects were moved into one part of the house, which was falling apart. The museum was neglected, but we should be proud of that culture. Mexico has a museum of the Indian—the Museo Nacional de Antropología—that is a marvel. Guatemala, which is a small country, has an exquisite museum. Peru has the Museo Oro, with its fantastic jeweled creations. We have the material culture of the Indian, but we look down on it. Look what happened in Brasília, where a Pataxó Indian was burned alive and the crime was not considered heinous. This conduct horrifies me. I feel indignation at the fact that people are ashamed to be Indian—are ashamed to have black blood. Like it or not, racial mixture is part of our culture. It is our reality, and we need to create our space with it. In spite of being slightly pedantic, the anthropologist Darcy Ribeiro possessed this admirable awareness, as did his wife and fellow anthropologist Berta Ribeiro, a woman of shining intelligence. Like Darcy and Berta, Mário Pedrosa was fully conscious about what it means to be born here. This is very important. . . .

Brazil is made of perpetual disasters. Whenever something grows, it becomes unsettling and is knocked down. We are underdeveloped through omission. Despite having such a rich and fantastic culture, we call ourselves the Third World because we build and destroy. The School of Medicine building on the Praia Vermelha, for instance, was torn down because it was a symbol of student struggle, a place of thought. A scientist who worked there told me that Brazil never again had a research laboratory like it. The Universidade de Brasília, which was also truly wonderful, was demolished and transformed into something of the greatest mediocrity. We build the way Penelope weaves, and then someone undoes it. By choice, we're always giving in.

. . . Búzios, too, is an anthill of people these days. Wonderful beaches have been destroyed in the name of progress. There's no respect whatsoever for the beauty created by nature. In no way does this mean I'm an unhappy or a pessimistic person. On the contrary, I believe art possesses such vitality; it is so powerful that it conquers all. I say this not in idealistic or utopian terms. Art is a creative energy we all carry within ourselves. And I believe we need to use it really well.

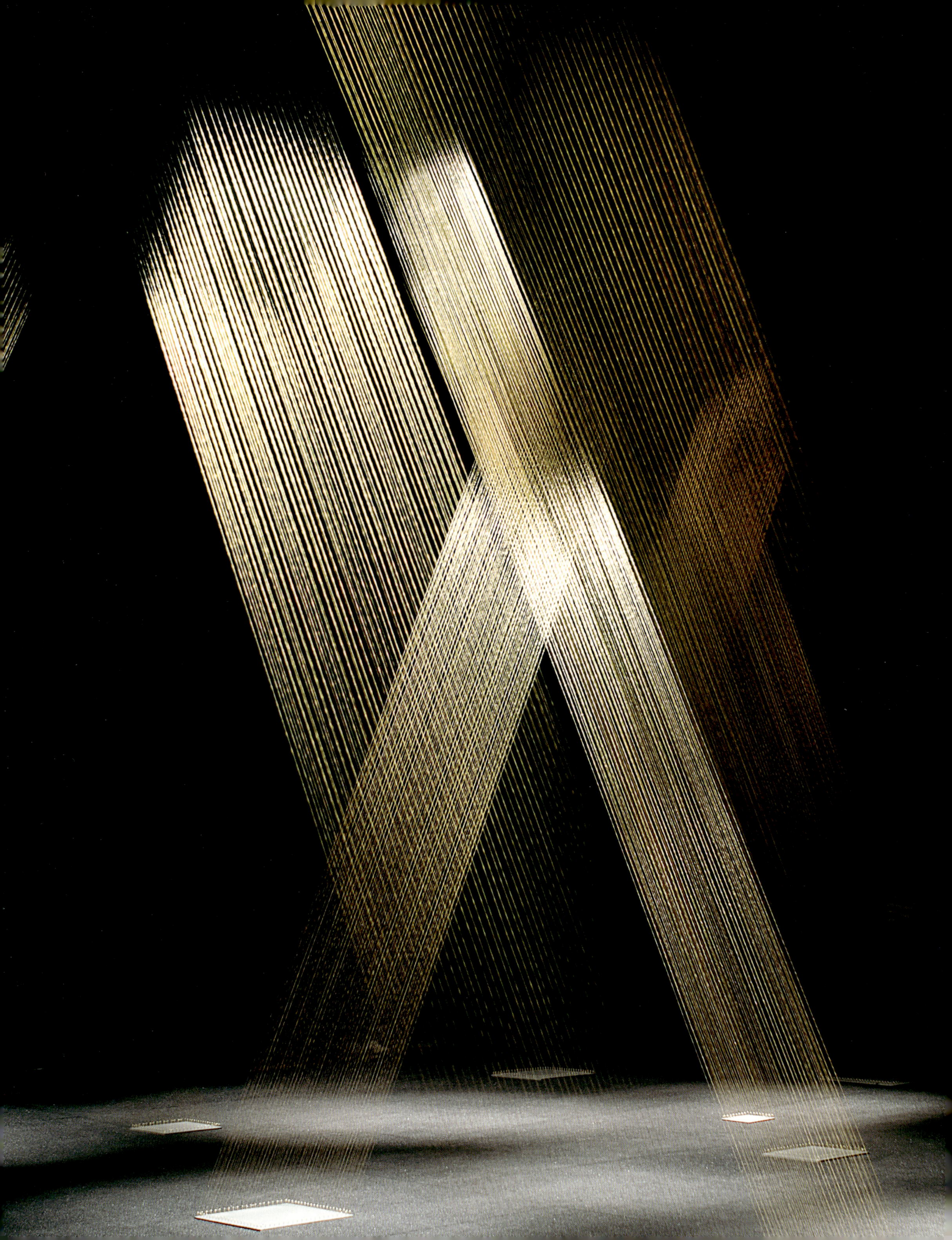

SÉRGIO B. MARTINS

an anticlass in avant-gardism

In the late 1990s, close to retiring from the Universidade Federal do Rio de Janeiro (UFRJ), Lygia Pape once again asked her students to bring wax pastels and sheets of newspaper to their next class. As one of them recalls, many of his graphic design classmates frowned upon the request.[1] To this young, middle-class cohort, mostly eager to master the computing skills the field increasingly required, the very mention of such materials meant that they were bound to waste their time with some childish drawing assignment. Pape's elusive demeanor during that class reportedly did little to assuage their mood: she gave virtually no instructions on how to proceed and spent a long time looking out the window to the mountains across the Guanabara Bay. Toward the end of the class, she finally inspected the students' work, offering stark comments and dismissing drawings that resorted either to traditional figuration or to well-rehearsed graphic solutions. The same student remembers her saying, "Why didn't you stop before? It was perfect, but now you have ruined it."

Unbeknown to her students, Pape's unorthodox teaching methods—her "anticlasses," as she termed them—were no personal idiosyncrasy.[2] Indeed, they were heavily indebted to the pedagogic environment she herself had frequented four decades earlier at the school of the Museu de Arte Moderna, Rio de Janeiro (MAM-RJ), where painter and Grupo Frente leader Ivan Serpa taught. Yet, whereas Serpa countered the kind of conservative artistic training epitomized by the nearby Escola Nacional de Belas Artes (ENBA), Pape sought to resist didactic schematism in general, regardless of whether it came from academic arts teaching or from the technologically determined mindset of her market-driven pupils.[3] Both Serpa and Pape frustrated their students' willingness to follow step-by-step instructions, privileging experimentalism over expertise, but she added a further twist of her own by having them draw on newspaper rather than on blank sheets. "The student starts out by acknowledging a newspaper page as a drawing," she once explained, "perceiving all the shades of gray, the stains, and the interference of the photographic images."[4]

Pape conceived of experimentation not as the result of subjective voluntarism or unbridled expression, but as the outcome of structural rigor and spontaneity in tandem. As her close friend Hélio Oiticica might have put it, experimentation relied on a previous process of *deconditioning*, that is, of eroding the constraints of internalized cultural and social norms.[5] The frustration her students experienced was thus an integral part of the teaching process, and the challenge of using newspaper pages as drawing structures represented her conviction that every artistic act had to be considered first and foremost as an intervention against the grain of culture and history. From her initial fascination with the veins of wood as "preexisting printed elements" in the *Tecelares* to her interest in spontaneous precipitations of urban sociability in *Espaços imantados* (*Magnetized Spaces*, 1968–95), Pape is often at odds in her work with the typically avant-gardist ethos of wiping the slate in order to affirm a new beginning.[6] True, she repeatedly resorted to metaphors of birth and creation—as in the *Livro da criação* (*Book of Creation*, 1959–60), *O ovo* (*The Egg*, 1967), and *La nouvelle création* (*The New Creation*, 1967), just to name a few examples—but their meaning is far from straightforward. Her work is shot through with a temporal complexity that divests these metaphors from a clear-cut sense of rupture and gives rise instead to a mythical sense of recurrence, repetition, and re-creation.[7]

Pape's preference for woodcut printing during the 1950s was a charged one. At the time, the medium was most often associated either with the popular tradition of cordel literature from the Brazilian Northeast or with an expressionist vein, represented in the work of the great—albeit unorthodox—printmaker Oswaldo Goeldi (1895–1961).[8] Goeldi and his assistant Adir Botelho (born 1932) ran an important printmaking workshop at the ENBA that was active into the late 1950s, and their teaching was influential even for artists younger than Pape, such as Antonio Dias (born 1944) and Anna Maria Maiolino (born 1942), who began their training at the ENBA before joining the MAM-RJ's avant-garde milieu. But ever since the early 1950s, Pape had been invested in the Brazilian constructive avant-garde's radical revision of modernist history, which sought to secure the movement's rightful place within this legacy. The MAM-RJ was vital in this regard, since the museum's intended role as a beacon of modern art in the country involved not only the formation of a dedicated public, but also the cultivation of artists. This aspect of the MAM-RJ's activity would remain crucial in the following two decades, even as the language of experimentation shifted away from geometric abstraction, as evident in such initiatives as the "Unidade experimental" ("Experimental Unit"), launched in 1969, and the "Domingos da criação" ("Sundays of Creation"; fig. 19), mounted between January and July 1971, during the height of the military regime.[9] As a member of Grupo Frente, more specifically, Pape was exposed to a rather different set of references very early in her career, including Josef Albers, who in 1957 figured prominently in the IV Bienal de São Paulo. It is to his work that we must first turn in order to appreciate Pape's unique development of Concretist woodcutting.[10]

Many of Albers's woodcuts play linear and reversible geometric forms against wood-grain background patterns. Such oppositions are not static, though. In *Tlaloc* (fig. 20), as the two "base" lines of the etched forms become parallel to one another and to their fine-grained background, the figure and ground relation suddenly changes from opposition (still operative in the section where carved diagonals stand against curved ripples) to implication (the fine pattern allows for a regular sense of spatial recession between the lines, as if they were two legs of a folding chair). This is the sort of play that prompted Rosalind Krauss to cast Albers

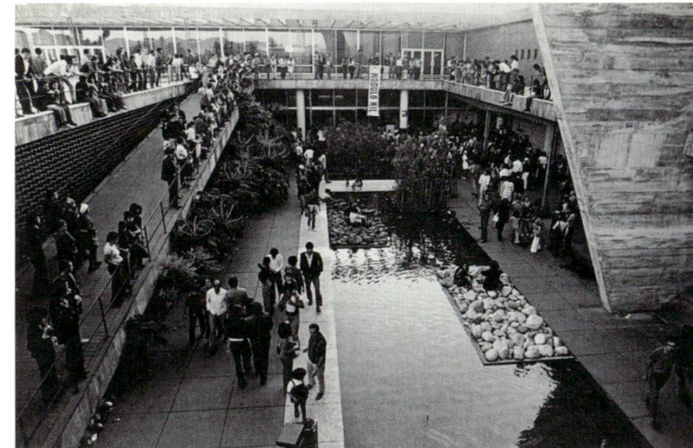

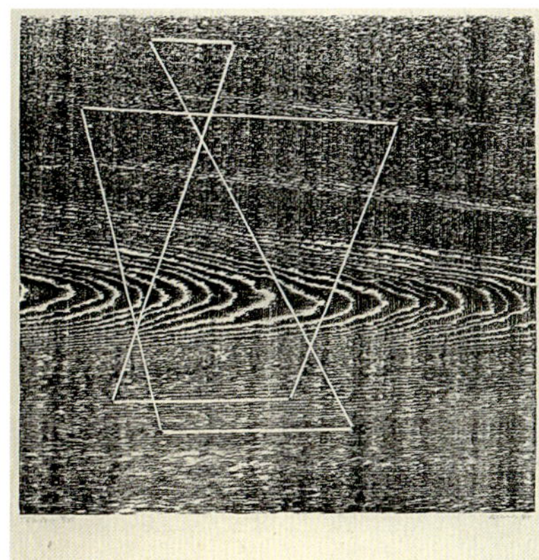

FIG. 19. "Domingos da criação" at Museu de Arte Moderna, Rio de Janeiro, 1971

FIG. 20. Josef Albers (American [born Germany], 1888–1976). *Tlaloc*, 1944. Woodcut in rough pine board, 12 × 12³⁄₈ in. (30.5 × 31.4 cm). The Metropolitan Museum of Art, New York, John B. Turner Fund, 1966 (66.685.4)

as a late modernist champion of the "fertility of the picture plane," with the plane understood as a kind of modernist golden cage that offered a seemingly unending repository of potential meanings.[11] But Pape approached Albers from a different perspective, one deeply informed by discussions she had had at Serpa's gatherings and at Mário Pedrosa's apartment. These ideas resonated throughout the decade not only in Pape's own writings and statements, but also in the rising voices of Lygia Clark and Ferreira Gullar.[12]

In these conversations, on the one hand, Albers's Bauhausian experimentalism converged with the philosophy of Susanne K. Langer, who insisted that the studio, like the laboratory in science, is where "the most vital issues in the philosophy of art" originate.[13] On the other hand, such discussions often returned to the topics of the crisis of modernism and the avowed death—or historical exhaustion—of its foremost constructive avatar: the picture plane.[14] Pape experimented with the construction of multi-element matrices for her printing blocks instead of using a single plank, in which the wood grain acts as an organic unifying pattern. In this way, she joined Clark in testing the line as a limit *of* the plane rather than a

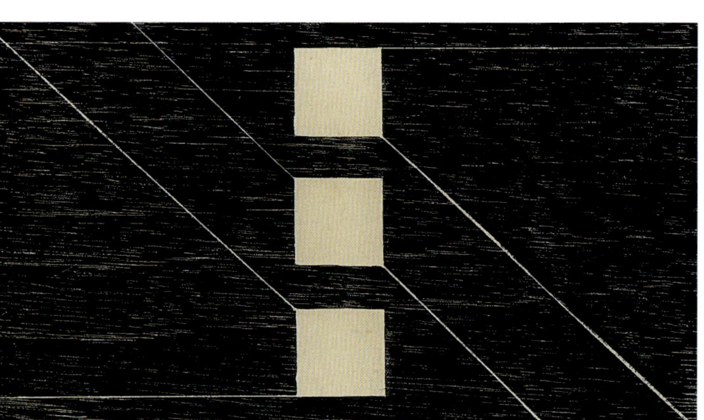

FIG. 21. Lygia Pape. *Tecelar*, 1957–58. Woodcut on Japanese paper, 8 × 13½ in. (20.3 × 34.3 cm). Museu de Arte Moderna, Rio de Janeiro, Gift of Fininvest S.A.

sign functioning strictly *within* the plane (conversely, even when Albers used elaborately constructed matrices, he still insisted on the nature/culture opposition as the ultimate ground of meaning, thus remaining firmly within the metaphysical confines of the plane).[15] Pape distinguished between lines obtained by juxtaposing sawn wood blocks from those that resulted from etching into or sanding down their surfaces, arguing that the former offered "a perfect identity with the material" and presented a unique set of problems for her own woodcut laboratory.[16] Her use of this kind of sawn line in *Tecelar* from 1960 (pl. 54) formally recalls Clark's *Planos em superfície modulada no. 5* (*Planes on a Modulated Surface No. 5*, 1957), although the visible texture and distinct graphic register of lines and planes in Pape's work suggest a different spatiality from that of the rather neat topological reversals of the smooth surfaces in Clark's painting. In Pape's woodcuts, geometric mirroring operates as a kind of standard against which the strikingly material but nevertheless subtle sense of temporal dilation of her incisions can palpably be felt.

This is where Pape's updating of the Brazilian printmaking tradition comes into play. As a matter of fact, her husband, Günther, owned a substantial collection of prints by Goeldi, who would later become the subject of her short film *O guarda-chuva vermelho* (*The Red Umbrella*, 1971). In a different woodcut from 1957–58 (fig. 21), Pape is able to turn what might have been yet another Concretist exercise in symmetry into a subtle, temporally inflected meditation on planar cohesion by translating Goeldi's masterful handling of luminosity to a constructive idiom.[17] Goeldi envisaged white and black not as stable graphic complementaries, but rather as an intricate struggle of light and dark. It is as if his printed surfaces were, to borrow artist and writer Nuno Ramos's evocative metaphor, "a black-painted window whose darkness blocks the light emanating from behind, and what we see is what breaches through its cracks, through the drawing's grooves, in a phosphorescence

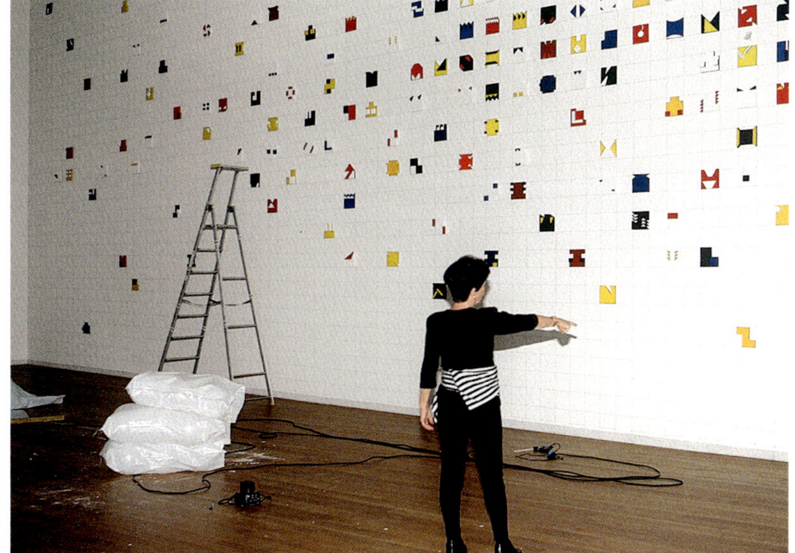

FIG. 22. Lygia Pape installing *Livro do tempo* at Fundação de Serralves—Museu de Arte Contemporânea, Porto, Portugal, 2000

always on the verge of petering out."[18] Pape's choice to print on Japanese paper makes Ramos's metaphor almost literal, as white and black become materially equated with translucence and opaqueness (the *Poemas-luz* [*Light-Poems*] are equally staked on this opposition, with the words as the opaque visual element).[19] The lines in that same 1957–58 woodcut are strikingly Goeldian in this particular sense. Instead of locking the three central squares to the plane—that is, instead of delivering the surface to the mandate of geometric rationality—they seem to project from it, like solitary scouts with flickering lanterns always on the brink of disappearing amid a dark expanse. They ultimately do not disappear, but the experience of the work remains indelibly marked by the sense of temporal unfolding those lines evoke by virtue of the palpable materiality that results from the etching and printing process. In short, Pape's prints translate luminosity into duration.

Duration and the death of the plane were two key subjects of Neoconcretism, but this is not to say that the movement's artists subscribed to a homogeneous program. Pape was actually skeptical of Gullar's concept of "non-object," believing it to be relevant for Clark's work but unfitting for her own.[20] Still, Pape's and Gullar's trajectories mirror each other rather uncannily. Just as the poet challenged the single-page graphic paradigm that informed Concrete poetry by privileging the temporality of the book form, Pape's own temporal investigation led her beyond the graphic limits of the *Tecelares* toward the making of books (Pape even incorporated woodcut prints in her 1960 *Livro-poema* [*Book-Poem*]). Her books also build off of the Grupo Frente reliefs, the square format of which was punctuated by smaller and unevenly colored square surface accretions that prompted viewers to try to encounter the work from different vantage points, thus tensioning the initial gestalt of the square base. This is especially true of the *Livro do tempo* (*Book of Time*; fig. 22), in which the saw-and-assemble procedure of the *Tecelares* morphs into a virtuoso array of variations on the dismantling of the square. Each of the 365 elements of the *Livro do tempo*—one for each day of the year—was sawn and

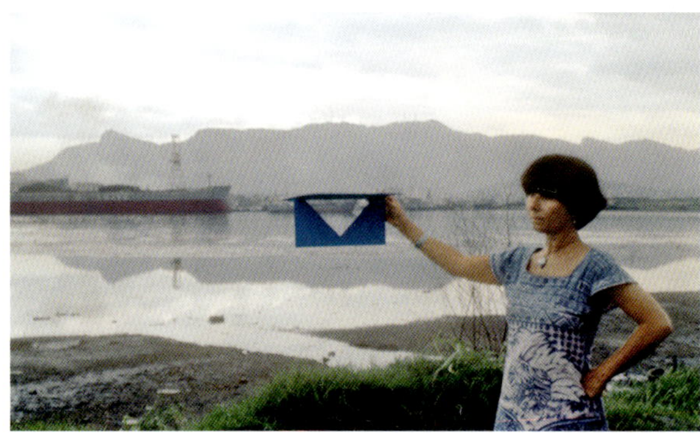

FIG. 23. Lygia Pape with *Livro da criação* (1959–60), in front of Favela da Maré, 1980s

FIG. 24. Page featuring "Olho-Alvo" by Reynaldo Jardim and photographs of *Ballet neoconcreto I*, *Suplemento dominical*, *Jornal do Brasil*, Rio de Janeiro, August 31, 1958

painted in a different way, with the sawn fragments reattached onto the surface of their respective squares in the manner of a Grupo Frente relief. The result is dizzying temporal concatenation, in which eventual perspectives of the plane's stability are swallowed by the rhythm of its fragmentations. Other books, such as the *Livro da criação* (*Book of Creation*; fig. 23) and the *Livro da arquitetura* (*Book of Architecture*, 1959–60), also take the square as their departure point; their formal and narrative unfolding (which is not as linear as the titles might imply) often begins, once again, with simple incisions that fragment the plane both actually and virtually. This places Pape's books, alongside Clark's *Unidades* (*Unities*, 1958–59) and Oiticica's *Invenções* (*Inventions*, 1959–62), at the core of the Neoconcrete subversion of the picture plane via its foremost geometric figure.[21]

Prior to the books, Pape's effacement of the body in her Neoconcrete ballets can be read as analogous to her engagement with the idea of the death of the plane and also as an extension of the rigorous control she exerted over the incisions in the printing blocks for the *Tecelares*.[22] For all their obvious differences, both woodcut printing and dance are media in which traditional gestural expressiveness normally takes hold. Strictly speaking, it was this kind of expressiveness, or rather expressionism, and not gesture, that Pape's ballets resisted. Pape's criticism of conventional interpretation was that it framed gesture in a kind of figure/ground opposition against the ensemble of the dancer's movements, which, in turn, led to a second-degree opposition between the acting human figure and the conventional spatial frame of the stage. Therefore, by restricting dancers to the task of bestowing movement to geometric forms that entirely covered their bodies, Pape sought to complicate theatrical framing in a twofold manner: on the one hand, in relation to the body vis-à-vis interpretation, and, on the other, by disrupting the spatial homology between stage and plane.[23]

Crucially, the ballets were conceived not as a substitution of the mechanic for the organic. Pape and Reynaldo Jardim were critical of Nicolas Schöffer's concept of spatiodynamism and adamant in rejecting the use of "cybernetic motors" in place of human ones.[24] *Ballet neoconcreto I* (*Neoconcrete Ballet I*, 1958) enacts Jardim's poem "Olho-Alvo" as if it were a score, with dancers wearing either cylinders or vertical parallelepipeds in lieu of the poem's words *olho* (eye) and *alvo* (target), respectively (fig. 24). The dancers' cyclical movement follows the words' rotation in Jardim's five-page piece. For Pape, translating the temporality of page turning to the continuum of dance was tantamount to recasting gesture beyond the confines of individual expression(ism).[25] From this perspective, expressiveness lay instead in the objective unfolding of forms and their concomitant complication of theatrical space; only then, and by extension, could the viewing subject be potentially implied, as the stage would lose its traditional metaphorical distance. The effect was reinforced by the carefully controlled lighting that slowly intensified the colors and shapes onstage and by the electronic soundtrack that heightened "the conflict between the curves and edges," in Gullar's lively description.[26] Pape envisaged the result as an organic spatial and temporal whole: "The space between the solids becomes form in a logical and continuous development."[27]

How to explain, then, the emergence of the body in *O ovo*, a work so formally indebted to the ballets? Hélio Oiticica offers a clue when he insists that the work enacts a passage, or *"body-object-environment,"* that begins not as participants break out of their cube-shaped "eggs" but rather as they enter them.[28] For the setting was no longer a stage, but the conflictive and precarious public space of 1960s Rio de Janeiro, marked as it was by social, cultural, and political struggles.[29] Oiticica adds that the egg is like a "shelter," a term he draws from The Rolling Stones song "Gimme Shelter" (1969), and interprets the work as the birth of a community initially driven by the need for sanctuary in the face of menacing or oppressive forces. As such, the egg would stand as a metaphor for the communal rebirth of the subject, or as Oiticica explains, "to be SHELTER is to open one's self to the WORLD which is created from these multipossibilities."[30] Indeed, Oiticica, Pape, and Clark often oscillate between offering an intimate abode and projecting a collective ethos in their works, and *O ovo* is no exception.[31] Here the egg is a kind of hideout that is not so much effective as affective, as hiding in it is reminiscent of the childhood experience of ensconcing oneself under a table or behind a curtain. In *Eros and Civilization* (1955), a book both Pape and Oiticica admired, philosopher Herbert Marcuse diagnoses that "the animal drives become human instincts under the influence of the external reality" and suggests that "the restoration of memory" of a past that preceded this cultural "reality principle" is crucial for the hope of bringing about a "nonrepressive civilization."[32] From this perspective, it is as if the bodies that tear their way out of the eggs had already undergone their cultural deconditioning by hiding in them and becoming ready to reemerge publicly as heralds of a community to come. This explains why participants in the short 1968 film of *Trio do embalo maluco* (*Crazy Rocking Trio*) are Mangueira *passistas* (plus Oiticica) who emerge from the eggs playing samba instruments. The samba school offered Pape and Oiticica, who jointly frequented Mangueira hangouts, a transformative communal blueprint (though not necessarily a benign one). Pape had *O ovo*—as well as *Roda dos prazeres* (*Wheel of Pleasures*, 1967)—photographed and filmed on deserted beaches and empty lots with no visible urban traces; such settings suggest a primitive and fantastic mythscape that frames both the experience of the proposition[33] and its utopian, countercultural hopes for society and culture.

Marcuse's attempt to rethink the psychoanalytic theory of the drives from a historical materialist standpoint is epitomized in his assertion that "Freud's individual psychology is in its very essence social psychology."[34] Such a shortcircuit between the individual and the social would no doubt be appealing to artists whose formation had largely sidestepped any consequential take on collective praxis now that the latter had become a sine qua non condition for their renewed

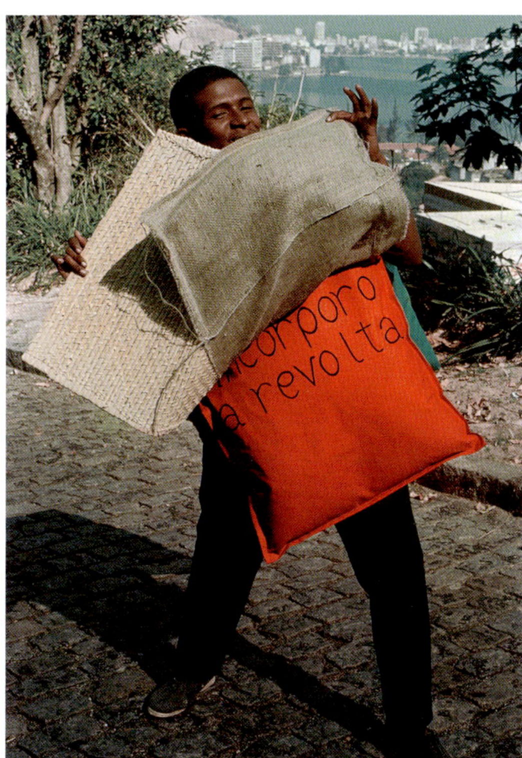

FIG. 25. Nildo da Mangueira wearing Hélio Oiticica's *P15 Parangolé capa 11—"Eu incorporo a revolta"* (*Parangolé P15 Cape 11—"I Embody Revolt,"* 1967), photograph ca. 1968

utopian gambit.[35] The square sheet that participants wear like a collective mantle in *Divisor* (*Divider*, 1968) is symptomatic of this appeal. Like color in the earlier Grupo Frente reliefs (and light in the 1976 *Ttéia quadrada*), the unorchestrated movement of participants tensions the square, which registers both their being together and their irreducible individualities. Previously a means of questioning the viewer's perception, the square now becomes a means of visualizing and interrogating the social, without disregarding the role of individual impulses. It is important to remember that samba in Oiticica's *Parangolés* (fig. 25)—a proposal with which *Divisor* is in direct dialogue—is not a celebration of unbridled communion, but rather an antagonistic display of physical enjoyment to a culturally constrained middle-class audience unable to partake in it.[36] It is hard to imagine the bourgeois public of the MAM-RJ feeling as comfortable as either Mangueira *passistas* or Oiticica's avant-garde colleagues wearing the capes the artist designed—some of them displaying defiant statements coined by the *passistas* themselves—and dancing to the sound of samba percussion. In other words, Oiticica casts the dancing (or danceless) body as a marker of sociocultural tensions between individualism and communitarianism. *Divisor*, in turn, plays the individual against the communal by means of a sensory split of the body. Pape initially conceived the piece as a gallery-based work in which participants would simultaneously feel cold air blowing from above the sheet and hot air from below. By abandoning this initial plan and relocating *Divisor* to the streets, Pape displaces sensorial heightening to the public space in the guise of the latter's "eroticization," that is, of the charting and mobilization of its nonrepressive aspects.[37]

None of this is to say that Pape's trajectory from her participation with Grupo Frente to the strident avant-gardist exhibitions and events of the 1960s and beyond was a straight, continuous development; suffice it to point out that she temporarily distanced herself from the visual arts in the period immediately following the breakdown of the Neoconcrete group in order to work in graphic design and on film projects, often in conjunction with Cinema Novo filmmakers.[38] But the path traced here does evidence the construction of a rigorous poetic backbone that served as a platform from which the artist launched an array of formal, conceptual, material, and political experiments that never coalesced in an easily recognizable individual style. Her preferred metaphor of the magnet, around which disparate elements remain bound by an invisible force, is apposite in this respect. In the pedagogic context, this vast experimental repertoire enabled Pape to respond to various situations and even turn them into the generative principle of new work.[39] Such a radical but not dispersive plasticity is undoubtedly one of the most valuable lessons of Pape's avant-gardist anticlasses.

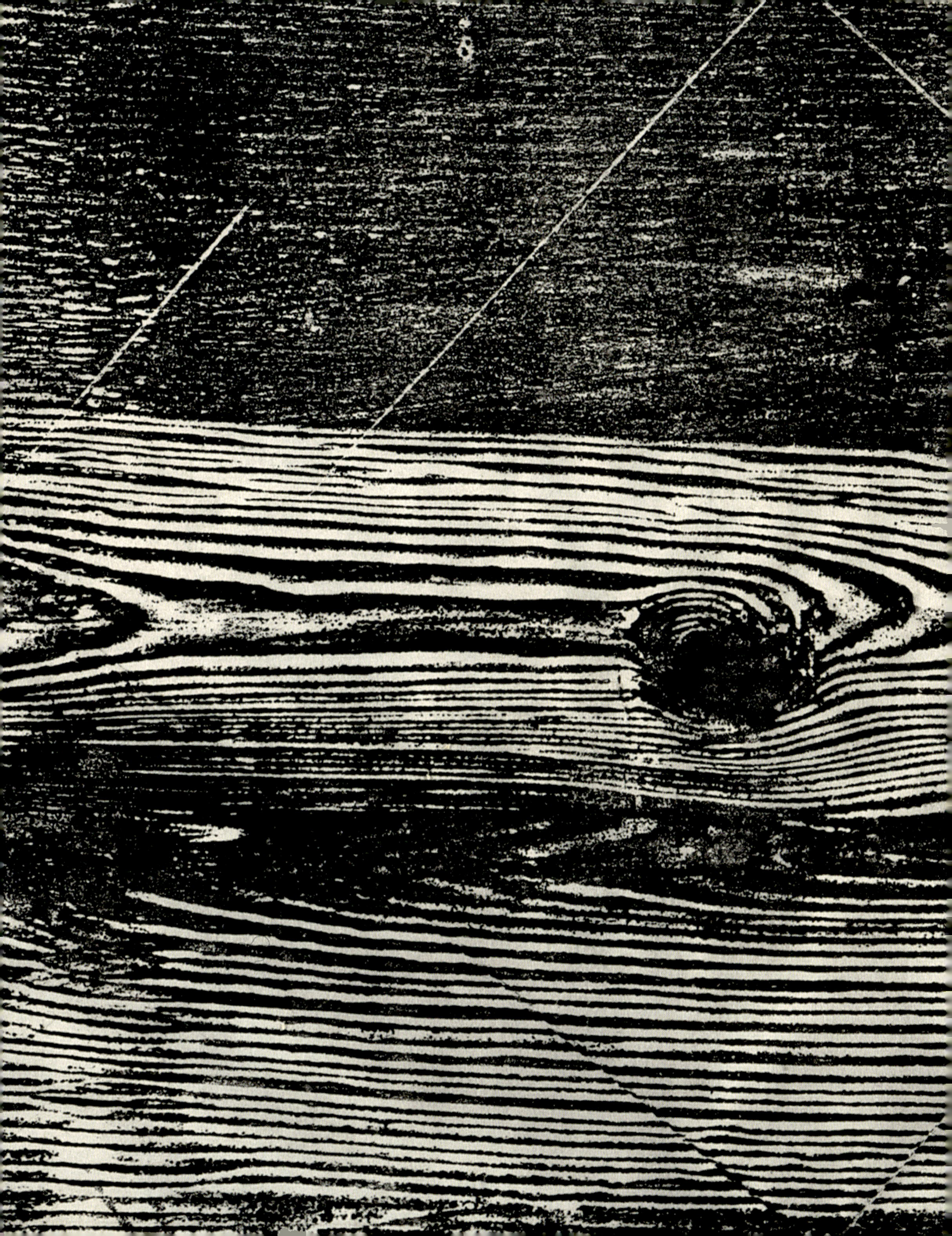

JOHN RAJCHMAN

lygia pape's vital ideas

Of all the artists in Brazil, none was "richer in ideas" than Lygia Pape—so Mário Pedrosa, great mentor and critic, declared in 1979.[1] The artist herself would never stop saying as much; what mattered to her above all were ideas, not the market nor the finished work nor securing a place in settled stories or institutions. Restless, recalcitrant, indefatigable, she would always go outside to find something new, ever revising, recasting, revitalizing what had come before. In this way, she took part in all the groups, preoccupations, and media of one of the most inventive and fraught times in Brazilian—and global—art history. That is why to her artist-friend Hélio Oiticica she seemed like a "permanently open seed," irreducible to fixed codes, emerging rather from a prior web of overlapping currents.[2] It is also why, in her master's thesis in philosophy (fig. 26), she tried to draw a picture of artists as savage "artist-inventors" of ideas, of a sort that might arise yet again out of the misery of the Third World, like a "new moon" in the lands of Brazil.[3] Later, in 1995, looking back again in a magazine article titled "What I Do Not Know," she insisted that ideas in art, in products of artistic invention, are never mere illustrations of any philosophy, adding that one's work, born rather of always risking new ideas, leaves in its wake a cluster of idiosyncrasies, a new potential for what is yet to come.[4]

Perhaps we are only now starting to untangle all the ideas thus encapsulated in Pape's long artistic itinerary, taking off from her early inspiration in Ivan Serpa's circle, passing through the great moment of Neoconcretism, then, against the growing adversity of the dictatorship, moving into film, pedagogical explorations of urban spaces and curation, working across many forms, materials, and projects, finished and unfinished—in the words of Pedrosa, ever spinning out from a "tiny particle, the breath of life," from somewhere deep within. Because ideas, for Pape, were in fact strange, wild things—"fragments of sensations," Pedrosa called them.[5] Coming to one unexpectedly, ideas always survive their initial formulations and so are irreducible to any one discursive definition. Developed instead through the materials and practices of the visual arts or film, they always remain poetic. Never alone, they fall into constellations with others, as if the fragments were suddenly brought together in a kind of magnetic force field, at once aesthetic and social or political. To attain them is to get out from one's conditioned clichéd sensibilities and unitary identities. They thus help mobilize new relations with others —friendships and ephemeral groups brought together through experiment rather than prior method or doctrine, freely meeting, thinking, inventing together; "special, good for nothing gratuitous beings," she called them at one point.[6] Such not knowing was what had already impressed Pedrosa about Paul Klee in the 1960s: one thinks in art just in those moments when there is no prior doctrine, method, or given sensibility, when one cannot yet know what to do, when one must risk trying out, experimenting with new things.[7] In the end, to live is to invent.

The resultant richness in ideas in the work Pape has left us is now rather like an entangled message in a bottle, as if thrown into the new seas of the art world of the 1980s, whose limitations a pessimistic Pedrosa already keenly sensed at the time (fig. 27).[8] It now forms part of her difficult and singular legacy, how we see and think about her work today. Like Pedrosa, Pape was long interested in finding a place for the new Brazilian art in a world dominated by the stories and the categories of a hegemonic North, taking up instead the legacies of the Russian avant-garde and the Bauhaus, broken off by fascism or Stalinism in Europe, and launching them on a new and vital Brazilian path. But what new life might her work yet have for us in the twenty-first century, with our own new narratives and geographies? Perhaps we can at least unpack a few points.

A great question in Neoconcretism was how to recast the legacy of geometric abstraction in a new Brazilian manner, aesthetically, socially, and politically. In her thesis, Pape argues that a key influence in this pursuit was Russian Constructivism, as if, in Brazil, one were free to develop Kazimir Malevich's own turn to social and architectural space, rather like her own eventual turn to what Oiticica called a social ecology. But retrospectively at least, Pape's peculiar path into the question of abstraction is already to be found in her striking early woodcuts and reliefs. In the woodcuts, later called *Tecelares* (translated as "weavings"), printed in black and white on Japanese paper, we find an adventure of lines no longer contained by contours or objects, as in an imaginary frame or window, and almost calligraphic in nature; and, in the reliefs, moving out into space from the picture plane, geometric figures recur in an irregular, nonmetric or unmechanical movement. In both cases, with both lines and figures and their interrelations, we thus find a kind of vital rhythm or dance and, with it, a new experimental intuition of space and time, no longer governed by fixed objects presented to external subjects. In this lies a first fertile seed in the germination of Pape's artistic ideas. As the new space in which abstract geometries figure became open or unlimited, no longer containing or enclosing them, the new time of their vital spin, movement, or repetition became free, no longer ordered in advance, as with mechanical or industrial means. At the time, of course, the Neoconcretists were responding to the more structuralist Grupo Ruptura in São Paulo, bent on defeating all expressive subjectivity through automatic means and industrial colors. But Pape later came to see this division between the two cities as part of a larger Brazilian movement in abstraction in which this sort of "eye-machine" would give way, in Rio de Janeiro, to a new "eye-body" *dispositif*, overcoming the very division between expressive subjectivity and mechanical reproduction.

The vital rhythm, the new dance of lines and shapes in Pape's early work, was accompanied at the same time by a philosophical search for a new role of bodily experience in art, a mad, vital *vivência*. For before seeing external objects,

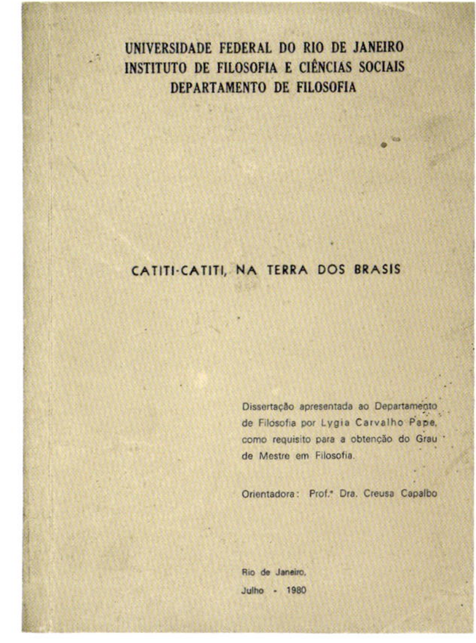

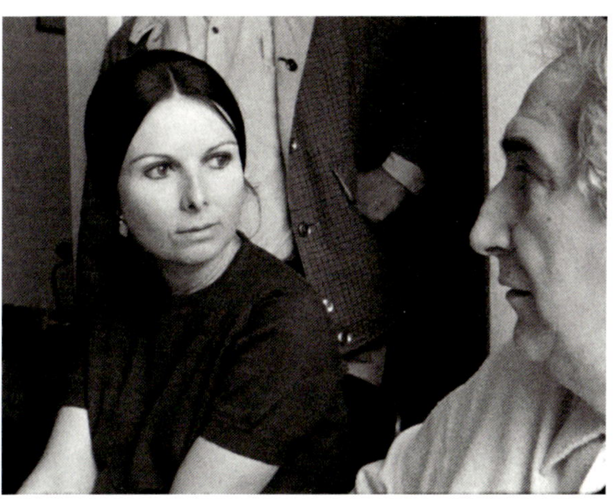

FIG. 26. Lygia Pape. "Catiti-Catiti, na terra dos Brasis." Master's thesis, Instituto de Filosofia e Ciências Sociais, Universidade Federal do Rio de Janeiro, 1980

FIG. 27. Lygia Pape interviewing Mário Pedrosa about *Opção brasileira* (*The Brazilian Option*) at Pedrosa's home, Rio de Janeiro, 1970

as if through a window, the body is in fact plunged into a chaos of sensations from which the new abstract art would emerge. To discover the new abstract dance was thus to plunge oneself into this prior chaotic sensory field, finding ways to make it visible or sensible. It was in this context that Brazilian artists turned to the new philosophical picture of "eye and mind" offered by Maurice Merleau-Ponty, which, interrupted by his untimely death in 1961, had inspired many artists and critics at the time—in Paris, in relation to Giacometti, and in New York, with the great passage of sculpture from the figure on the pedestal into a new "chiasmic" space, where it would encounter dance and performance.[9] Today we might thus see Pape, along with the other Neoconcretists, as offering already in the 1950s another artistic reading and use of Merleau-Ponty, closer to the vital chaos so central in Klee, which would move them in the new direction of social participation and media manipulation, drawing on other currents in the Bauhaus and Constructivist legacies.

If the new adventure in lines and shapes Pape was exploring in the woodcuts and reliefs was thus a kind of new abstract dance, it was because it was born from a vital chaotic bodily experience—that was the idea. More precisely, it was given through an experimental sort of intuition of space and time freed from any prior organizing gestalt of the sort still found in Josef Albers's great Bauhaus exercises: figure and ground, center and periphery, horizon and plane. That is exactly what made the work open. Art itself became an "experimental exercise"[10] prior to the kind of a priori forms still found in Ernst Cassirer or indeed in the lingering hopes for an eidetic reduction found in Edmund Husserl's 1936 "The Origin of Geometry." Thus freeing themselves, artistically and intellectually, the experimentally minded Brazilian artists were in effect moving away from any centered anchorage in the life-world, in which such forms of intuition might be relocated. In this they were already moving in the same direction as Pierre Boulez in Paris around the same time; Boulez, starting from Klee's ideas of pictorial chaos and nonretrogradable rhythms, was trying to develop a new picture of what it is to have ideas in music. Indeed, retrospectively, we find a fertile, uncanny match between what Boulez was then calling "smooth" and "striated" spaces and "non-pulsed" and "pulsed" rhythms and the new experimental abstraction in Rio de Janeiro, itself tied up with the new music and dance of the day.[11] Gilles Deleuze would later isolate and develop the central artistico-philosophical question Boulez was thus posing: how, in music, art, and writing alike, to "occupy space without counting"?[12] Together with Félix Guattari, Deleuze went on to extend the idea of the smooth and the striated into social spaces and cultural practices in a way that might now shed light on Pape's own turn to the irregular quilts and disparate weavings she sought in Amerindian art—outside the modernist divisions between figurative and abstract, decorative and artistic—as well as in the vital rhythmic sense of the sea she would explore in the Favela da Maré.[13]

But there is another singularity in Pape's path into these questions, found early on in the woodcuts. Unlike other Neoconcretists, she started with print, with which many of her evolving ideas and practices would continue to be associated.[14] Impressed early on by the woodcuts of Oswaldo Goeldi, which she and her husband collected and about which she would later make a film, Pape pushed the practice of woodcuts in a new direction. Already in Pedrosa's 1933 essay on Käthe Kollwitz, we see that the question of woodcuts was central in his Trotsky-inspired ambition to find a new Brazilian practice of abstraction outside what he saw as the empty formalism to which abstraction elsewhere seemed to be leading. Woodcuts mattered in this larger question because of the key role they had acquired in the turn to Soviet Socialist Realism and its global influence, notably in Asia.[15] Looked at in this light, what is remarkable in Pape's early woodcuts is not only that she released abstract lines from the grain of the wood instead of creating great expressive images as Kollwitz did, but also that, using the same medium, she deliberately freed them from any mechanical reproduction, making them more like unique or auratic objects—perhaps, more precisely, vital ones. Her invention of abstract woodcuts thus formed part of a larger search for a new path for abstraction, outside sterile medium divisions, moving instead into public forms of participation associated with the great questions of the book: language, writing, image, text, discourse.

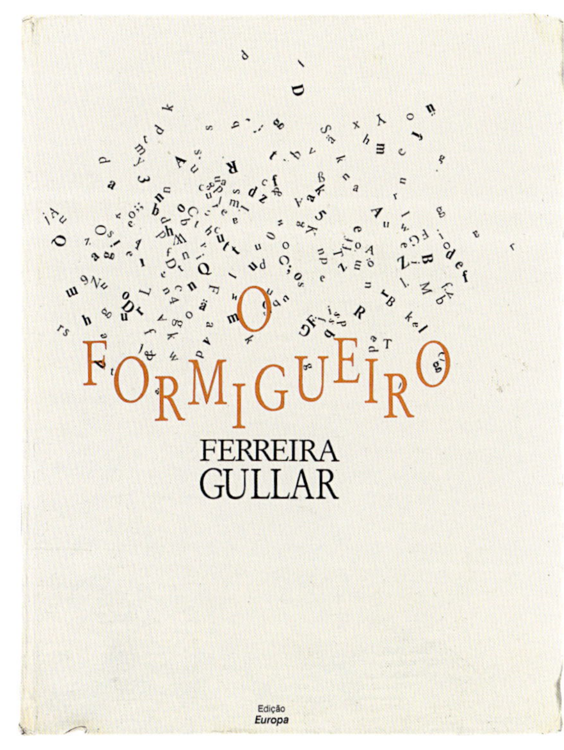

Pape's vital ideas were thus fertilized through print, not painting, a practice to which she later confessed she was never really drawn. In this she was hardly alone. Indeed, we find a long line of artists coming to abstraction through the legacy of Stéphane Mallarmé and the idea of the book, intersecting with the great political preoccupations about whether poetry is in books or in the streets, in handwriting or in industrialized print. Drawing on the Brazilian movement in Concrete poetry, Pape was very much involved with such questions, writing Concrete poems herself, collaborating with the poet Reynaldo Jardim on *Ballet neoconcreto I* (*Neoconcrete Ballet I*, 1958), inspired by the work of Ferreira Gullar (figs. 28, 29), the poet-critic who wrote the "Manifesto neoconcreto" and later created the "Poema enterrado" ("Buried Poem," 1959). Indeed, as Pedrosa declared at the time, the Neoconcretists were "poets all."[16] We might thus retrospectively see the questions of image and text (or the "verbivocovisual") in Pape's work as part of a larger story of art and poetry, reflected at the time in the media theory of Marshall McLuhan or, in Brazil, Vilém Flusser.[17] The role of print in Pape's woodcuts had already pushed her in this direction. Vital material objects, poems were, for her, things of this world, which, not necessarily confined to the page, could be disassembled, opened up in other ways. Indeed, perhaps neither canvas nor page is ever blank in quite the way the spiritualist-minded Mallarmé had imagined; instead, they are manipulable material things that can be moved by art into the public realm rather than being read alone or in private. The book, in other words, could be freed from the cover in much the same way that, for Gullar, painting was being freed from the framed object, opening onto new kinds of relations to be explored in galleries, theaters, or the

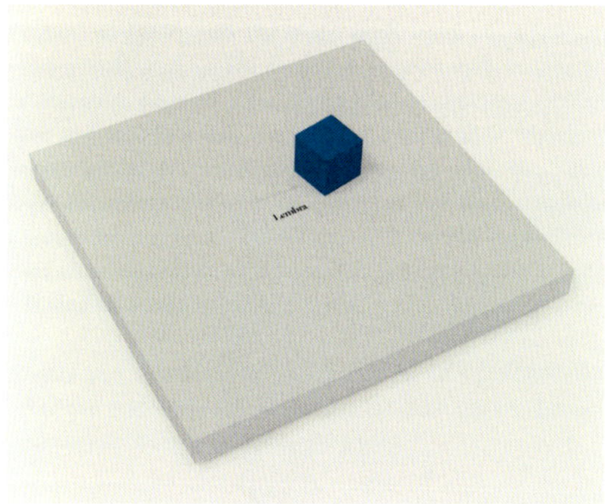

FIG. 28 Ferreira Gullar (Brazilian, born 1930). Page from "O formigueiro" ("The Anthill"), 1955; published 1991

FIG. 29. Ferreira Gullar (Brazilian, born 1930). "Lembra" ("Remember"), 1954; reconstructed 2004. Acrylic on wood and vinyl, 15¾ × 15¾ × 2 in. (40 × 40 × 5 cm). Paço Imperial—Centro Cultural do Iphan/MinC, Rio de Janeiro

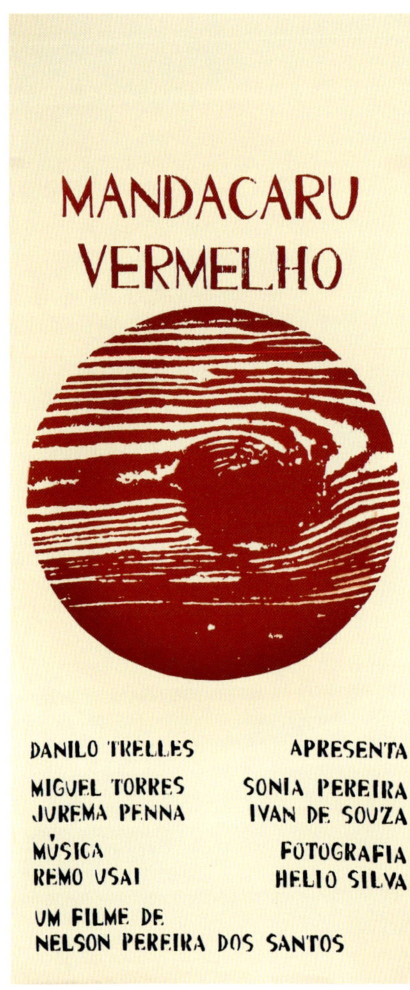

FIG. 30. Lygia Pape. Poster for *Mandacaru vermelho* (*Red Mandacaru*), 1961. Screenprint on paper, 30½ × 13 in. (77.5 × 33 cm). Projeto Lygia Pape

street. We thus find the aesthetic questions of inner and outer, open and enclosed, later explored by Guy Brett in his suggestive study of the box and the book in Brazilian art.[18] In this way the Brazilian artist-poets created a whole new *dispositif* of image, language, and writing, rather different from Marcel Broodthaers's picture of the "end of poetry"—the book as frozen, its pages unable to be opened, without a public—and much closer in many ways to the experiments in poetry and art carried out at the time by Henri Michaux.

In the Neoconcrete ballets, and in the series of works she called books, Pape would develop these questions, inflecting them in a distinctive manner that might be called allegorical. Using new means taken from poetry or music, she tried to retell the story of creation itself, dramatizing the role of images in it. We see this in a very striking manner in the ballets, which themselves recall Malevich's Cubo-Futurist opera of 1913, *Victory over the Sun*, but with a new sense of how images are born.[19] In Pape's ballets, abstract geometrical figures, thanks to special contrivances, were set into motion by the invisible bodies of actual ballet dancers within.[20] In these early balletic visual poems and allegories of creation we thus find many of the elements of the distinctive idiom Pape would go on to develop in her *Divisor* (*Divider*, 1968) and her *O ovo* (*The Egg*, 1967), one version of which was filmed on the beach. With the membrane of the white sheet dividing individual heads from the rhythm of the collective movement beneath, or the birth out of white cubes called "eggs," we find the emergence of a new public and, with it, a kind of becoming feminine and becoming Brazilian, of the very idea of magnetized space.

In these works and with this new idiom there is a turn from the earlier allegories of creation prominent in the books to something more like a social immanence of the process of creation, of having ideas, with the magnetized spaces now located in urban or social space, forming part of larger collective movements. The great question of invention or creation then assumes a new form: not simply how to open up the spaces of abstract art, but how, at the same time, to invent those called upon to give birth to vital ideas, to think together in art, through art, as part of larger movements. For the inventors are not given but must themselves be born in and through the process of invention. In this way, Pape thought one might rejoin those anonymous inventors found in the favelas and in the Amerindian labor of weaving, in tandem with the larger Tropicalist movement of the time.[21]

One of the key forms through which Pape developed this larger social sense of invention was film: the Cinema Novo, her friendship with director Glauber Rocha—whose first film, *O pátio* (*The Patio*, 1959), was in fact first screened in Pape's house—and what she thought was misleadingly called "marginal" film.[22] In much the same way as the Anthology Film Archives in New York operated, it was a time of mix and crossover between film and the visual arts. The Neoconcretists would not only see films together but also participate in them; at Rocha's suggestion, Pape edited one with the musician Caetano Veloso. Apart from this filmic fertilization in her ideas, Pape worked on publicity for films, making striking posters (fig. 30), and, like Richard Serra for example in New York, she would go on, using many formats, to make her own films (fig. 31), from an early allegory of space exploration to poetic film documents in the favelas. In cinema, she loved above all the mad silent voyages of Georges Méliès, and it was in unedited film footage that she thought one discovered the sort of open work that descends from Mallarmé's idea of the book. It was thus not at all that in film an image culture was taking over from a book culture but rather that the creative energies in both were meeting in a new terrain, a new Brazilian space, opening up new ideas.

In this way, Pape would come to the key problem Deleuze later found in Rocha and more generally in Third World and minority filmmakers: the great principle that "the people are not already there," in contrast to the masses in Sergei Eisenstein's Revolutionary cinema.[23] With Rocha in particular this principle would be developed in the Tropicalist and anthropophagic manners of mixing up many sources, outside any linear passage of tradition to modernity (or of craft to automated production, aura to mechanical reproduction). Thus Rocha, using the peculiarities of the industrial cinematic *dispositif*, would instead superimpose traditional with modern strata, inducing a kind of trance of a people in the making. The idea that the people are missing and must themselves be created would assume a striking role in Brazil in relation to both poetry and the arts. Indeed, it was this vision of a Tropicalist Third World that Pape hoped to elaborate in the exhibition she was working on in 1977 and 1978 with Pedrosa, canceled due to a fire, called "Alegria de viver, alegria de criar" ("Joy of Living, Joy of Creating").

What then is the act of invention and who then are the artist-inventors in the lands of Brazil? In her thesis, written at the same time as she was working on the exhibition, Pape took up precisely this question. Perhaps it is the privilege of eccentric places of invention to work outside the constraints of market and state of more hegemonic centers like New York or Paris; one is then free to take up ideas from many places, mixing them with others, pushing them along new creative paths. That in effect is how Pape came to see the new experiments in which she had taken part. The picture of artists as artist-inventors of fresh ideas and sensibilities that she develops in her thesis was very much opposed to any nationalism or exoticism, even and especially with respect to Brazilian native art, to which she was nevertheless drawn. At the same time, she rejected the notion that everything exists in some great imaginary Western museum or dialogue. Her artist-inventors instead were always starting things up again, from fresh points of view, outside such official narratives and categories, while avoiding a reactive retreat into a national

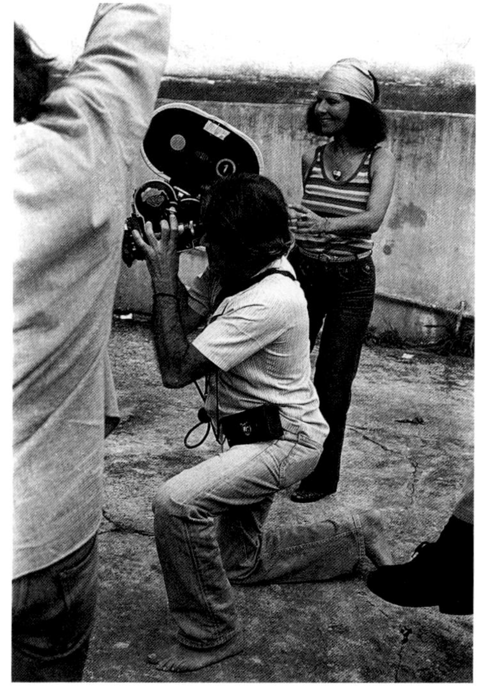

FIG. 31. Lygia Pape during filming of *Catiti-Catiti*, Rio de Janeiro, 1978

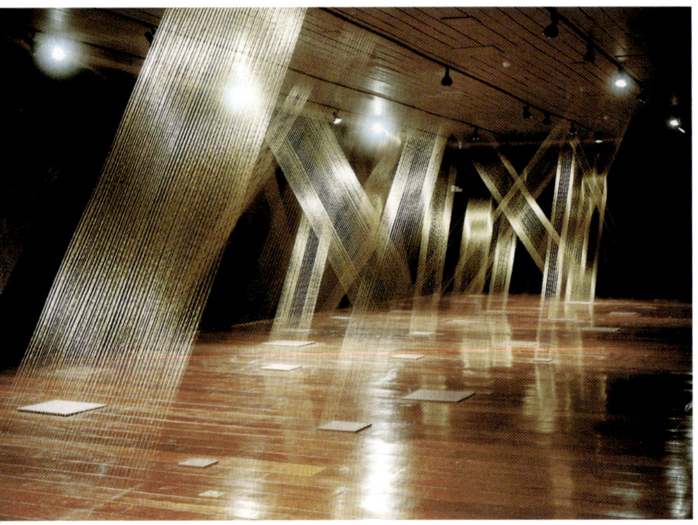

FIG. 32. Lygia Pape. *Ttéia 1, C*, 1976–2004. Golden thread. Installation view, Paço Imperial, Rio de Janeiro, 2002

cultural identity or any simple anxiety of influence. Instead, as already with what Oswald de Andrade had called "antropofagia" in his manifesto of 1928, they devour everything, including philosophies and ideas, mixing all together in such a way as to open up new inventions, new creations, vital ideas to be taken up later in turn.[24]

Perhaps today we might see this grand Brazilian vision of creation born of Pape's singular passage through the Brazilian art of her day in relation to our own questions about transnational art and citizenship and the role of ideas in it. Pape shared with Pedrosa the assumption that the history of art is more than a transmission, migration, or survival of images or forms, but something of an open work itself, always to be rewritten, punctuated by larger sociopolitical crises creating the new questions that fall to exhibition and criticism to pose. That is why, as earlier with Klee in 1902, artist-inventors, confronted with new forces knocking at the door, cannot know in advance and must invent new modes of creation and of thinking together, opening up stories, geographies, and ideas. Pape's notions of "weaving" and "web," which assumed increasing importance in her late writings, might be read in this light. In one of those writings she develops the idea of a spiderlike weave in relation to an aerial map of Rio de Janeiro.[25] Unlike Michel de Certeau's contrast between this view from above and everyday life on the ground, Pape saw a vast web containing the magnetized spaces from which the urban fabric might be rewoven, creating potentials of the sort she was trying to document in her research, teaching, and poetic film. In this picture we find a theme running throughout the many adventures of this ever-open seed: one never creates from nothing, the problem instead being, against all adversity, to reinvent art from the multiple threads of one's time and milieu, for a new people that does not yet exist. Pape's *Tecelares* might thus belong to a larger series of related conceptions of art history going back to Aby Warburg's archival configurations or to Walter Benjamin's baroque convolutions in Paris. Indeed, it is as though the archive, in cities or collections, had moved out into materials and bodies in a world whose vital potential would be released through fresh acts of invention. Pape's late installation simply called *Ttéia 1, C* (fig. 32), which focuses on the great questions of light, sensation, and material running throughout her work, might be seen as encapsulating this vision.[26]

But this vision may be found as well in the title of the show she was working on with Pedrosa at a moment of crisis in Brazil when, returning from exile, he declared that the energies of the great Neoconcretist experiment were spent. "Alegria de viver, alegria de criar" would then serve as a new springboard from which things might yet take off again. Perhaps we can now read the "joy" of the title of this unrealized exhibition in a Spinozistic spirit of multiplicity and multitude, posed against the sad passions of fixed identities and the pious, nationalist violence to which they lead. For to live is always to invent.

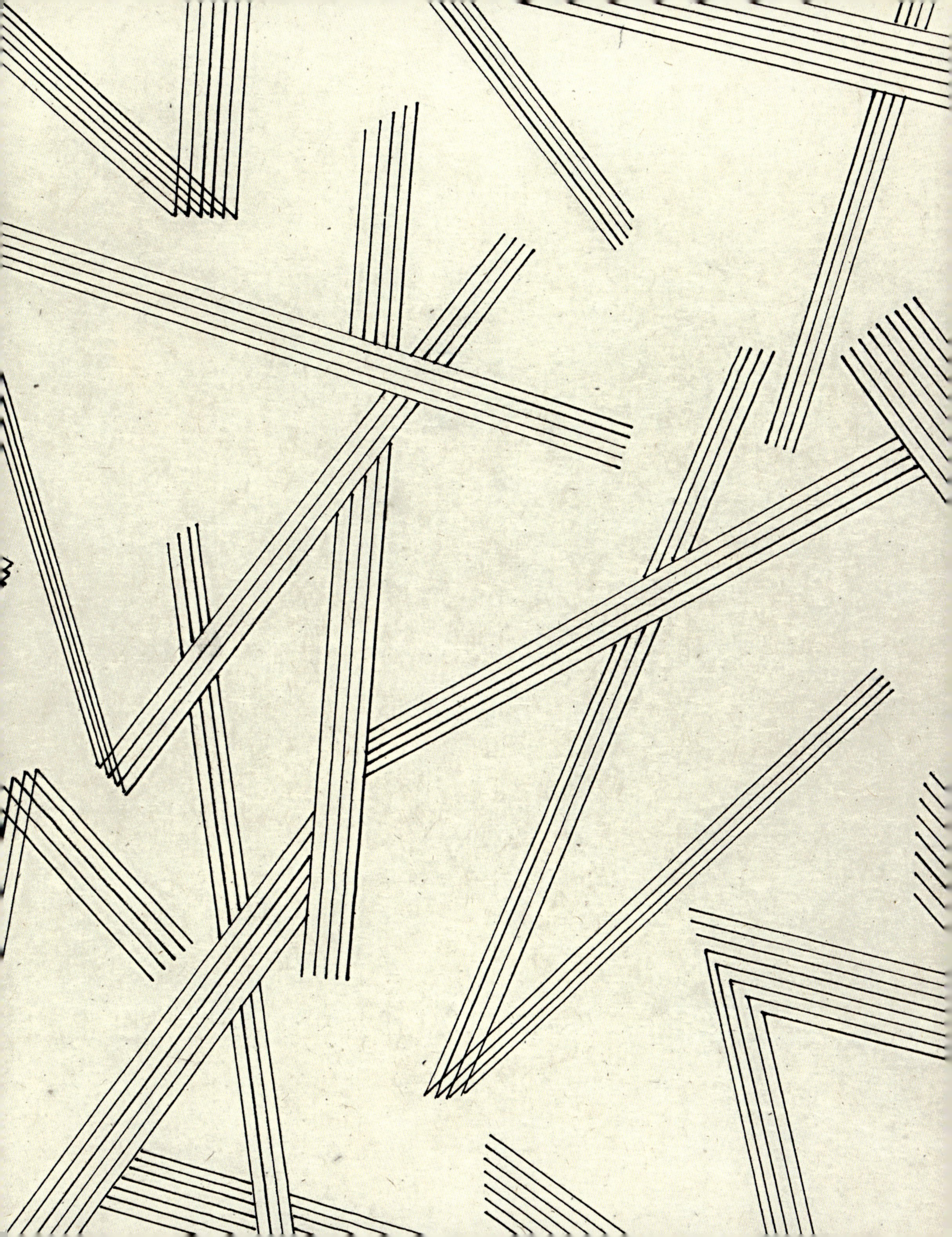

outside the frame of the screen

LYGIA PAPE INTERVIEWED BY ANGÉLICA DE MORAES

This interview was conducted across a number of sessions in March 1998. A total of eleven hours were taped during daily meetings at Lygia Pape's home. This translated text is excerpted from a longer, unpublished transcript.

Angélica de Moraes: When did you take the plunge into film-making and begin interacting with the Cinema Novo group? Was it around 1958?

Lygia Pape: It was just before the end of the Neoconcrete group, which broke up after 1962. In 1958, I created the ballets and the book-poems. But I had always been involved with the matter of light. Before the cinema, I worked with the projection of words and color planes.

AM: What were those projections like? Did they move?

LP: No, they were fixed. They were slide projections. I projected a word onto a colored background, then another word. Around the same time, the cartoonist Reginaldo José Azevedo Fortuna invited me to contribute to a humor magazine in Brasília. So I decided to make about twenty extremely interesting works, which were adventures with geometric forms. They were sequential. For example, a ball would enter the frame and then another very small one would begin to swell and swell and push the other ball out of the picture. All of this was done in a sequence of about eight frames on foolscap. Visually, they were beautiful. Naively, I handed over almost all of the originals to Fortuna and he lost them. I only kept two or three of those pieces. Those works had movement, only it was edited into drawings. I'd previously considered the idea of working outside the frame of the screen in film, with an action taking place outside it. For example, a hand might appear to enter the frame and then leave it.

AM: Might these poem-projections be considered sources for the *Livro da criação* (*Book of Creation*, 1959–60) insofar as each frame or slide could be a page from it?

LP: Partially, though they were not necessarily *the* source. It was a nourishing thing. The book-poems were already precursors to the *Livro da criação*.

AM: You made the poem-projections prior to the sequential drawings you just mentioned?

LP: They were more or less parallel. I used to do lots of things simultaneously. I had a small manually operated slide projector that I brought from Europe that had an extremely powerful light. I wanted to do things with light. I wanted an invasion of light. I envisioned something similar to what later became known as a holograph, with rays of colored light in motion and the emergence of one word and then another. Around this time, a coincidence occurred. Nelson Pereira dos Santos, who worked at the copy desk of the *Jornal do Brasil*, asked Amilcar de Castro, a graphic designer, whether he knew an engraver who could do titles with wood textures for his film. Amilcar recommended me for the job. At home I was already experimenting with 16mm and Super 8 film. Soon I began designing the titles and posters for all the Cinema Novo films. The first one I worked on was Nelson's *Mandacaru vermelho* (*Red Mandacaru*, 1961). It had a texture and a red ball that resembled a sun. That poster was sort of Japanese even though the setting of the film was the Northeast of Brazil. The black lettering had subtle textures, and they were printed on almost transparent Japanese paper. Nowadays I keep thinking how I wasted that wonderful paper to make film titles! When I showed my designs for the titles to Nelson, I told him I could produce an even better effect, and then I crumpled one of them. Nelson almost died of fright. I crumpled the paper and opened it up again, and it looked even more interesting.

AM: Nelson thought you had destroyed the work?

LP: Yes. Nelson thought I'd torn it up. He wasn't used to such things. Later I did the titles for another one of his films, *Vidas secas* (*Barren Lives*, 1963). I also did them for *Deus e o diabo na terra do sol* (*Black God, White Devil*, 1964), directed by Glauber Rocha. And so on.

I also screened films here at home. Glauber's first film, *O pátio* (*The Patio*, 1959), premiered in the living room we are sitting in. Paulo César Saraceni's first film also premiered in this house. Mário Pedrosa, Lygia Clark, and Hélio Oiticica, everyone came to express their convictions. It was the age of the *Suplemento dominical* of the *Jornal do Brasil*. Reynaldo Jardim and Ferreira Gullar attended . . . it was effervescent. Every once in a while some big shot would come from Germany, especially from Ulm. I'd bring them over to the house. I was very sociable then. I gave parties and invited everyone. There was this extraordinary coming and going. Once, we held the screening here in this room and light from a lamppost in front of the house was interfering with the projection. The room wasn't dark enough. So Jean Boghici, who was Lygia Clark's boyfriend, threw a stone at it and broke the lamp. From then on I became persona non grata in this ultra-conservative neighborhood.

AM: There are accounts that say you were a sort of muse to the Cinema Novo. Is that true?

LP: I didn't bring the Cinema Novo people over to the house. I invited the visual arts people, my colleagues in the Neoconcrete movement. Sometimes I would have film people over, but rarely. Once I brought Luiz Carlos Barreto and Nelson Pereira dos Santos to show them Humberto Mauro's *Ganga bruta* from 1933. They had never seen it. There is a beautiful moment in this film when a woman falls and rolls across a lawn. You see this white figure rolling away. While watching it, I said: "It looks like a bólide." Hélio Oiticica later used the word "*bólide*" as a title for a series of works. Because the filming technique in *Ganga bruta* was very rudimentary, the whites were overexposed. And I believe it was because of Mauro's film that Barreto and Nelson overexposed the light in *Vidas secas*.

AM: Those meetings were inspirational—

LP: I was very ecumenical about passing along information and bringing people together to show them things I liked. I was always like that.

AM: Your connection with cinema is a greatly enthusiastic one.

LP: No doubt. I had the amazing experience of watching the Cinema Novo films at Líder, the laboratory that developed their film. With the exception of the Barreto family, I was the only person here in Rio who was allowed to see the rough cut of *Vidas secas*. It was wonderful stuff. After the film was edited and the sound was added, it got boring because it became this little story with a beginning, a middle, and an ending. Before that, it had an open structure that one fantasized about and marveled at. I used to spend whole days at Líder watching rushes. I sat in on all the editing work for *Vidas secas* because I did all the titles and the poster. The titles were extremely laborious and only appeared in the lower part of the screen, where there was earth, on fade in and fade out. It was a hell of a job to do because Líder was very precarious, but there was no other place. Nowadays editing is computerized. In those days, you had to hold the projector so it wouldn't tremble and so that the titles would always imprint the same place on the frame. They were made frame by frame.

AM: What a lot of work.

LP: I used to adore doing this stuff. The more complicated the assignment, the greater the challenge. What really impressed me, and I said this to Nelson, is that the book by Graciliano Ramos—on which the film is based—has an open structure. You can open it at any chapter and start to read and it doesn't make the slightest difference to your understanding of that family saga in the Northeast. And I was drawn to this style because I came from the Neoconcrete and from that type of engagement with an open structure. . . . Nelson would be a little surprised by my ideas but he liked the fact that I was very theoretical and said these things. So did Glauber. So much so that once I was standing at a bar and along came Glauber, and he said: "Do you want to help some boys from Bahia to edit a film?" The film was by a fellow called Álvaro (Alvinho) Guimarães and the young editors were Caetano Veloso and Torquato Neto. We edited from the projector. Stop, glue the film, move on . . . it was an unbelievable amount of work. The name of the film was *Meninos de rua* (*Street Boys*, 1987).

AM: Shall we talk about your own work in film?

LP: While I was doing graphic design for the Cinema Novo, I was working for myself, too. I made lots of short films. I made *Eat Me* (1975). I made *Catiti-Catiti* (1978), a film about Mário Pedrosa, another one about a favela. Later, I filmed some northeastern markets in Paraíba. I did tons of stuff.

AM: Have these films survived?

LP: Some of them were stolen from my car in the parking lot of the Museu de Arte Moderna, Rio de Janeiro (MAM-RJ). Because they were originals, they are lost. The projector and two lots of films were stolen.

I made a very nice short nearby here. There used to be a favela on that hill there [points to the landscape through the window]. It wasn't a favela with wood houses; they were brick. When they razed the favela, they removed the roofs of the houses and left the walls. They were very colorful houses. I made a very funny little film of the area. I walked around the ruins of the favela with a camera and the only sound was that of a woman calling her son. It was a faraway voice, almost a Gregorian chant. It is a very beautiful film.

AM: What is the subject of *Catiti-Catiti*?

LP: *Catiti-Catiti* means "New Moon, oh New Moon" in the indigenous language of the Tupi. I wanted to make a short film about cannibalism. In the film there is a figure who continually eats, devours things. The actor is Luís Otávio Pimentel. The film, shot in black and white using 16mm, also shows forests with the sound of a sawmill in the background. It ends with a speech by a congressman, one of those grandiloquent, inflated speeches about Brazil.

In 1975, I made a short film for a competition sponsored by the Ministry of Education. The short was called *A mão do povo* (*The Hand of the People*) and, for it, I filmed folk art and anything made by hand. I was interested in the subject of identity loss in people who move from rural to urban areas. I showed objects that belong to popular culture, such as geometric quilts from Minas Gerais, ceramics from the Jequitinhonha valley, an endless amount of stuff. Then I showed how those people become consumers of industrialized plastic objects, such as flowers, etc. They lost an identity and had not yet gained a new one in the urban space. I find that film very interesting.

AM: Your short *Eat Me* has the same title as your solo show held in São Paulo during the military dictatorship, the one that was censored for being allegedly pornographic. Is the short part of it?

LP: The film should be regarded as an independent work; although it was shown during the exhibition I opened—and which was closed down—in 1976 in São Paulo and later traveled to the MAM-RJ. The exhibition had a teaser that aired on TV Globo, which sponsored Galeria Arte Global, where the show was held in São Paulo. This teaser consisted of a close-up of a frankly pornographic mouth [roars with laughter]. In Rio, the exhibition space was all black. It was an experimental room on the third floor of the museum, with a black floor and a very high ceiling. I made three completely black booths with the phrase "Eat Me: A gula ou a luxúria?" ("Eat Me: Gluttony or Lust?") written on them in neon. In the inside of one booth it was yellow neon, in another it was red, and in the third it was green. On the museum's external lateral wall, which is enormous and as smooth as a motion picture screen, I projected my own image making this gesture [she puts her index finger in front of her face and crooks it, signaling "come hither"]. There was an identical image of me inside the show, behind a curtain, also beckoning into the exhibition.

AM: You were already working with outer wall projections in the 1970s?

LP: Yes. It is interesting that, like a Moebius strip, what was happening inside the exhibition was happening outside it as well. Inside and outside became indistinguishable. The installation of the exhibition "Eat Me" at the MAM-RJ was much richer than the São Paulo version. It had a rush-hour appeal at twilight. I wanted to cover the museum floor with hair, but I wasn't able to gather all the material I needed. The hairdressers didn't want to collaborate because they thought I was going to do macumba with their clients' hair. I only got enough hair for the display cases. One of them had hair and apples, and there was another one with nothing but dentures. One day during the exhibition, I rode the elevator with a gentleman who had picked up one of the little bags, but when he saw the hair he felt a little nauseous and dropped it on the floor. However, he pocketed the small calendars of naked women. And the funny thing was that there I was, standing right beside him, observing his sensorial reactions quite anonymously.

AM: Those little bags contained a lot of stuff—

LP: There were peanuts, aphrodisiac potions, hair . . . the gentleman in the elevator also kept those potions, you know?

AM: I notice that you made several shorts in the early 1970s. The first was *The Super* (1971), then *Wampirou* (1973). Tell me about them.

LP: *Wampirou* is about a vampire who went nuts (*pirou*). Instead of biting, he used an electric drill on the necks of his victims before drinking their blood. It was great fun to make. I was one of the vampire's victims. I exposed myself to all sorts of craziness! The actors included Lygia Clark, the poet Waly Salomão, the *passista* Rose from the Mangueira samba school, lots of people. It was fictional. Reality is so much more brutal! I also made *Our Parents "Fossilis"* (1974), which uses postcards of Brazilian Indians. After showing the postcard, I would make a remark about it. I haven't seen this film in a long time and I don't even know what condition it's in now. It was shot on Super 8. I also made *Carnival in Rio* (1974) with the same camera. I shot the random characters I came upon at the carnival on the Avenida Rio Branco. There was a very hairy man who had tied ribbons around tufts of hair from head to toe—his body was covered in little bows. It was incredibly humorous. Later Thomaz Farkas said to me: "Gosh, Lygia, you have quite an eye, look at all these things you discovered!" That was because I spent all day on the avenida, just to find these characters.

AM: What is *Arenas calientes* (*Hot Sands*, 1974) about?

LP: It's about Palestinians stuck in sand dunes. Later they rob a gas station and drink gasoline while wearing full Arab garb—a very amusing and nonsensical thing. Raymundo Collares and Antonio Manuel were the Palestinians.

AM: Did you shoot your films yourself?

LP: Yes, always. I was even invited to make a feature, but I didn't have the patience for managing actors. That was never a part of my projects.

AM: Were you still editing films at the time?

LP: Yes, because it's a rhythm thing. I sat in on plenty of editing. I was even assistant editor to Leon Hirszman.

AM: What is your assessment of the Cinema Novo with regard to the rupture of language? Do you think the directors could have been more daring?

LP: I do. Unequivocally. I don't think they had the same notion of language that we had in the visual arts. Our readings of Ezra Pound, of Mallarmé, about the throw of the dice, about chance, were different. The directors had talent, some more than others, and they wanted to make films that had a message. The films have organized structures with clear discourses that are meant to be understood. To them, that was the most that should be done. But who would dare to make a film with a more open structure? Mallarmé made the great revolution in the word and in verse. He opened up the verse.

AM: To return to your short films: one of them was entered in an international competition. Which one?

LP: It was the short *La nouvelle création* (*The New Creation*), shot in 1967; it is just under sixty seconds long. The subject of the competition was the Land of Men. The first trip to the moon had just taken place, and I made something that went beyond man's gesture on earth all the way into space. I obtained an image from NASA of an astronaut leaving his ship, floating in space as if he were a newborn still connected by an umbilical cord. The beginning of the film is in black and white. Then the screen goes completely red and a child is heard crying. I won a prize in Canada for that work.

GLÓRIA FERREIRA

irreverence and marginality

"I always enjoyed marginality," Lygia Pape declared in 2000. "I made a point about staying in the periphery. I was very much an anarchist. I didn't sell work. I didn't hold gallery shows."[1] This marginality expressed itself in her contempt for galleries and the art world, as when in 1967 she presented her *Caixa das baratas* (*Box of Cockroaches*)—a work that contains large cockroaches that were sourced by children from a favela near her home—to the Museu de Arte Moderna, Rio de Janeiro (MAM-RJ), for purchase. The work was not acquired, but for Pape, the disgust felt when viewing the cockroaches was equivalent to her own rejection of the "dead art" of museums. Yet, as she explains in her undated text "Cinema marginal," she did not consider a place at the margin of society to be marginal because marginality is a bourgeois concept.[2] Having emerged in the 1950s within the context of the Brazilian constructive tradition, and in spite of her constant reiteration of the legacy of Neoconcretism, her own work evinced an ongoing openness to experimentation. Her trajectory, especially in the 1960s and 1970s, was informed by the irreverence of underground cinema and the influence of vernacular and indigenous cultures and shaped by a strong awareness of her role as a woman artist.

In the 1960s and 1970s, countless artists were focused on expanding the boundaries between the various arts and questioning the very concept of what constitutes art. Like photography, film became a means for investigating reality and its conditions for representation, expressed in the growth of the cinematic field to include structural cinema, mathematical montage, and expanded cinema, among other inventions. In the 1960s, Pape began to work with directors associated with Cinema Novo, creating the titles and posters for more than ten feature-length films, including Nelson Pereira dos Santos's *Vidas secas* (*Barren Lives*; fig. 33) and Glauber Rocha's *Deus e o diabo na terra do sol* (*Black God, White Devil*, 1964), and several shorts, including her 1963 design for the opening credits for the cinema program at the MAM-RJ; its irreverent soundtrack of cows mooing is an aural play on the pronunciation of the museum's acronym, MAM (fig. 34).

In parallel with her graphic design work, Pape embarked on her own investigation of the medium of film, and, by the late 1970s, she had made more than fifteen shorts, in both the fiction and documentary genres. Film offered Brazilian artists like Pape a new form of expression. In 1973, on the occasion of "Expo-Projeção 73," which presented sound, audiovisuals, and Super 8 and 16mm films by such artists as Antonio Manuel, Cildo Meireles, and Hélio Oiticica, Pape declared, "Super 8 is truly a new language, especially when it is also free of a more commercial involvement with the system. It is currently the only source of research, the touchstone of invention."[3] She elaborated on her vision of how to use film in her 1975 text

"Superoito" ("Super Eight"), explaining, "I do NOT want to communicate ANY-THING / what I want is to inform EVERYTHING."[4]

As early as 1967, in the award-winning *La nouvelle création* (*The New Creation*), made for Expo 67 in Montreal, Pape demonstrated her dexterity with the medium. For the competition, participants were instructed to make a film based on the subject of the Land of Men, which was taken from Antoine de Saint-Exupéry's 1939 book *Terre des hommes*. In Pape's submission, a NASA astronaut slowly exits his capsule and floats in space still connected to the ship by what looks like an umbilical cord. Toward the end of the short, the black-and-white image turns red, an effect achieved using a filter, and a crying child is heard, unmistakably equating the action of man moving into a new scientific frontier to a cosmic birth. Established in 1958, NASA was by the late 1960s deeply committed to its manned space program, a scientific advancement that captured the imagination of many, including Pape. *La nouvelle création* most directly addresses the experience of "birth," or more particularly "rebirth," and this theme, as well as the related notions of connection and rupture, recur in some of the artist's other works from the time, such as *O ovo* (*The Egg*, 1967) and *Divisor* (*Divider*, 1968). In addition, the film helped Pape to visualize her own mandate of constant renewal.

The historical period of the 1960s and 1970s was conflict ridden; the dictatorship in Brazil became increasingly oppressive toward the end of the 1960s, and thousands of people went into exile or were banished. But as Roberto Schwarz noted, government repression that was initially (and above all) focused on unions, or in rural areas, with the dissolution of student organizations, invasion of churches, military inquests into universities, censorship, and more, still allowed "a relative cultural hegemony of the left in the country."[5] Within this climate, artists responded with work in which the political dimension is not rhetorical; rather, it is present and being questioned. In their artwork, the dialogue artists established with politics as well as the facts of everyday life was intended to provoke the spectators' critical distance from the reality in which they lived. They wanted to remove the artistic debate from the ideological terrain—and its demand for an affirmation of a Brazilian identity—and orient it toward the field of ethics and aesthetics, an aim inherited from the Brazilian constructive project.

Of all Pape's films, *Wampirou,* made in 1973, is the closest in spirit to what was known as *undigrudi* (underground) cinema, a dynamic facet of Brazilian counterculture of the 1960s and 1970s. Pape greatly admired the work of Rogério Sganzerla and Júlio Bressane, two of the principal inventors of underground cinema, which made cynicism a banner of sorts for their protest.[6] *Wampirou* is about a vampire (played by Antonio Manuel) who preys on everyone and everything, starting with himself, drinking blood from his own arm and from the neck of Lygia Clark. The other participants are the poet Waly Salomão, the visual artist Jackson Ribeiro, and Lygia Pape. The vampire goes forth in daylight, wanders around the city, attempts to enter a church, drinks a Coca-Cola, becomes a little paranoid, removes his vampire dentures to take a nap, and dreams of other vampires. At one point, the vampire plays the role of an artist who is visited by a dealer (portrayed in the film by Ribeiro), who robs the artist of his clothes. In this way, the film presents an

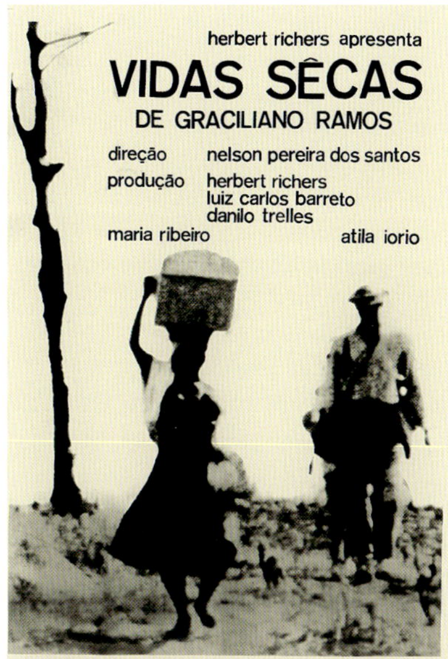

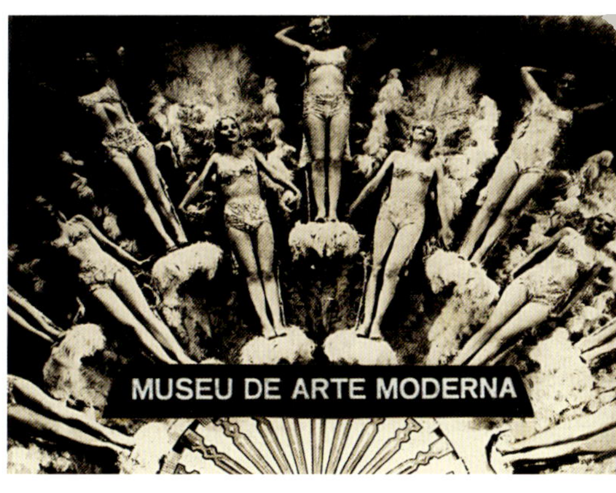

FIG. 33. Lygia Pape. Poster for *Vidas secas*, (*Barren Lives*), 1963. Offset print, 43⅜ × 28¾ in. (110 × 73 cm). Projeto Lygia Pape

FIG. 34. Lygia Pape. Film title design for *Cinemateca MAM-Rio*, 1963. Collage on paper, 9¾ × 13⅜ in. (24.5 × 34 cm). Projeto Lygia Pape

ironic parody of the artist's relationship to the market, a matter of crucial importance to Pape, who was then reluctant to sell her work or show it in the context of commercial galleries.

Throughout her career, Pape examined the role of urban spaces, as is evident in her interest in the "anti-architecture" of the favelas. She was drawn to what she saw as a marginalized building tradition that did not relate or belong to the dominant discourse on or practice of the discipline of architecture as executed by the ruling class in the city. Her documentary *Favela da Maré* (1972) explores all aspects of this section of Rio de Janeiro, from the buildings and alleyways to the children playing, the filthy living conditions, and the open sewage. According to Pape, it is only in such areas that we are able to find a sort of existential freedom "of self-expression in the collective space—turned outwards, open to the world like fruit that has broken through its rind; outside and inside as equals: a 'Moebius strip.'"[7] Pape's interest in exploring the creative potential of the common man in social space is further apparent in *Espaços imantados* (*Magnetized Spaces*, 1968–95), her photographic documentation of urban scenes, such as street vendors (known in Brazil as *camelôs*) selling their wares or people watching capoeira. "I believe that aesthetics are the foundation of ethics," Pape said. "I grew up with this perspective. Many of the things that dazzle me visually lie outside a so-called artistic context."[8] The street as an active arena of collective self-expression is also a central part of *Carnival in Rio* (1974). In this short, a group of costumed children from the favela at the end of the Rua Inglês de Souza, where the artist lived, joins a larger street *bloco*. The film proceeds to show typical carnival figures, such as men in drag and people costumed as animals. The *bloco* grows to mass proportions until it arrives on the Avenida Presidente Vargas, in Rio's business district, where carnival parades, samba schools, and *blocos* congregated during the popular festivities. This incursion into the public space, where artistic expression and political rallies were not allowed under the dictatorial regime, ends with the arrival of the repressive forces of the government, in the form of two police vehicles that enter the street.

In 1975 Pape made the documentary *A mão do povo* (*The Hand of the People*) for the Ministry of Education. With total freedom in spite of the dictatorship, she explored the affection with which migrants preserve cultural traditions—such as working the wicker—when they move from rural areas to the big city. At the same time, she also shows how, in acquiring objects for their new homes, these people turn to cheap industrial objects, leaving the material traces of their old traditions behind. With a varied soundtrack, including folk *sertanejo* music, samba, and pop, the film travels through various places and records several traditional arts, such as the ceramics of the Jequitinhonha valley, and analyzes the design of objects, such as the mathematical reasoning that goes into the geometric patchwork quilts of Minas Gerais.

Further exploring Brazilian culture in an attempt to reexamine hegemonic cultural assumptions, *Catiti-Catiti* (1978) is something of a film-manifesto that, according to Ivana Bentes, "fuses Tupinambá symbolism, cannibalism, Brazilian Romanticism, and modernism, with allusions to the historical avant-gardes and to perceptions of the tropical landscape as a conceptual character structuring that imagery."[9] The Tupinambá inhabited the Brazilian coastline before it was colonized, and only a small number of what are considered their descendants live in the southern region of the state of Bahia today. The tribe was known to practice cannibalism, and the film attempts a deconstruction of the anthropophagic ritual. It is no coincidence that the opening titles include prints of modern artist Tarsila do Amaral's *Abaporu* (1928) and the closing credits feature *A negra* (1923), both of which merge the depiction of landscape with the abstract language of modernism. Furthermore, *Abaporu,* a term of Tupi-Guarani origin, is an amalgam of the indigenous words *aba* (man), *pora* (people), and *ú* (eat), which together convey the meaning "man that eats people." Tarsila do Amaral had been a contributor to the *Revista de antropofagia* (1928) in São Paulo, which published the "Manifesto antropófago" ("Cannibalist Manifesto"), by author and poet Oswald de Andrade. This text proposed the deglutition of foreign culture and its incorporation into local traditions as the starting point for a new and transformed culture. The debate about whether or not to accept the principles of the manifesto—"Tupy, or not tupy that is the question"[10]—was revisited in the 1970s in the visual arts, film, music, and theater.

Over the course of ten minutes, *Catiti-Catiti* deconstructs the history and myths of cannibalism. Shots of the forest and the Indians are complemented by those of the bathers on Ipanema beach in the 1970s—an image circulated internationally at that time to attract tourists to Rio de Janeiro. Through the use of a voiceover, a man recites snippets from a letter written by Pêro Vaz de Caminha, a Portuguese knight who traveled to Brazil and encountered native tribes in Bahia in 1500, saying, "Ah, Jesus, and who will populate these lands?" It then responds with three questions: "The Indian? The white man? The black man?" As the film unfolds, it records the presence of the triad that is considered to be the foundation of Brazilian society: the Indian (who dons a feather headdress), the Portuguese (who sports a Vasco da Gama soccer team T-shirt), and the African (who wears a black stocking over his face), all played by poet Luís Otávio Pimentel. Writing in the 1930s, sociologist Gilberto Freyre claimed that Brazil offered the possibility of a harmonious coexistence, leading him to propose a racial democracy.[11] This ideal, however, did not manifest; the historical traces of slavery (which endure in Brazil to this day) were especially prevalent during the military dictatorship, which implemented policies of repression and censorship that aggravated racial and social segregation and led to the further decimation of the Indian population. Near the end of the film, the hope for the fulfillment of Freyre's proposition returns as the voice declares, "I don't care for exalted, patriotic talk, but, as a man who was born here, who raised his children and his grandchildren here, I have a citizen's right to believe deeply in our youth to carry out the dream of my maturity."

Presented in 1980, Pape's master's thesis in philosophy bears the same title as her film, "Catiti-Catiti, na terra dos Brasis." In the thesis, she turned to contemporary art "in the land of the Brasis," examining the crisis of art and upholding the ideas of her friend, the critic Mário Pedrosa. Like Pape, Pedrosa expressed dissatisfaction with the current direction of art, which seemed to cater to consumerism.

During the 1950s, Pedrosa defended and promoted abstraction and the Brazilian constructive tradition as the means through which to achieve modernity in the country, but he was also always interested in art produced by the mentally ill, children, Indians, and Africans. In a 1968 essay, "Arte dos Caduceus, arte negra, artistas de hoje" ("Art of the Caduveo, African Art, Contemporary Artists"), Pedrosa declared in connection to this topic that "the primitive artist creates an object 'that participates.'"[12] Both Pape and Pedrosa called upon the inhabitants of the Third World, the dispossessed, to take on creative leadership in the domain of the arts. "It is because we also believe in this destiny," Pape noted, "that we would like to point out the *artist-inventors* as the only ones capable of this function—as the *experimenters* of the new."[13]

Speaking of her experiences engaging with and researching the Brazilian Indian, the artist mourned that "the very heart of that culture—its manner of building and experiencing space—was destroyed. Origin myths were undoubtedly splintered."[14] She was outraged by the postcards that treated indigenous peoples—

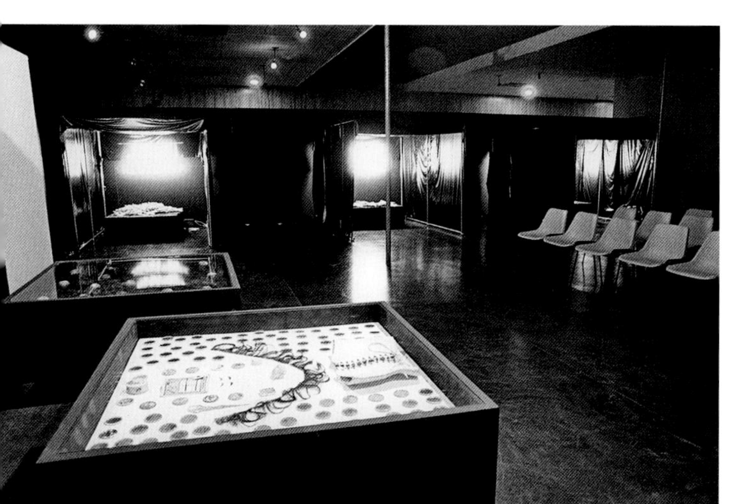

who had been largely dispossessed of their lands—as exotic souvenirs whose images were sold at kiosks in Rio de Janeiro alongside photographs of famous stars and naked women. Paula Pape recalled how her mother became so infuriated by this that she purchased nearly all the postcards of Indians from a given newsstand.[15] For the 1974 film *Our Parents "Fossilis,"* Lygia Pape appropriated these postcards to attempt a revised portrait of the Indians and their daily life, with an indigenous song as the soundtrack.

Although she did not feel much of an affinity toward the feminist discourse that was then being developed in Brazil, Pape was strongly opposed to the transformation of women into objects of seduction and explored the concept of seduction at different levels in several works. For the 1976 exhibition "Eat Me: A gula ou a luxúria?" ("Eat Me: Gluttony or Lust?"; fig. 35), held at the MAM-RJ (the show's second venue), Pape appeared in a video projected onto one of the museum's outer walls, facing lanes of traffic and beckoning to spectators like a prostitute calling out to her clients. The video was soon censored under the pretext that it interfered with the city's traffic. Within the museum, she placed little packets containing lipsticks, rouge, false eyelashes, dentures, hair, and other elements of women's makeup inside darkened booths illuminated with red, green, and yellow neon lights and sold these items at the price of one cruzeiro. In her installation Pape criticized the objectification of women by pointing to the marginal spheres of prostitution as well as to the societal pressure that drives female consumption of beauty products.

In *Sedução I e II* (*Seduction I and II*, 1974)*,* precise editing allows the words "come" and "go" to succeed one another on the screen in an almost hypnotic sexual rhythm. The film highlights Pape's skill as a filmmaker who experiments not only with content but also with the technical specificity of how a work is made. Her interest in editing went beyond the question of how to cut a scene for emotional impact toward a conceptual investigation of structure. For the later *Sedução III* (1999), Pape recorded people likely boarding the Rio de Janeiro–Niterói ferry and then manipulated the footage so that the people appear to move backward and forward at an accelerated speed "like endlessly returning waves."[16] The construction of *Sedução III* relied on camera positioning and manipulated frame-speeds, which allowed Pape to transform a documentary into a conceptual film that foregrounds motion, speed, and space.[17]

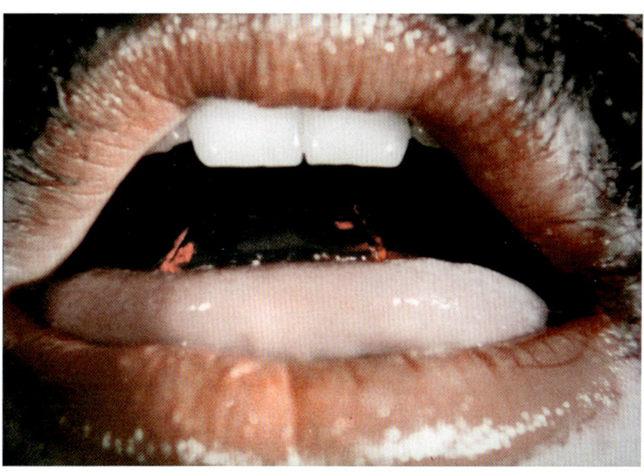

FIG. 36. Lygia Pape. *Eat Me*, 1975. 16mm film in color with sound, 9 min. Projeto Lygia Pape

Editing is also a key component of *Eat Me* (1975), which draws on several components of structural film. According to Regina Cornwell, the characteristic of a structural film is that its "form is defined before shooting."[18] *Eat Me* introduces the relationship between form and structure by using a fixed camera position and a pulsating effect. It presents close-ups of the mouths of two men, alternately sticking out and pulling back colored crystals on their tongues (fig. 36), as well as the mouth of a young woman eagerly sucking on a ketchup-slathered sausage. As the artist explains, "The film was edited mathematically, in that sections were cut by the meter, based on the following principle: I divided the film into two parts, then divided each half into two again, and so on, until I obtained a pulsation that grows into a crescendo up until the end. Images were cut without concern for describing the moment—a number alone (one meter) determined the cut."[19] With increasing speed, the editing creates a luminous pulsation and a sort of obscene rhythm. Repeated in German, English, Italian, Portuguese, and Spanish, the question "gluttony or lust?" accompanies the images. In this way, *Eat Me* draws attention to media manipulation and criticizes bodily pleasure and excess, analyzing the conflict between art and consumption.

In connection with the act of eating, Pape created an interactive work in which notions of seduction and consumption were tested through the spectator's experience. For *Roda dos prazeres* (*Wheel of Pleasures*, 1967), twelve white ceramic bowls, each containing a differently colored and flavored liquid, are arranged on the ground in a circle, with a dropper resting on a saucer placed beside each bowl so that the contents can be tasted. The participants' act of tasting the different flavors cannot fail to evoke cannibalism and seduction given that, no matter how beautiful and attractive the color, the taste may be unpleasant, bitter, or sour. As the artist once said, the most radical expression of this experiment would be to put poison in one of the bowls.

The idea of including poison, a transgressive proposal, embodies how Pape harnessed art as a means of challenging conventions and coming to terms with the present within the context of the complex history of Brazilian culture and society. Themes of irreverence and marginality are key to unraveling many of Pape's ideas, particularly in her films and installations from the 1960s and 1970s. They help to penetrate the lesser-known fields of experience and layers of history that define what it meant to live in Brazil in the decades following the 1964 coup d'etat.

PLATES

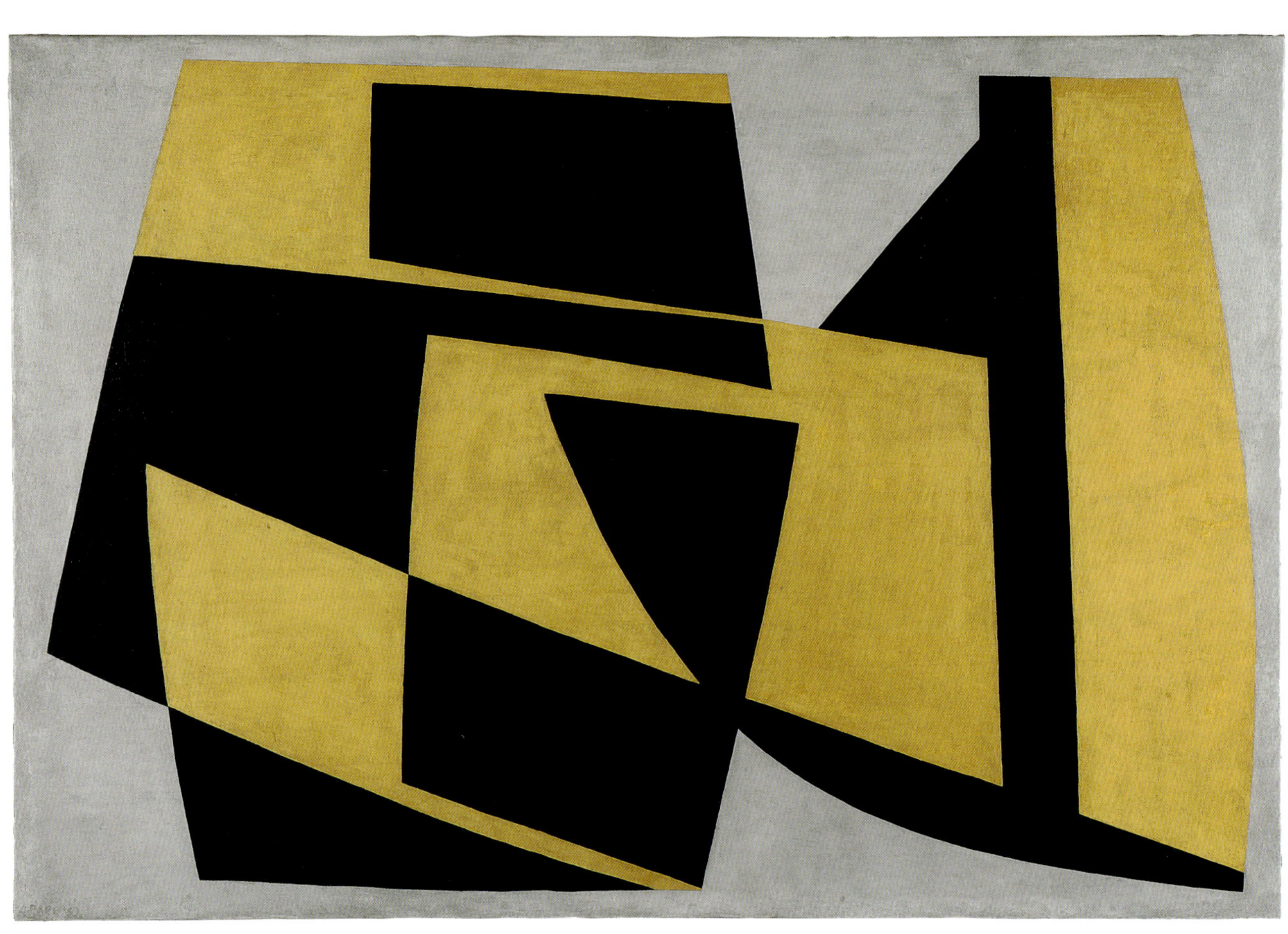

1. *Painting*, 1953

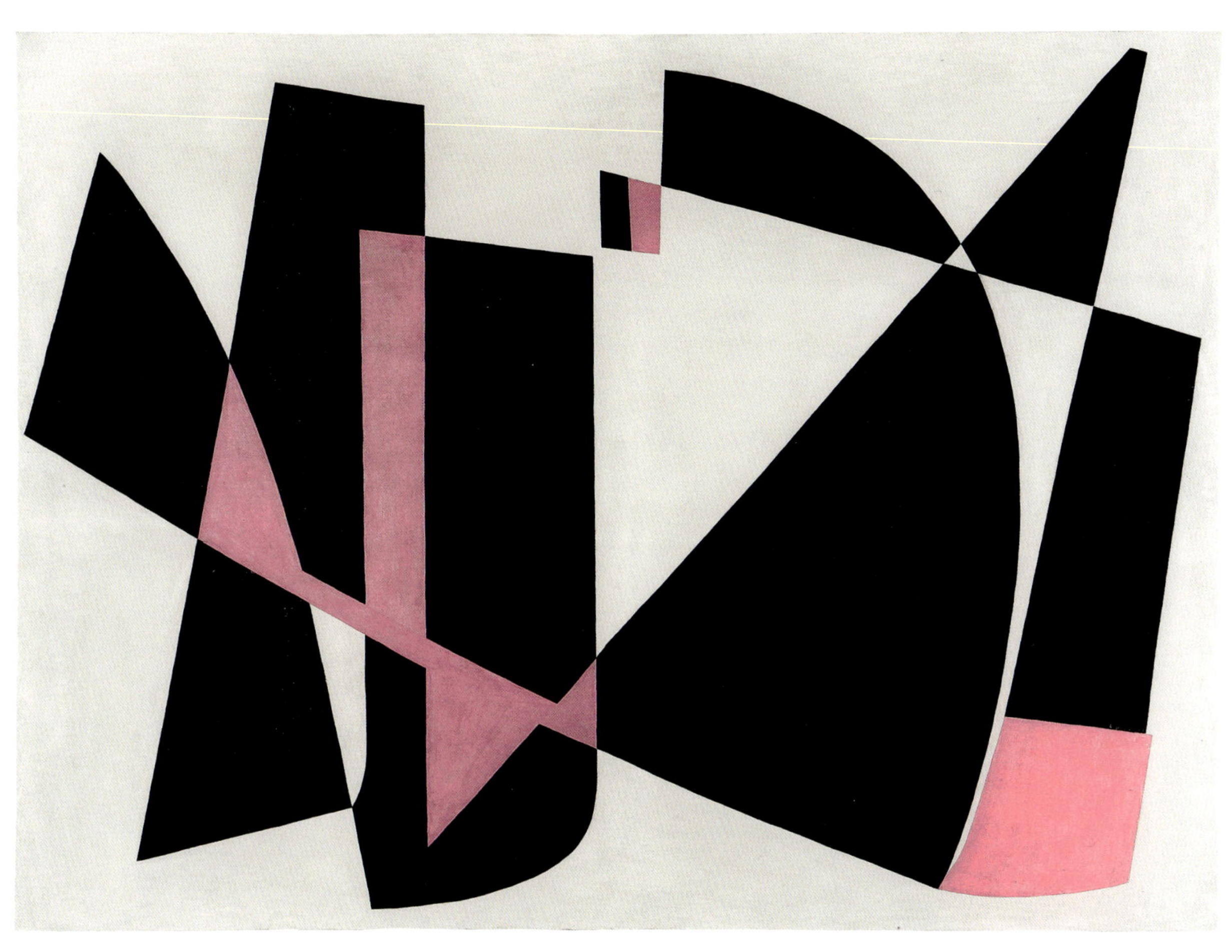

2. *Painting*, 1953

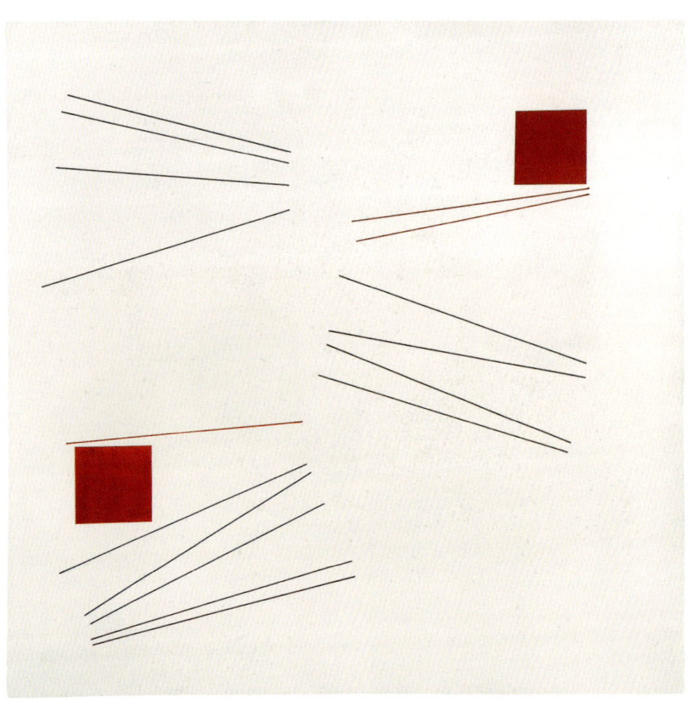

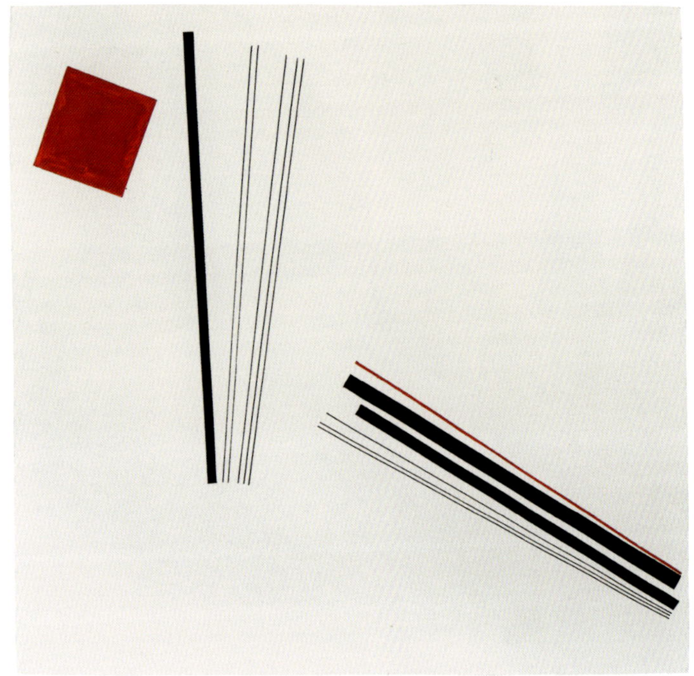

3. *Painting*, 1954–56

4. *Painting*, 1954

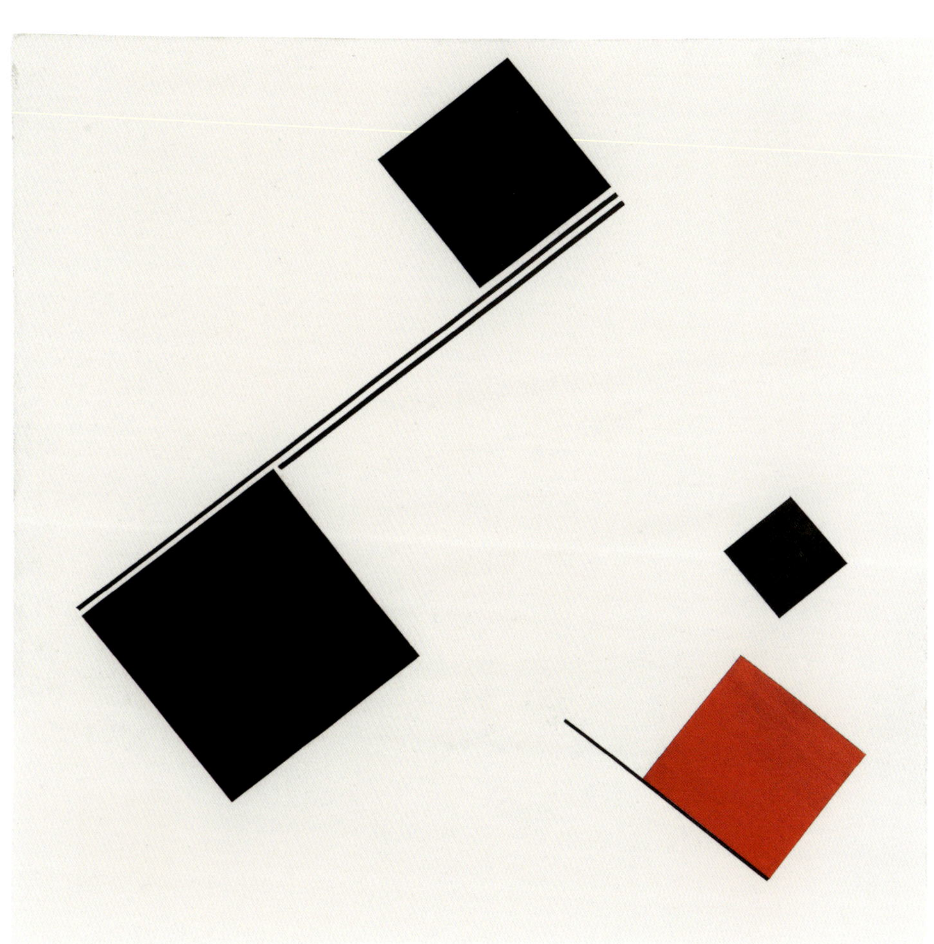

5. *Painting*, 1954–56

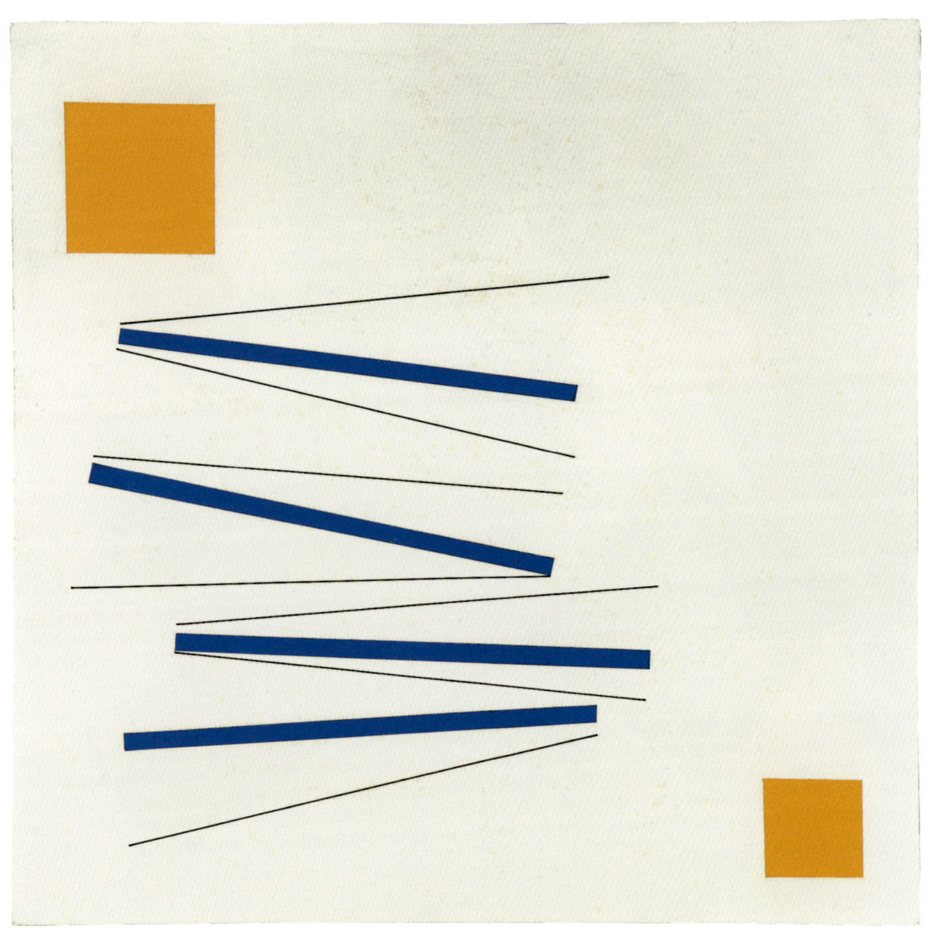

6. *Painting*, 1954–56

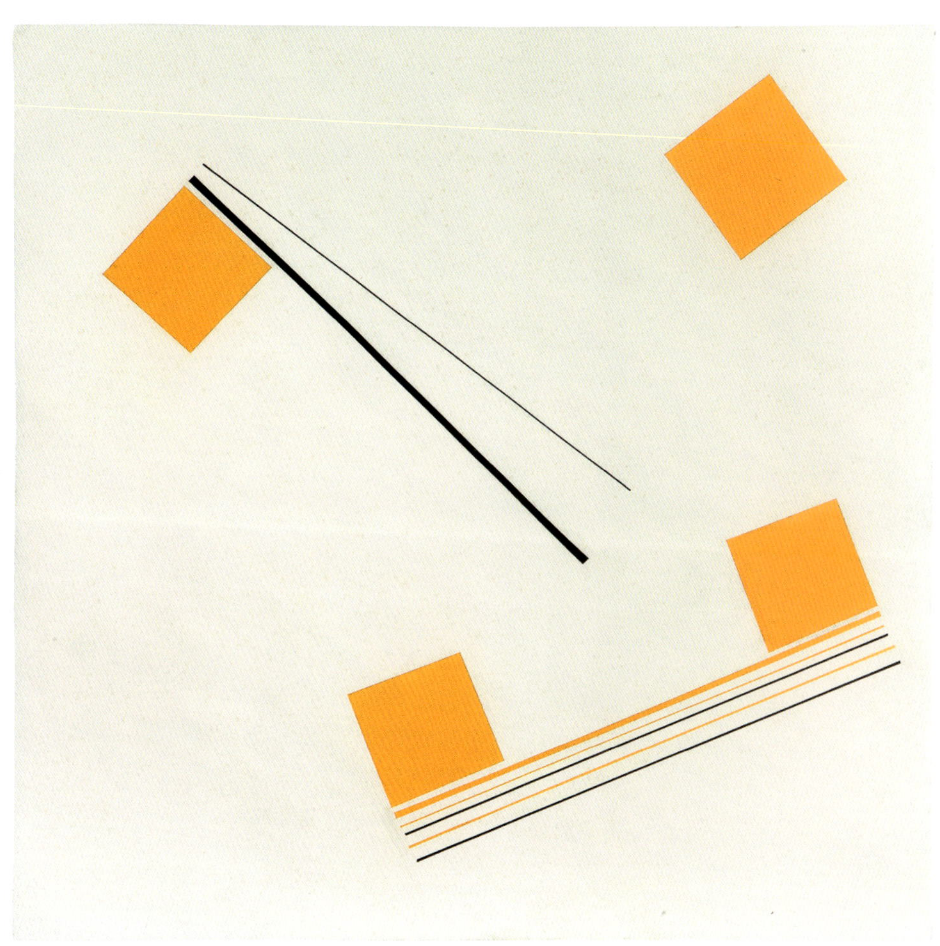

7. *Painting*, 1954–56

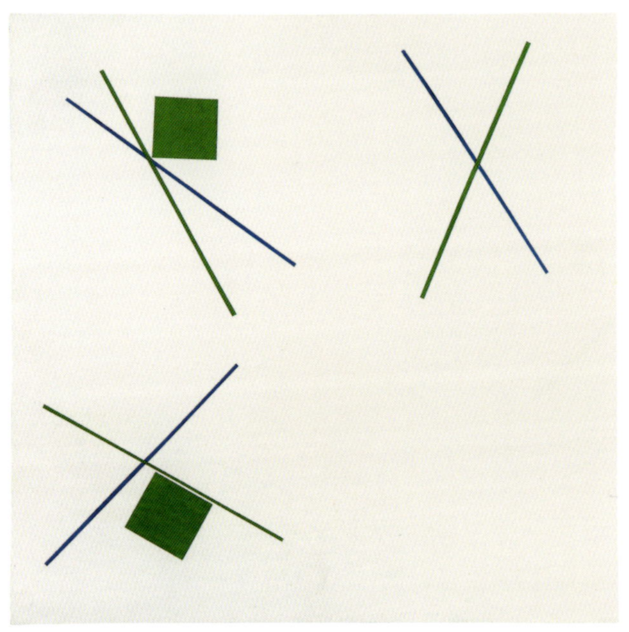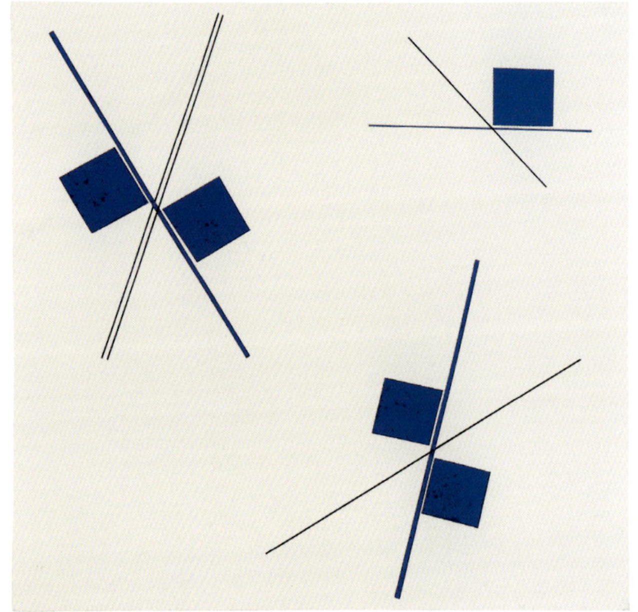

8. *Painting*, 1954–56
9. *Painting*, 1954–56

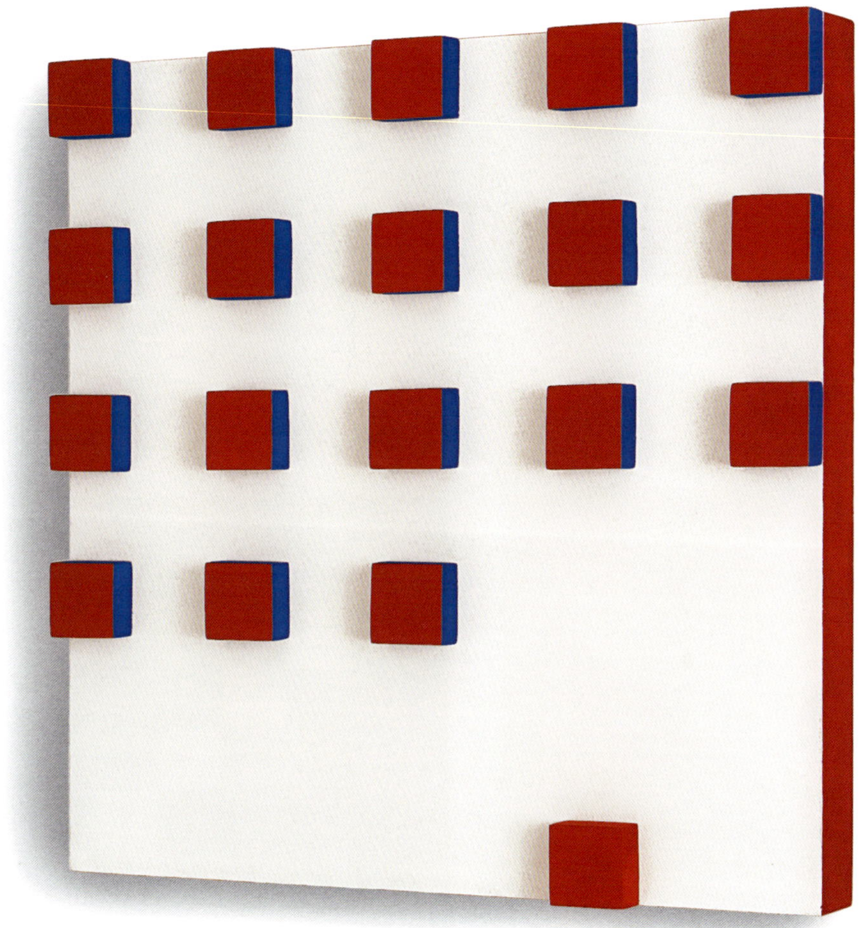

10. *Revelo*, 1954–56

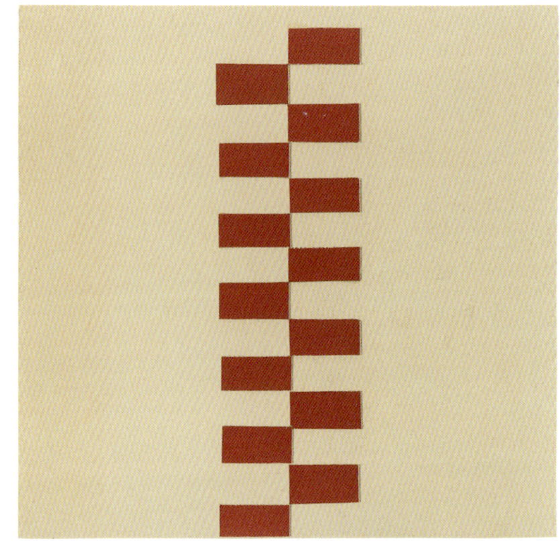

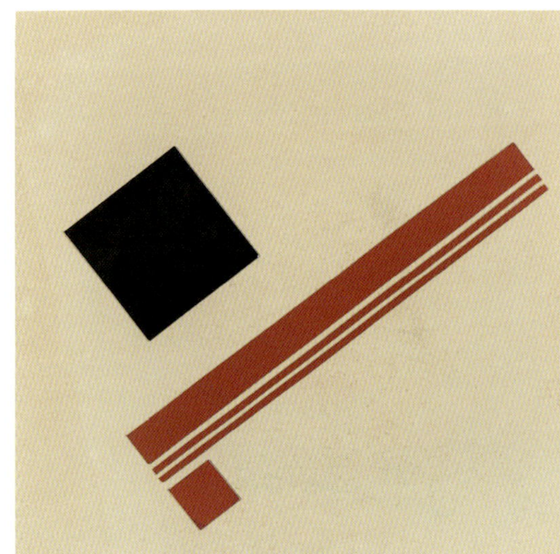

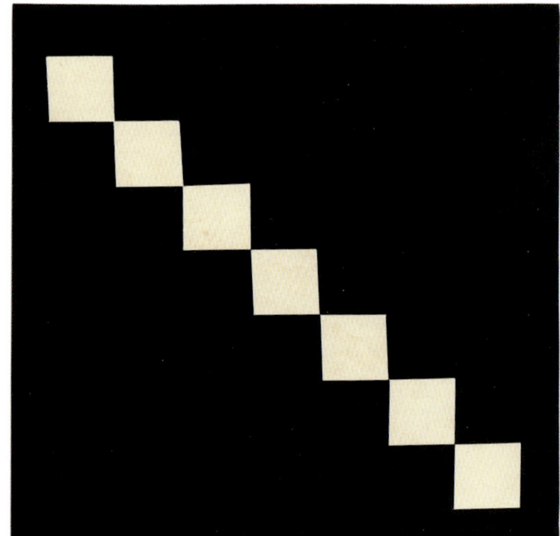

(clockwise from top)

11. *Study for a Relief*, 1955

12. *Study for a Relief*, 1955

13. *Study for a Painting*, 1955

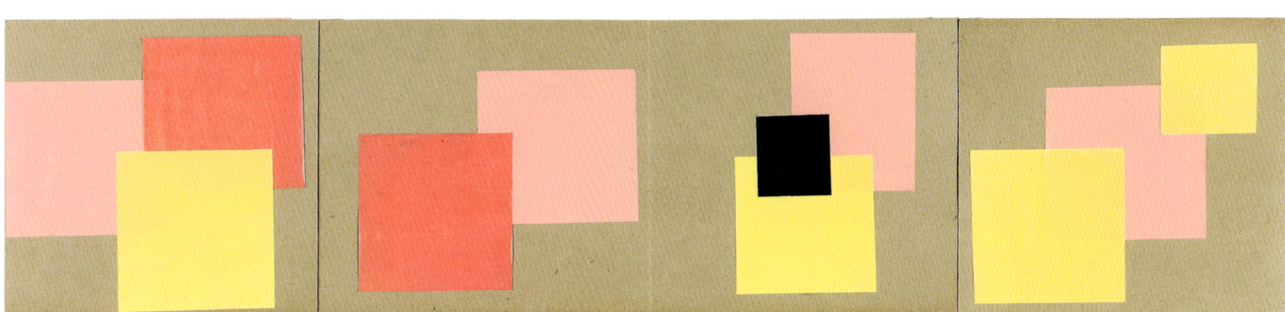

14. *Study for Ballet no. 3*, 1959

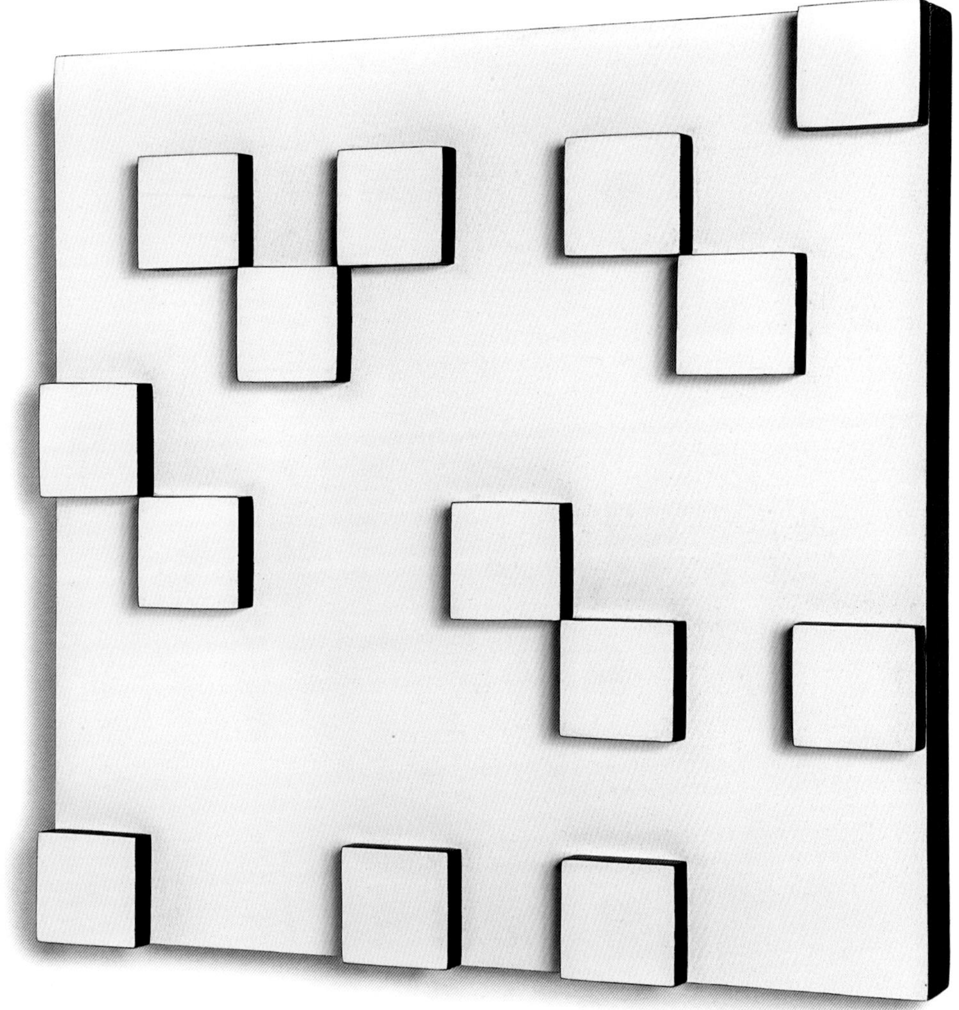

15. *Relevo*, 1954–56

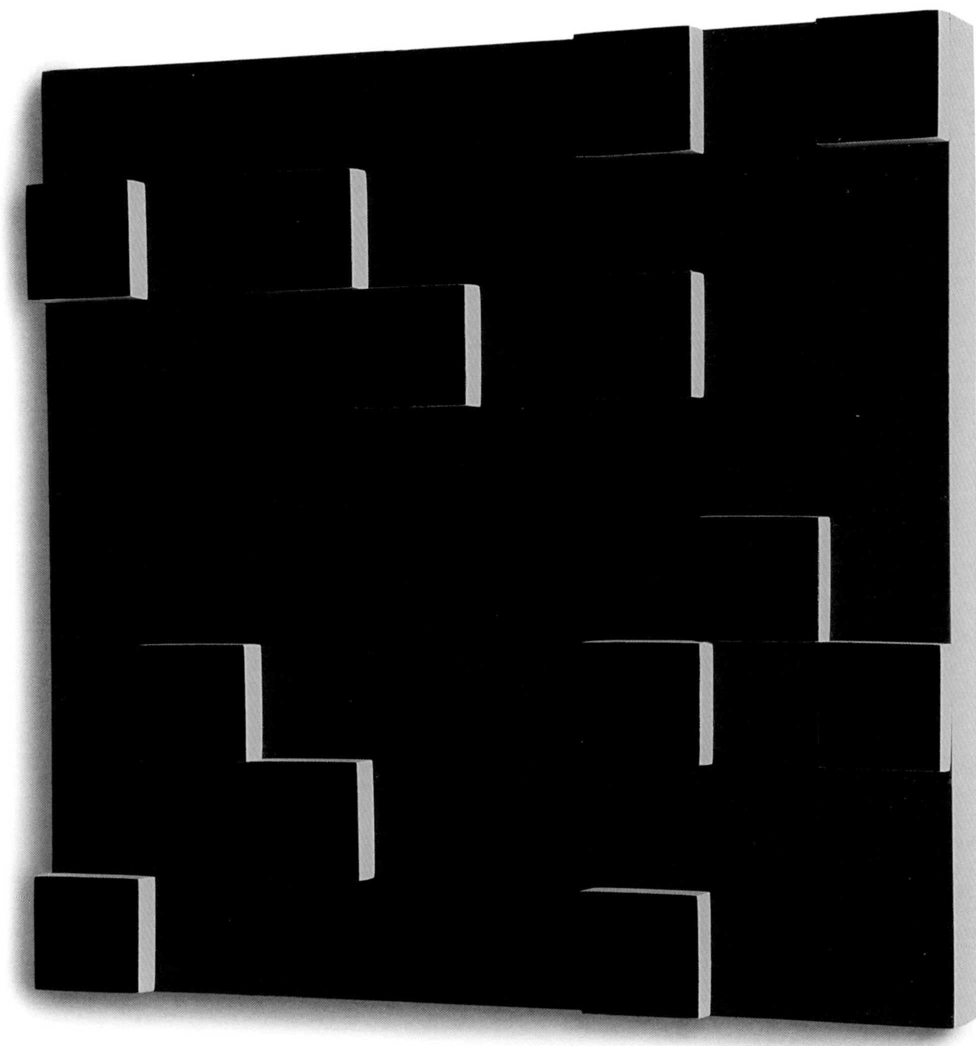

16. *Relevo*, 1954–56

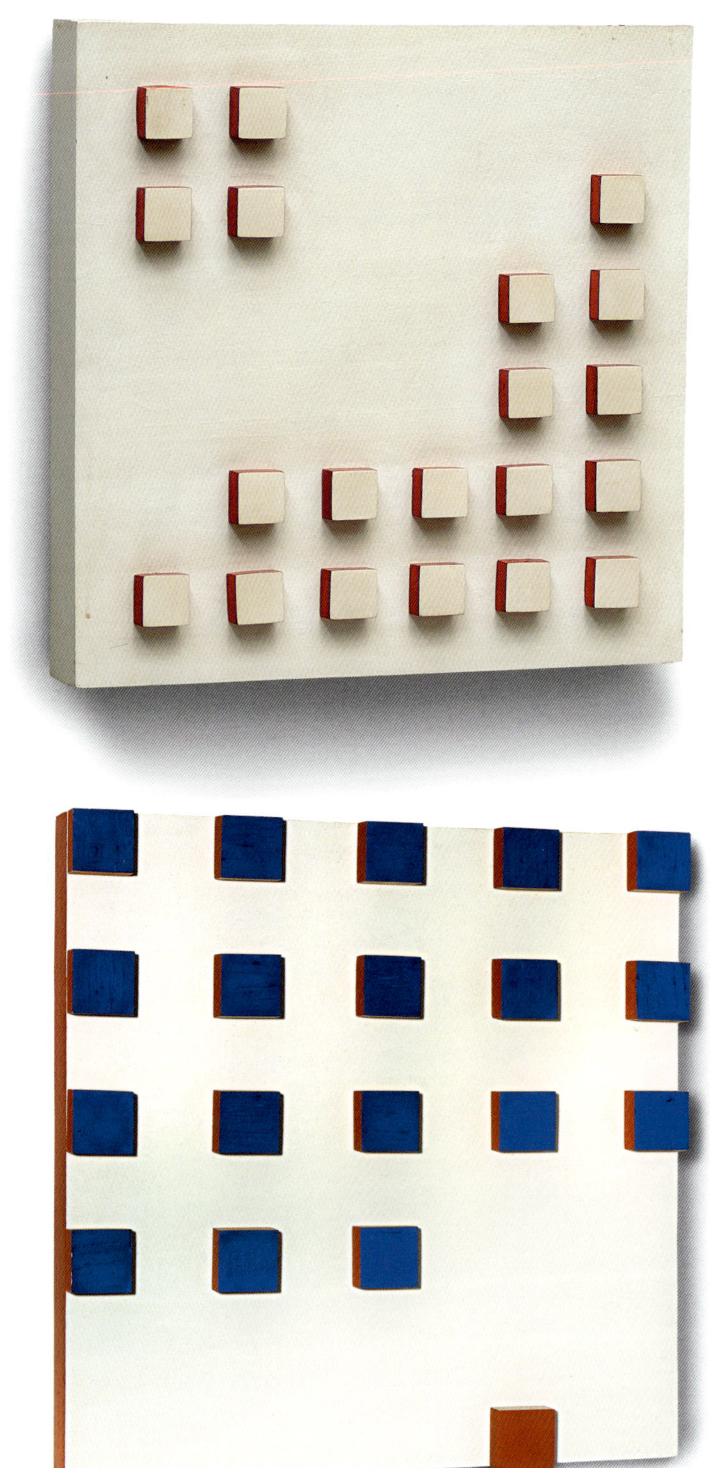

17. *Tarugo*, 1954

18. *Relevo*, 1955

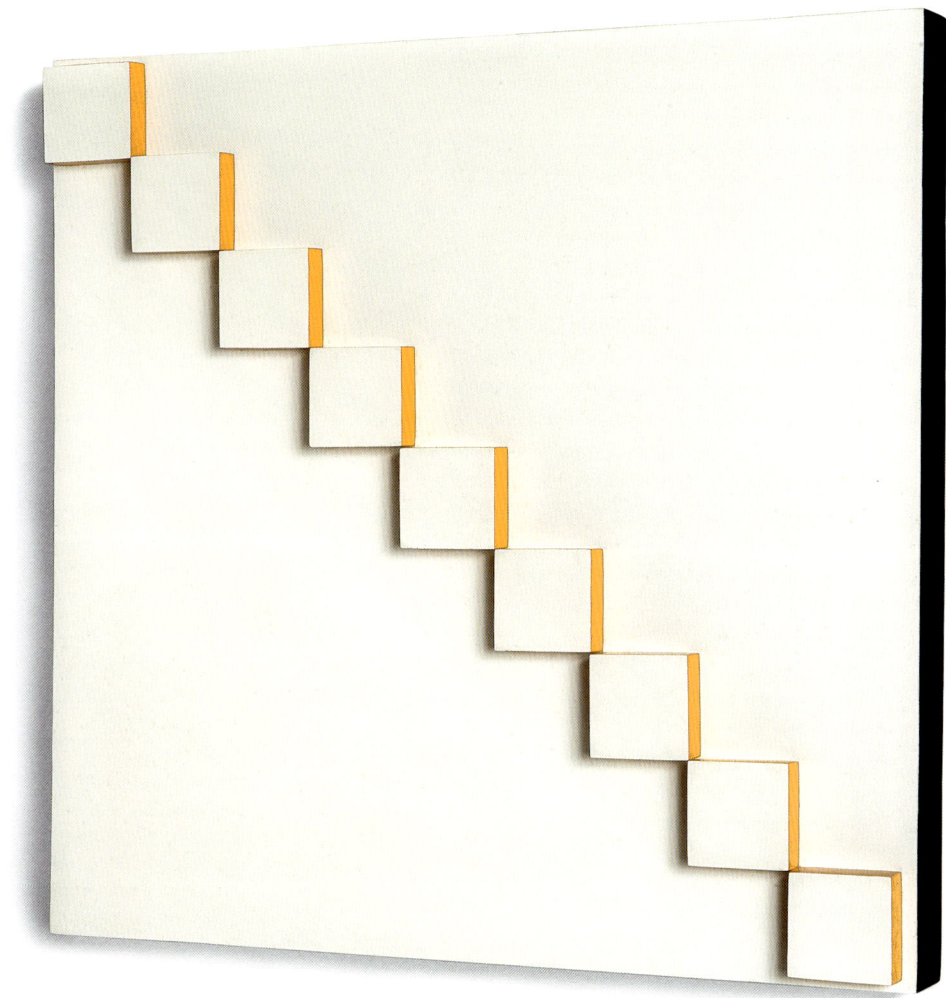

19. *Relevo*, 1954–56

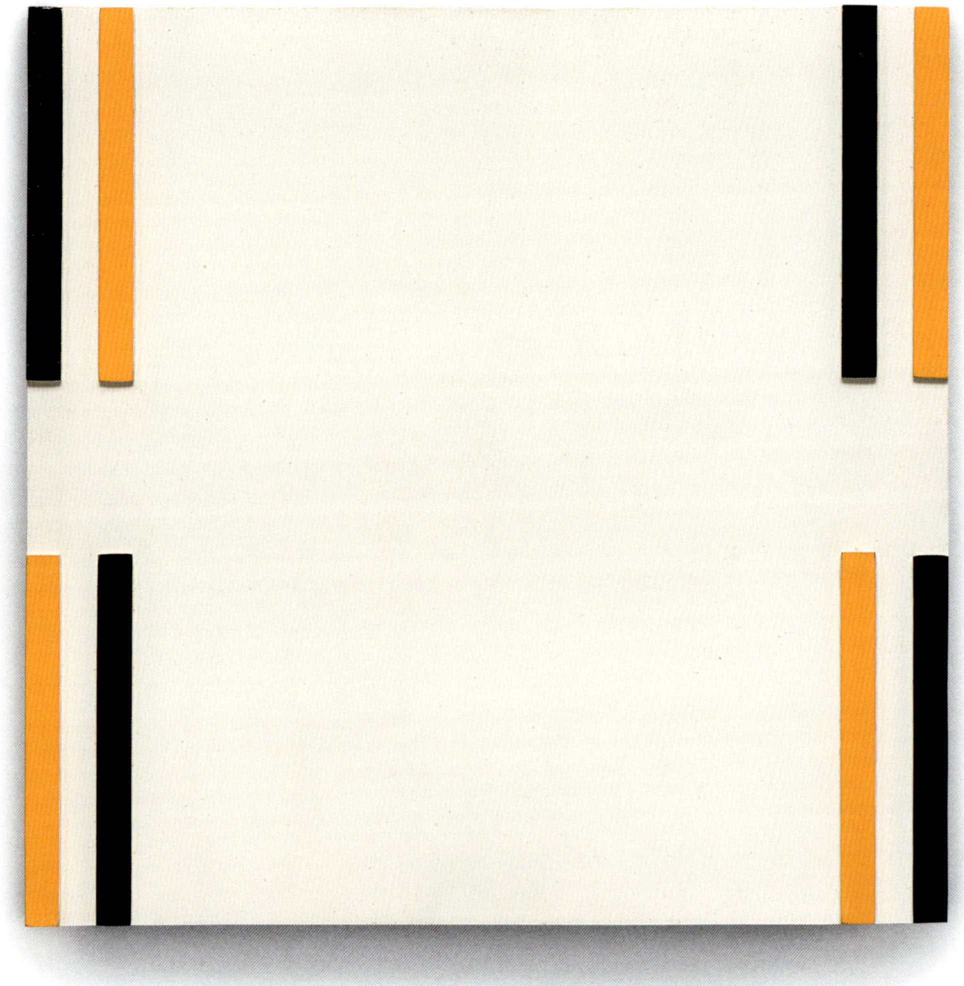

20. *Relevo*, 1954–56

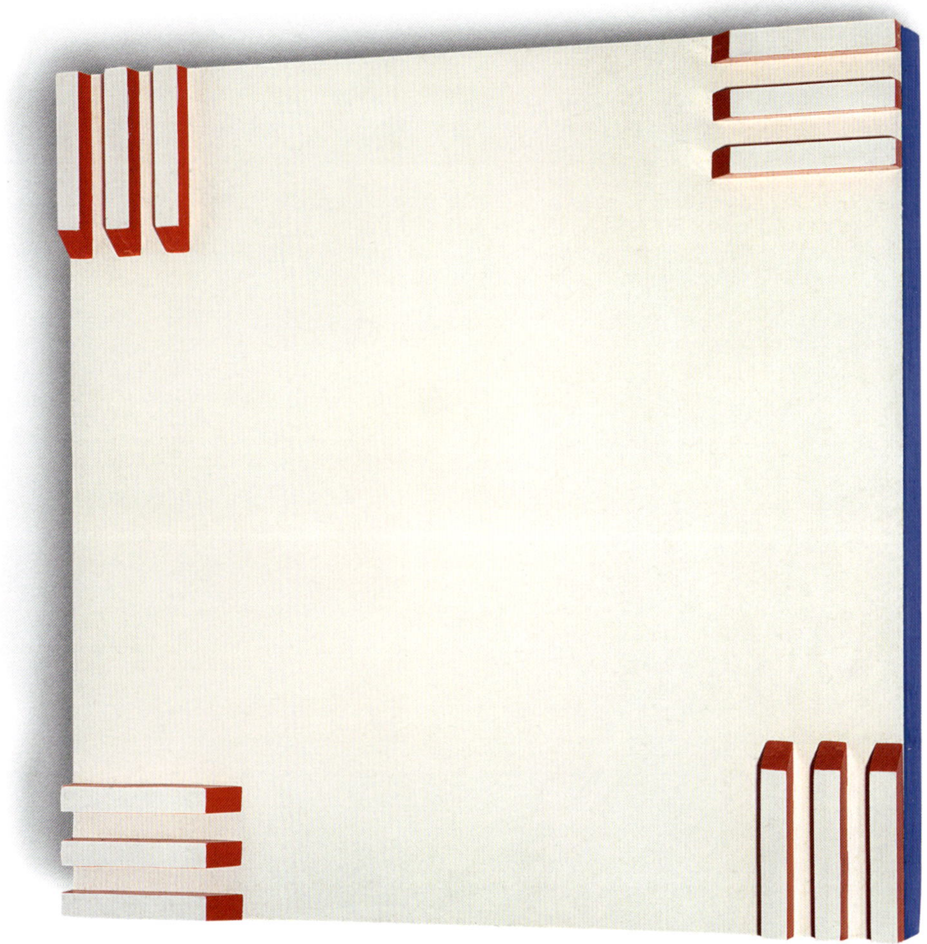

21. *Relevo*, 1955

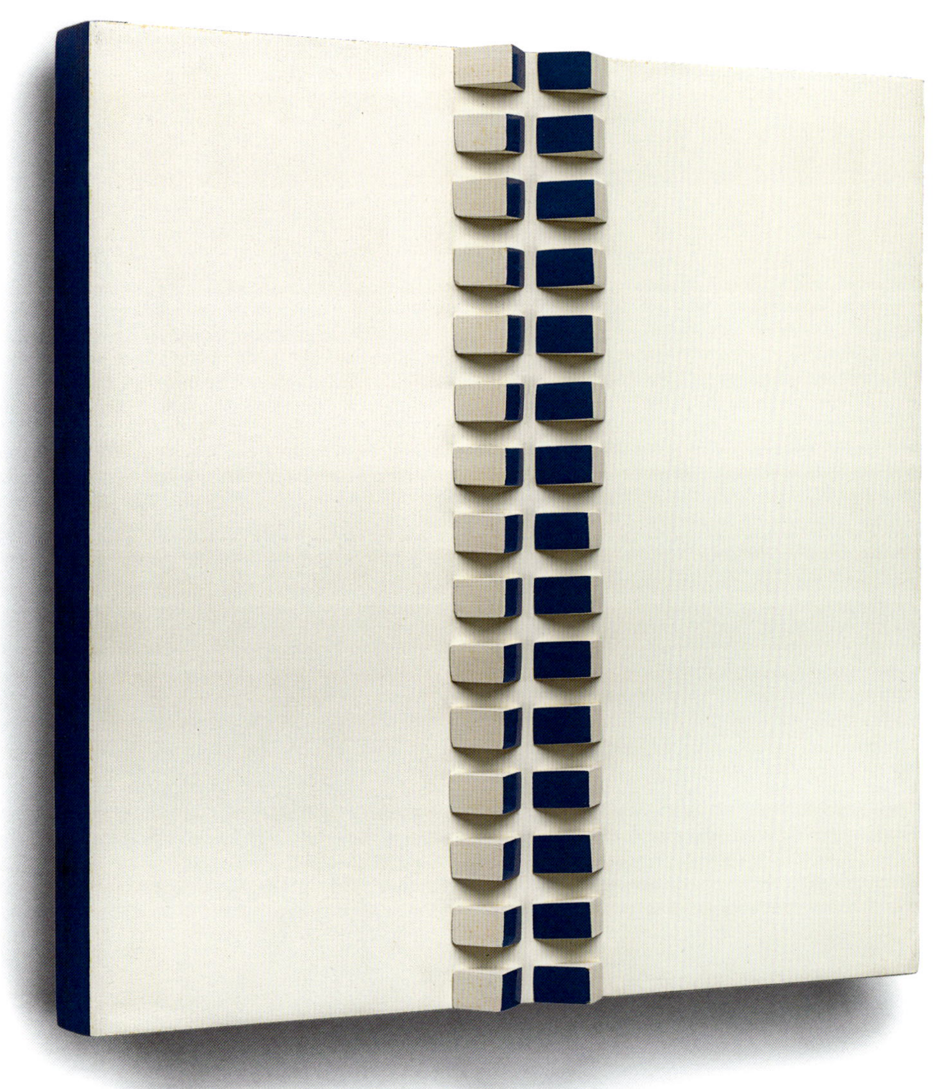

22. *Relevo*, 1954

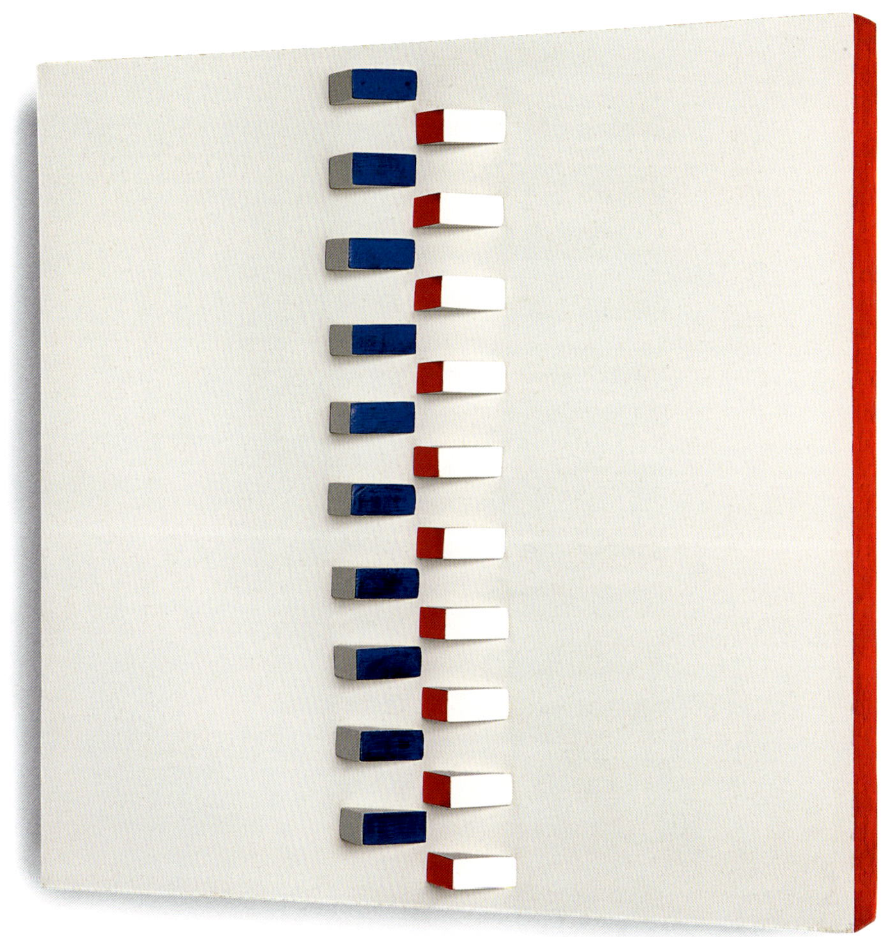

23. *Relevo*, 1954–56

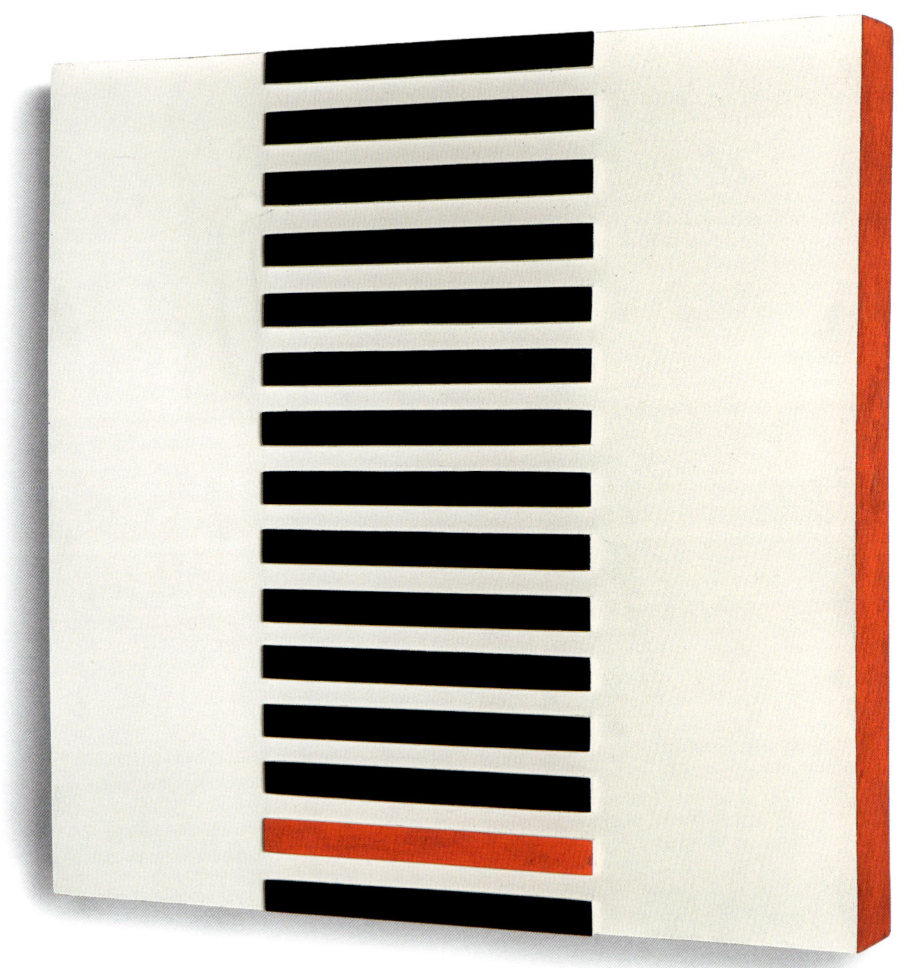

24. *Tarugo*, 1954–56

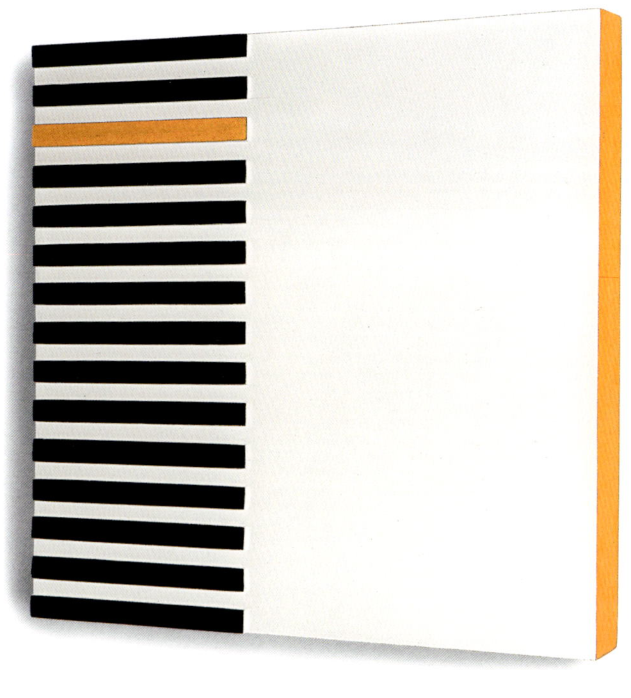

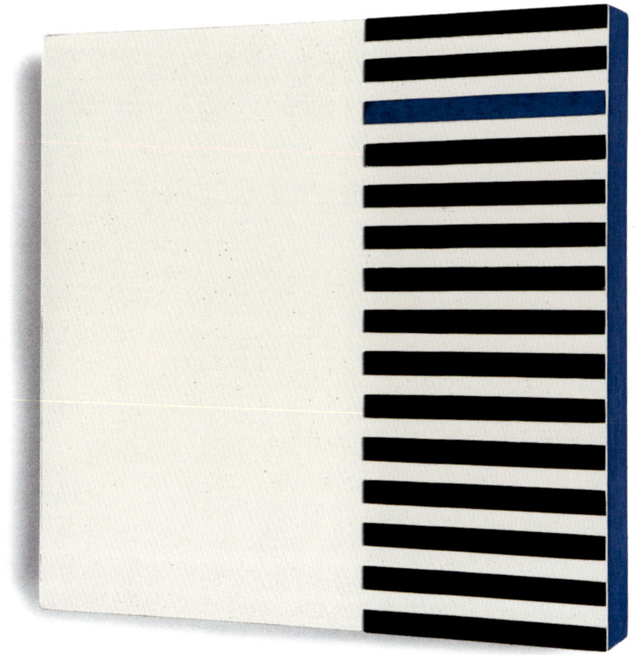

25. *Tarugo*, 1954–56

26. *Tarugo*, 1954–56

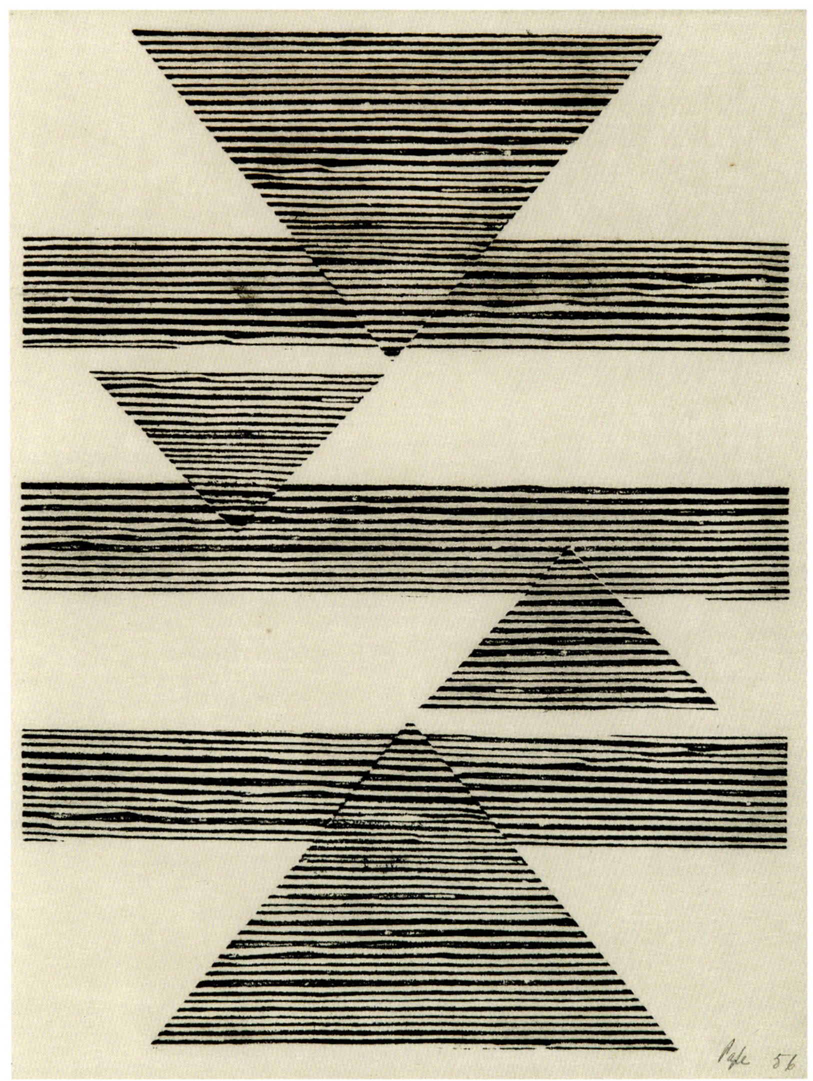

27. *Tecelar*, 1956

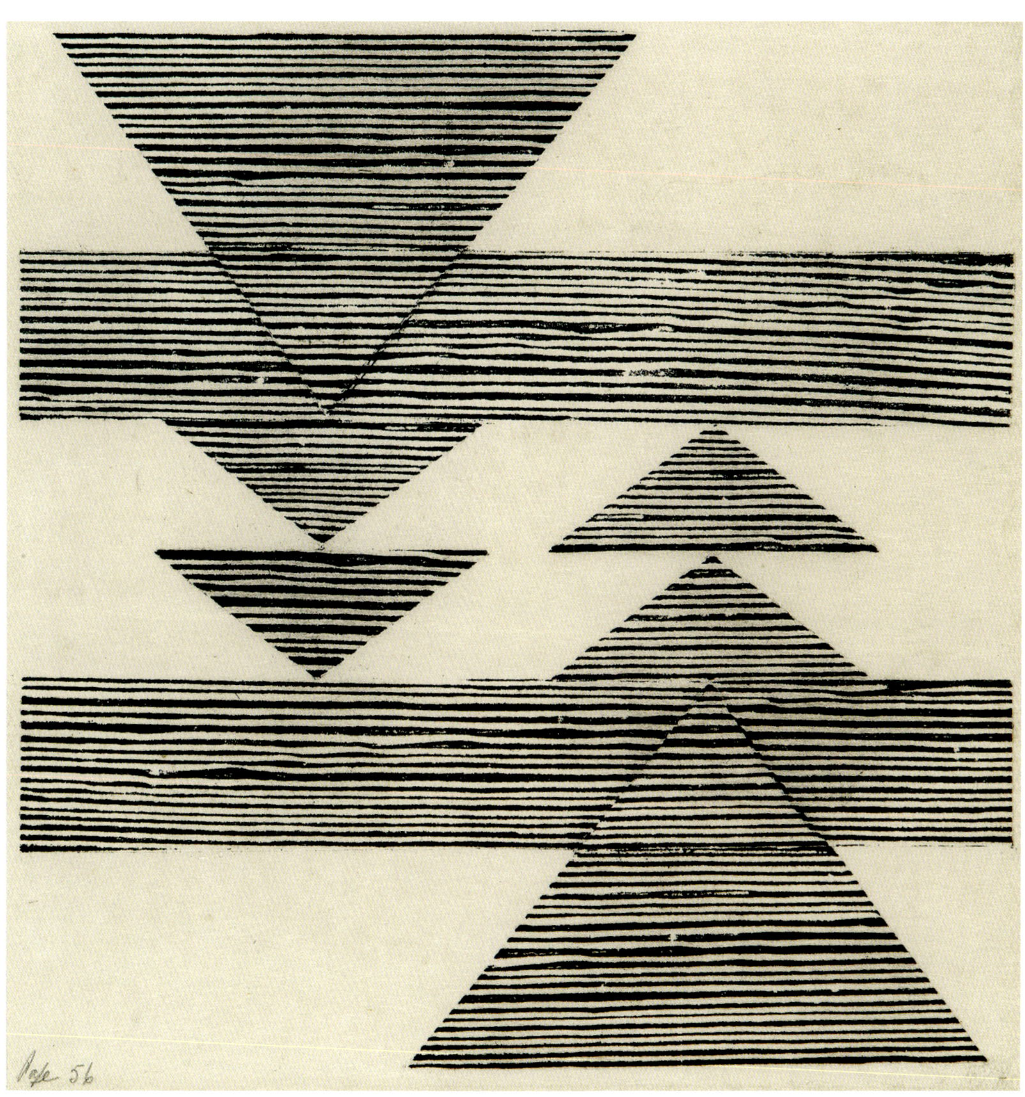

28. *Tecelar*, 1956

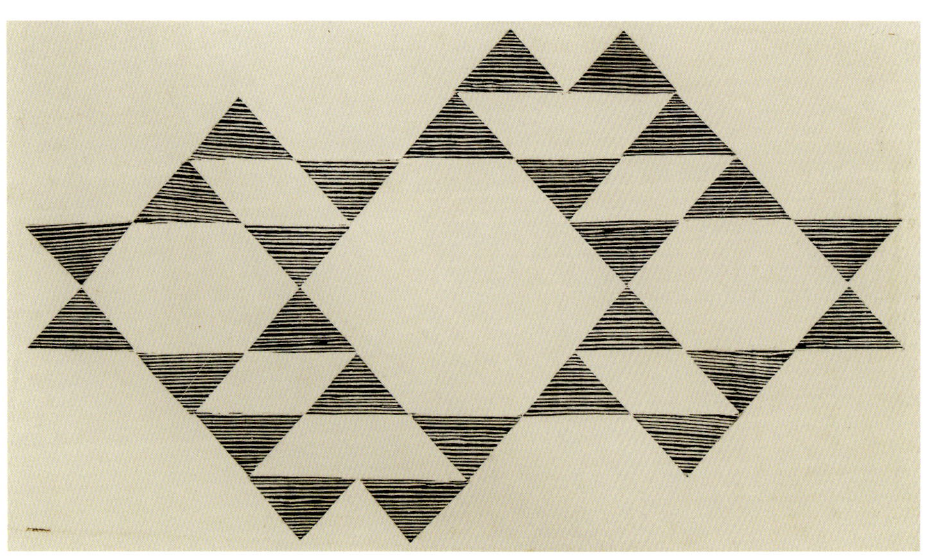

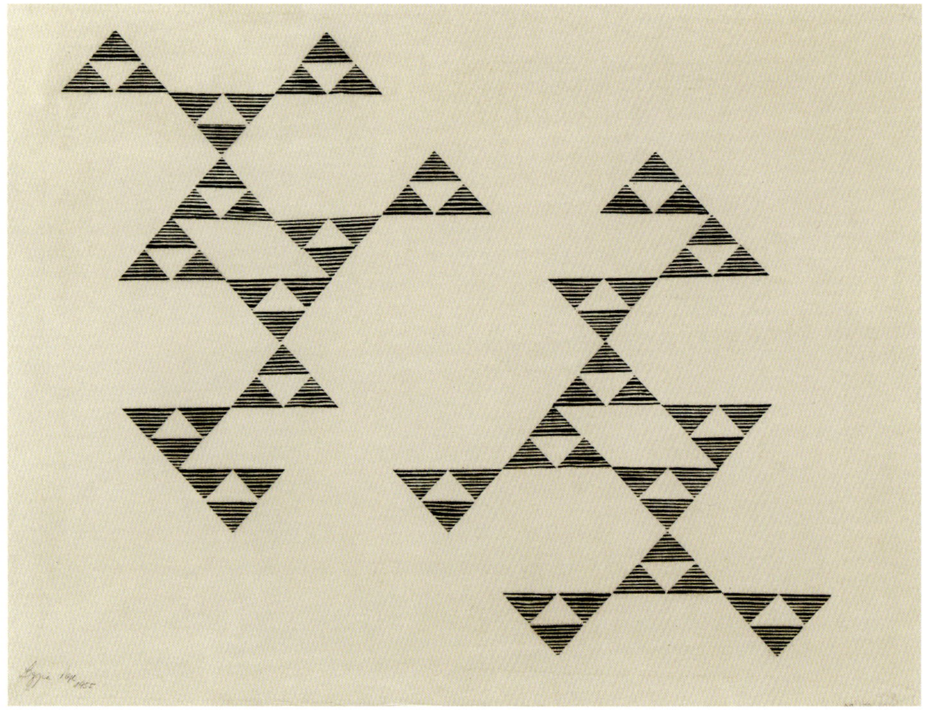

29. *Tecelar*, 1955

30. *Tecelar*, 1955

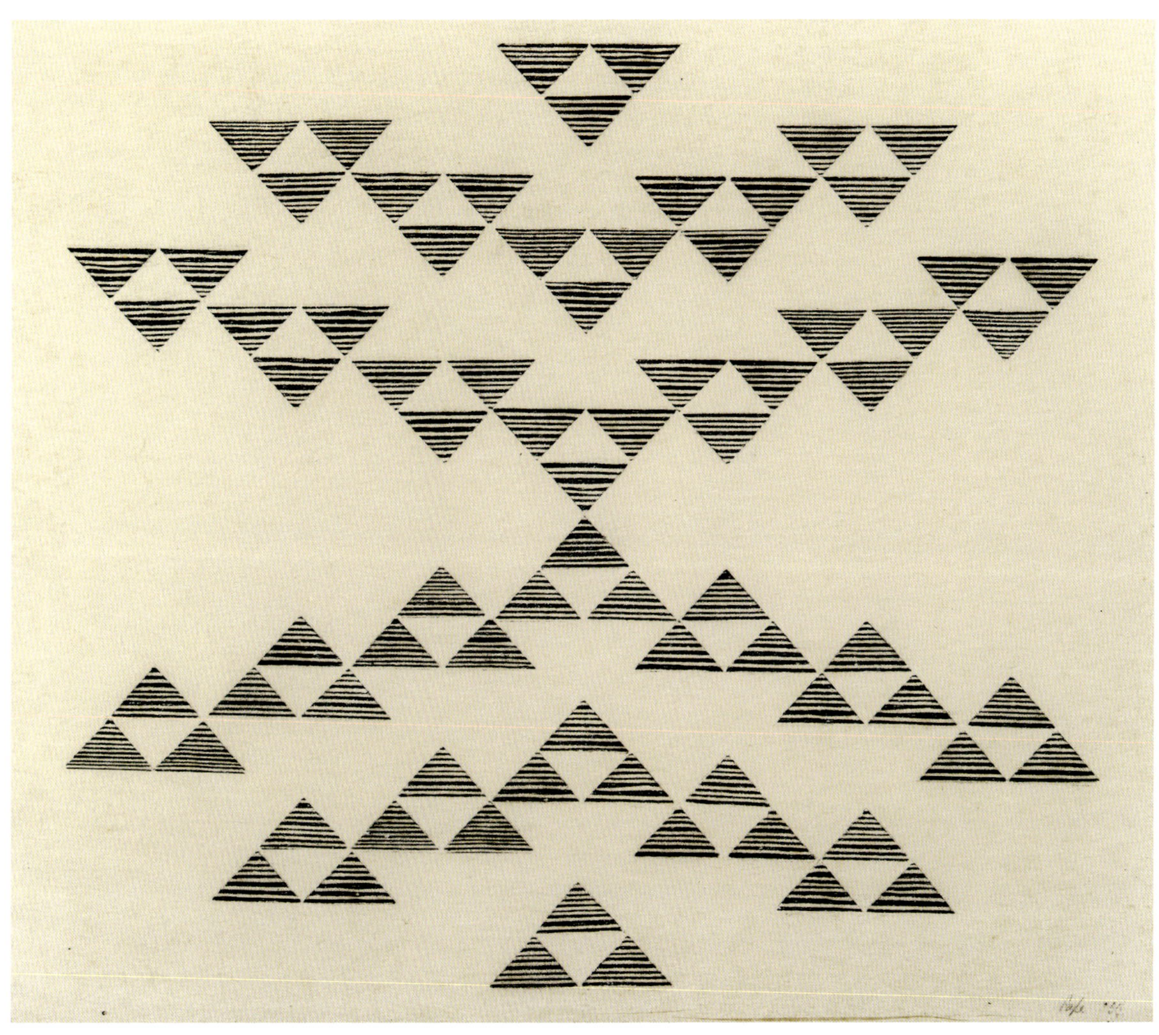

31. *Tecelar*, 1955

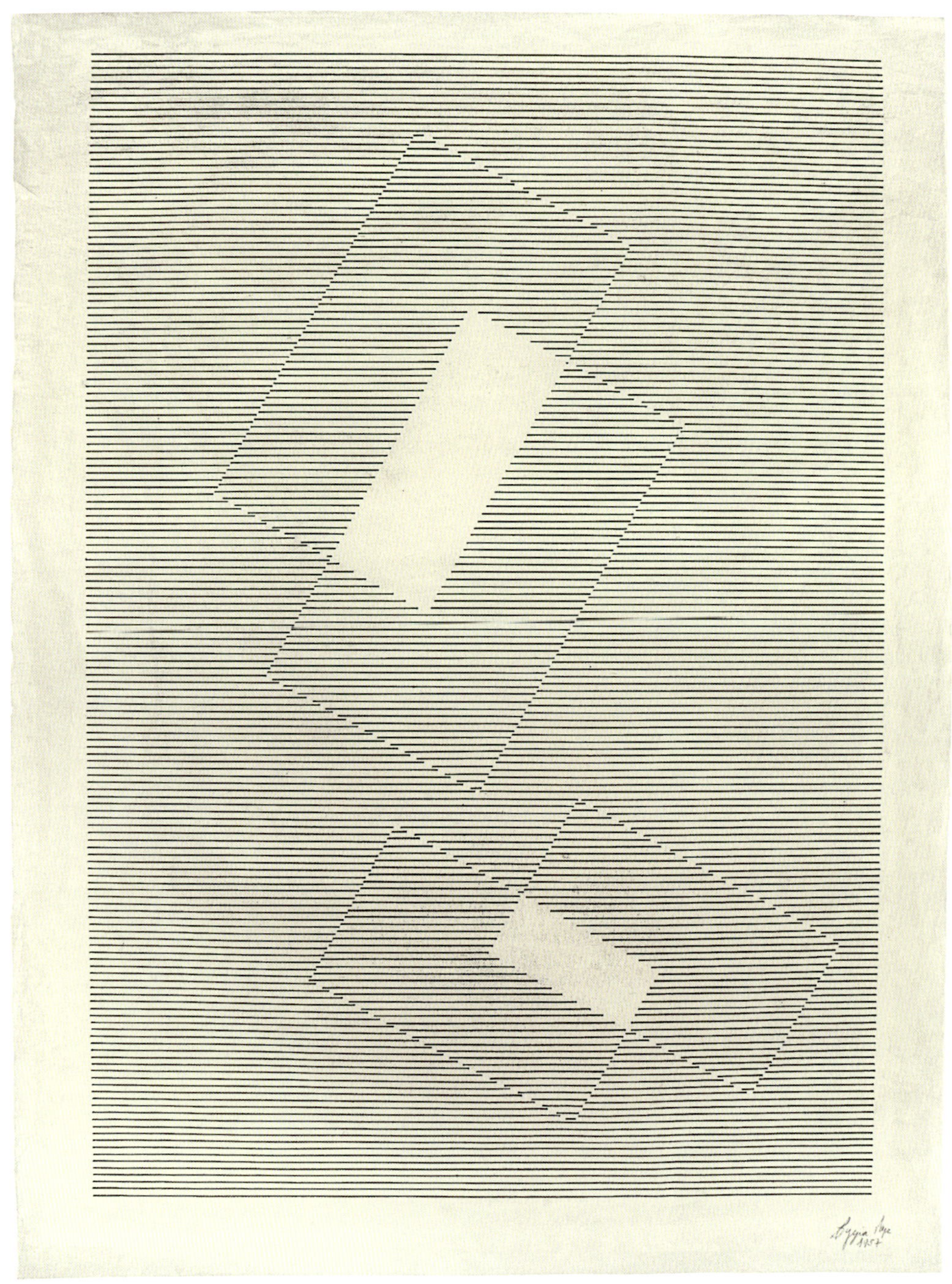

32. *Drawing*, 1957

33. *Drawing*, 1957

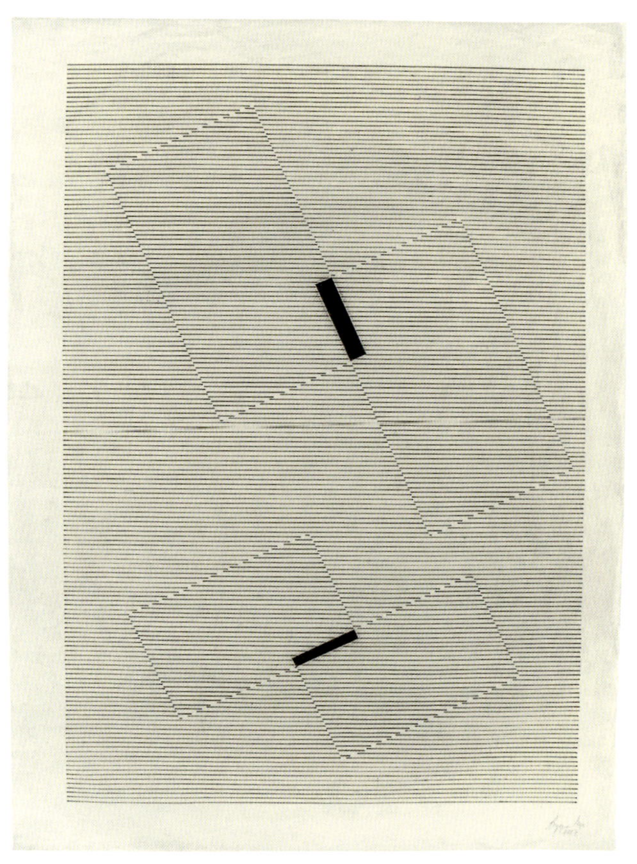 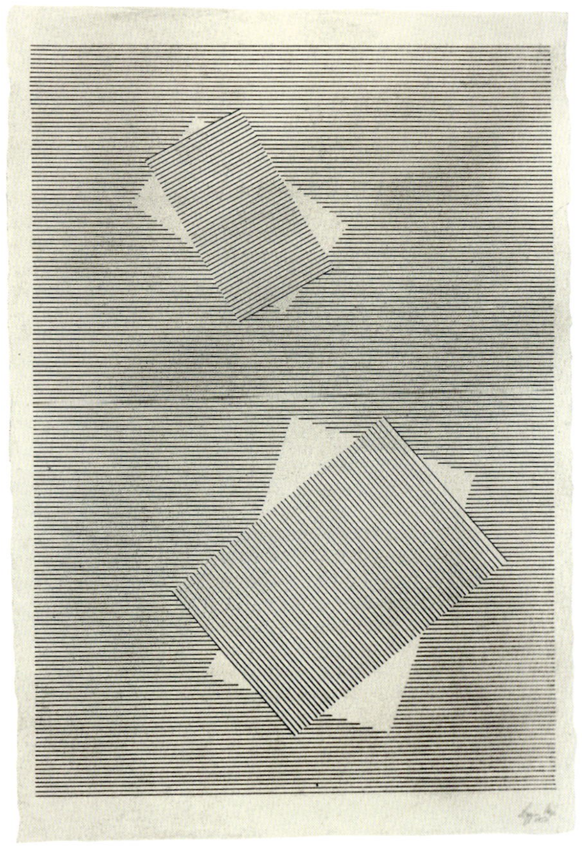

34. *Drawing*, 1957

35. *Drawing*, 1957

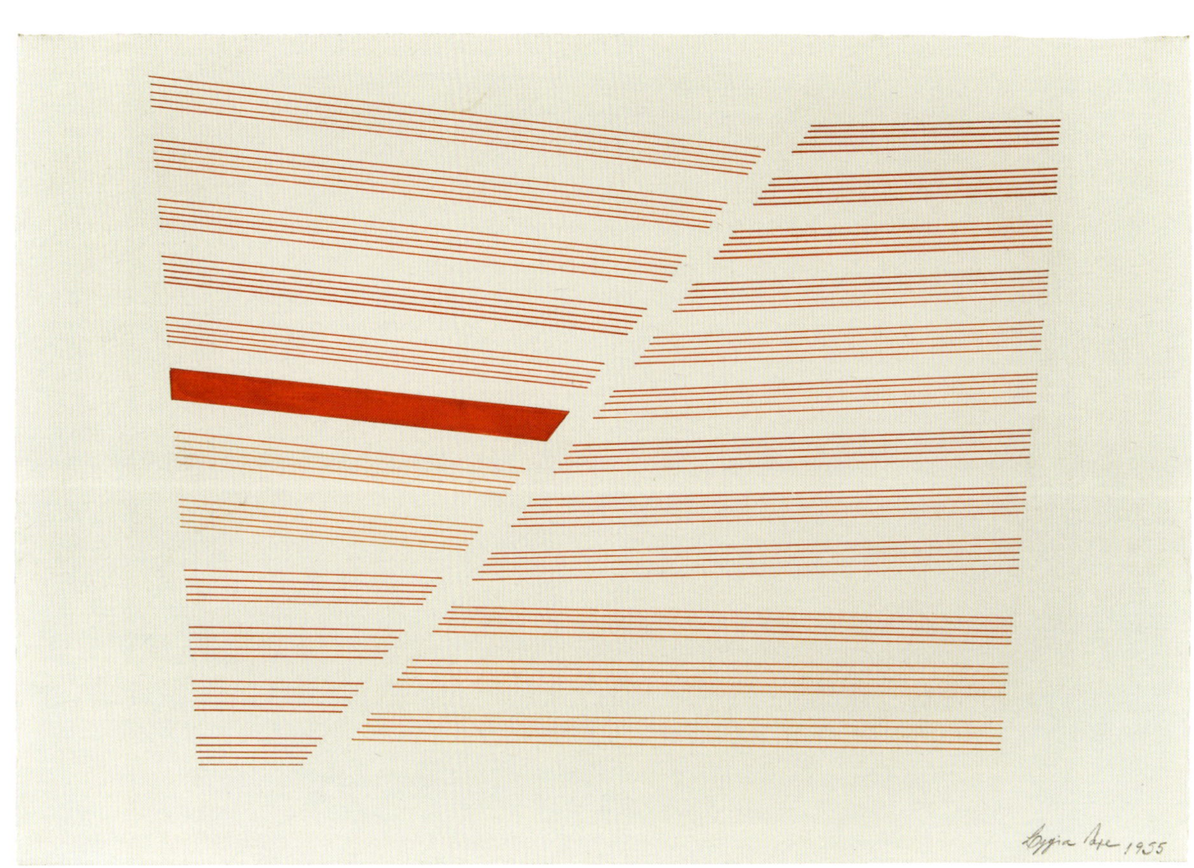

36. *Drawing*, 1955

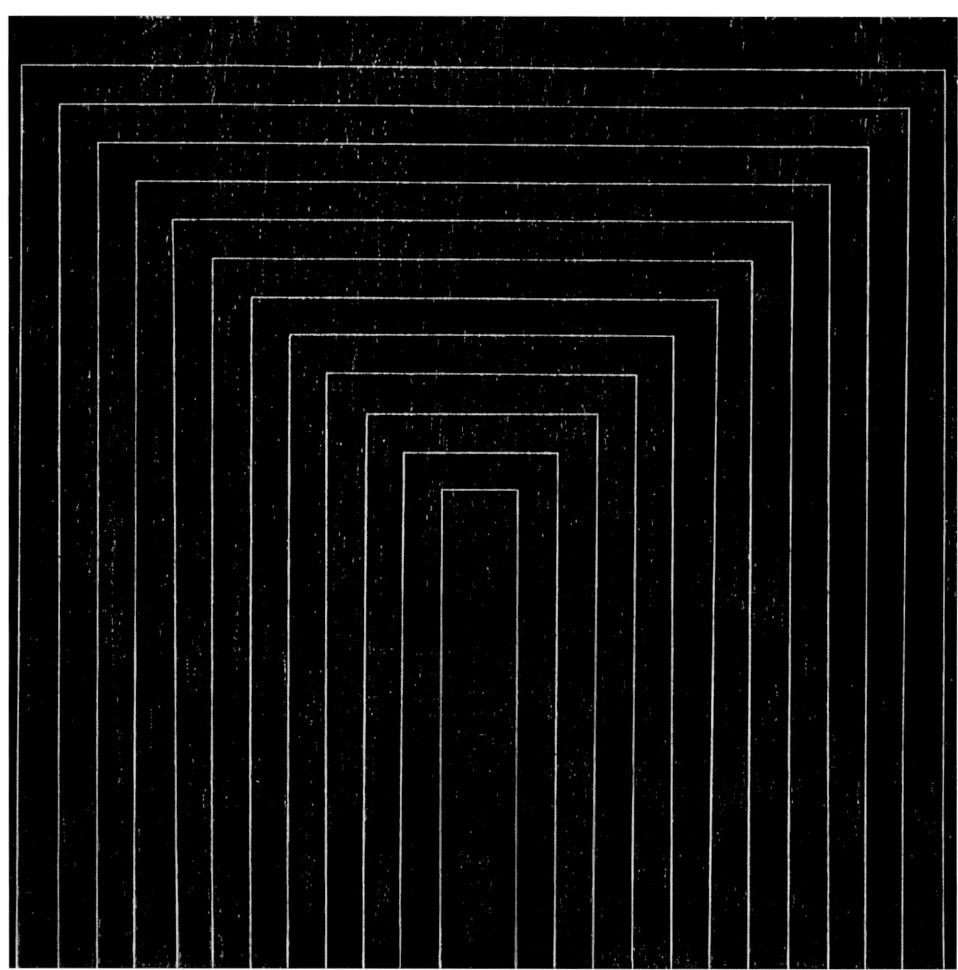

37. *Tecelar*, 1956

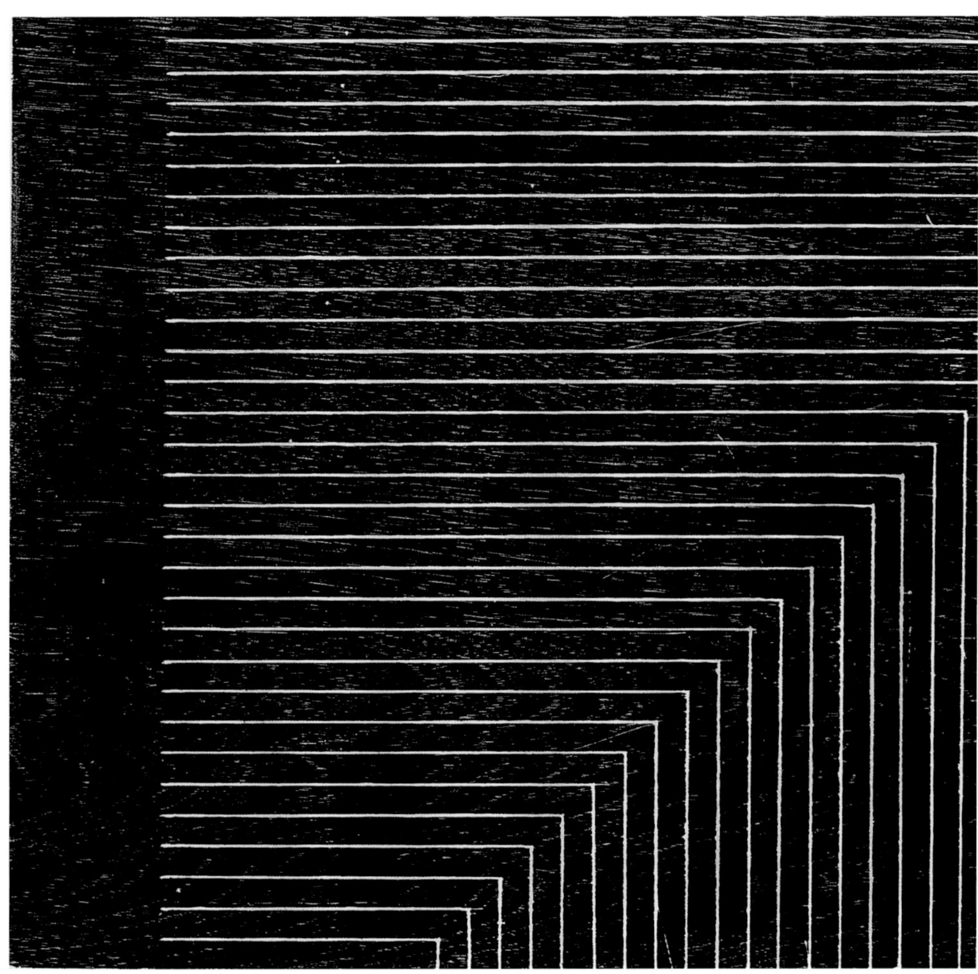

38. *Tecelar*, 1957

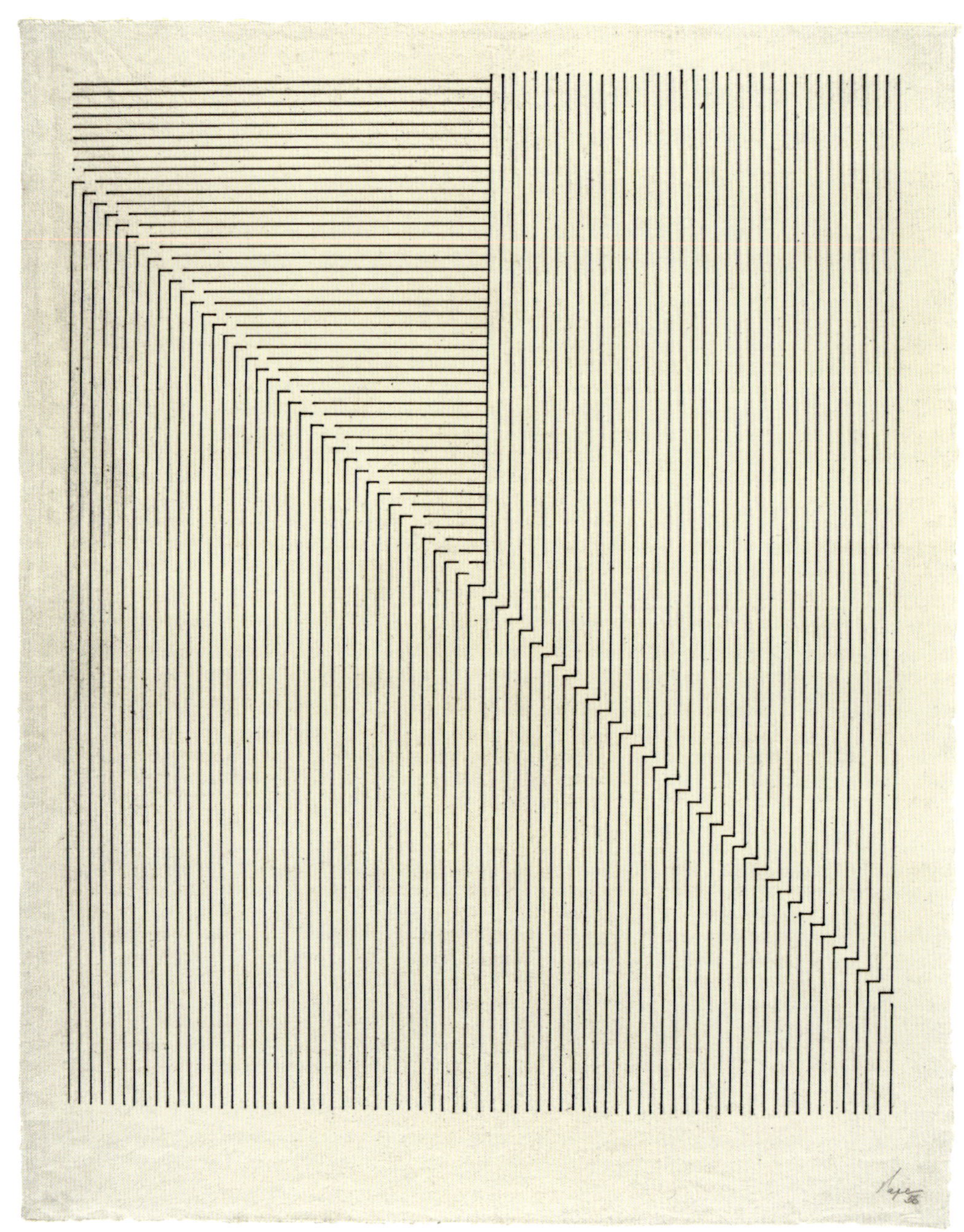

39. *Drawing*, 1956

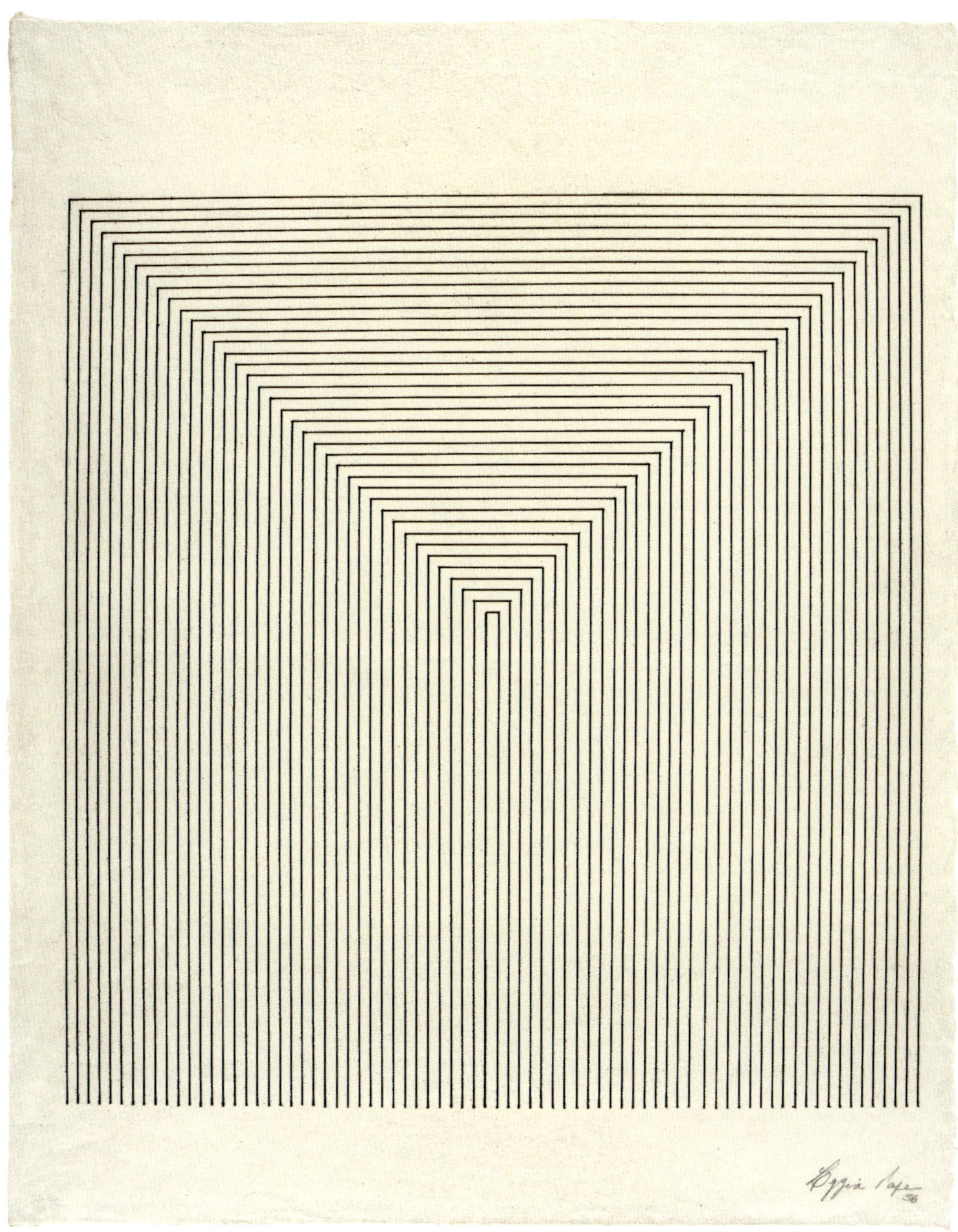

40. *Drawing*, 1956

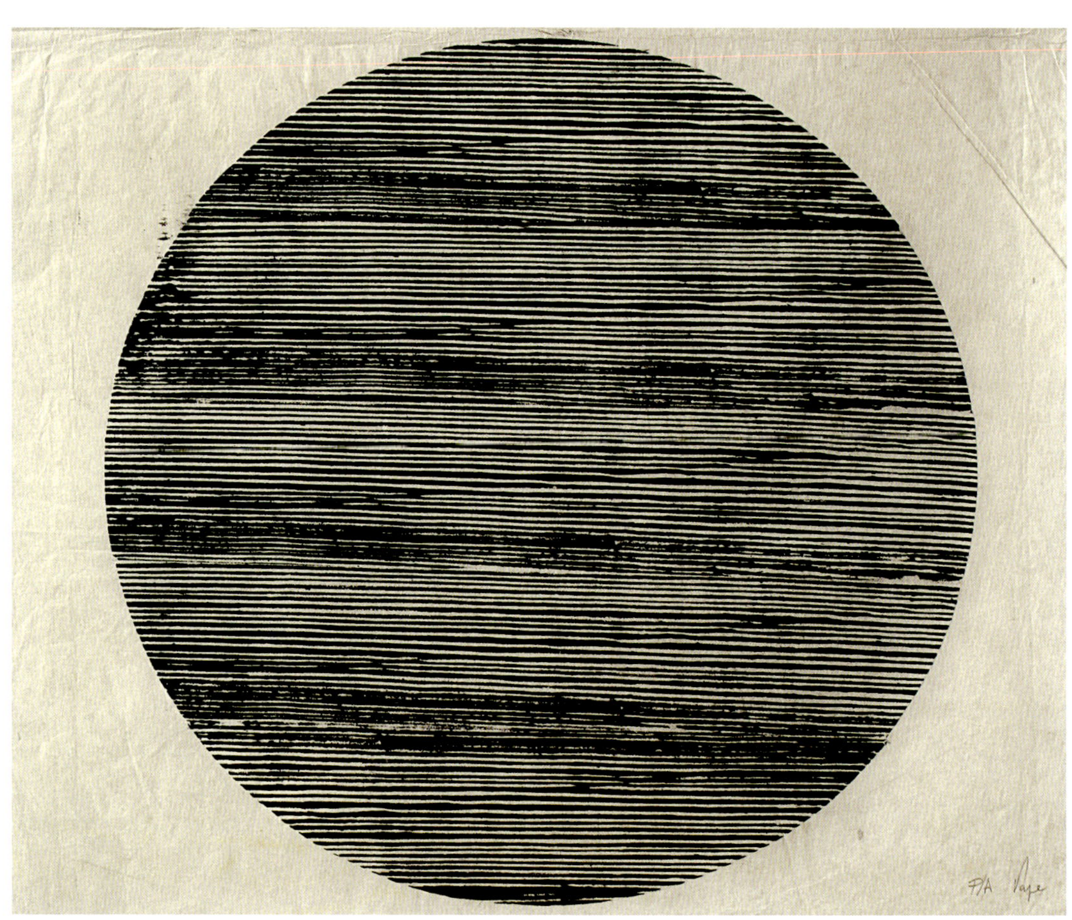

41. *Tecelar*, 1959

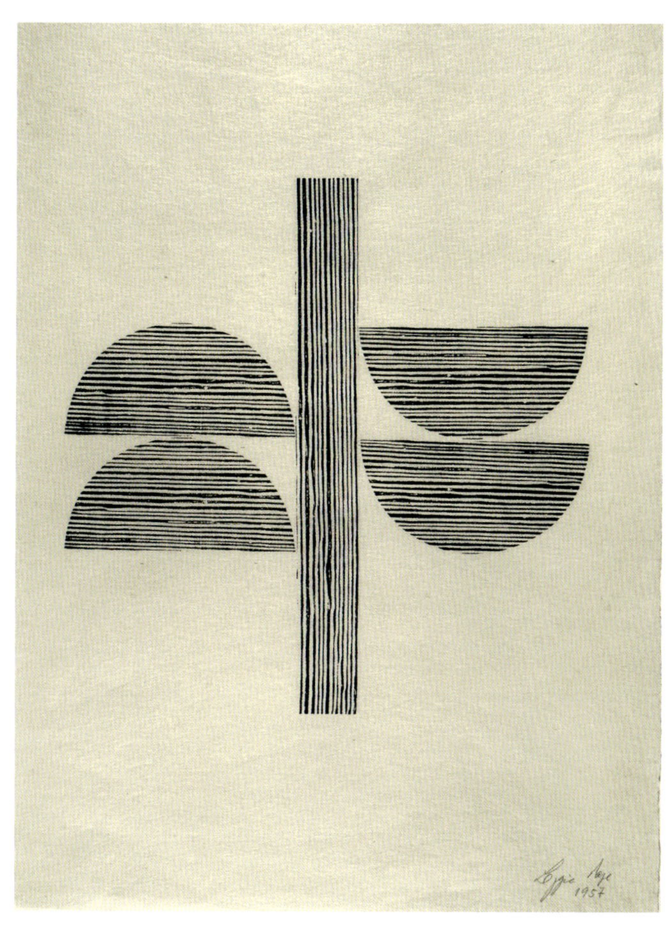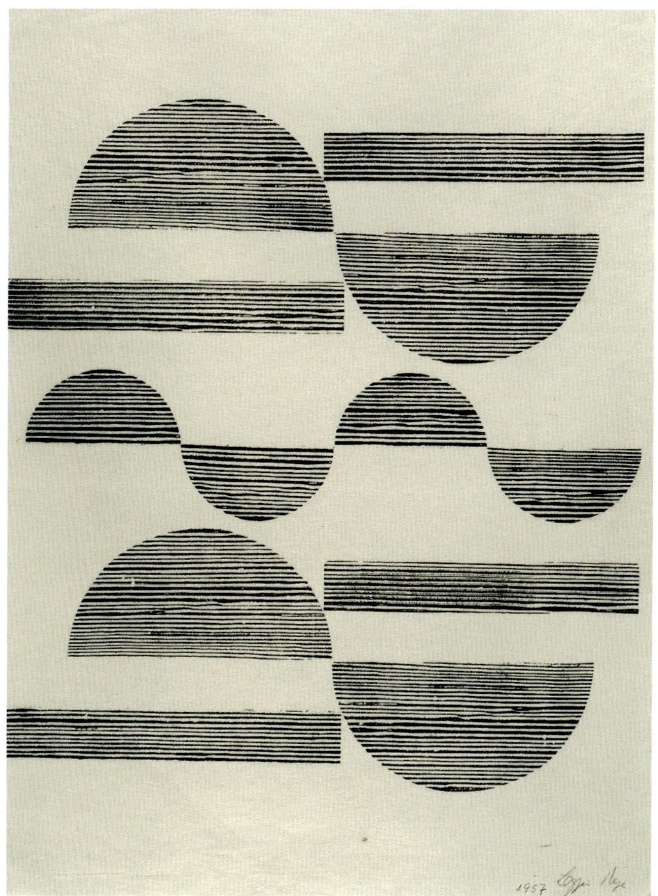

42. *Tecelar*, 1957

43. *Tecelar*, 1957

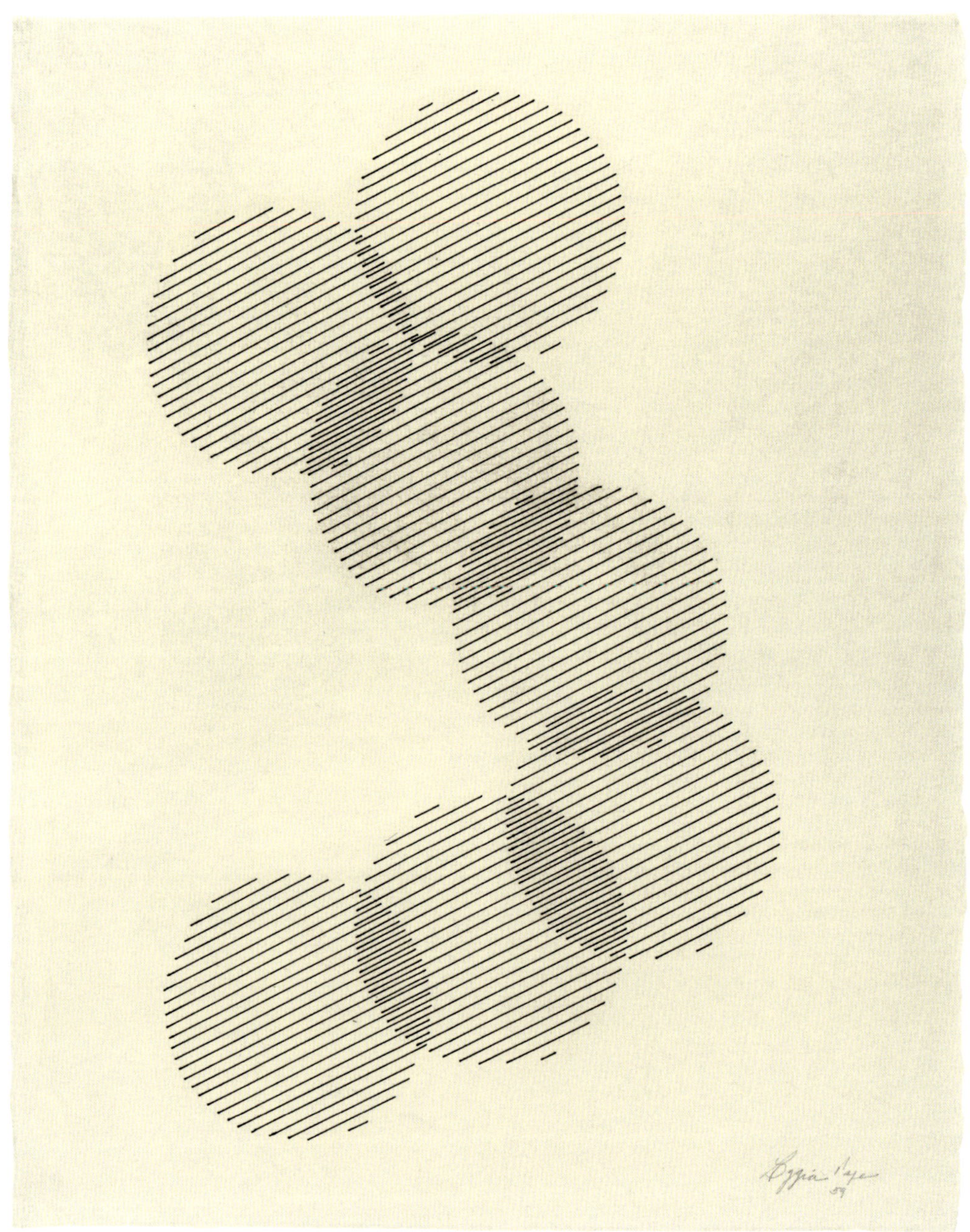

44. *Drawing*, 1959

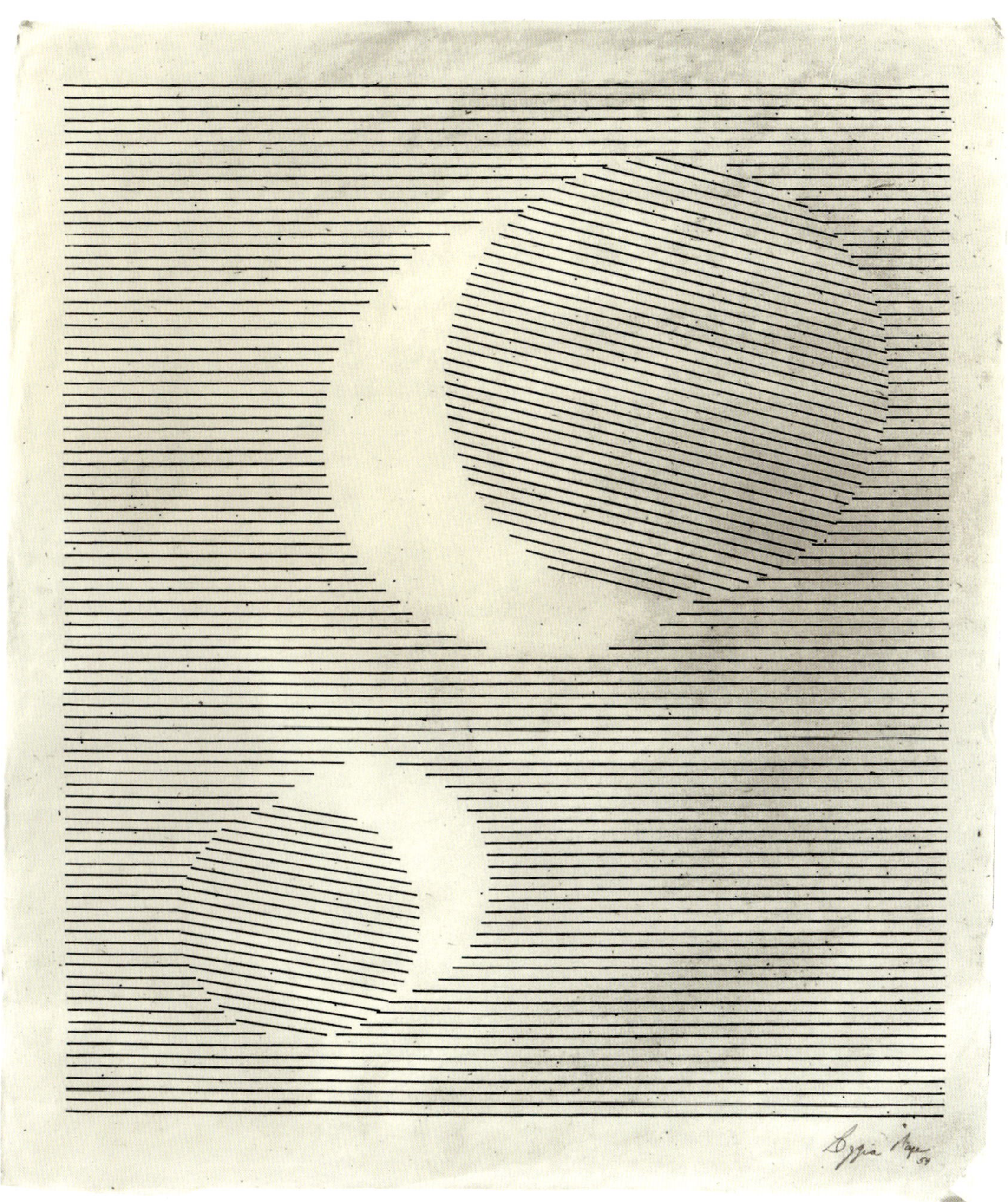

45. *Drawing*, 1959

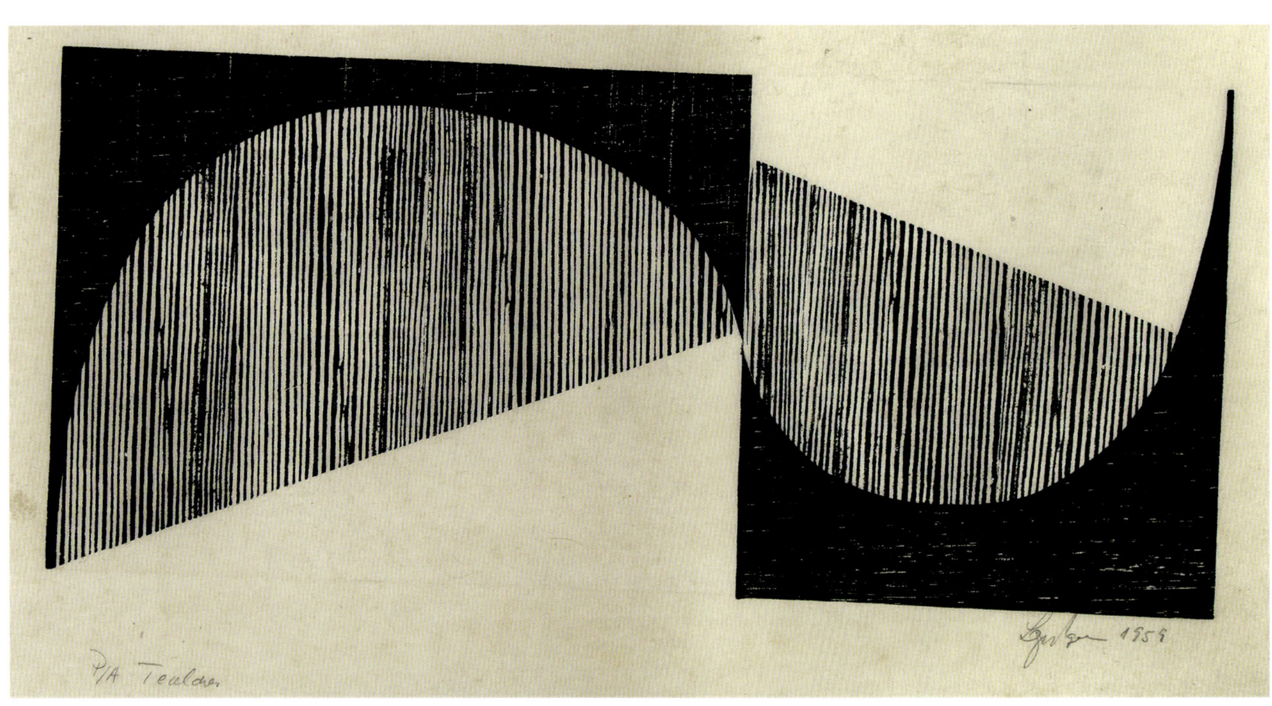

46. *Tecelar*, 1959

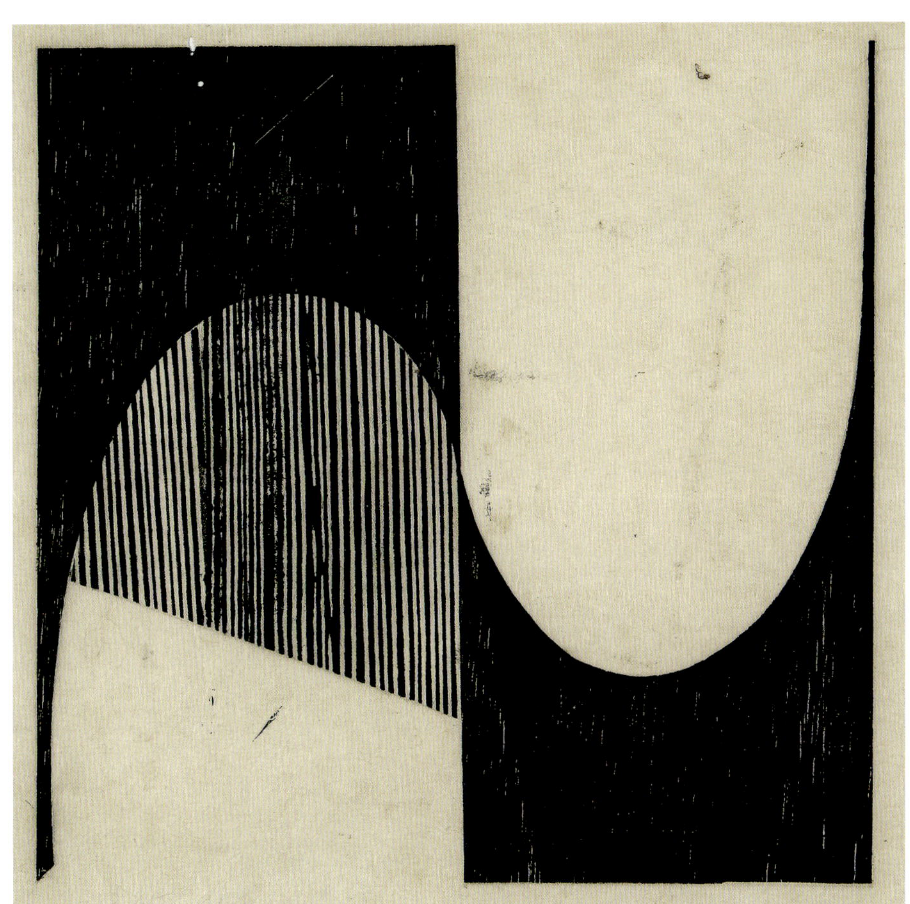

47. *Tecelar*, 1959

48. *Tecelar*, 1959

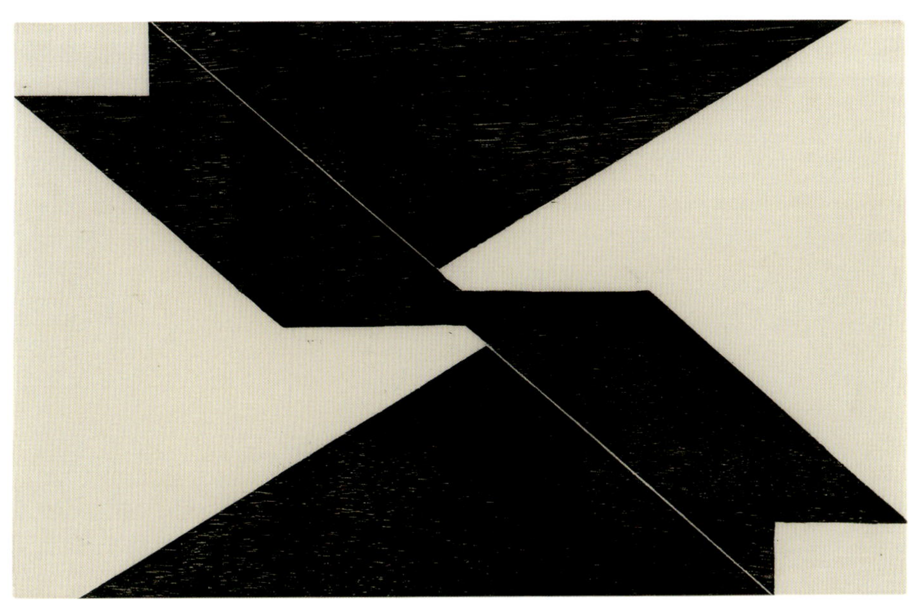

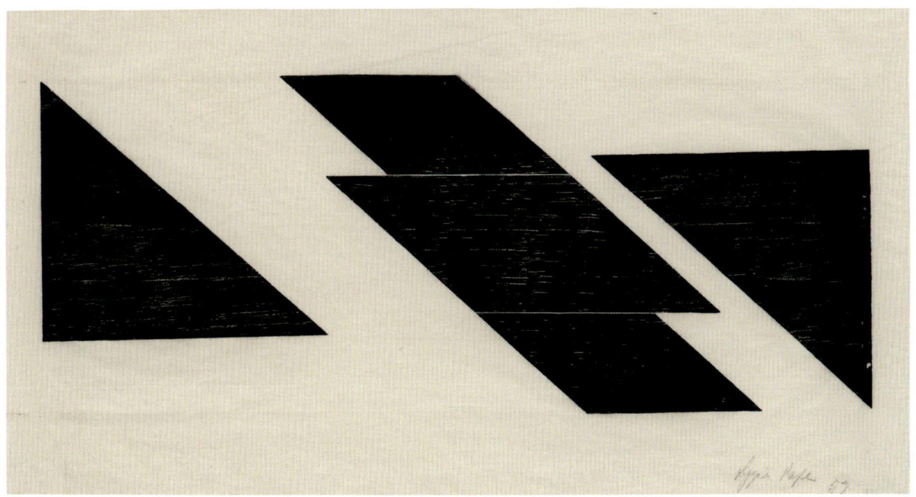

49. *Tecelar*, 1958

50. *Tecelar*, 1959

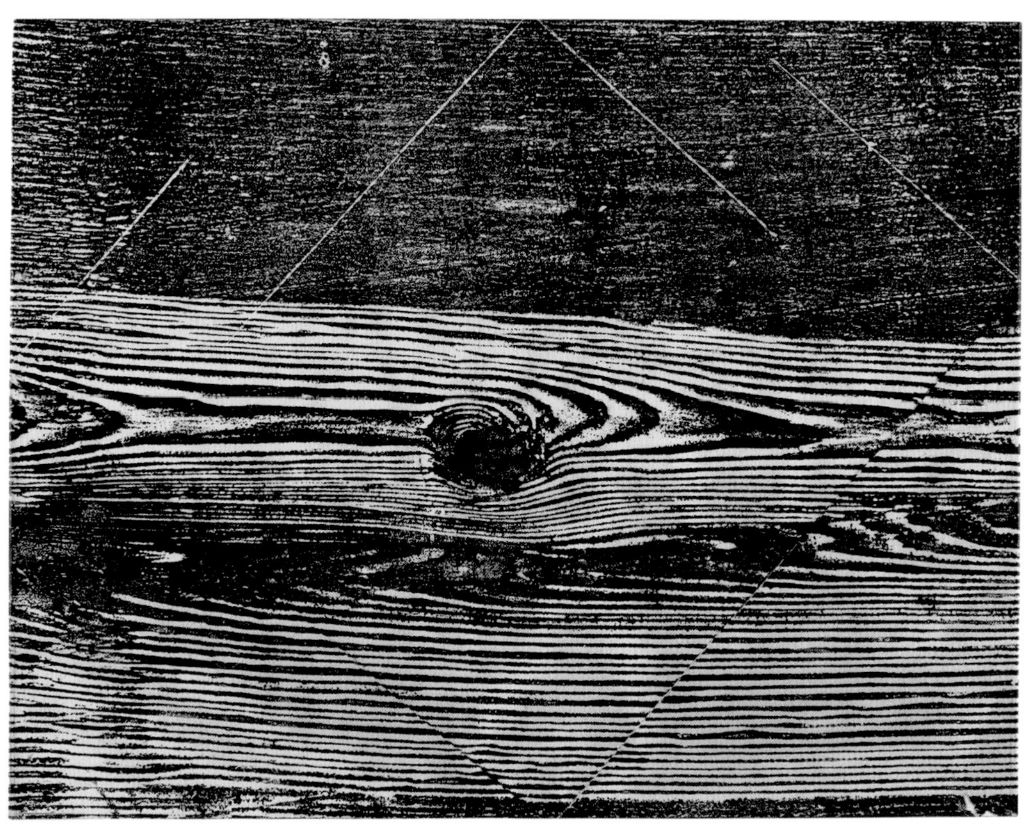

51. *Tecelar*, 1960

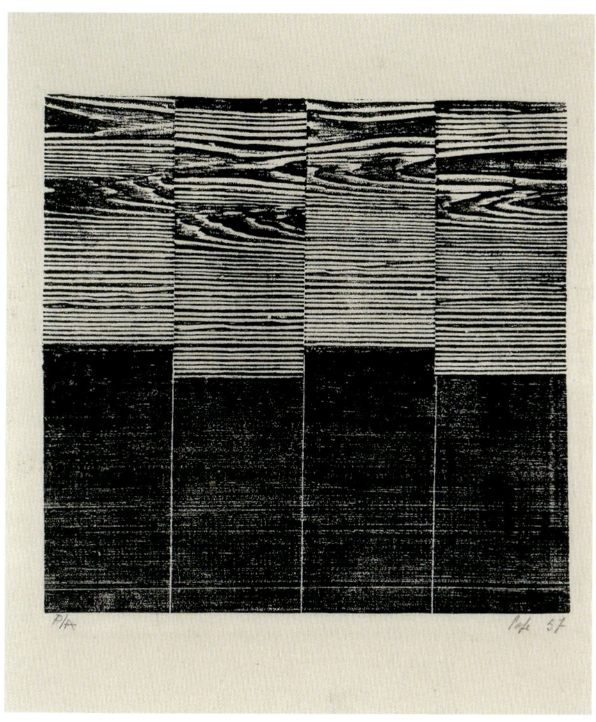 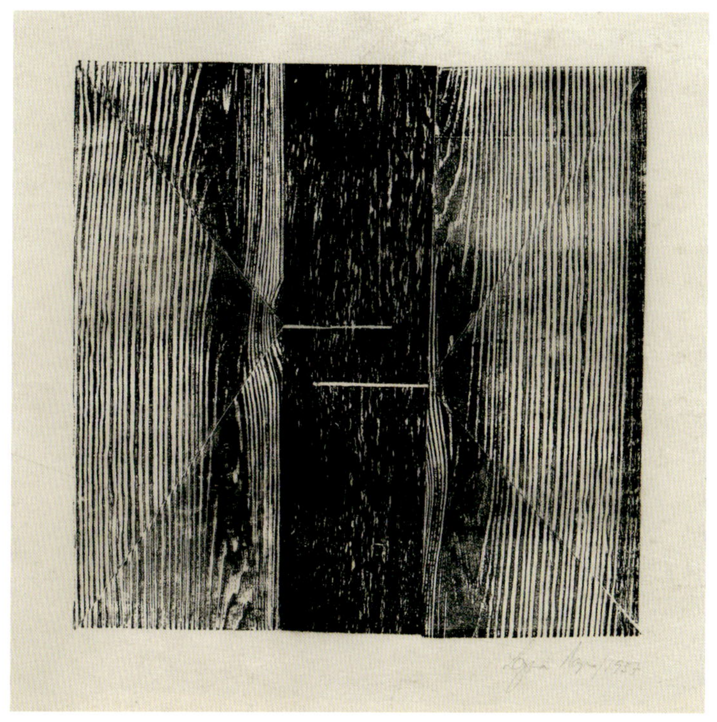

52. *Tecelar*, 1957

53. *Tecelar*, 1957

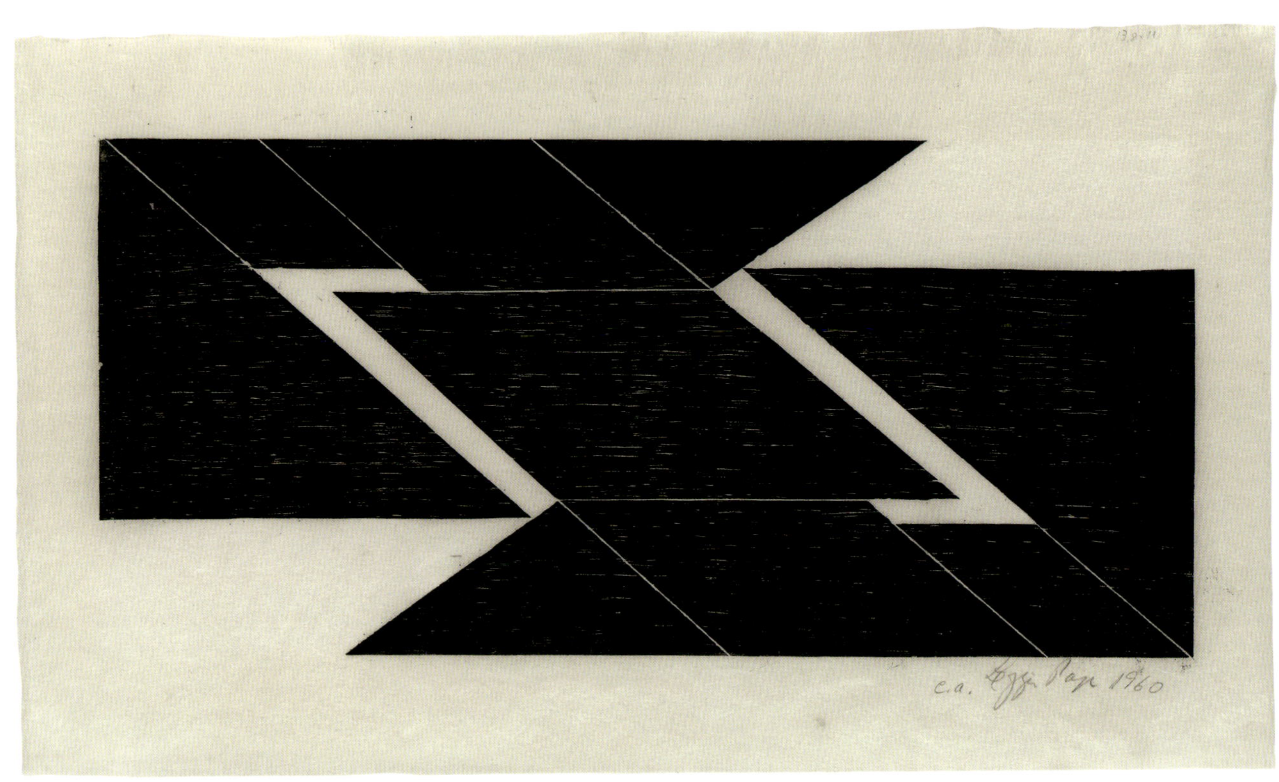

54. *Tecelar*, 1960

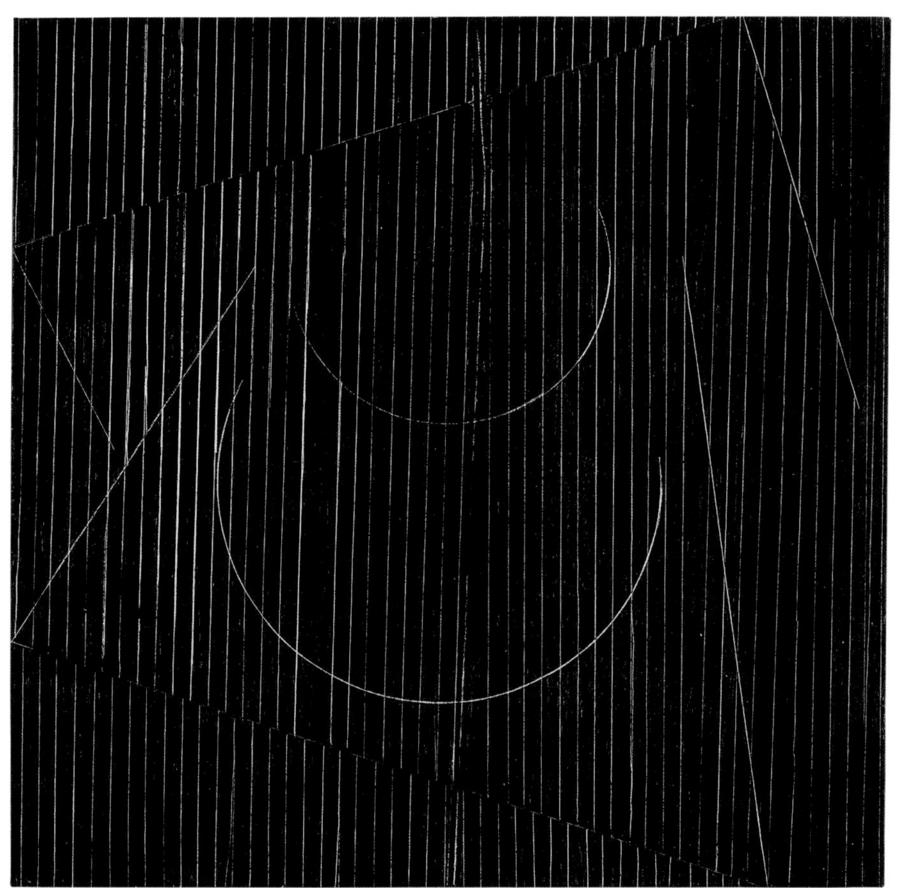

55. *Tecelar*, 1959

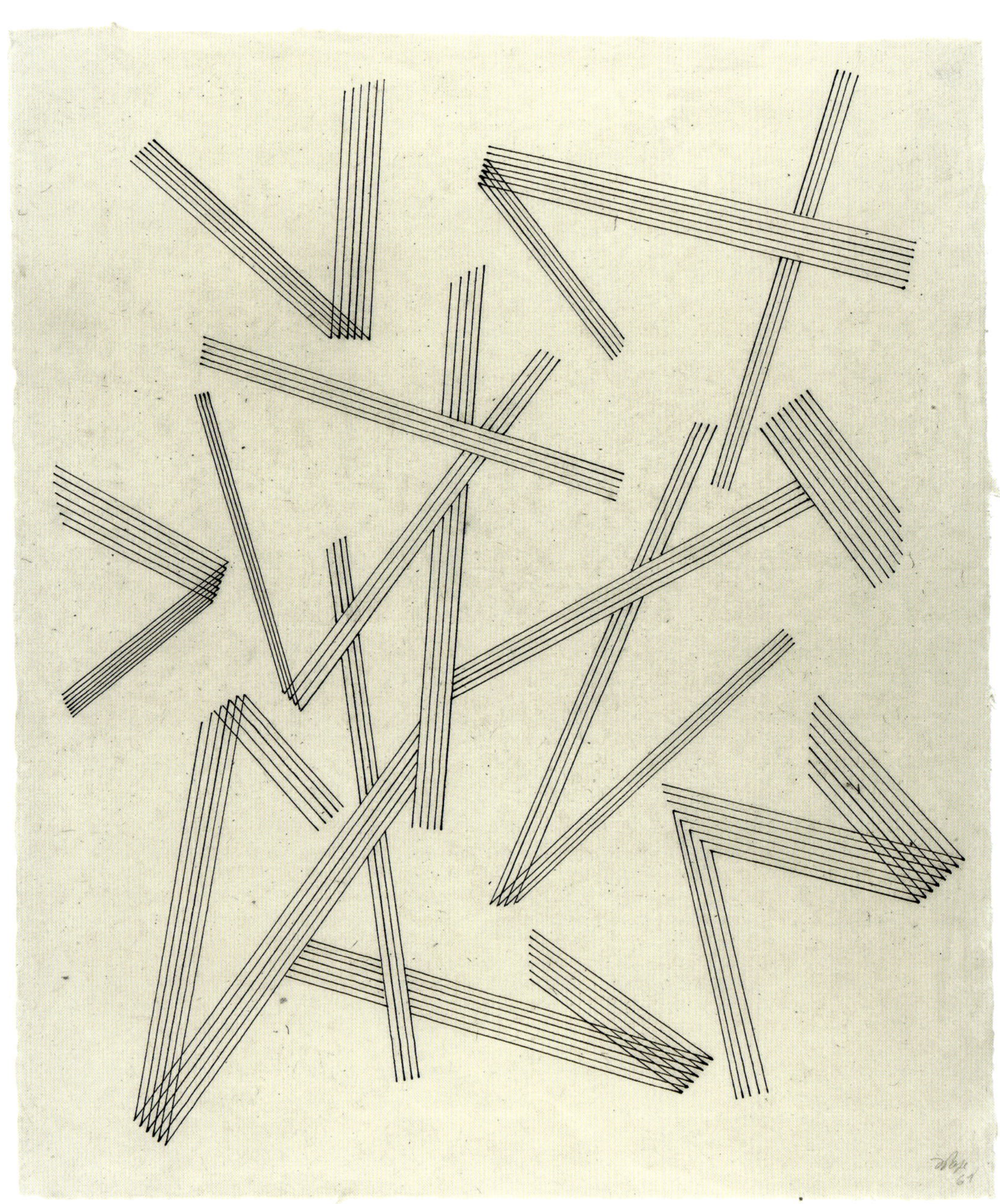

56. *Drawing*, 1961

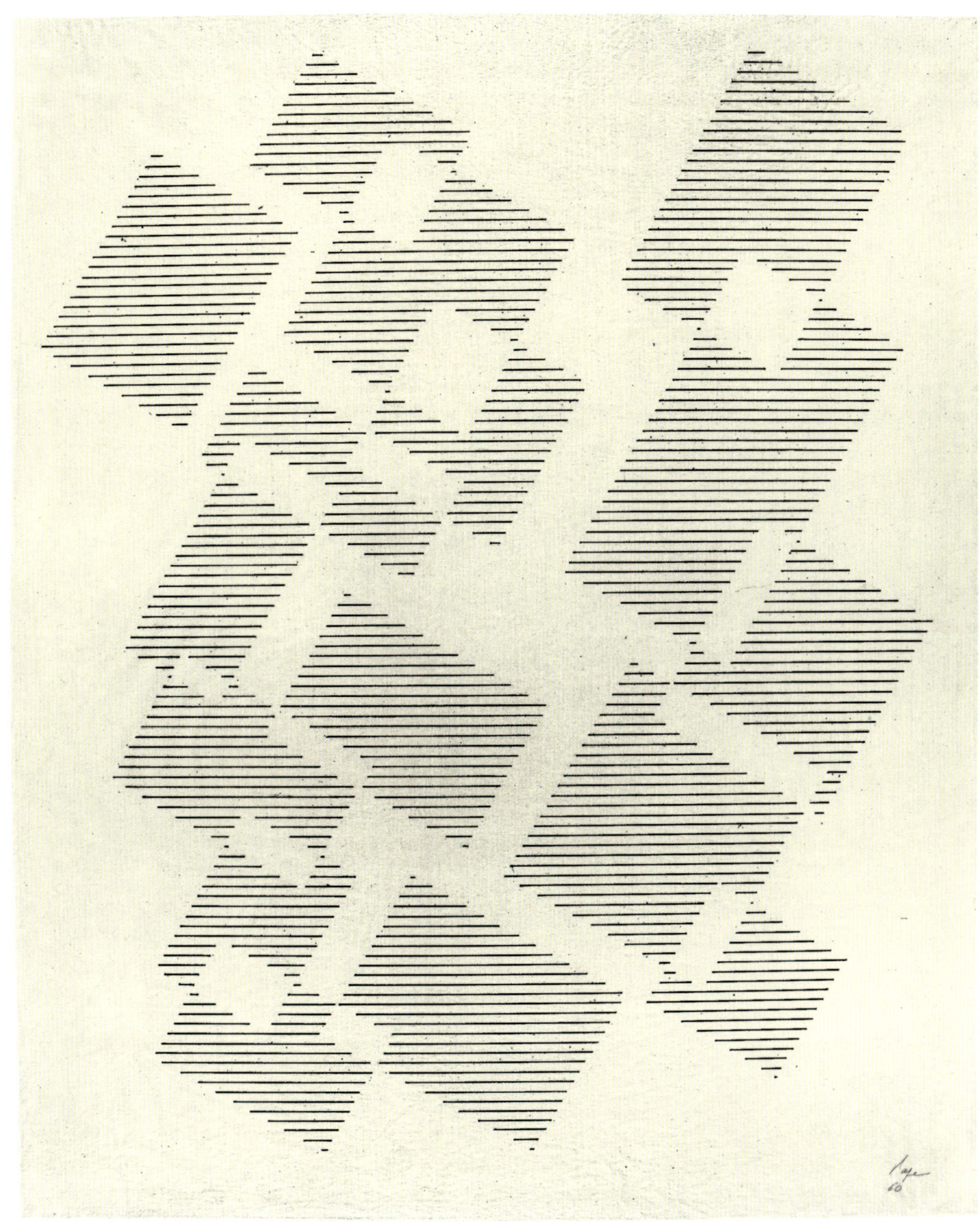

57. *Drawing*, 1960

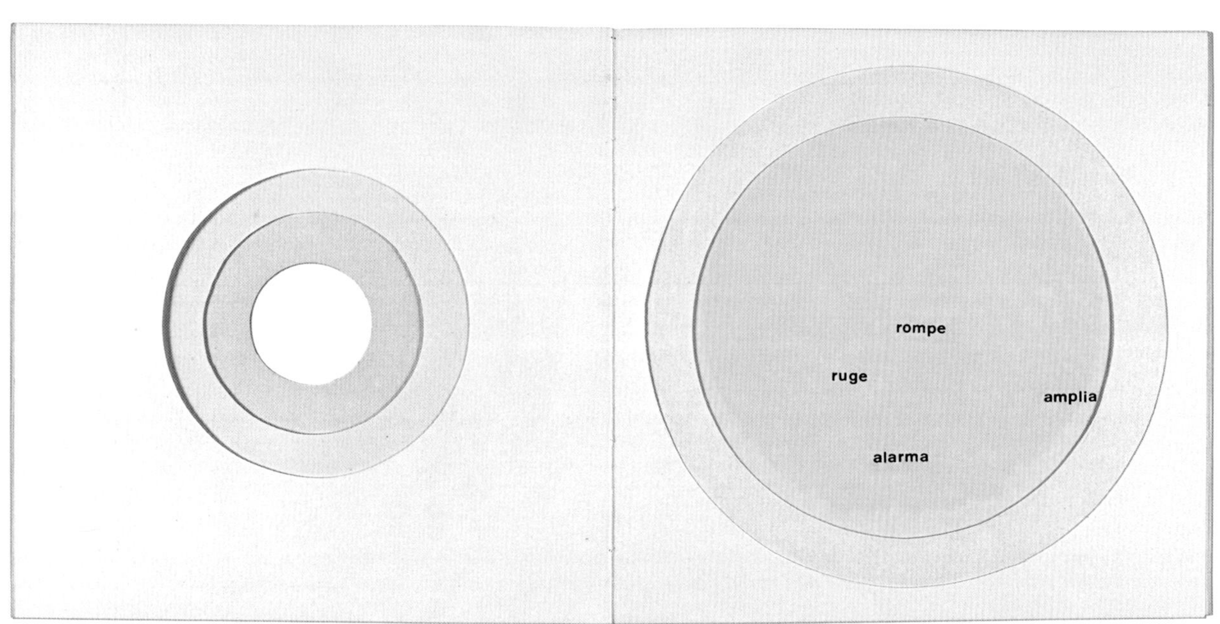

58. *Rompe* (*Burst*), 1957

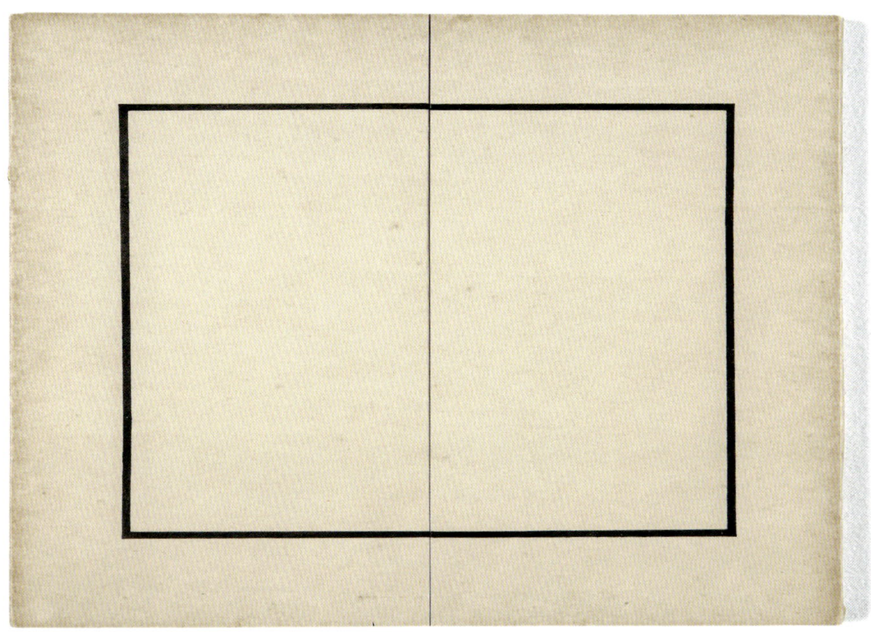

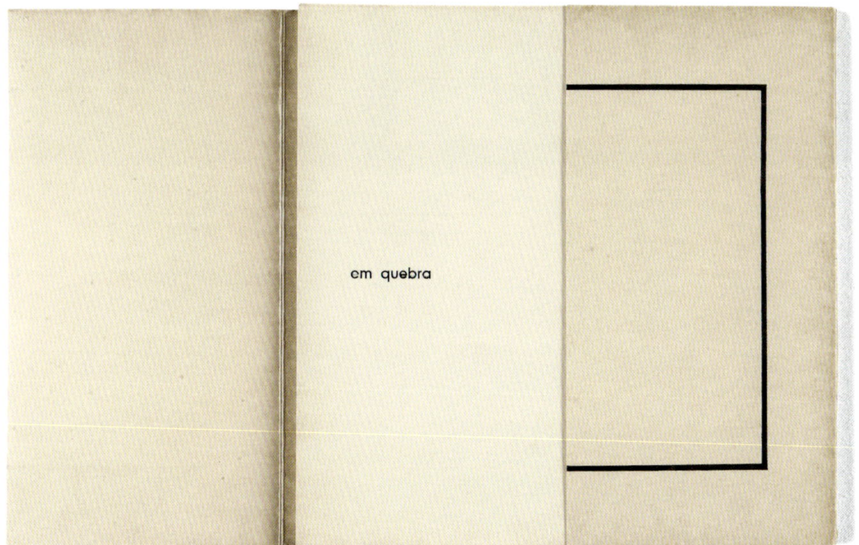

59. *Coleção espaço #5* (*Spatial Collection #5*), 1960

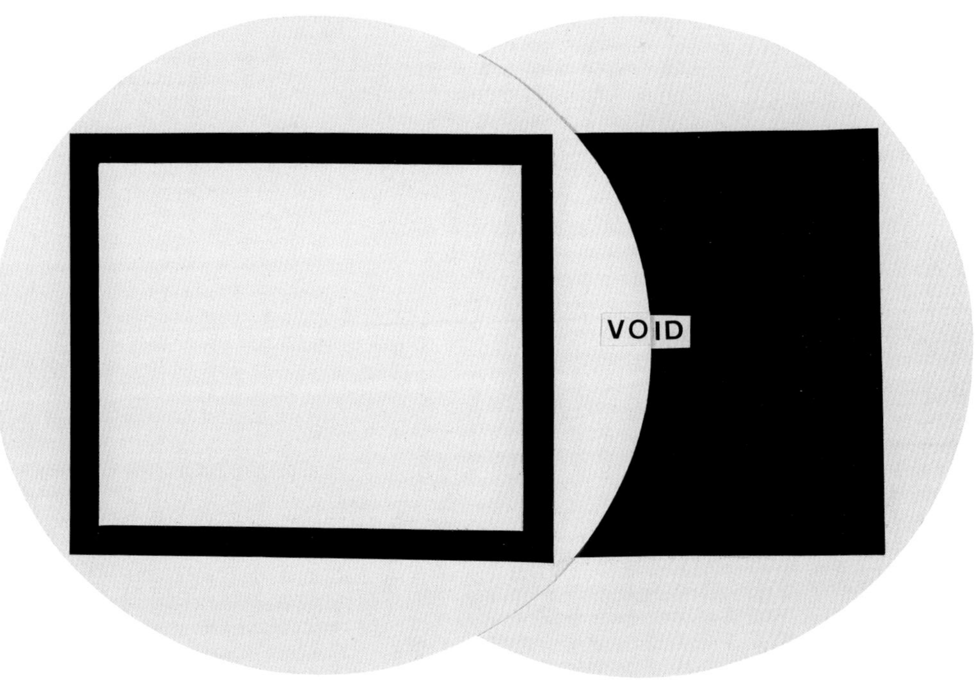

60. *Vazio* (*Void*), 1957

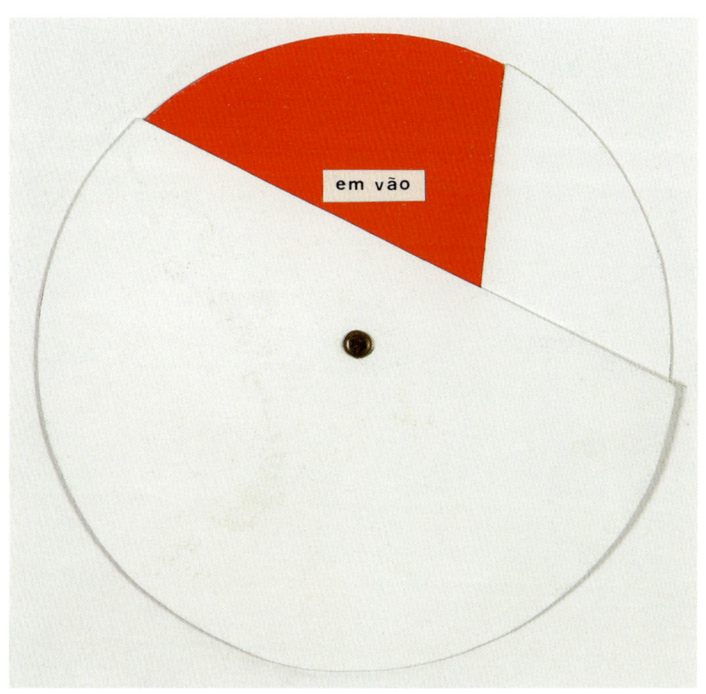

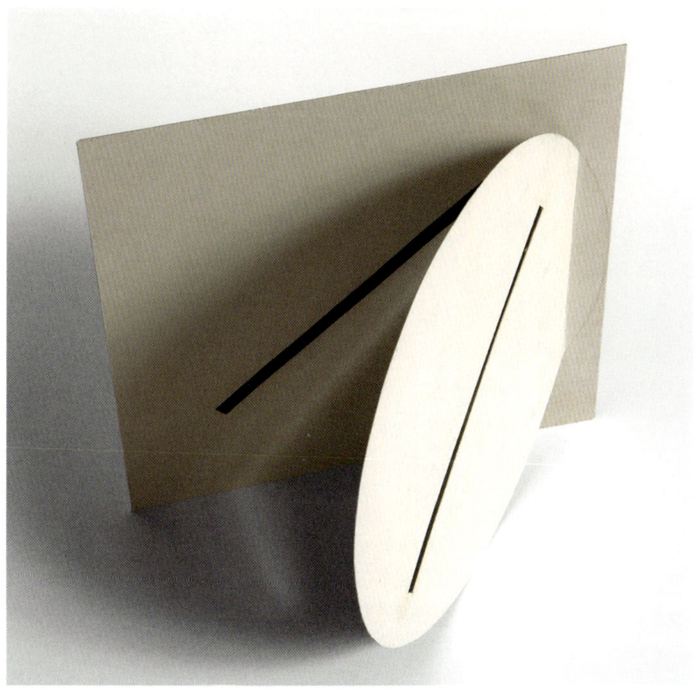

61. *Em vão* (*In Vain*), 1957

62. *Traço* (*Line*), 1957

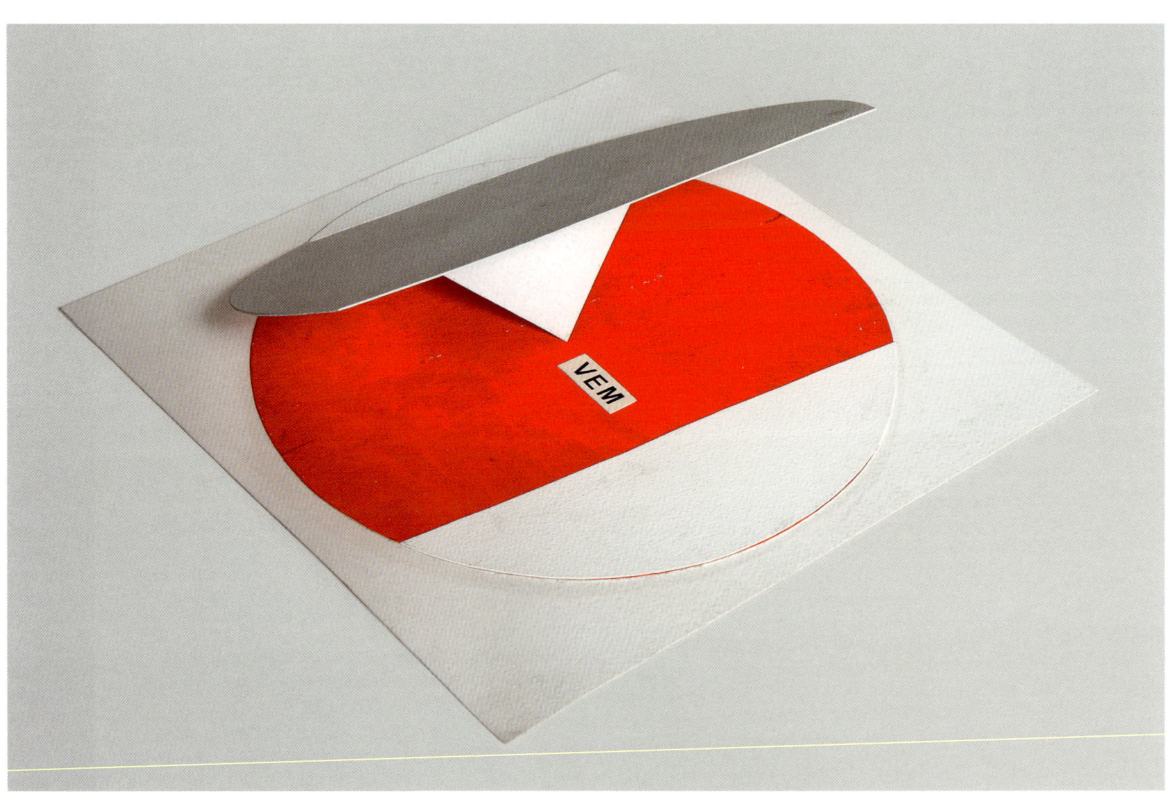

63. *Vem (Come)*, 1957

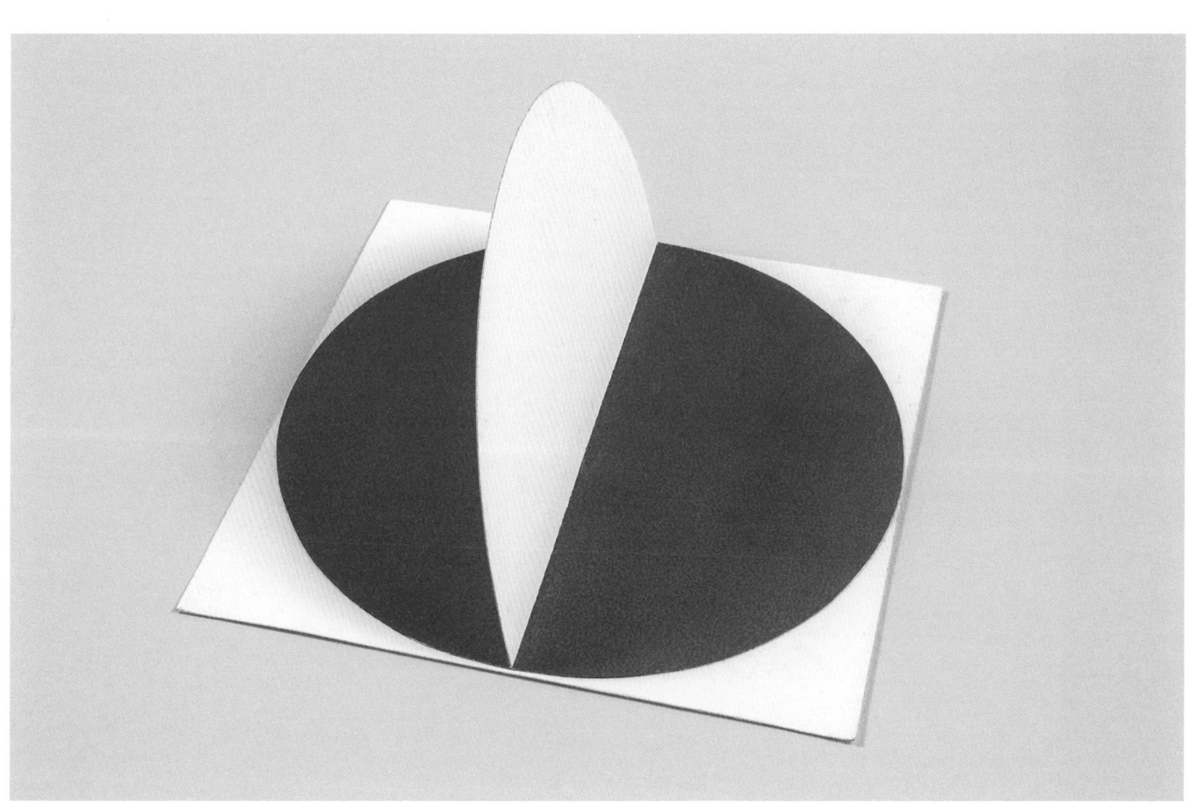

64. *Verde* (*Green*), 1957

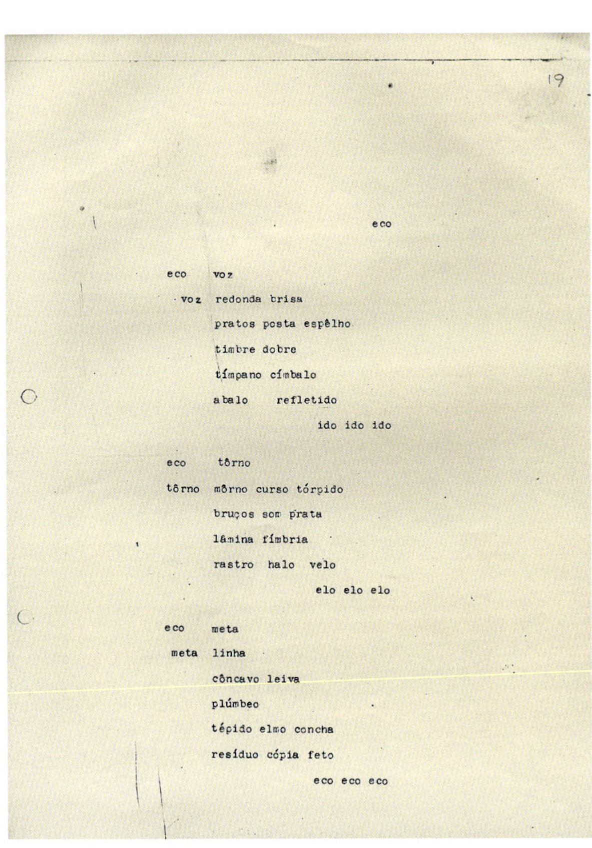

```
                              eco

eco    voz
   voz  redonda brisa
        pratos posta espêlho
        timbre dobre
        tímpano címbalo
        abalo    refletido
                    ido ido ido

eco    tôrno
tôrno  môrno curso tórpido
       bruços som prata
       lâmina fímbria
       rastro  halo  velo
                   elo elo elo

eco    meta
meta   linha
       côncavo leiva
       plúmbeo
       tépido elmo concha
       resíduo cópia feto
                   eco eco eco
```

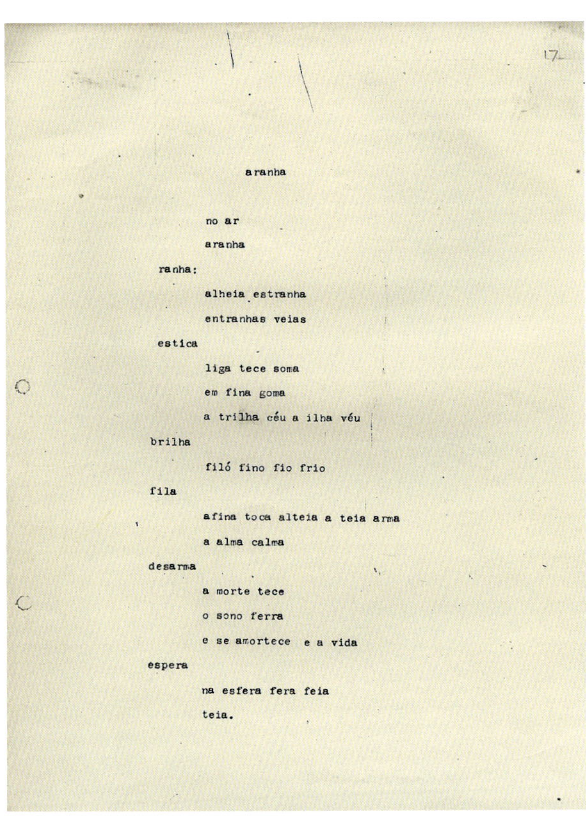

```
                    aranha

            no ar
            aranha
       ranha:
            alheia estranha
            entranhas veias
       estica
            liga tece soma
            em fina goma
            a trilha céu a ilha véu
       brilha
            filó fino fio frio
       fila
            afina toca alteia a teia arma
            a alma calma
       desarma
            a morte tece
            o sono ferra
            e se amortece  e a vida
       espera
            na esfera fera feia
            teia.
```

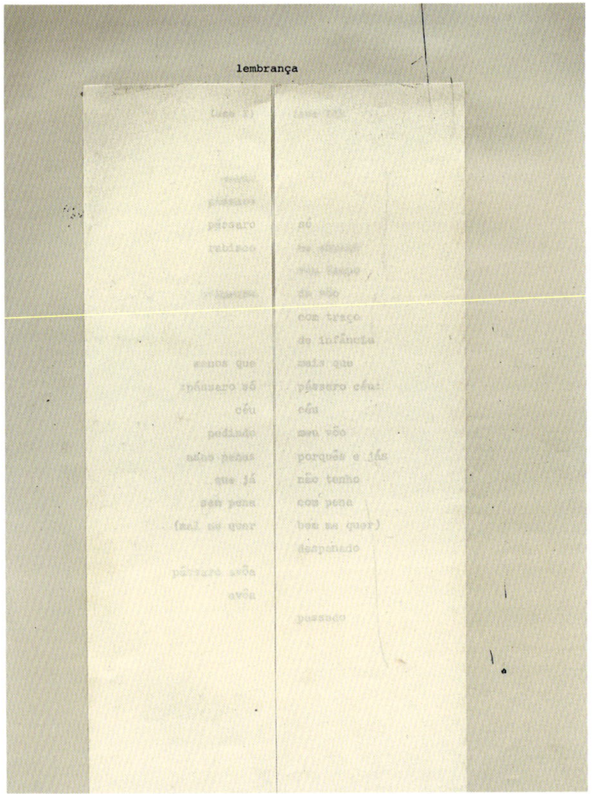

```
                    lembrança

              (lado I)        (lado II)

              pássaro
              pássaro         só
              rabisco         se afasta
                              num tempo
                              do vôo
                              com traço
                              de infância
              senos que       mais que
              pássaro só      pássaro céu:
                 céu          céu
              pedindo         meu vôo
              suas penas      porquês e jás
              que já          não tenho
              sem pena        com pena
              (mal me quer    bem me quer)
                              despenado
              pássaro são
                 avôa
                              passado
```


65. *Eco* (*Echo*), ca. 1960s

66. *Aranha* (*Spider*), ca. 1960s

67. *Lembrança* (*Memory*), ca. 1960s

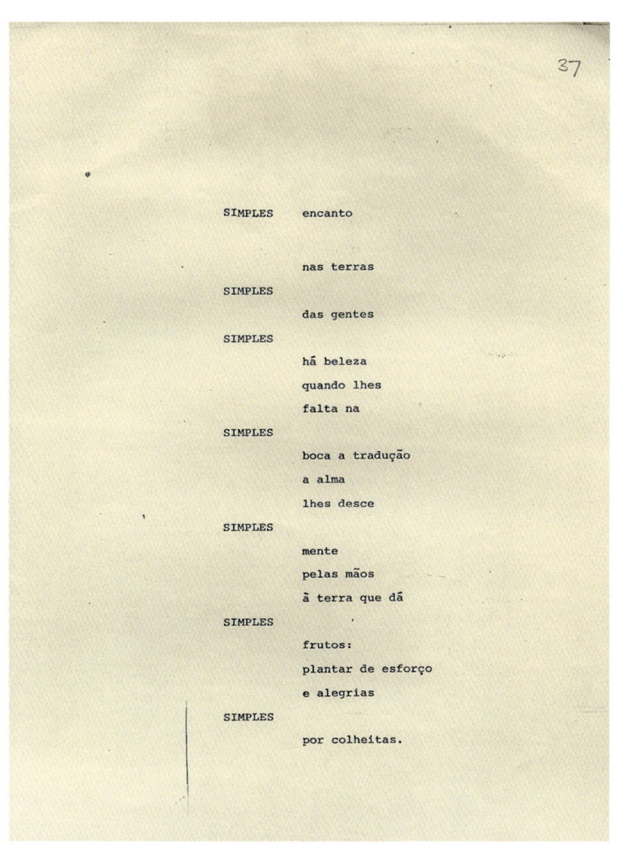

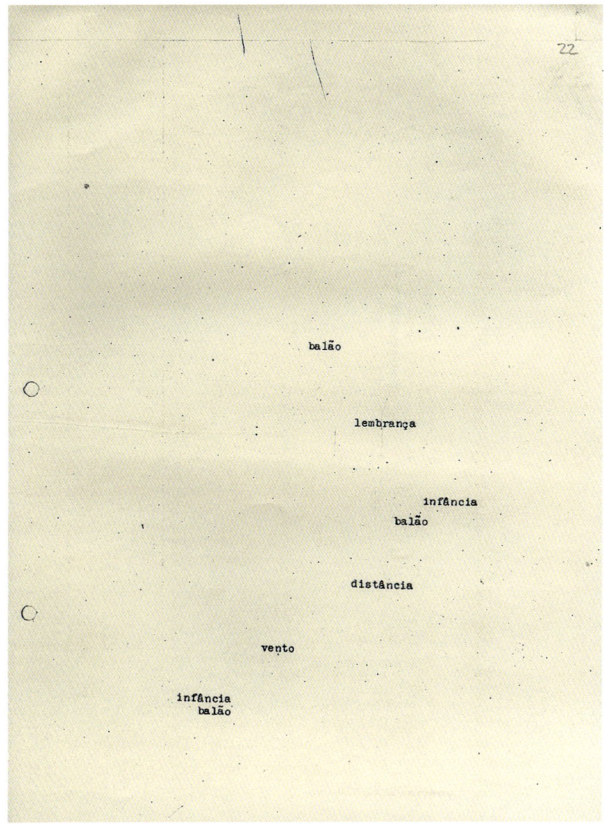

68. *Simples* (*Simple*), ca. 1960s

69. *Balão* (*Balloon*), ca. 1960s

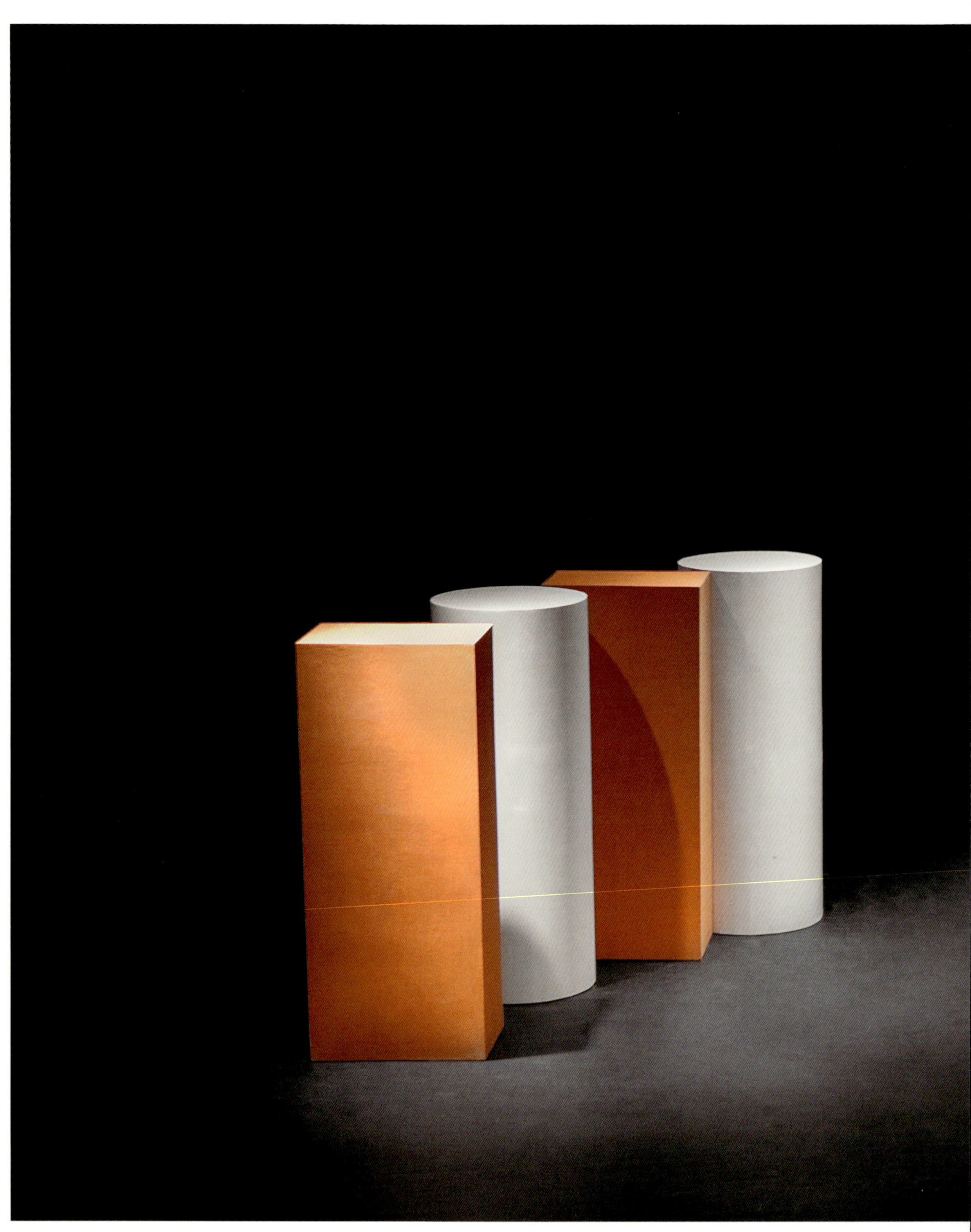

70. *Ballet neoconcreto I* (*Neoconcrete Ballet I*), 1958;
performance at Fundação de Serralves—Museu de Arte
Contemporânea, Porto, Portugal, 2000

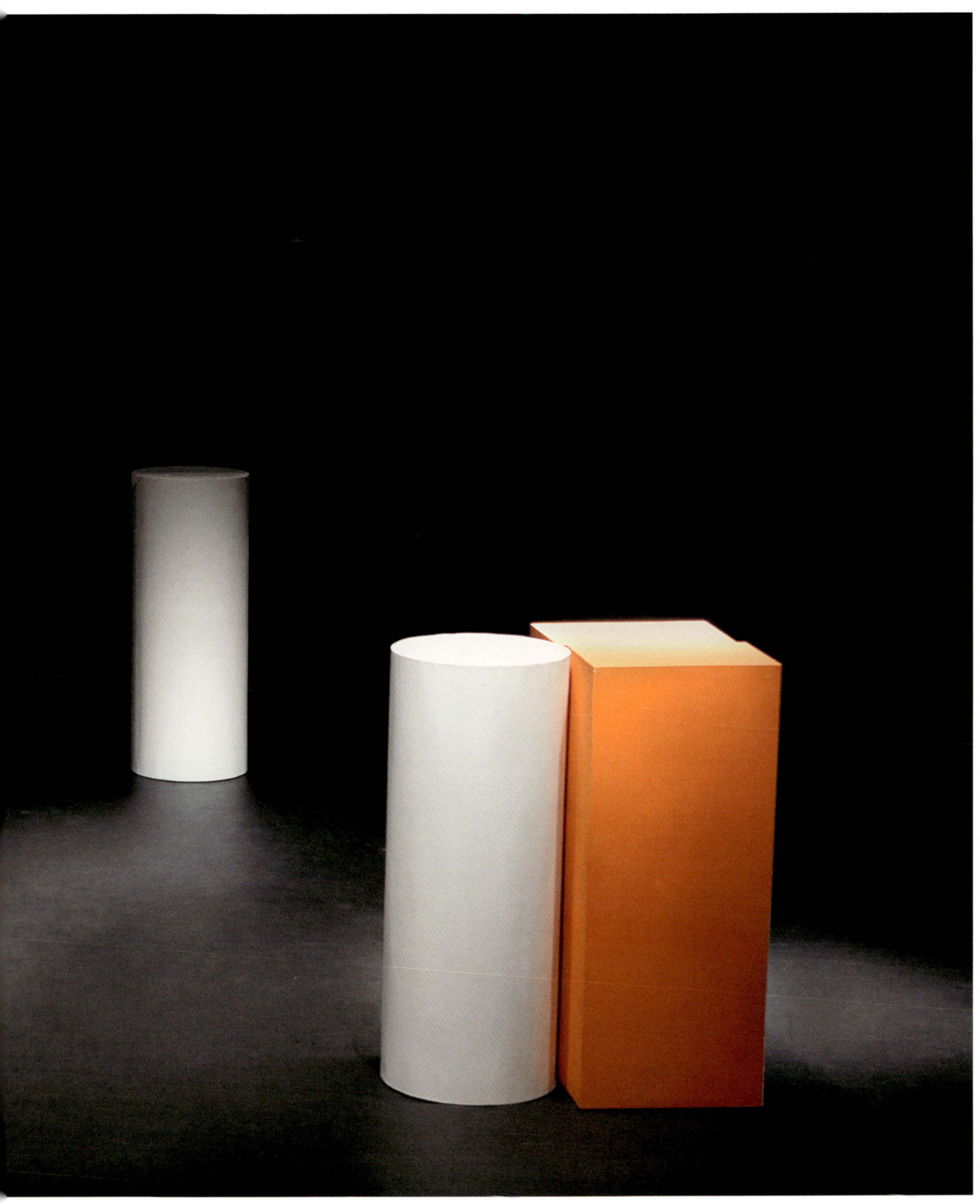

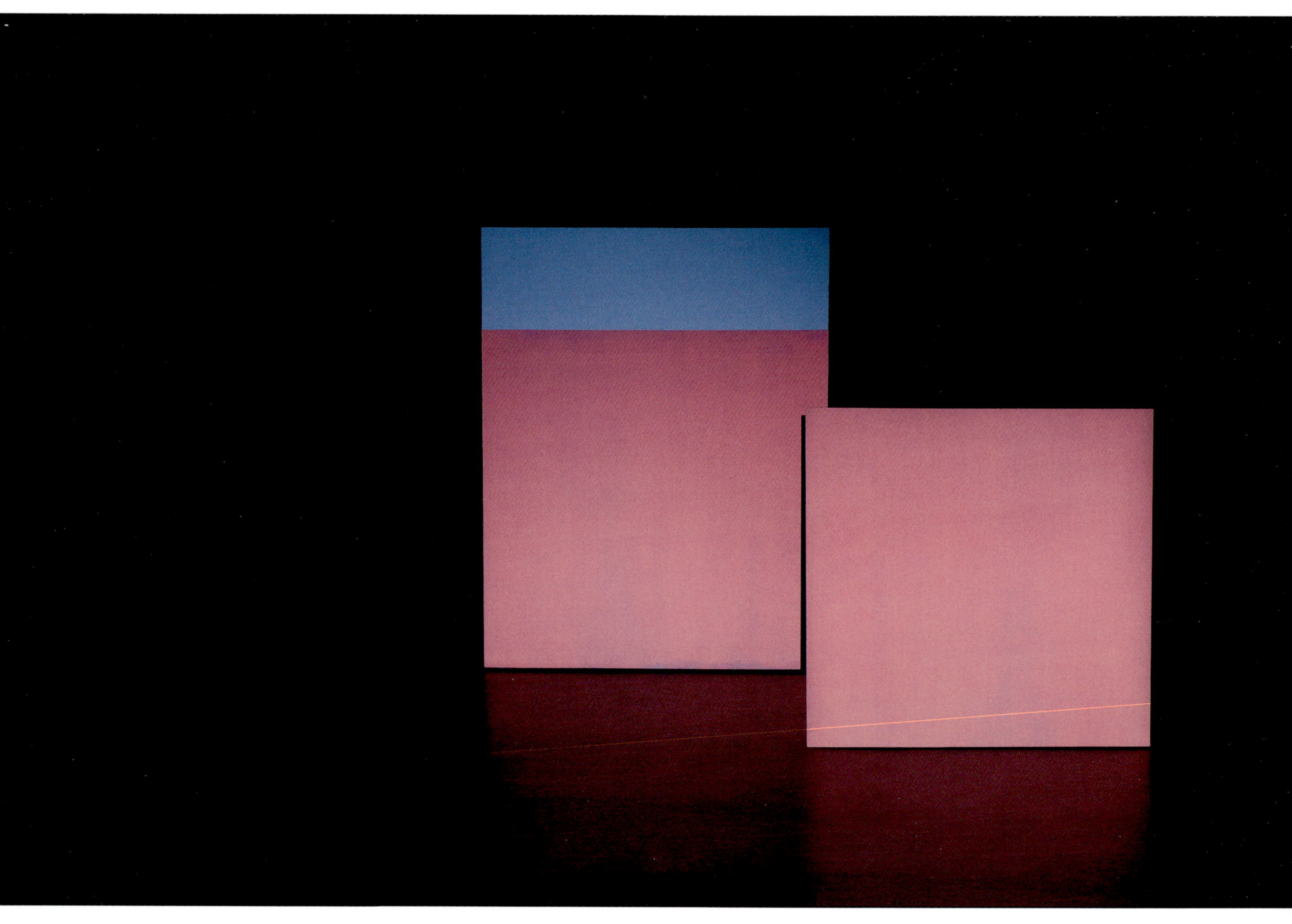

71. *Ballet neoconcreto II* (*Neoconcrete Ballet II*), 1959;
performance at Fundação de Serralves—Museu de Arte
Contemporânea, Porto, Portugal, 2000

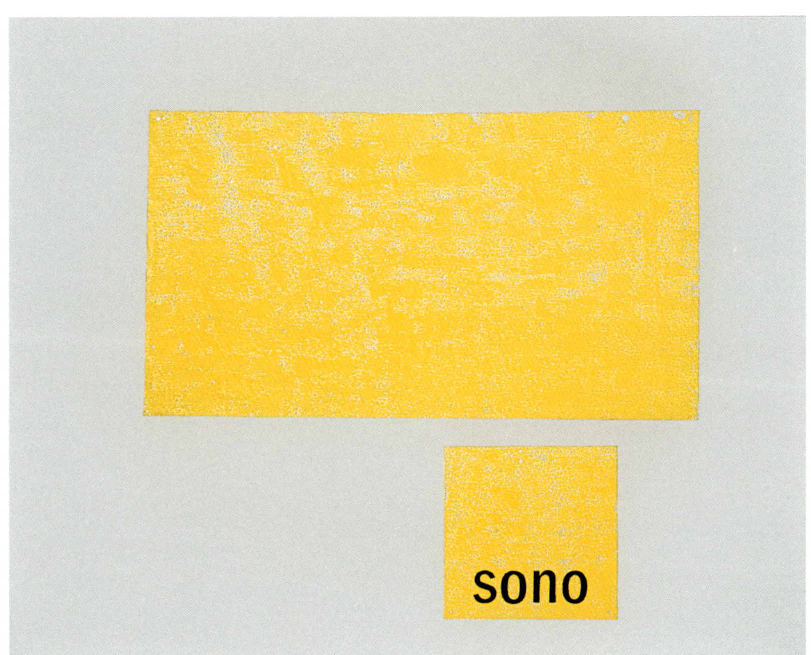

72. *Poema-luz* (*Light-Poem*), 1956–57

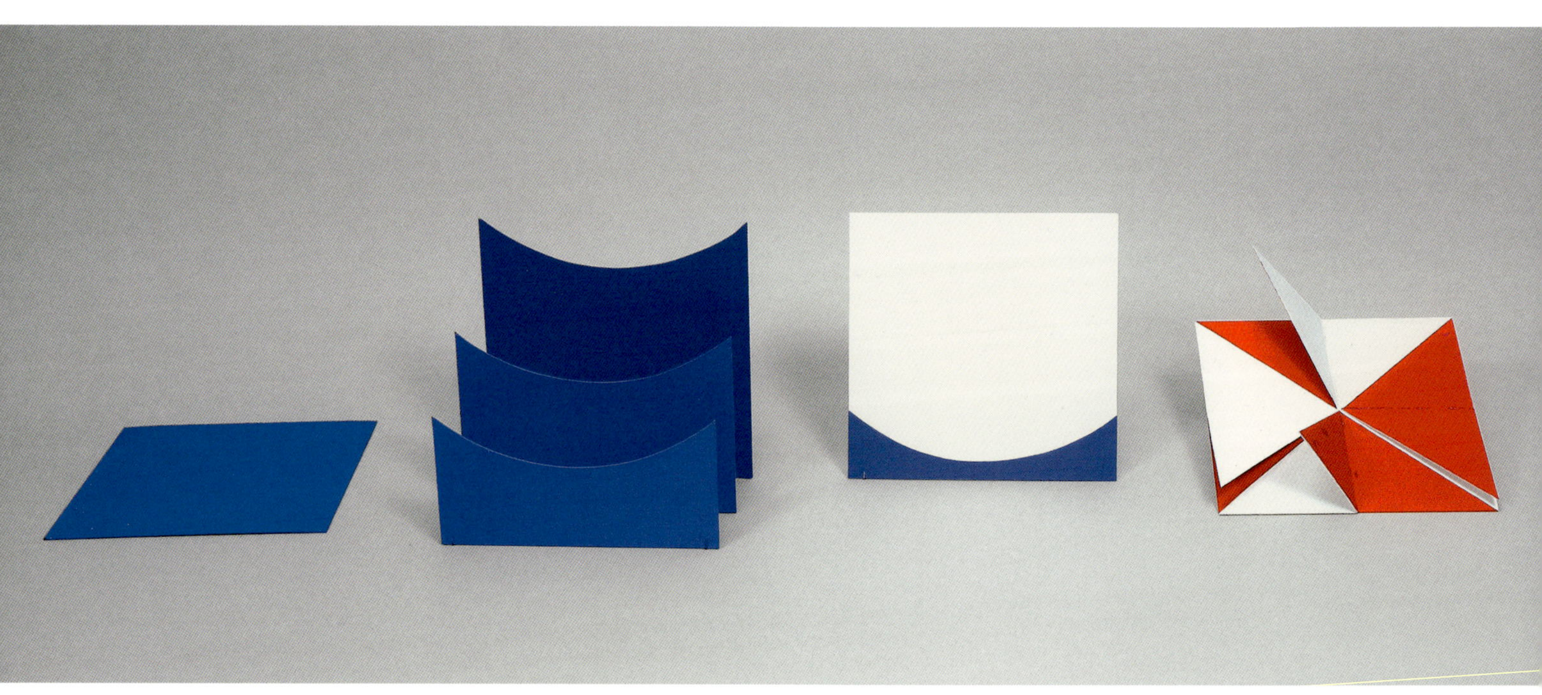

73a. *Livro da criação* (*Book of Creation*), 1959–60

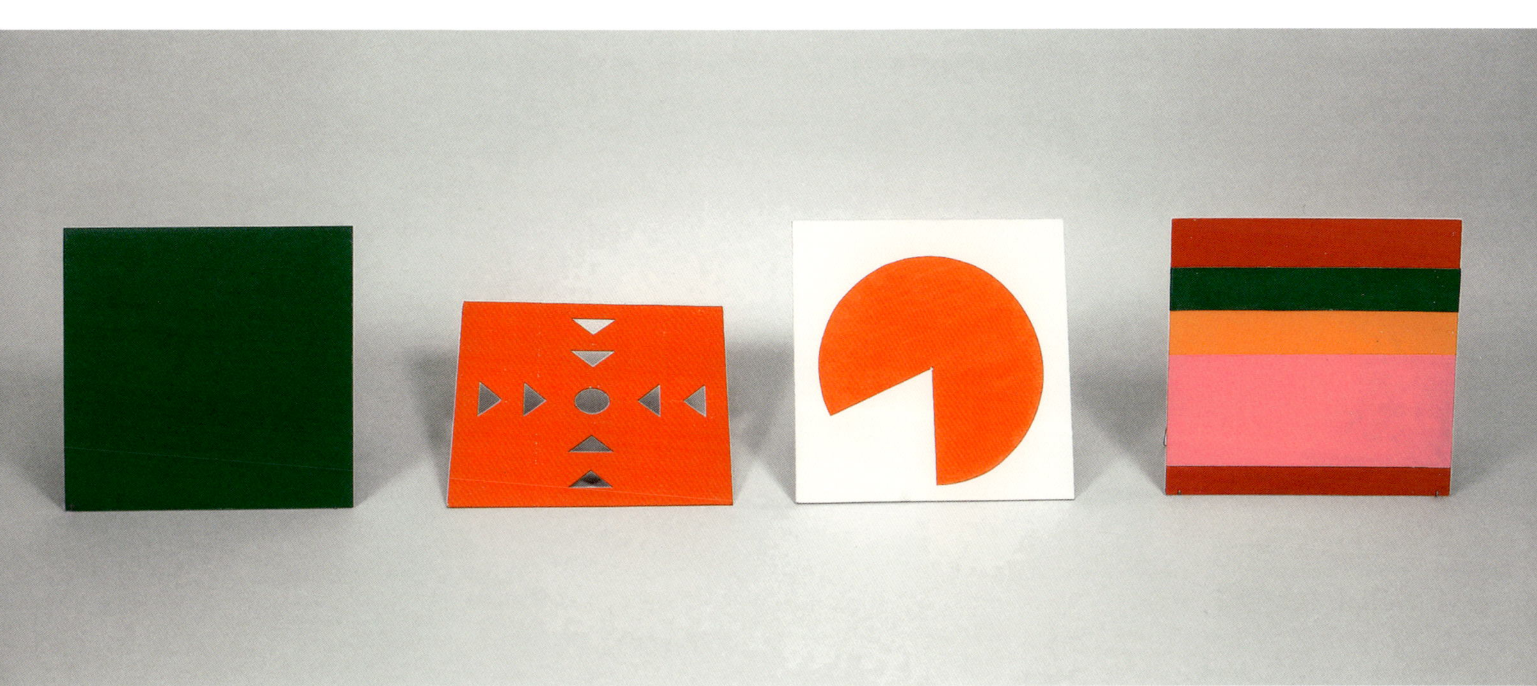

Na floresta (In the Forest)
O homem era nômade e caçador (Man Was a Nomad and a Hunter)
O homem começou a marcar o tempo (Man Began to Measure Time)
E a terra floresceu (And the Land Flourished)

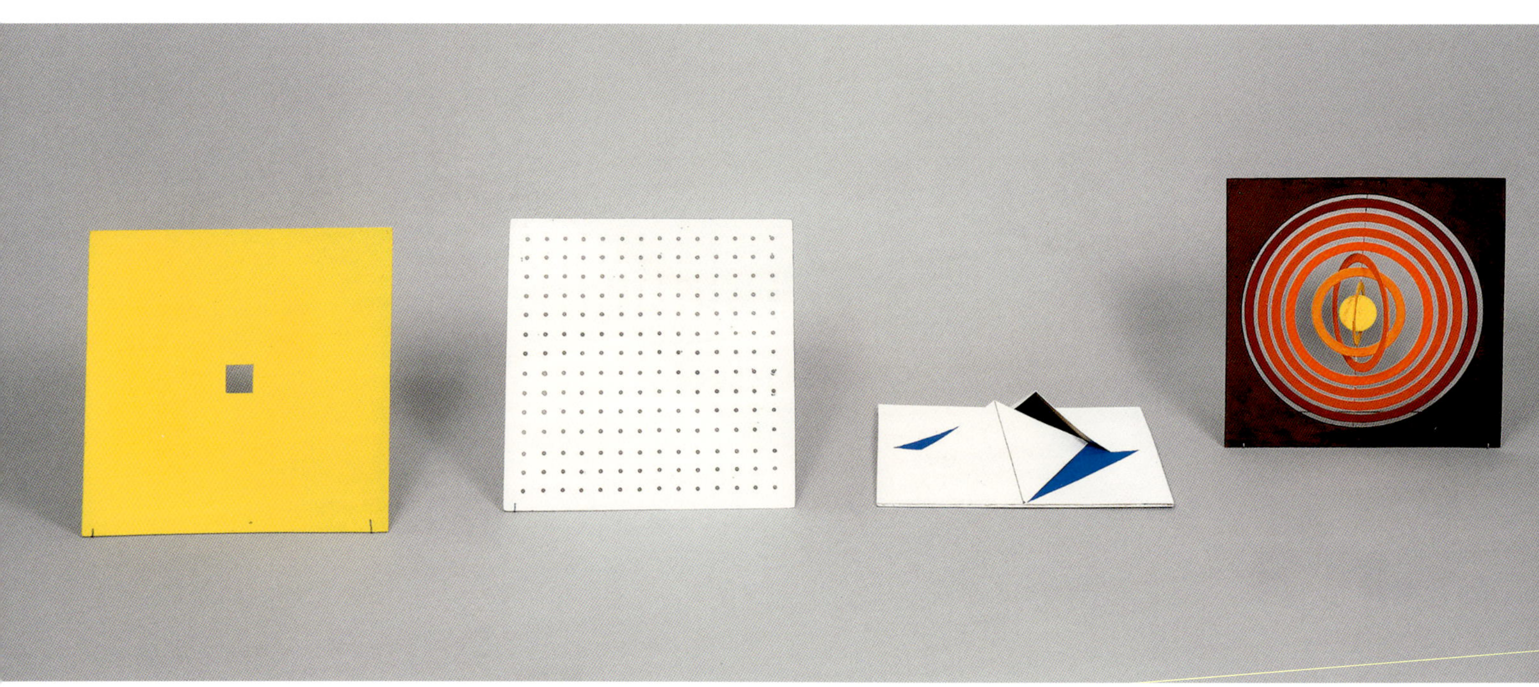

Luz (Light)

O homem era gregário e semeou a terra (Man Was Gregarious and Sowed Seeds on the Land)

O homem construiu sobre a água: palafita (Man Built on Water: A Stilt House)

O homem descobriu que o sol era o centro do sistema planetário
(Man Discovered that the Sun Was the Centrer of the Planetary System)

73b. Livro da criação (Book of Creation), 1959–60

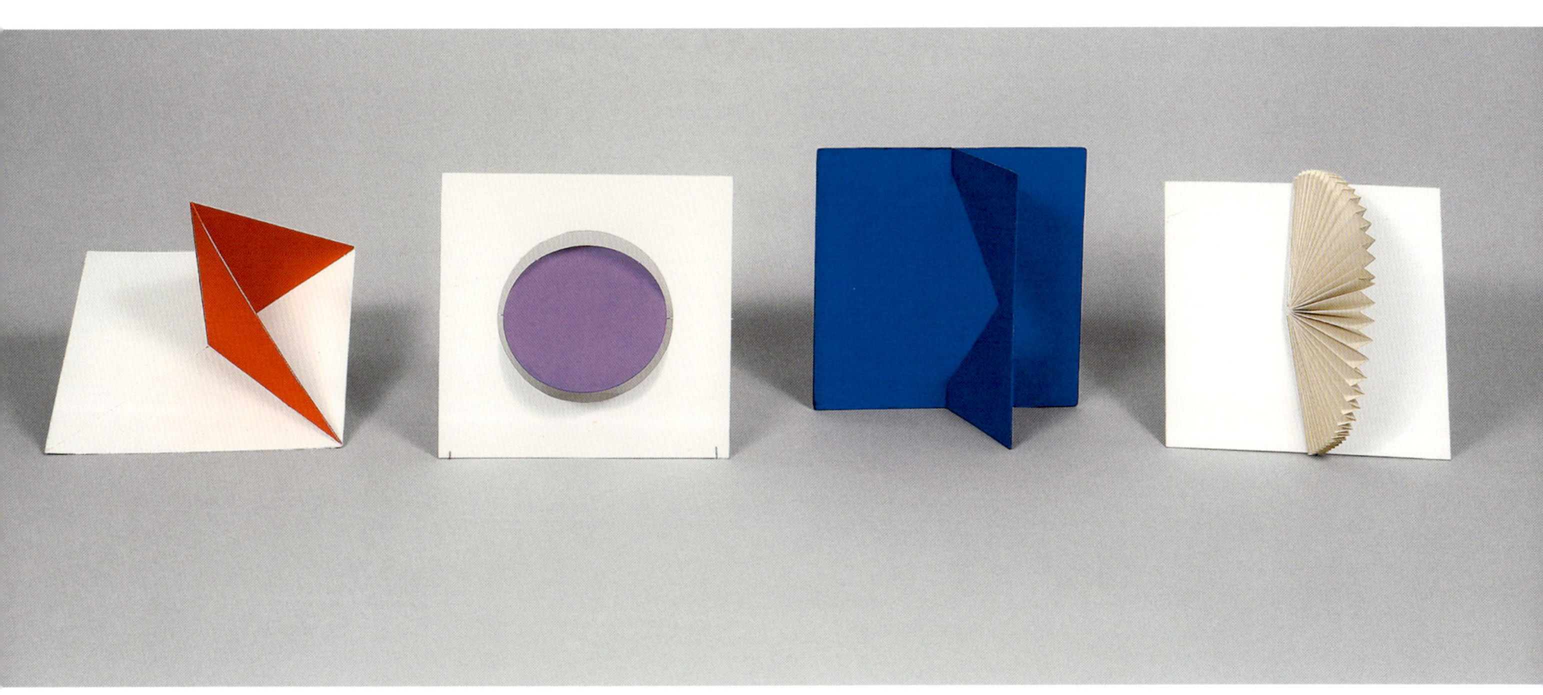

A quilha navegando no tempo (The Keel Navigating Through Time)

Que a terra era redonda e girava sobre seu próprio eixo (That the Earth Was Round and Rotated on its Own Axis)

Submarino: o vazado é o cheio sob a agua (Submarine: The Excavation Is Full Under Water)

O homem inventou a roda (Man Invented the Wheel)

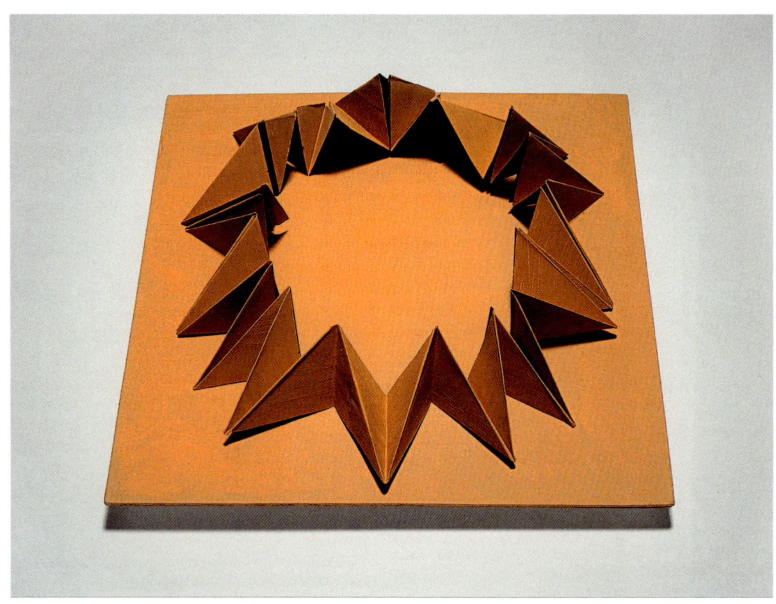

Árabe (*Arab*)

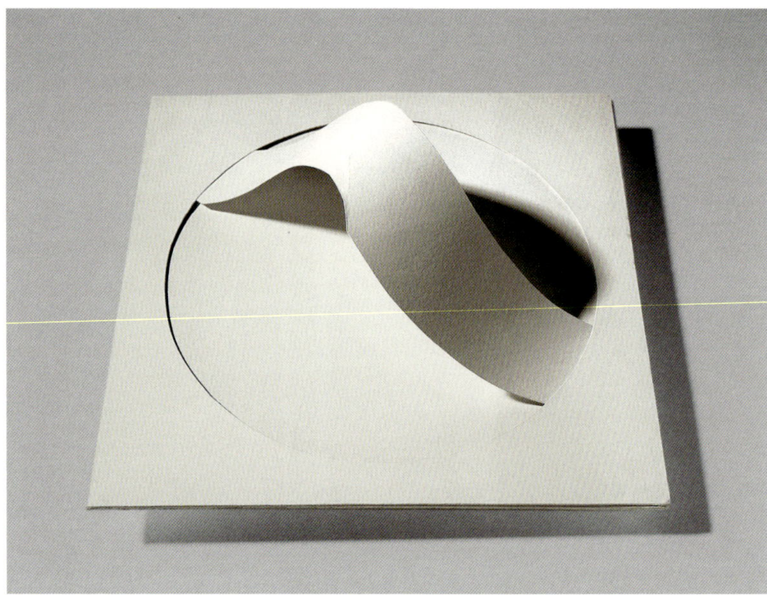

Lance de concreto (*Concrete Stairway*)

74. Four of twelve pieces of *Livro da arquitetura* (*Book of Architecture*), 1959–60

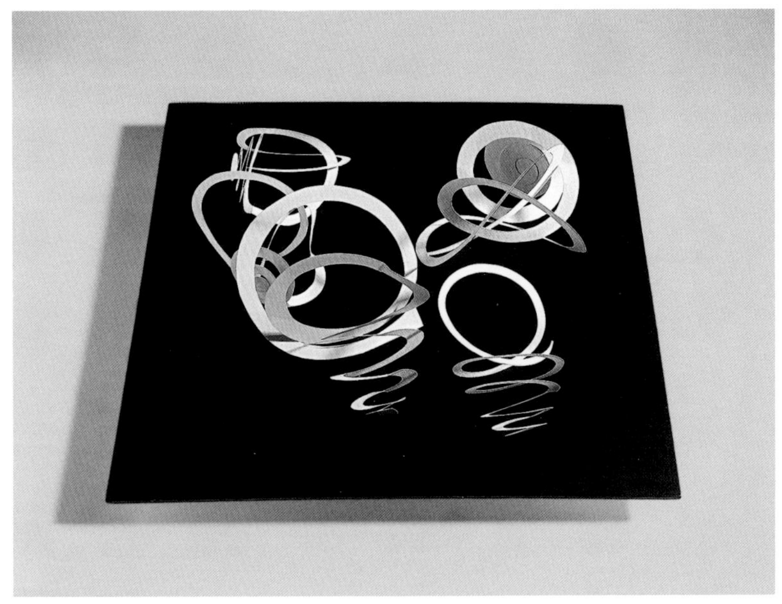

Barroco (Baroque)

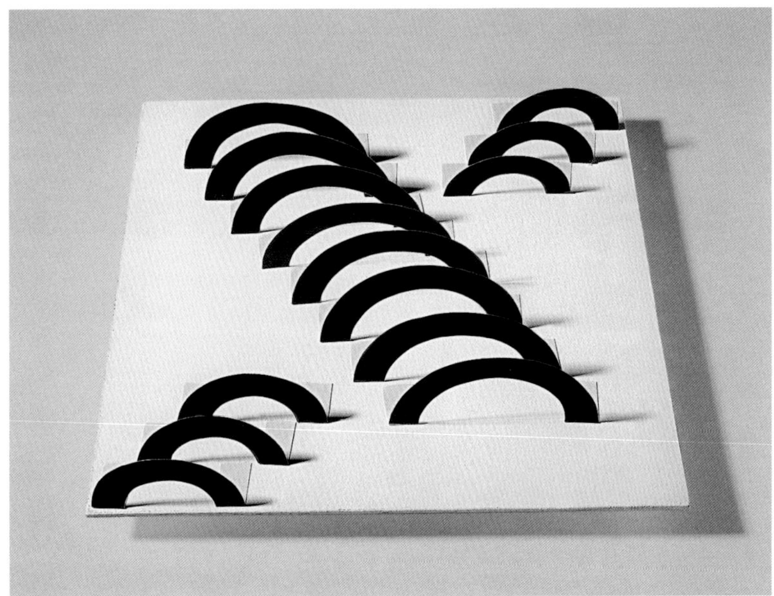

Romano (Roman)

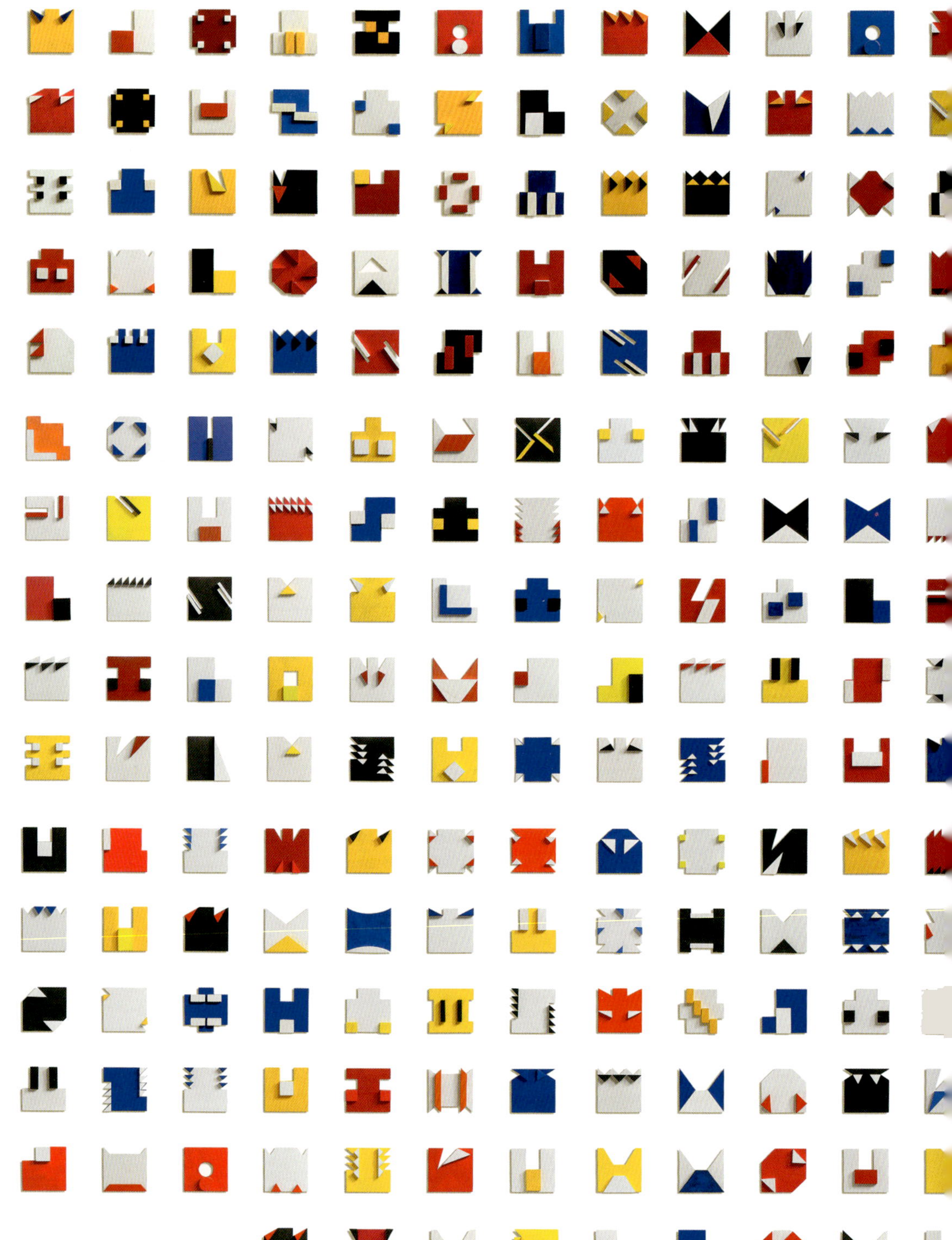

75. *Livro do tempo* (*Book of Time*), 1961–63

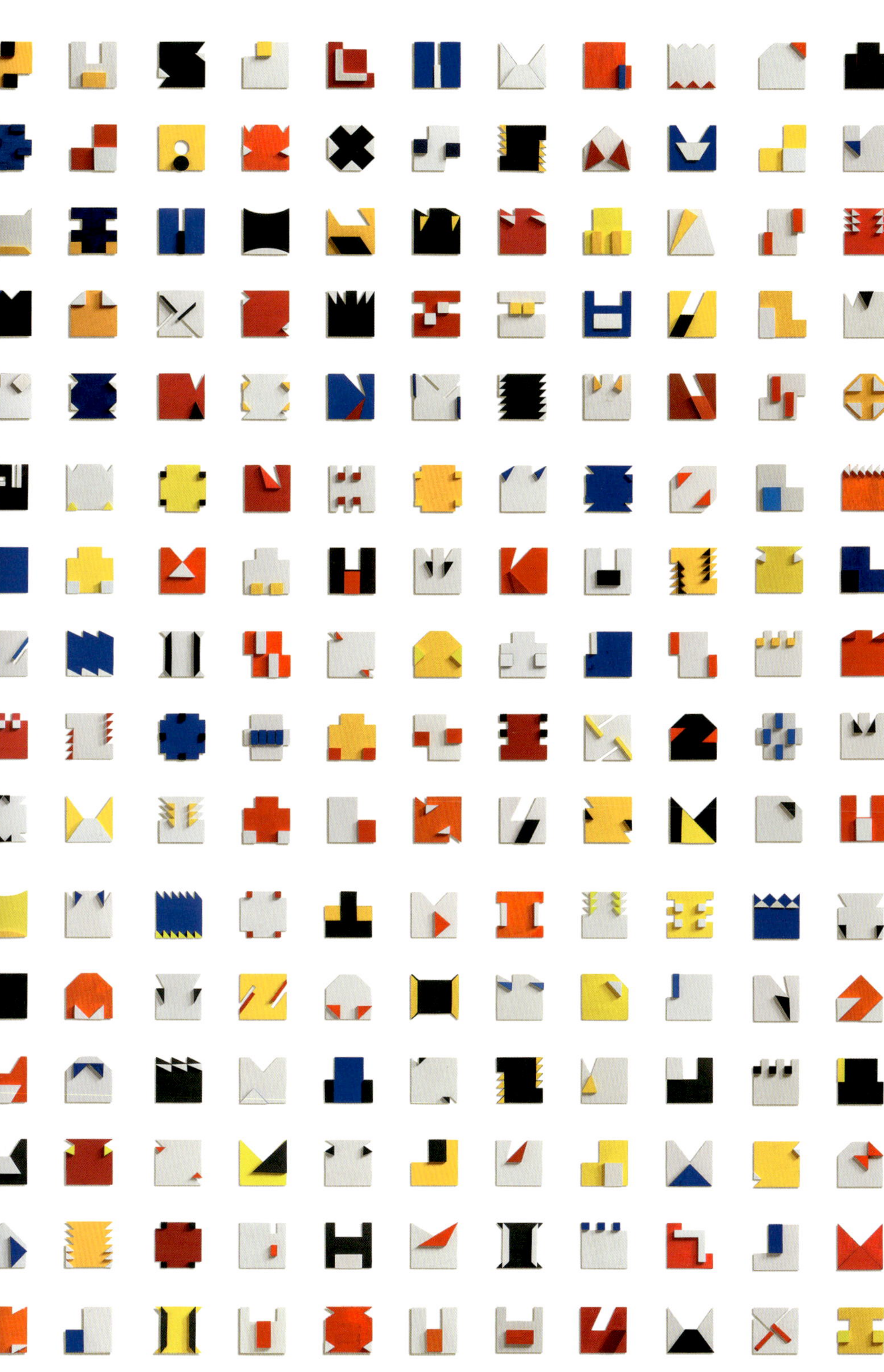

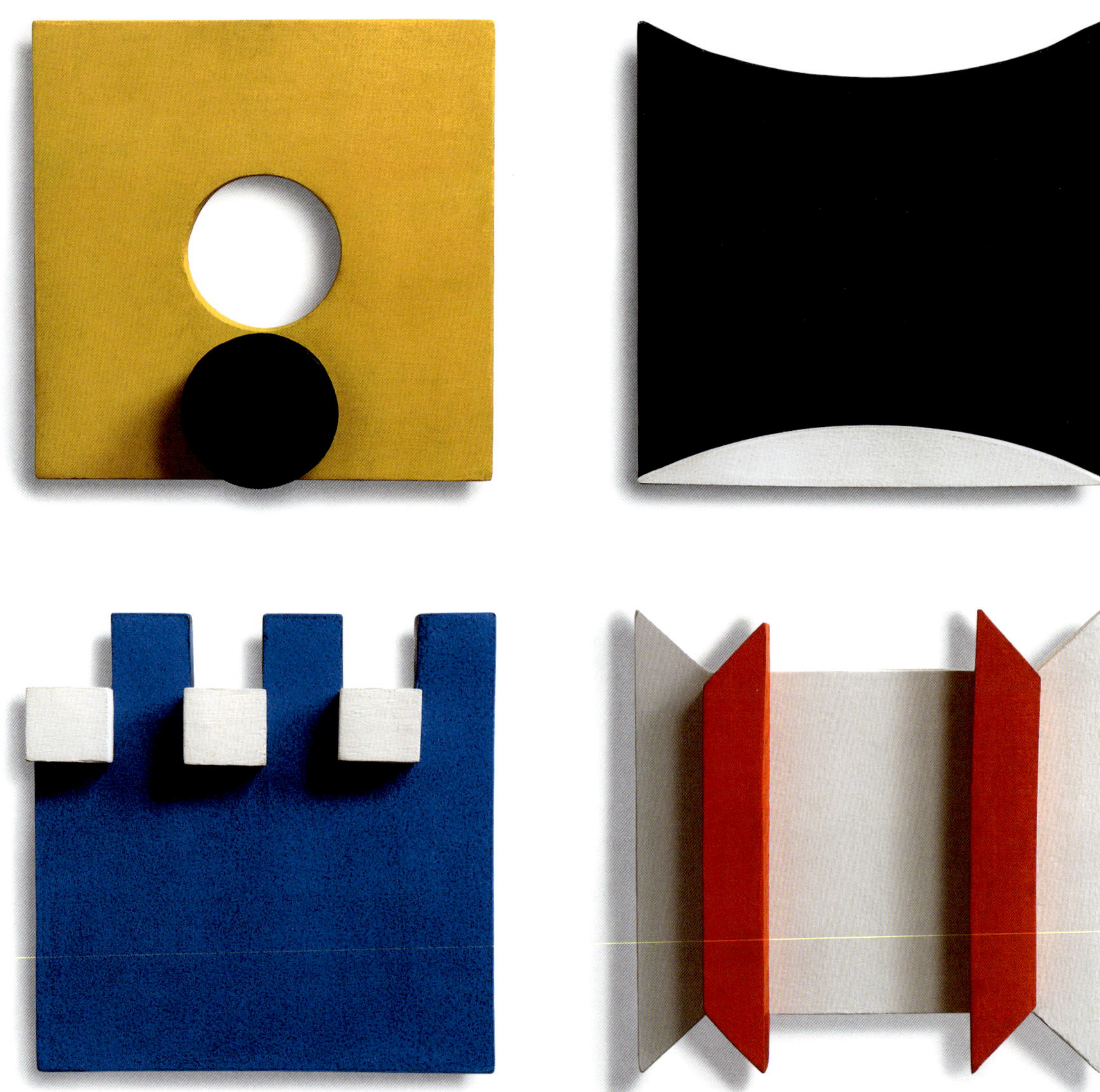

Details of *Livro do tempo*

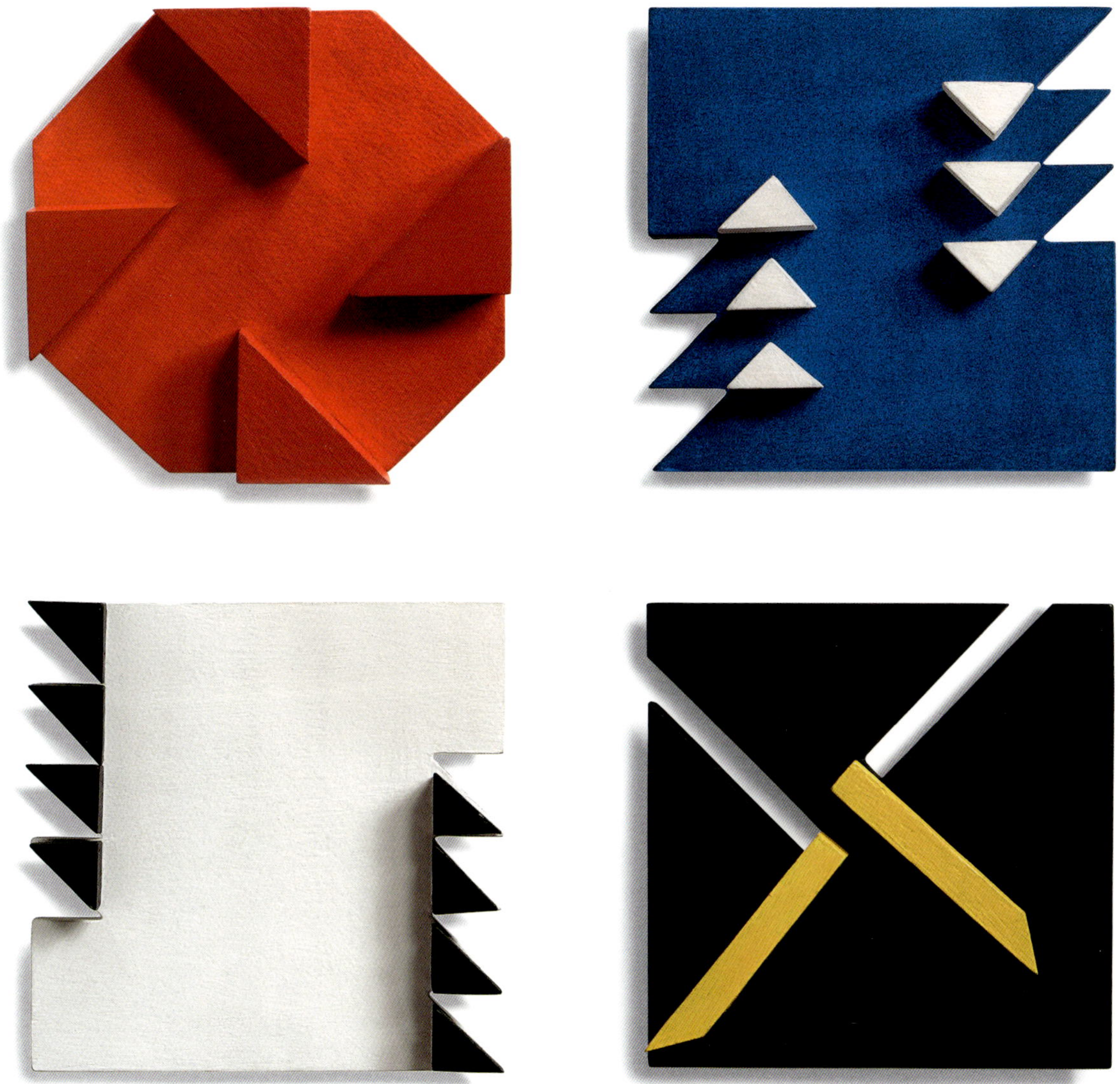

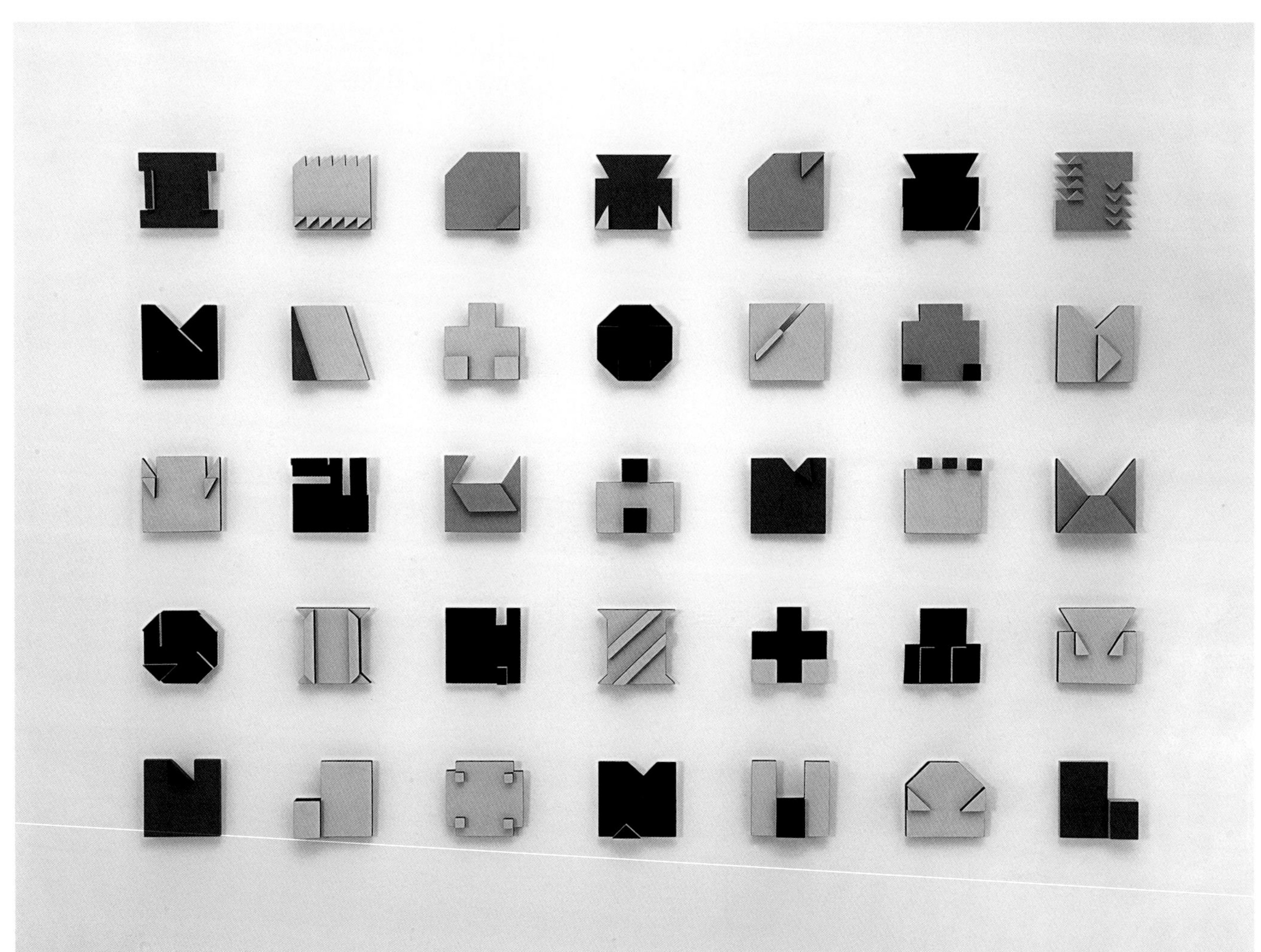

76. *Livro noite e dia (Book Night and Day)*, 1963–76

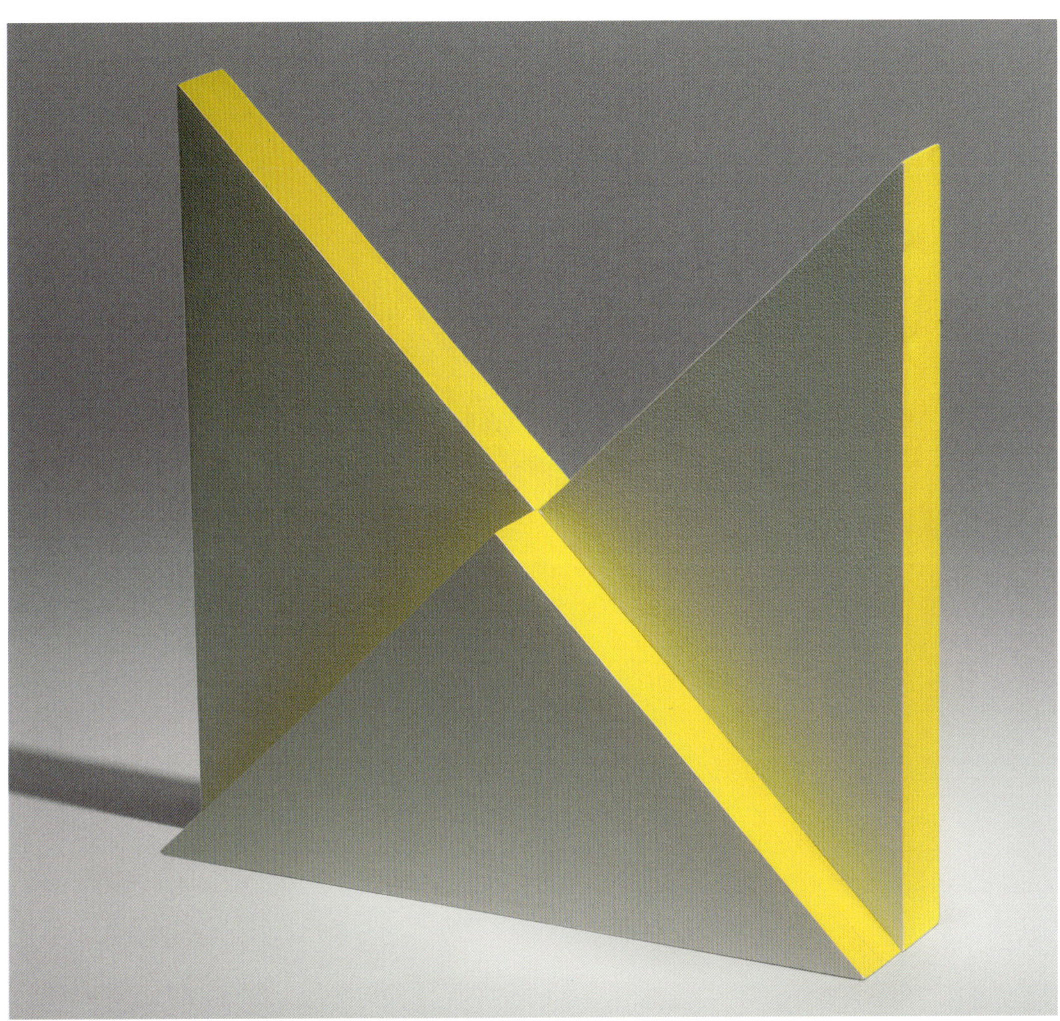

77. *Livro do tempo (médio)* (*Book of Time [medium]*), 1965

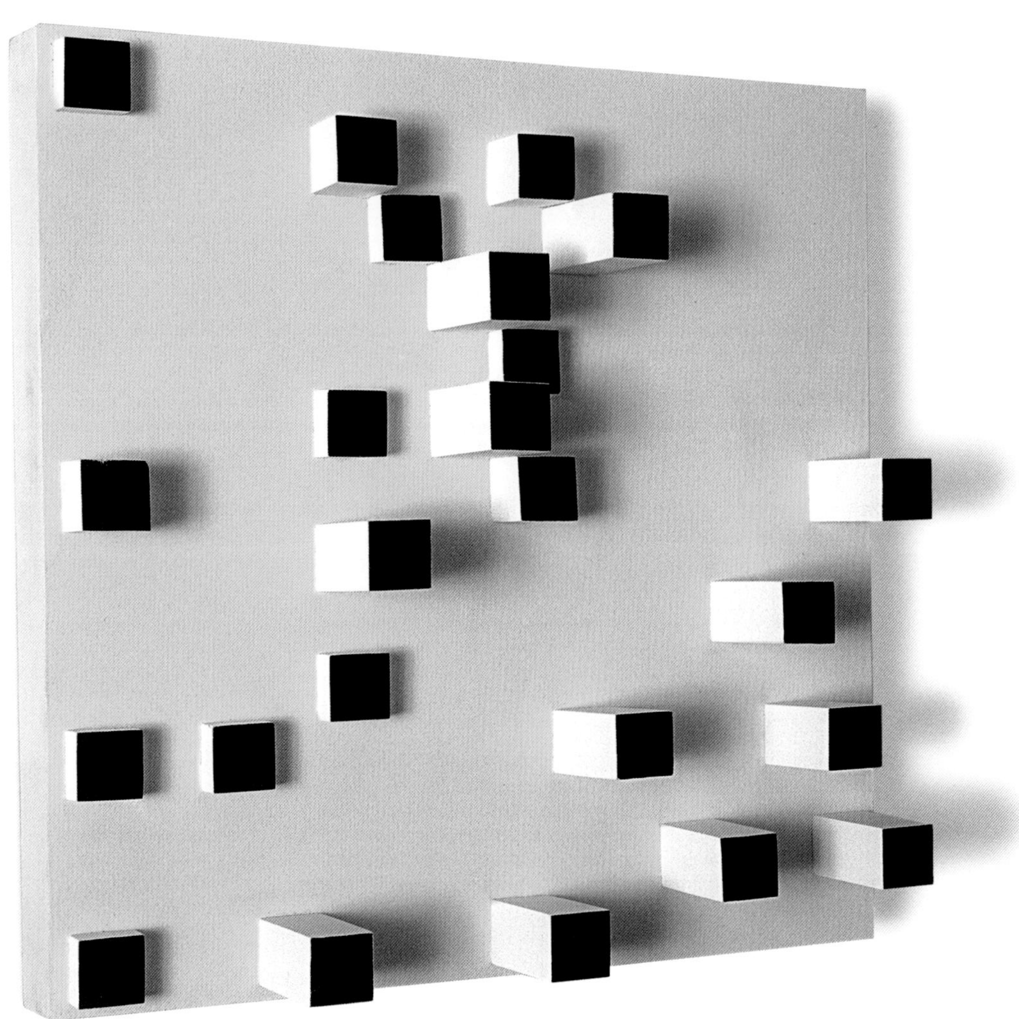

78. *Livro dos caminhos* (*Book of Paths*), 1963–76

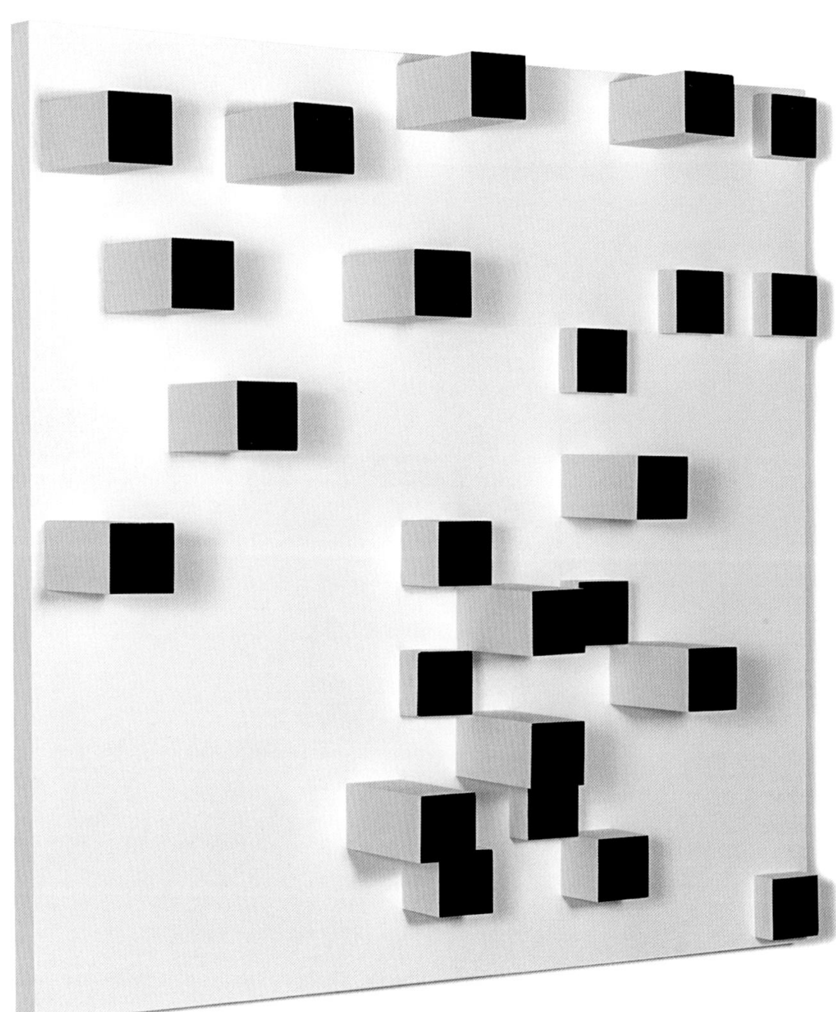

79. *Livro dos caminhos* (*Book of Paths*), 1963–76

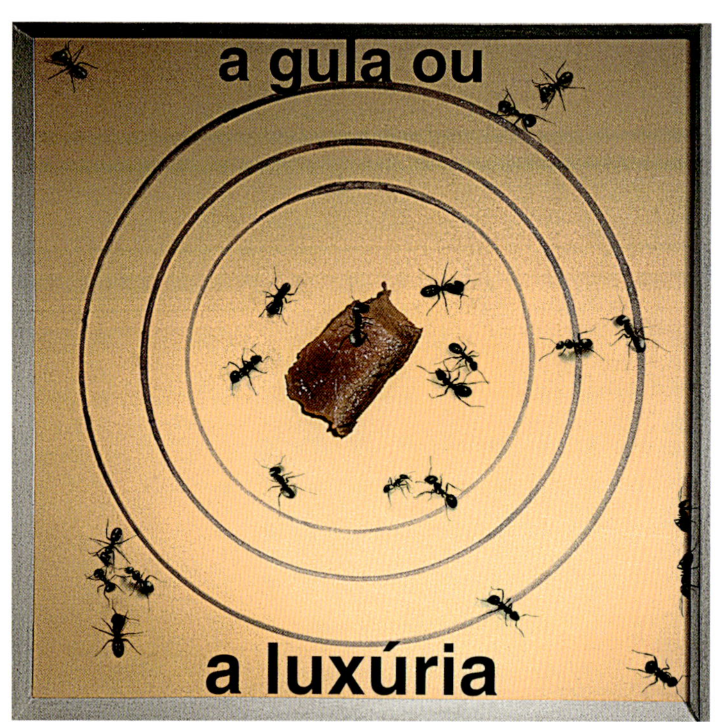

80. *Caixa das formigas* (*Box of Ants*), 1967

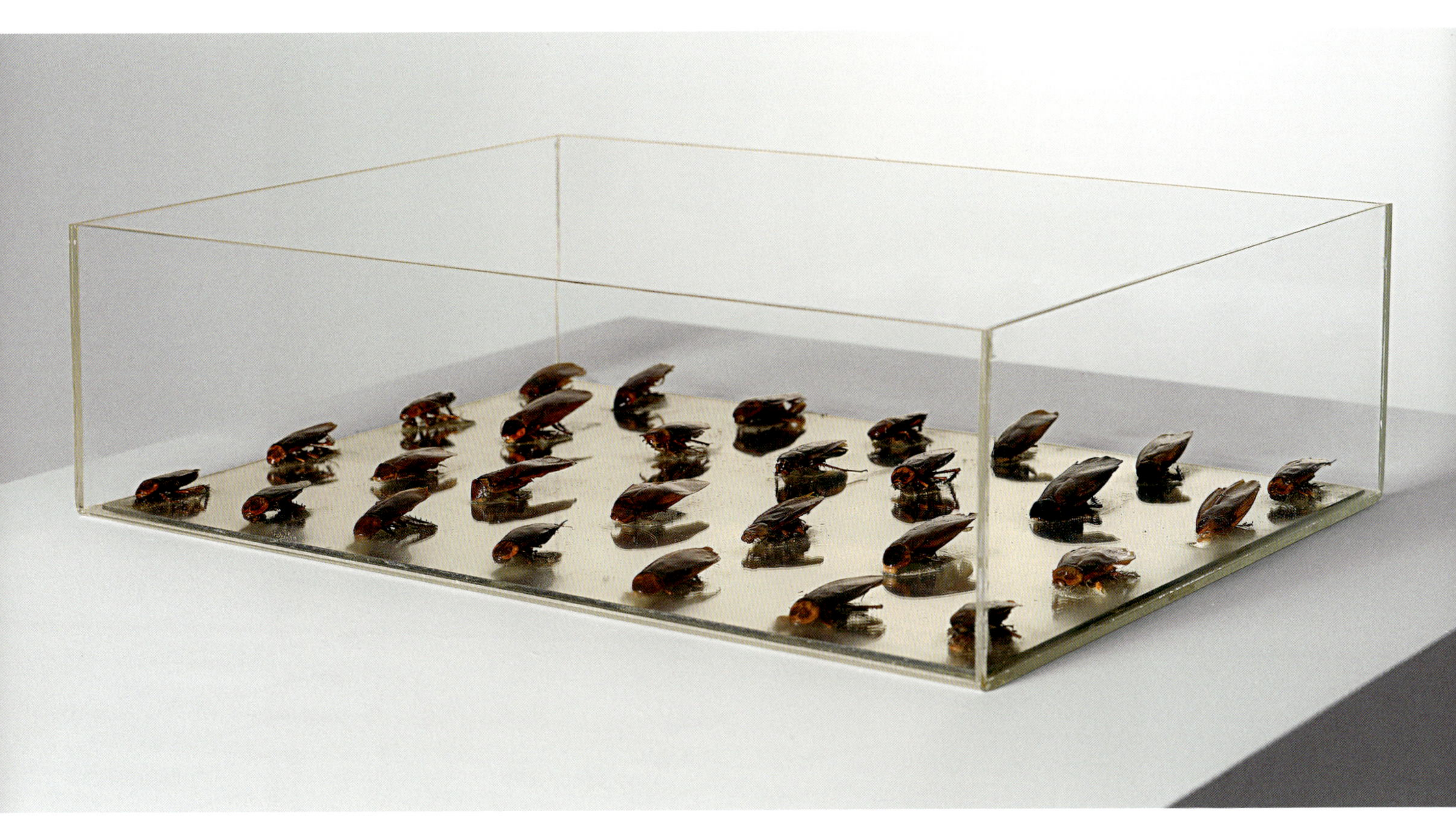

81. *Caixa das baratas* (*Box of Cockroaches*), 1967

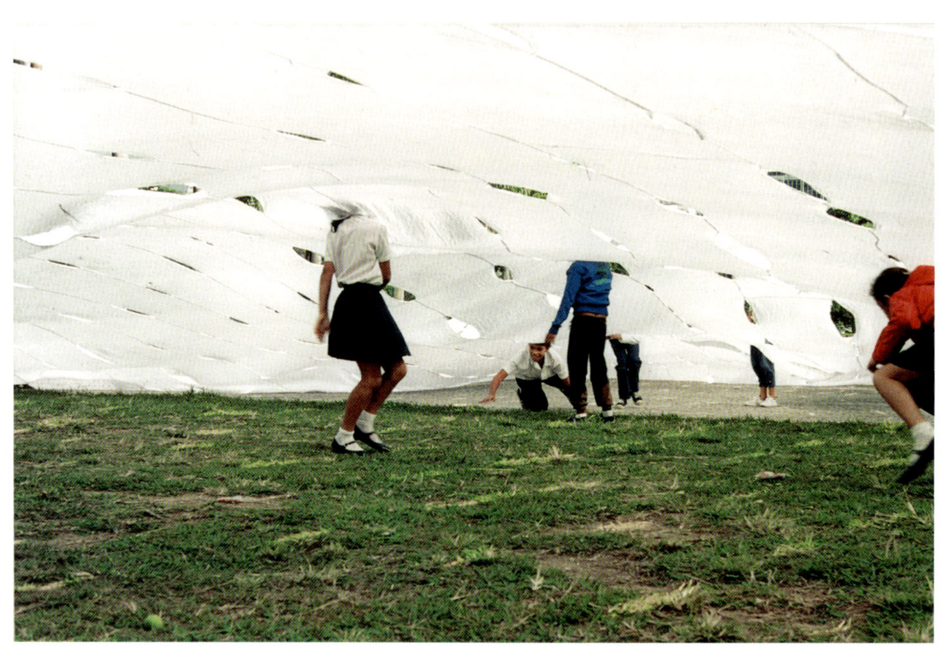

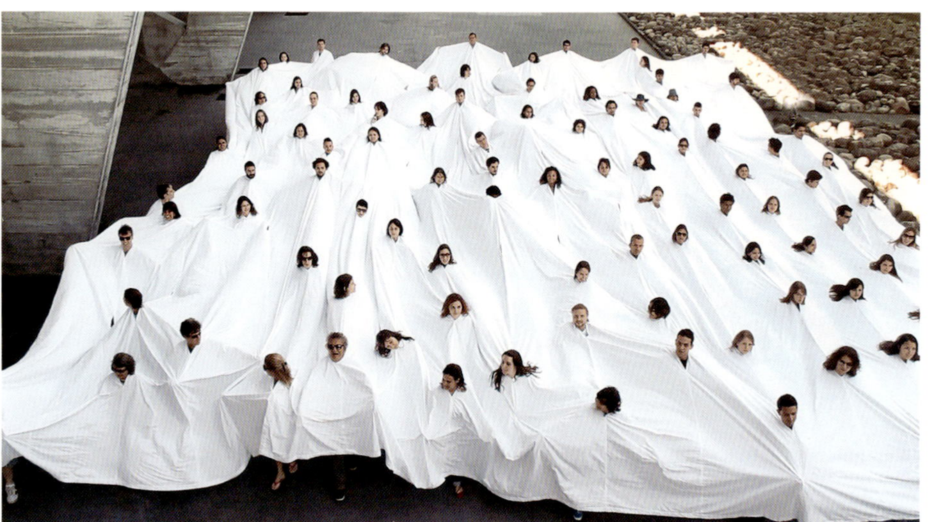

82. *Divisor* (*Divider*), 1968;
performance at Museu de Arte Moderna, Rio de Janeiro, 1990

83. *Divisor* (*Divider*), 1968;
performance at Museu de Arte Moderna, Rio de Janeiro, 2010

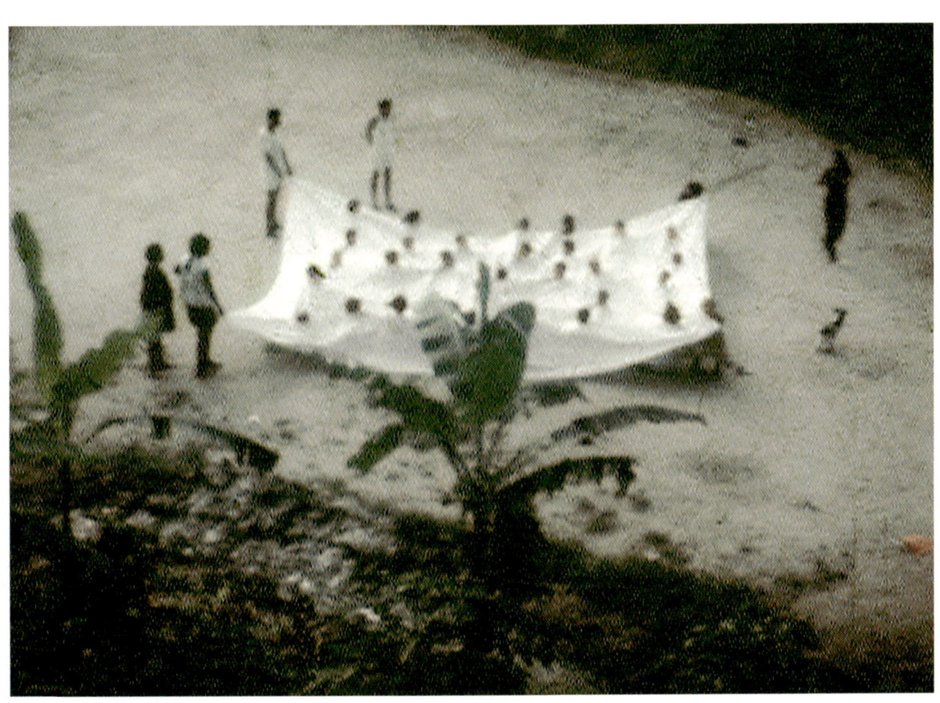

84. *Divisor* (*Divider*), 1967;
performance at Favela da Cabeça, Rio de Janeiro, 1967

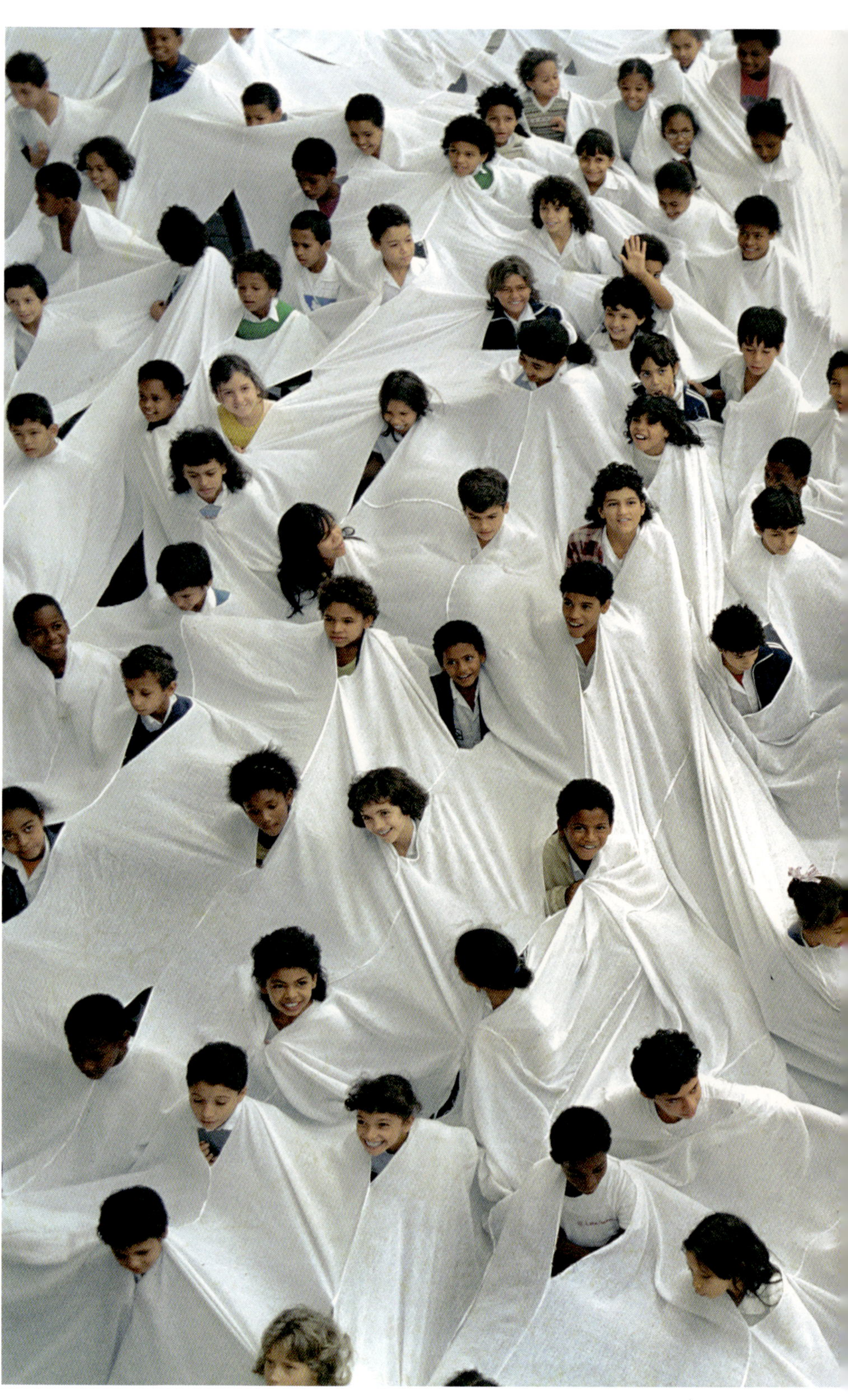

85. *Divisor* (*Divider*), 1968;
performance at Museu de Arte Moderna, Rio de Janeiro, 1990

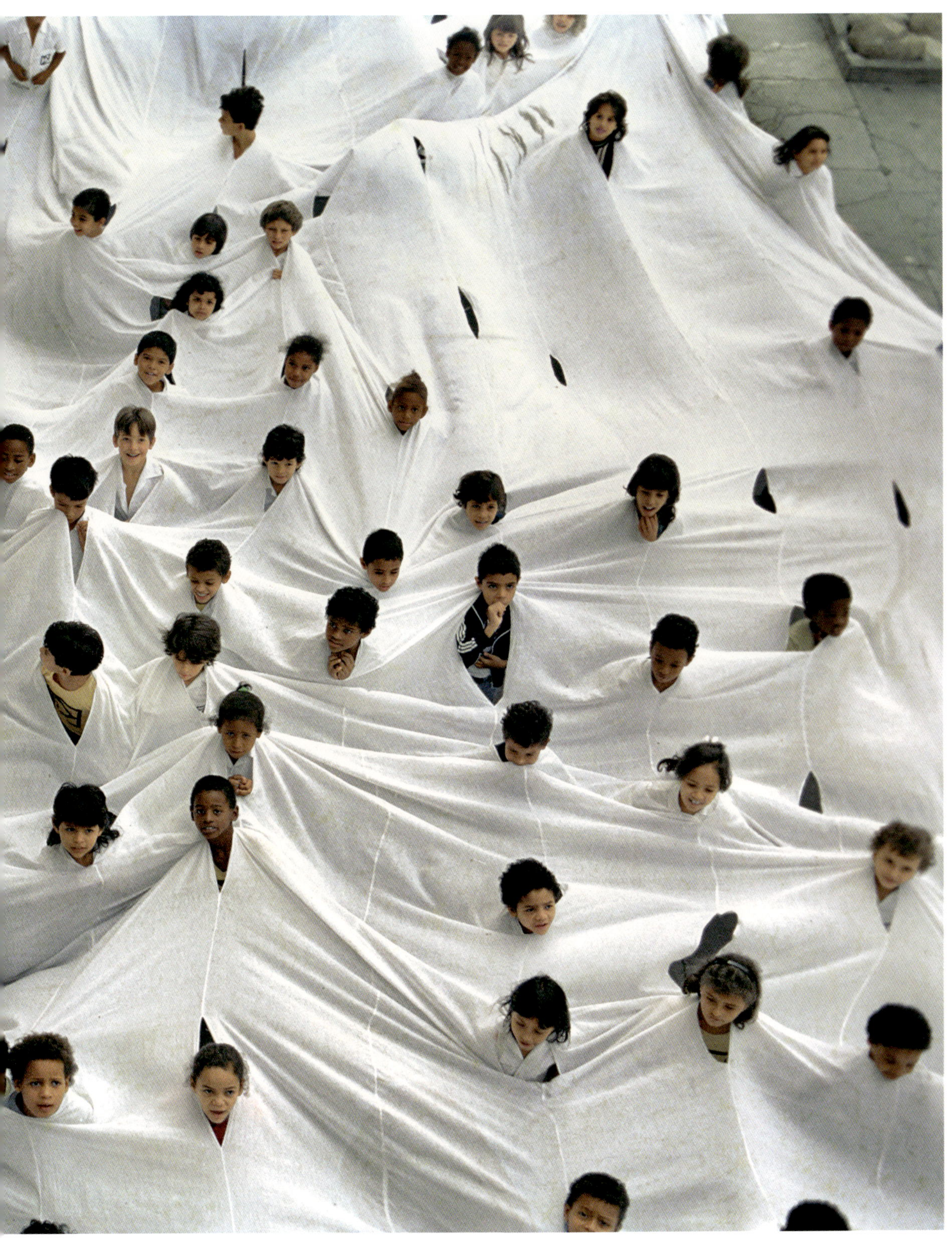

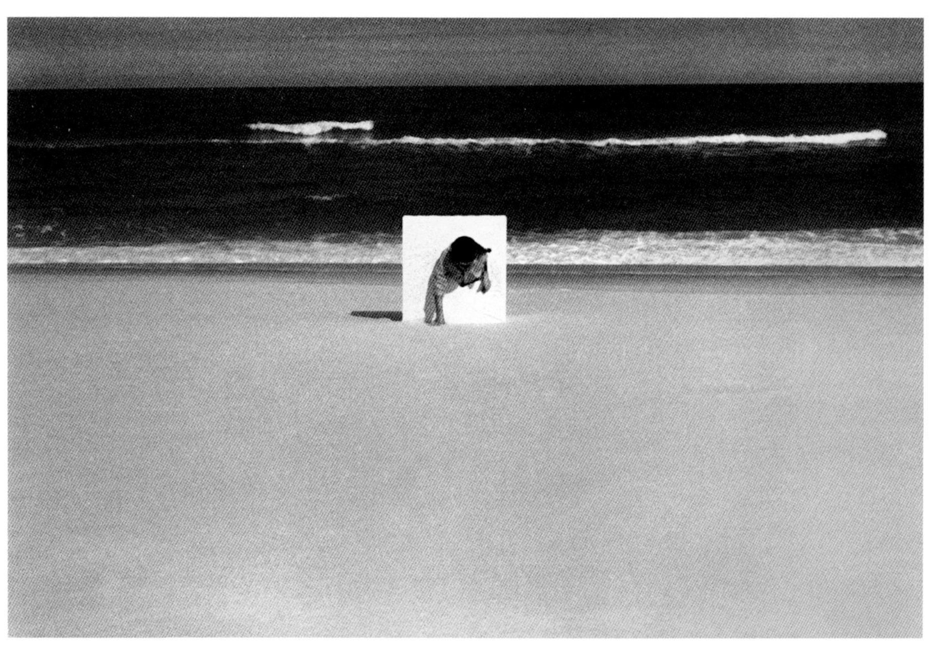

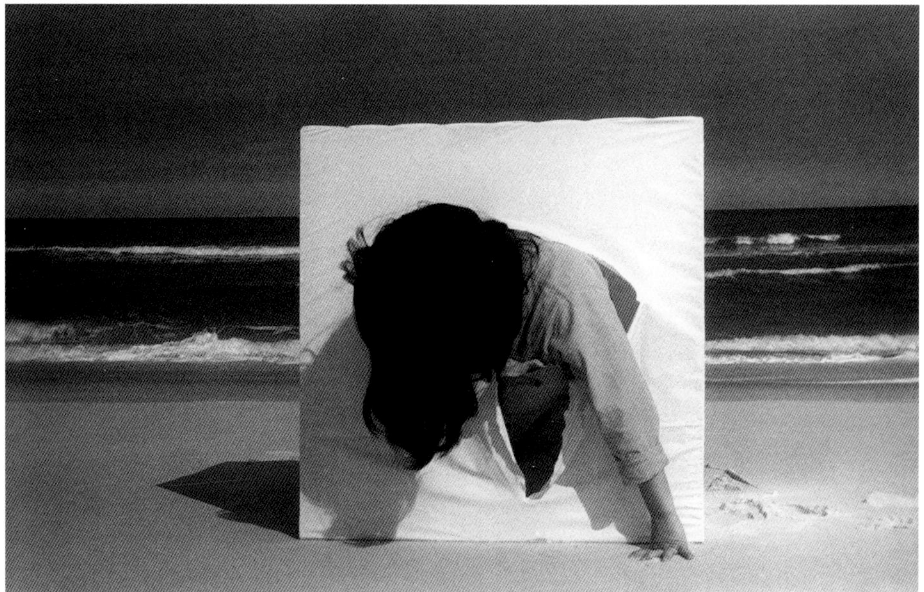

86. *O ovo* (*The Egg*), 1967;
performance at Barra da Tijuca beach, Rio de Janeiro, 1967

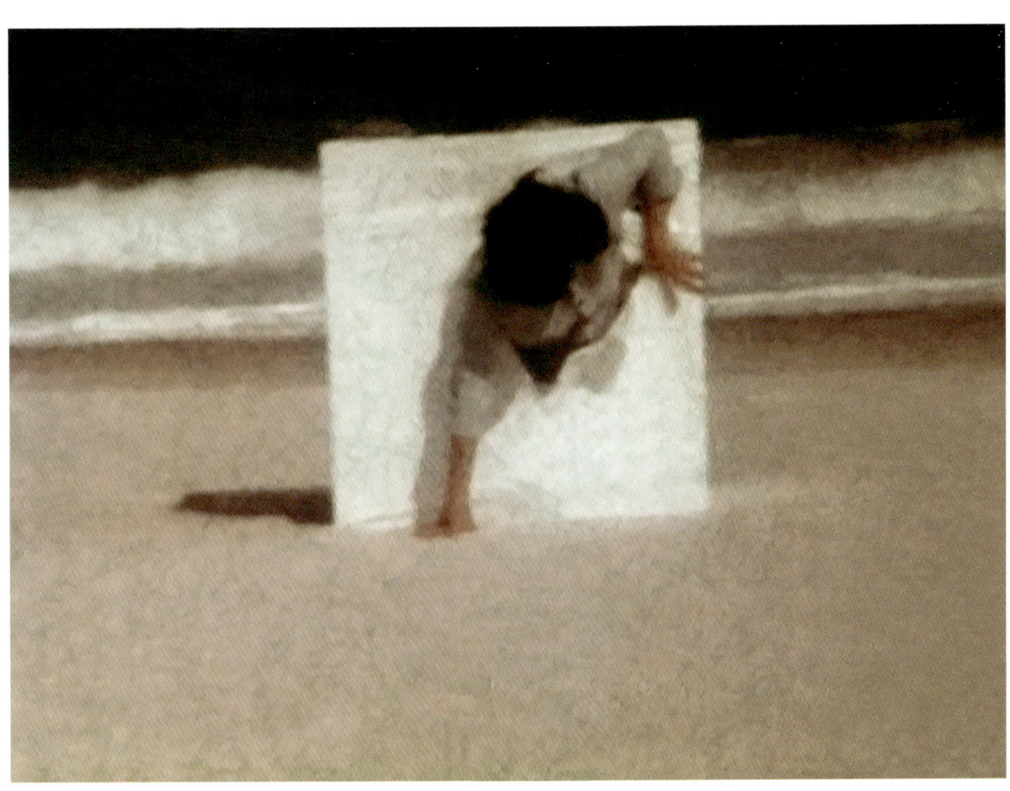

87. *O ovo* (*The Egg*), 1967;
performance at Barra da Tijuca beach, Rio de Janeiro, 1967

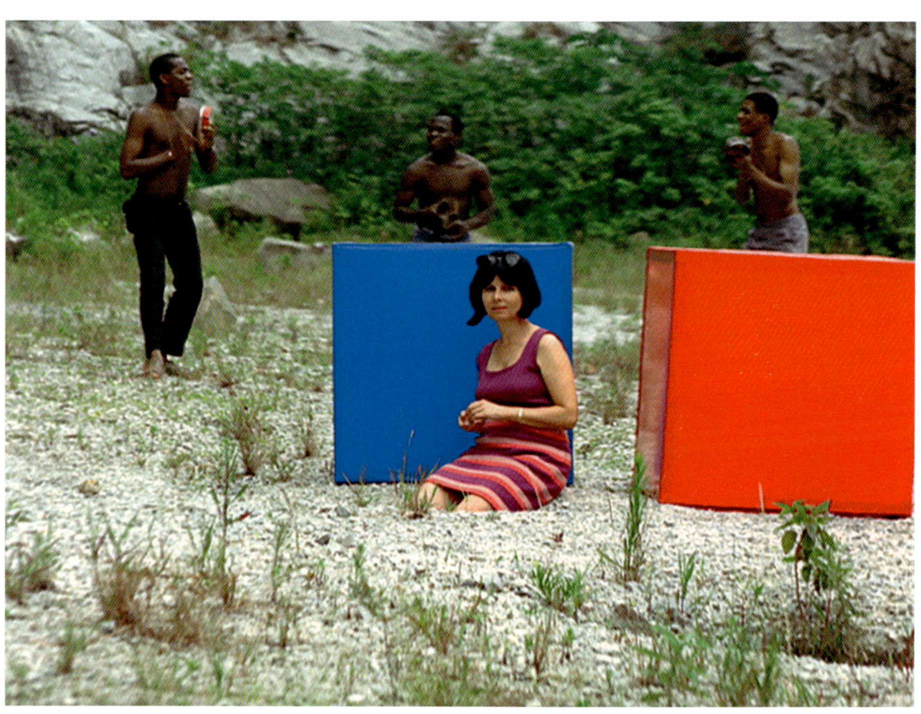

88. *Trio do embalo maluco (Crazy Rocking Trio)*, 1967;
performance at a quarry near the artist's home, Rio de Janeiro, 1967

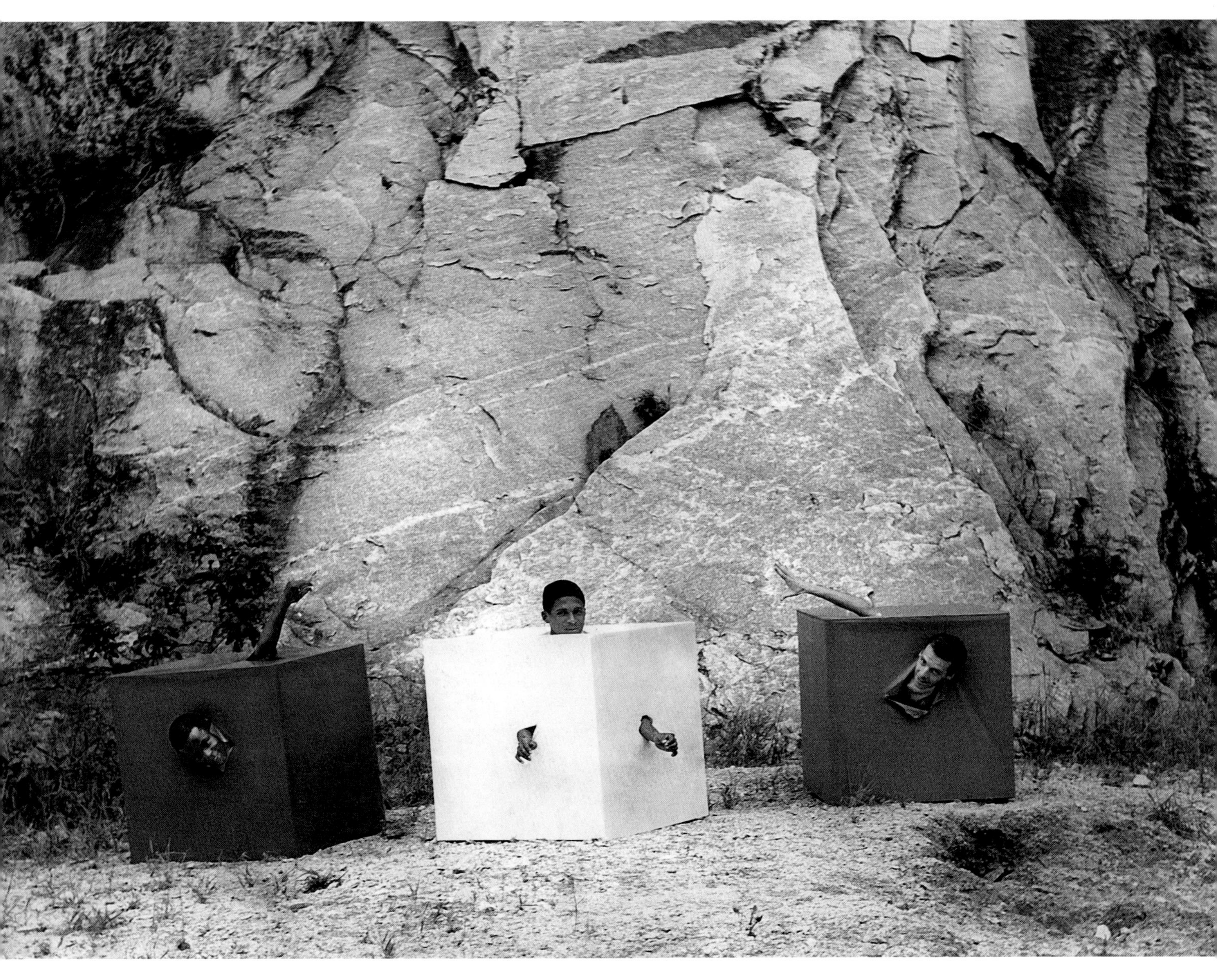

89. *Trio do embalo maluco* (*Crazy Rocking Trio*), 1967;
performance at a quarry near the artist's home, Rio de Janeiro, 1967

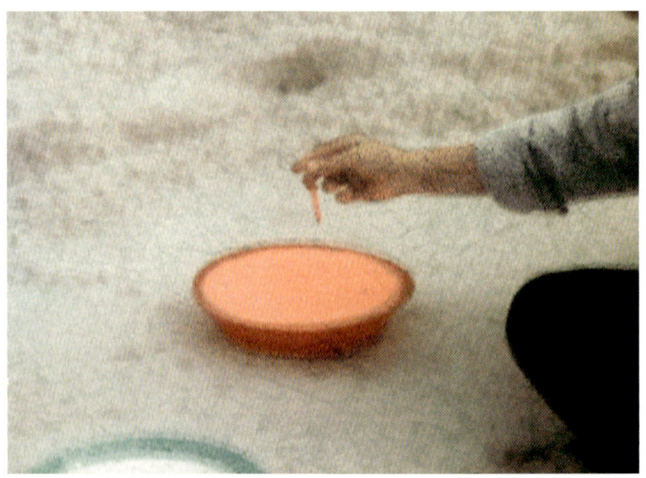

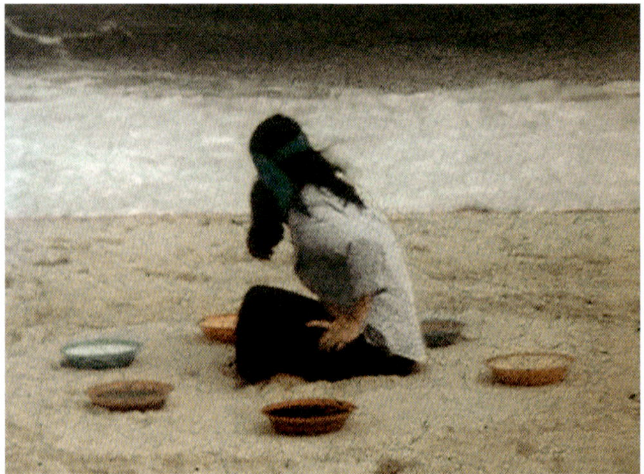

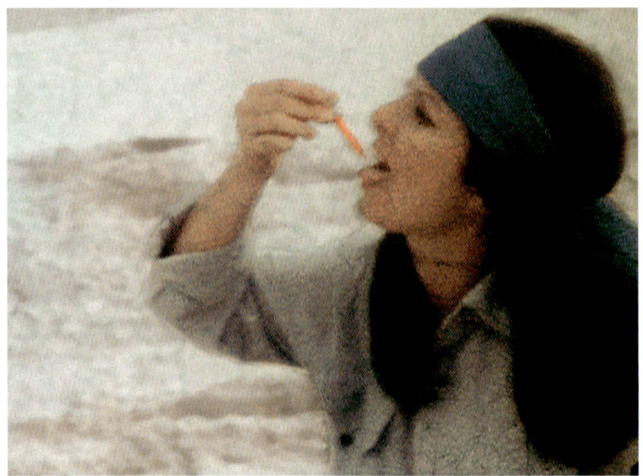

90. *Roda dos prazeres* (*Wheel of Pleasures*), 1967;
performance at Barra de Tijuca beach, Rio de Janeiro, 1967

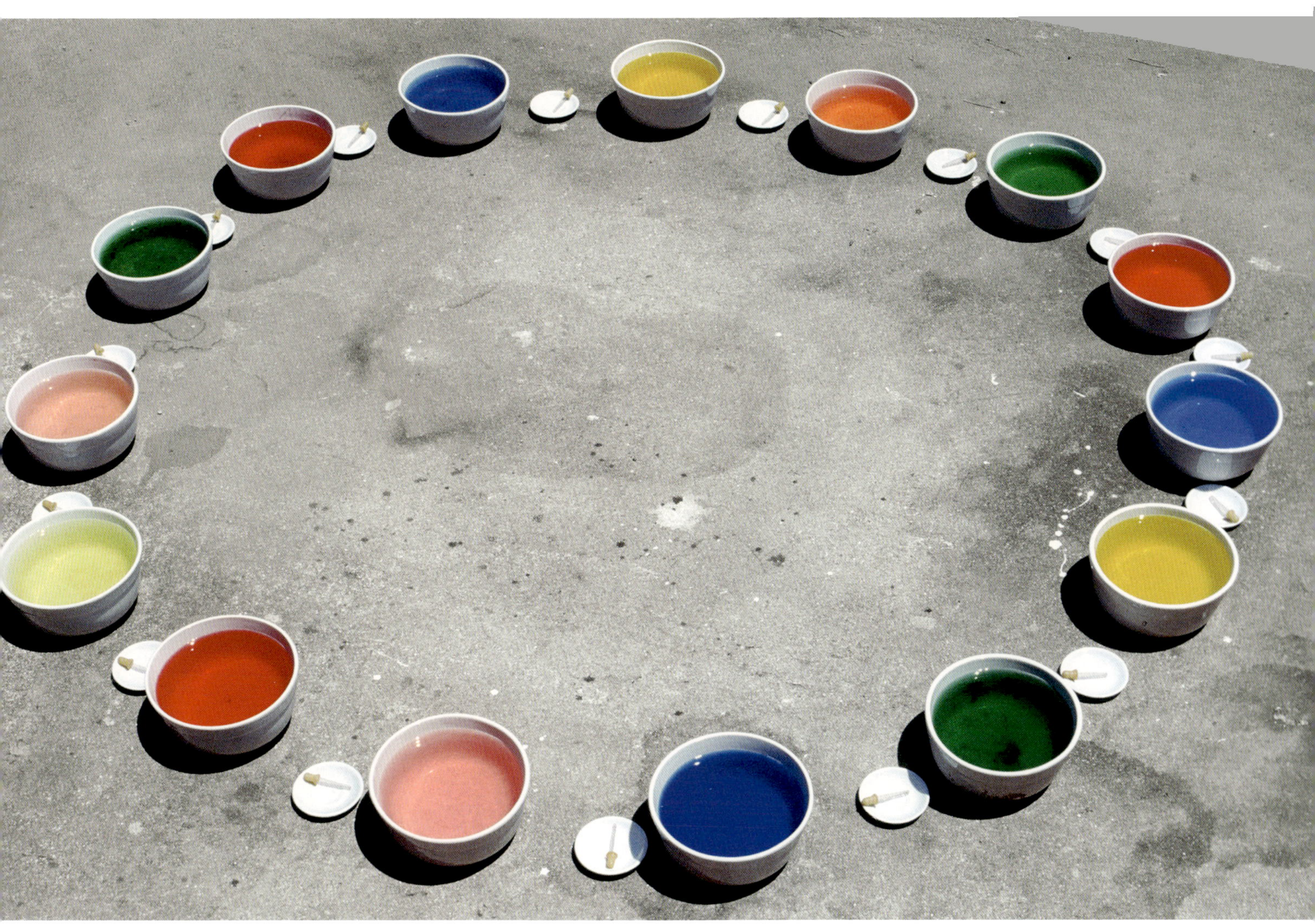

91. *Roda dos prazeres* (*Wheel of Pleasures*), 1967

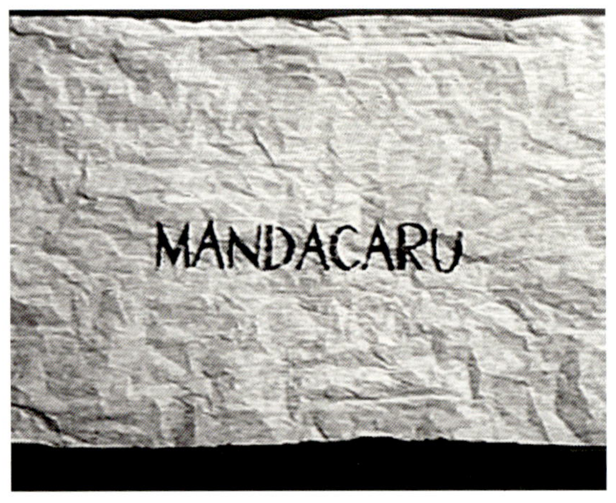

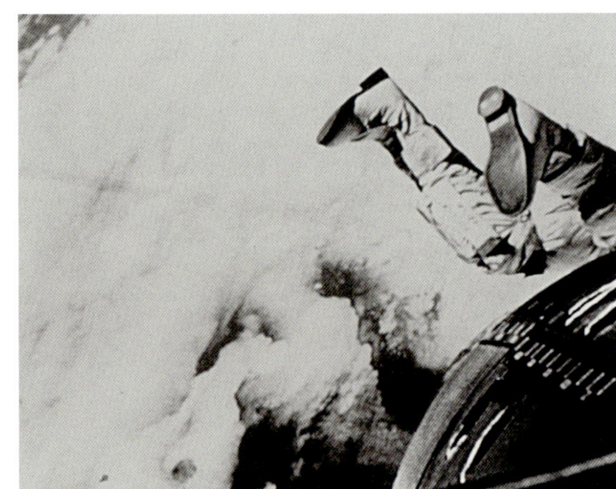

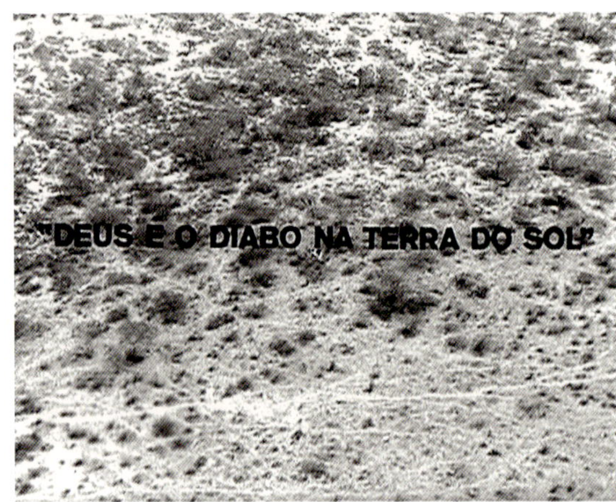

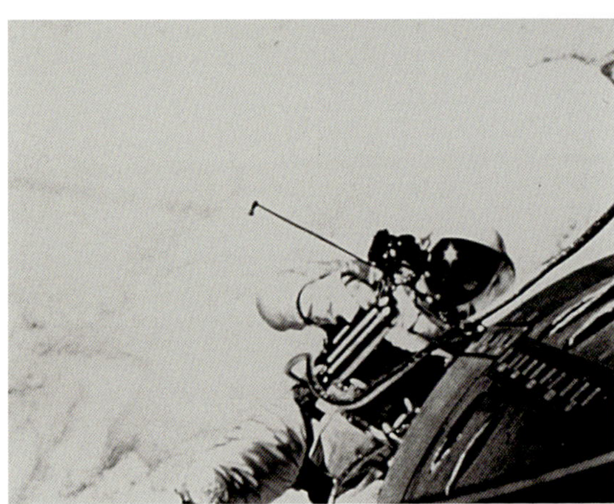

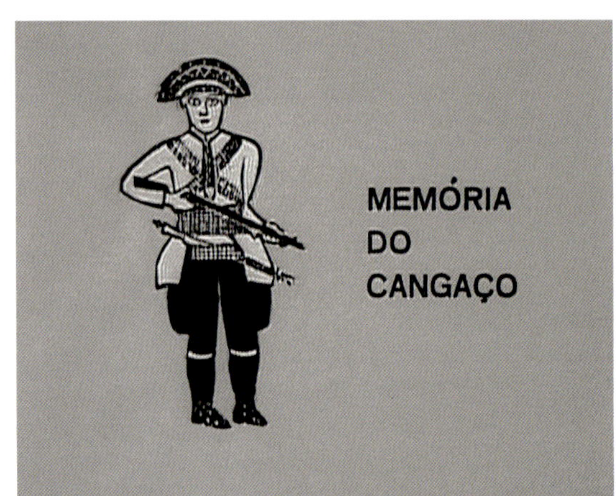

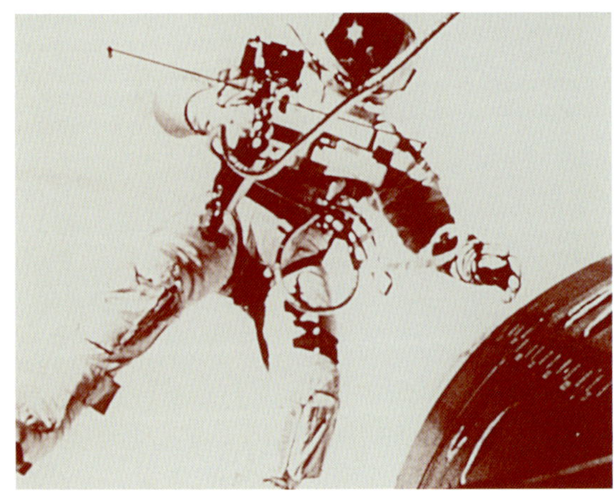

92. Title credits for Cinema Novo films, 1960s

Mandacaru vermelho (*Red Cactus*), 1961

Deus e o diablo na terra do sol (*Black God, White Devil*), 1964

Memória do Cangaço (*Memory of Cangaço*), 1964

93. *La nouvelle création* (*The New Creation*), 1967

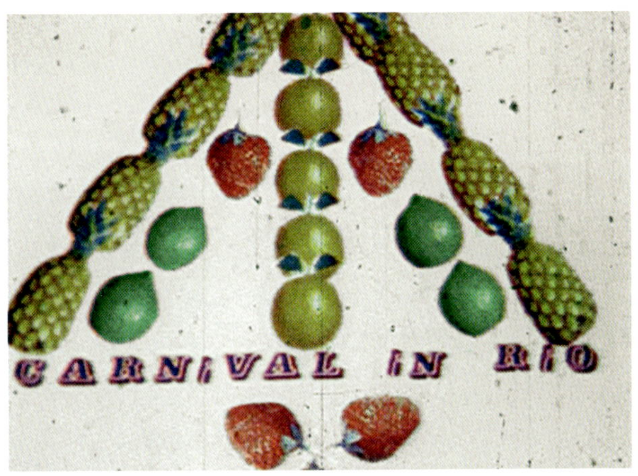

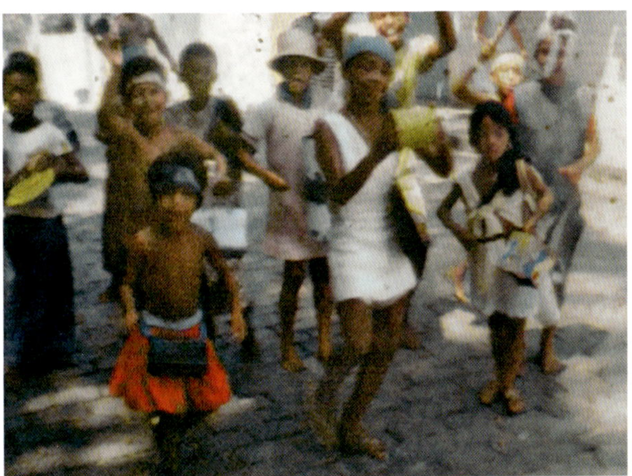

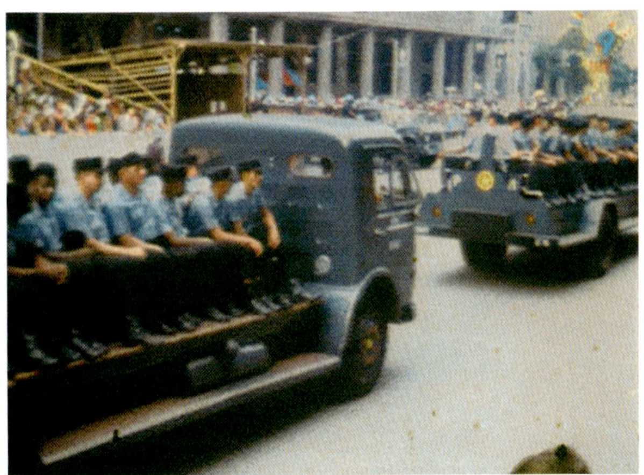

94. *Carnival in Rio*, 1974

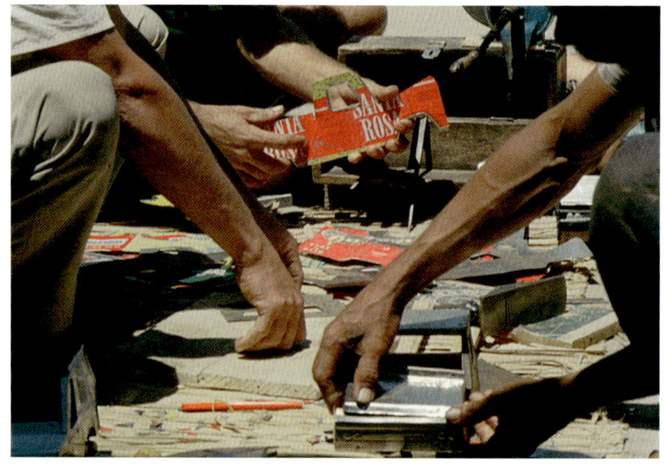

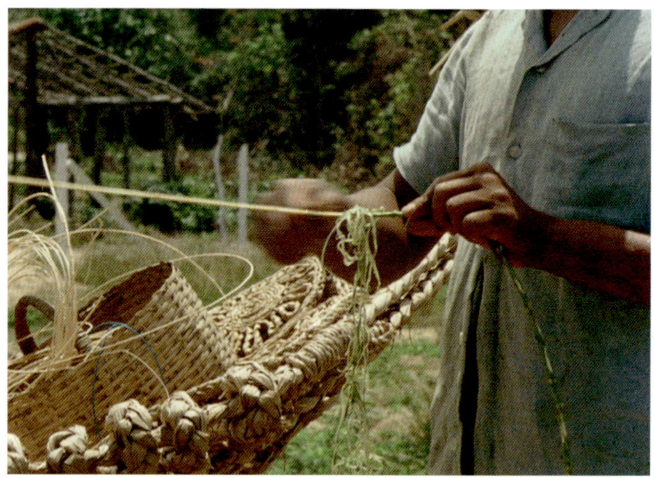

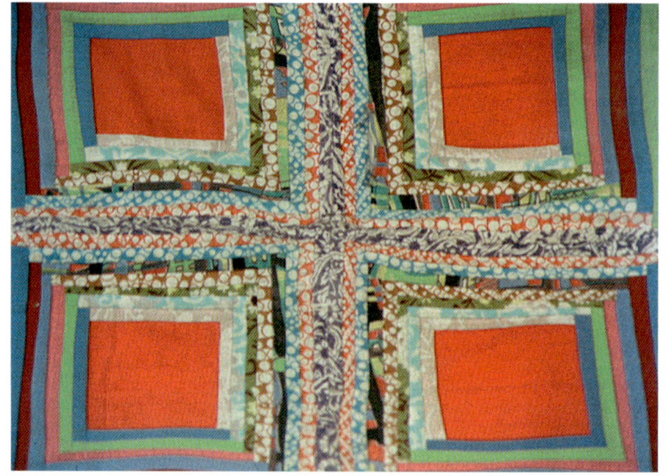

95. *A mão do povo* (*The Hand of the People*), 1975

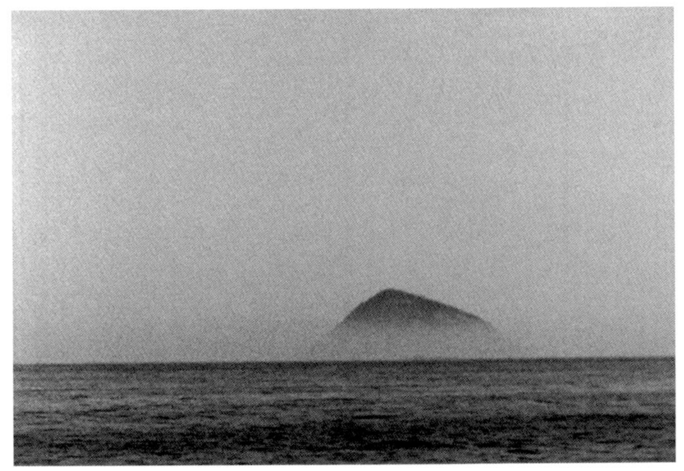

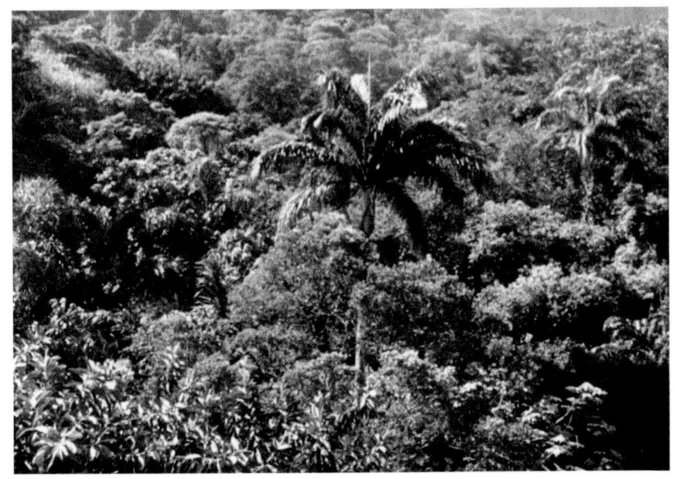

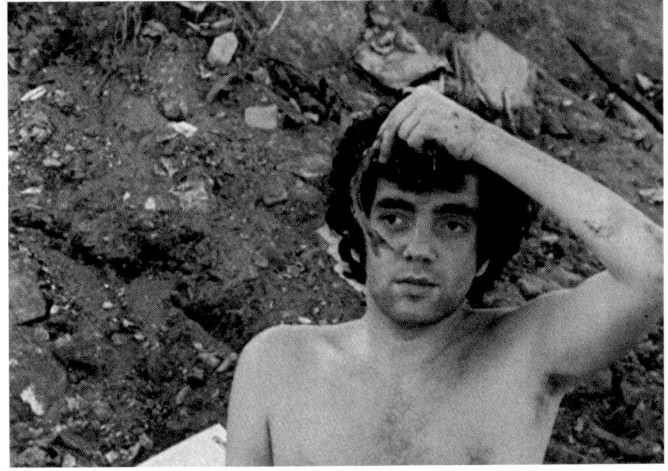

96. *Catiti-Catiti*, 1978

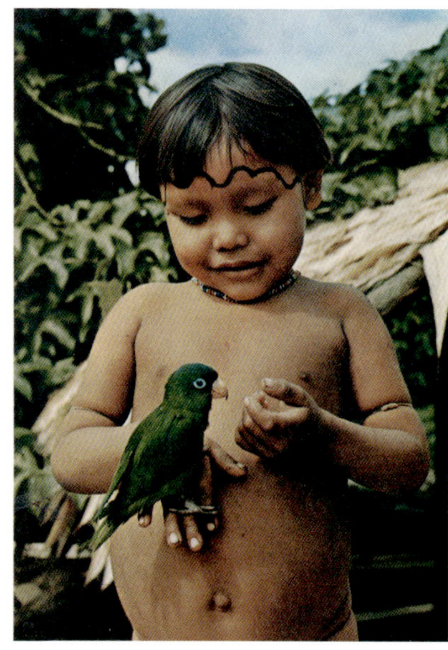
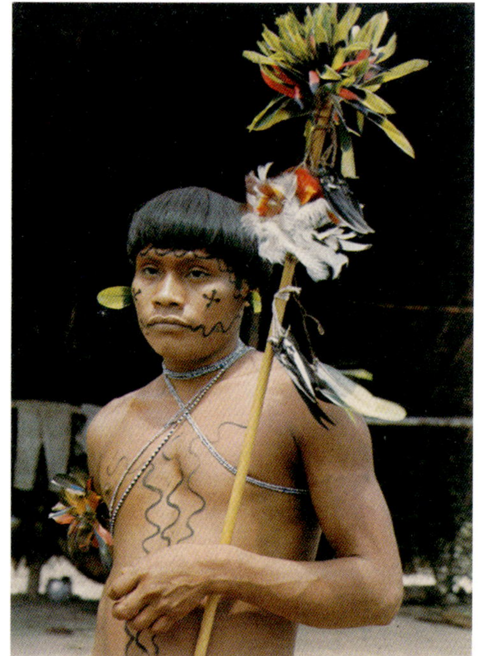
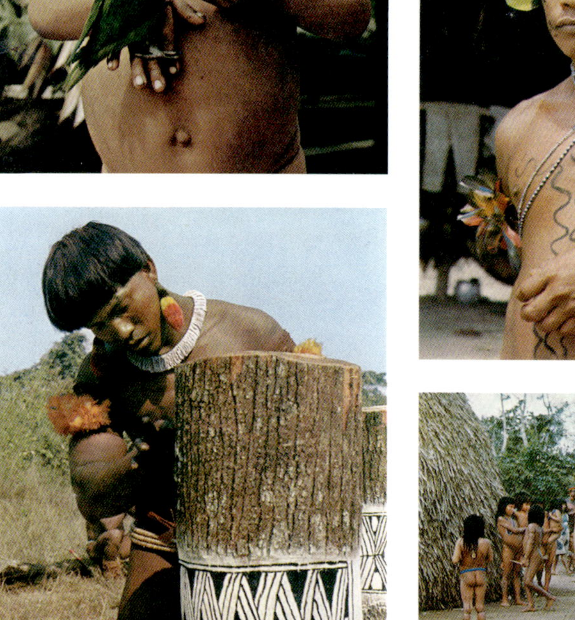
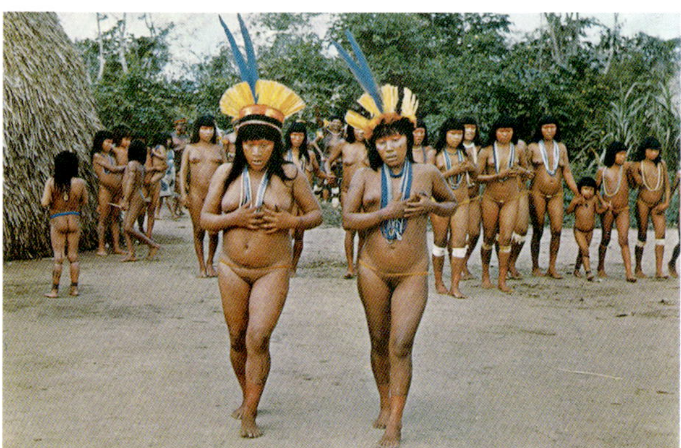

97. Commercial postcards of Indians used in *Our Parents "Fossilis"* (1974)

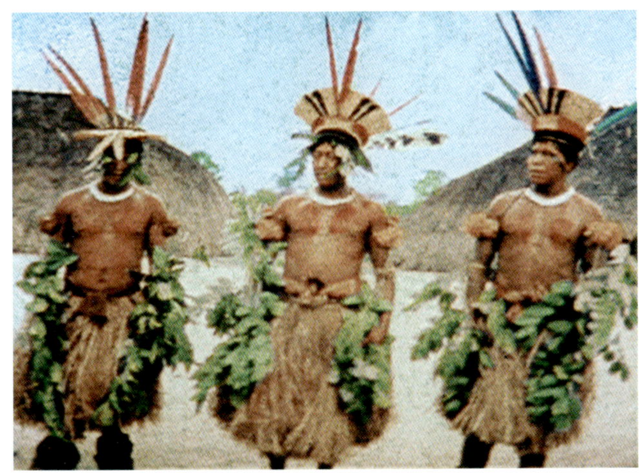

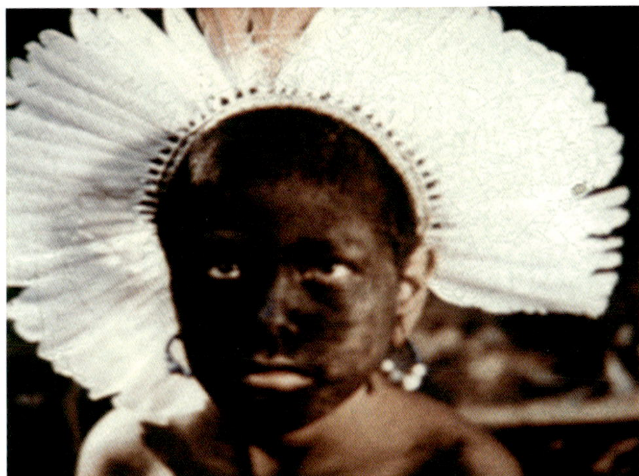

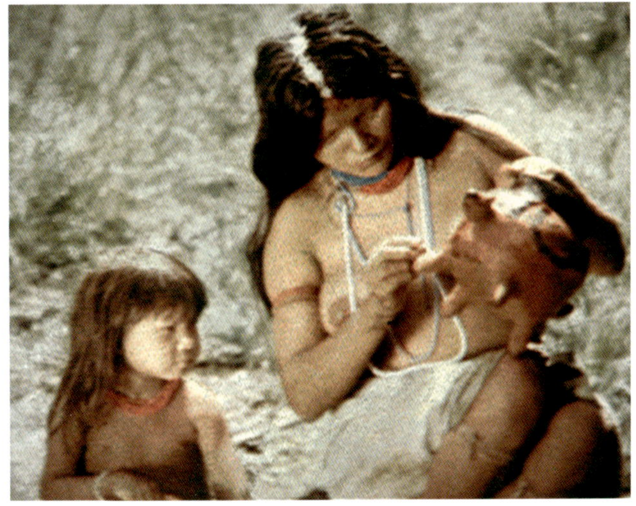

98. *Our Parents "Fossilis,"* 1974

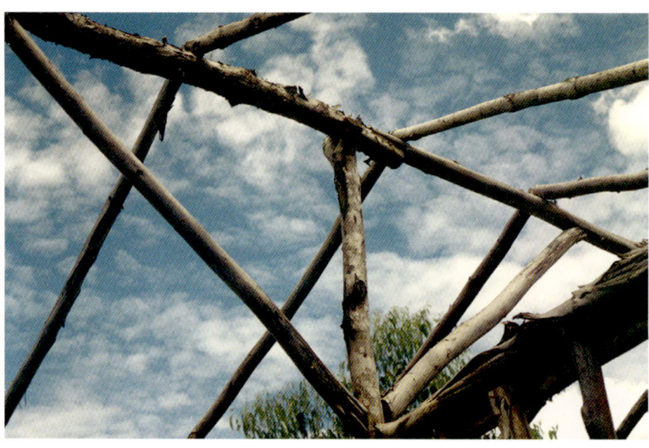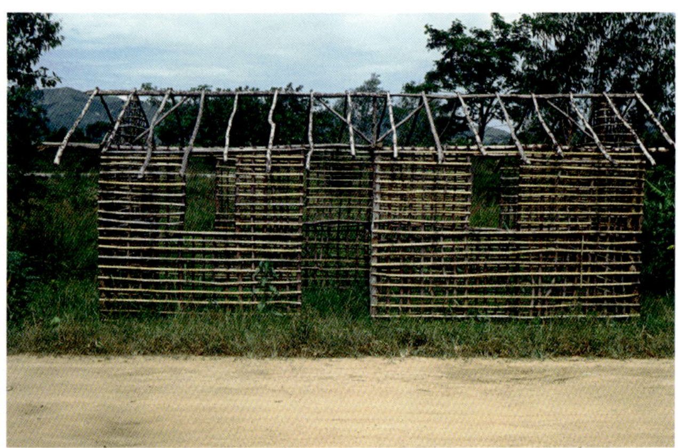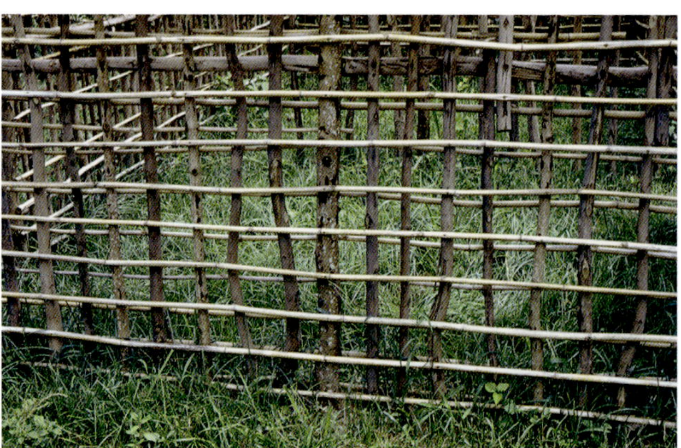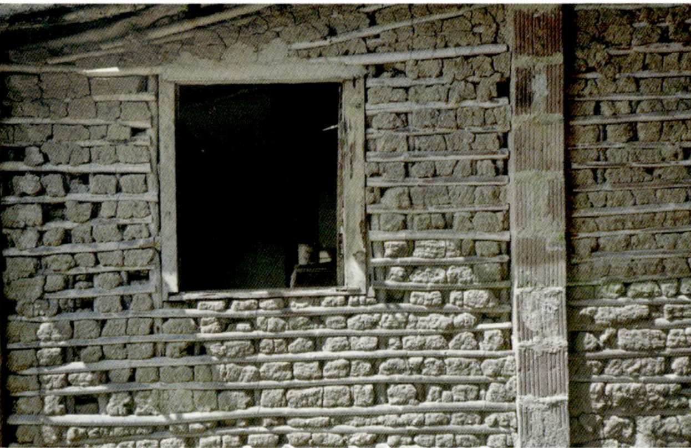

99. *Casa Sapé*, 1979

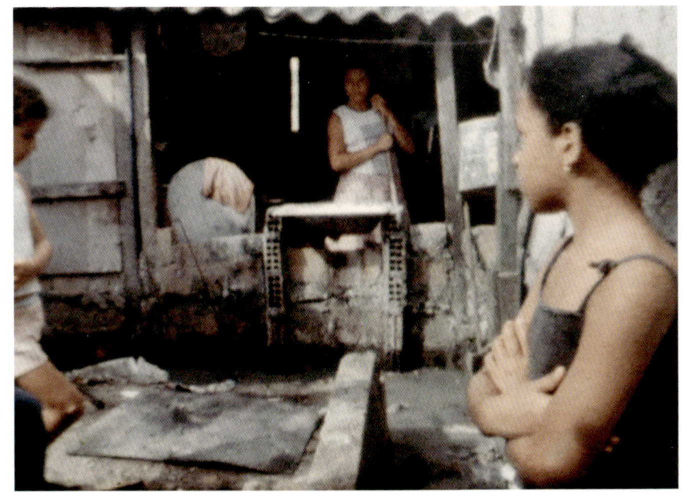

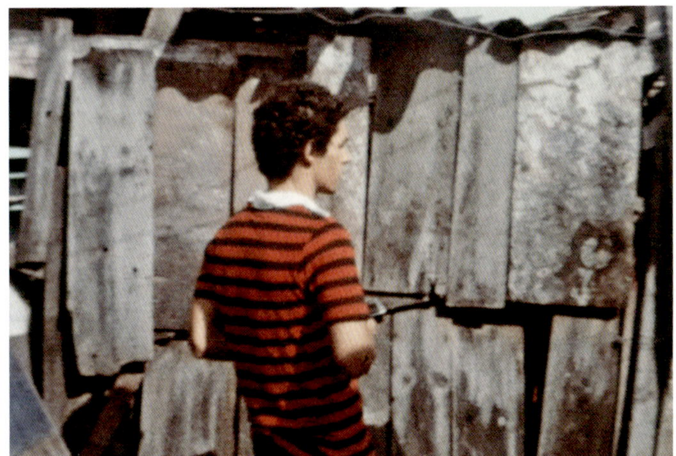

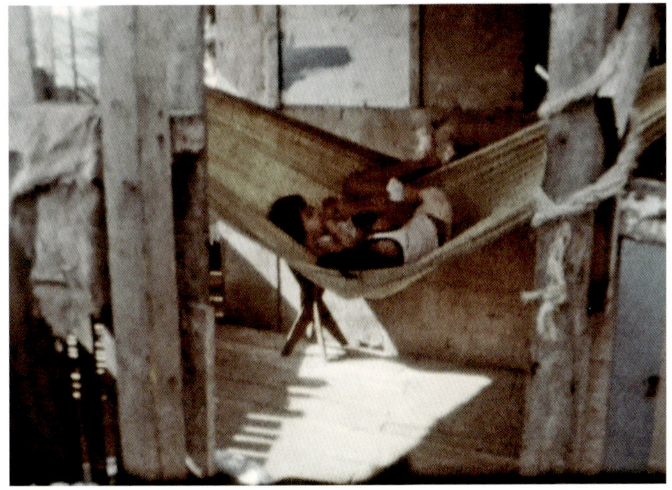

100. *Favela da Maré, 1972*

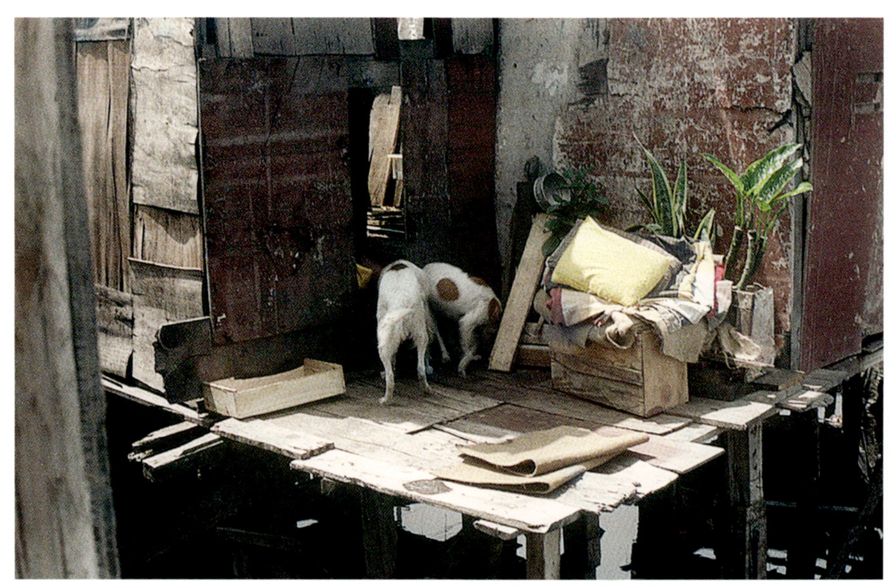

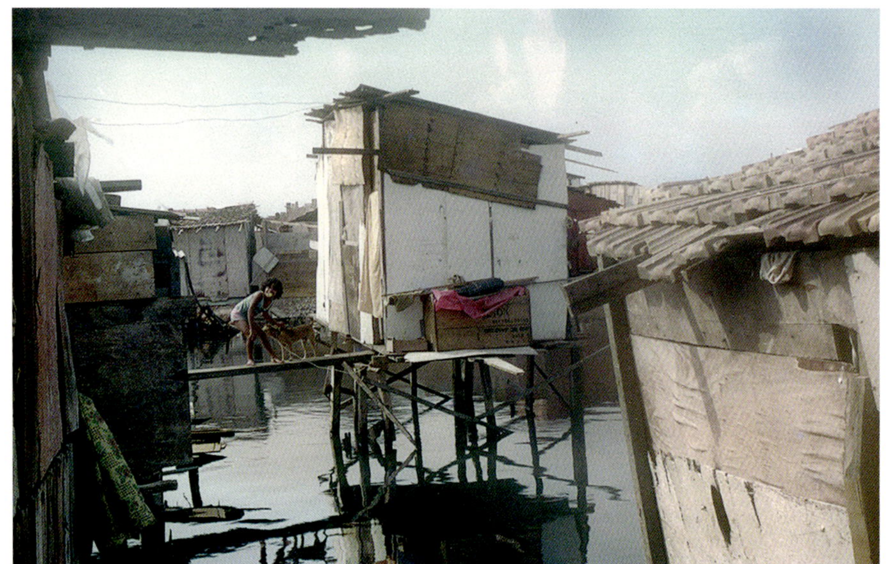

101. *Favela da Maré, 1974–76*

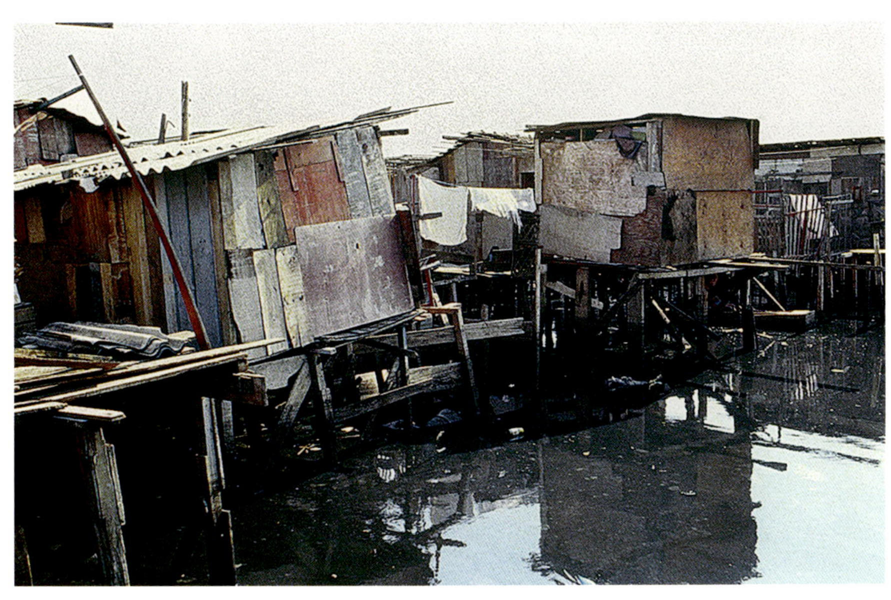

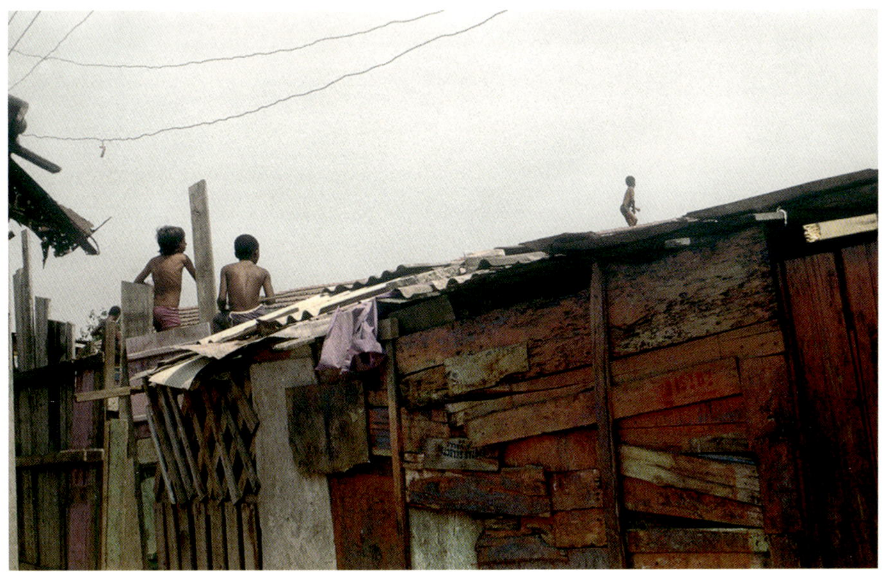

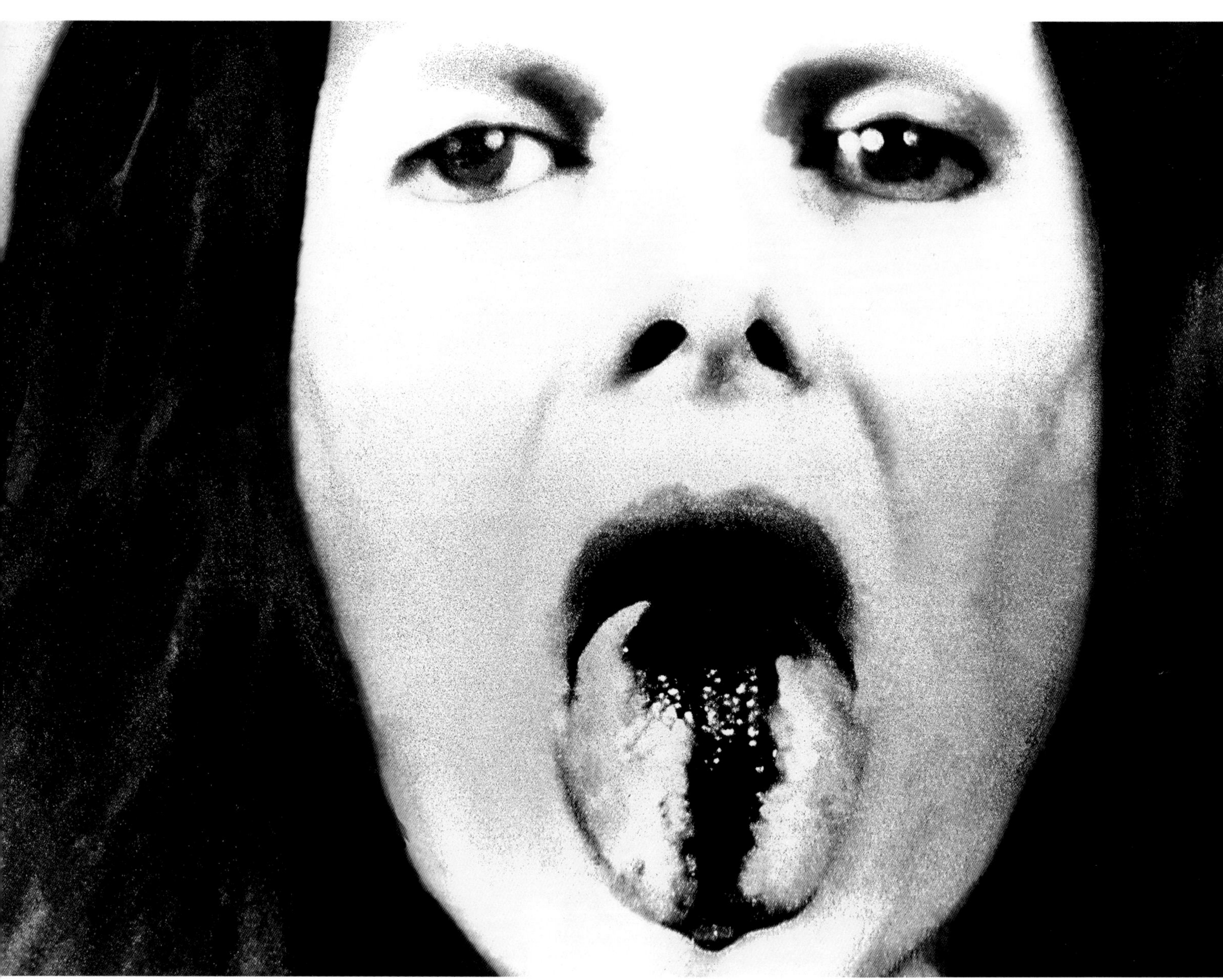

102. *Lingua apunhalada* (*Stabbed Tongue*), 1968

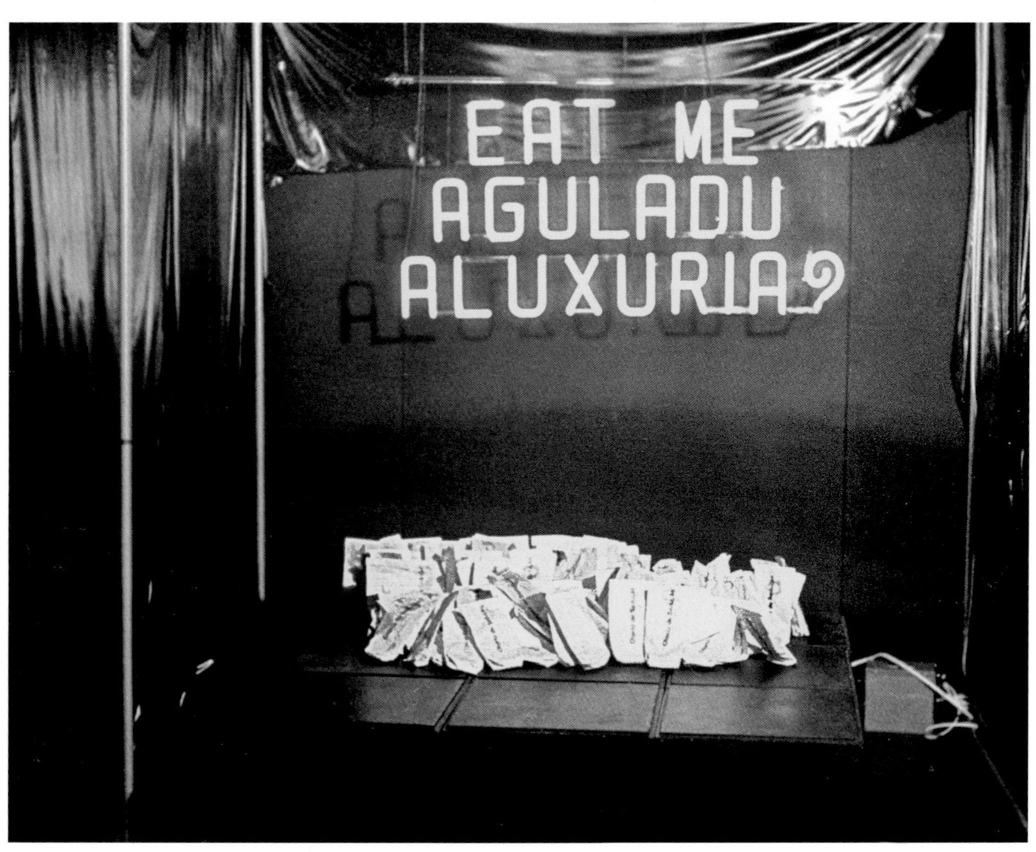

103. *Objetos de sedução* (*Objects of Seduction*), 1976; installation view
"Eat Me: A gula ou a luxúria?", Museu de Arte Moderna, Rio de Janeiro, 1976

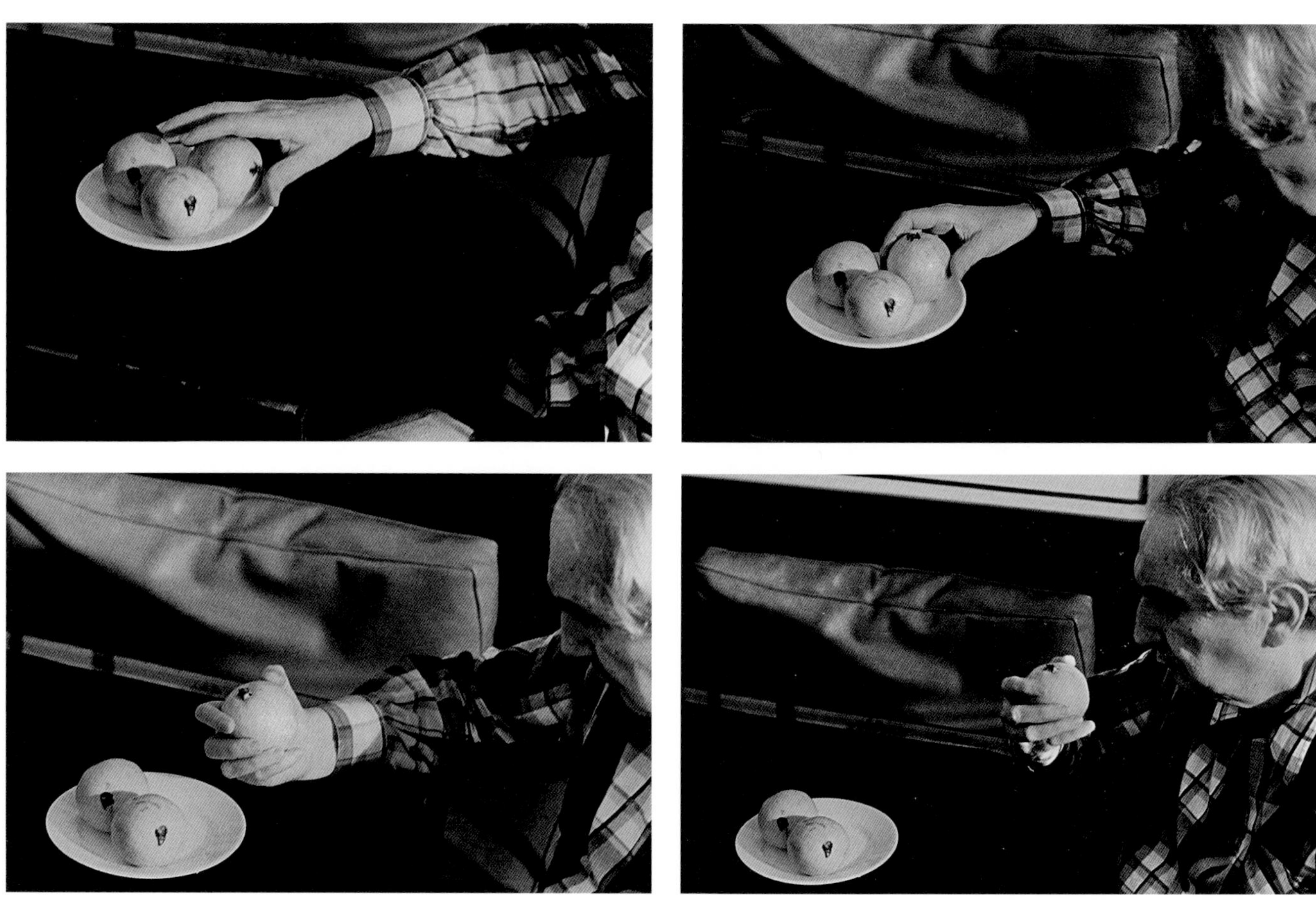

104. *Mário Pedrosa Eating Fruit*, 1978

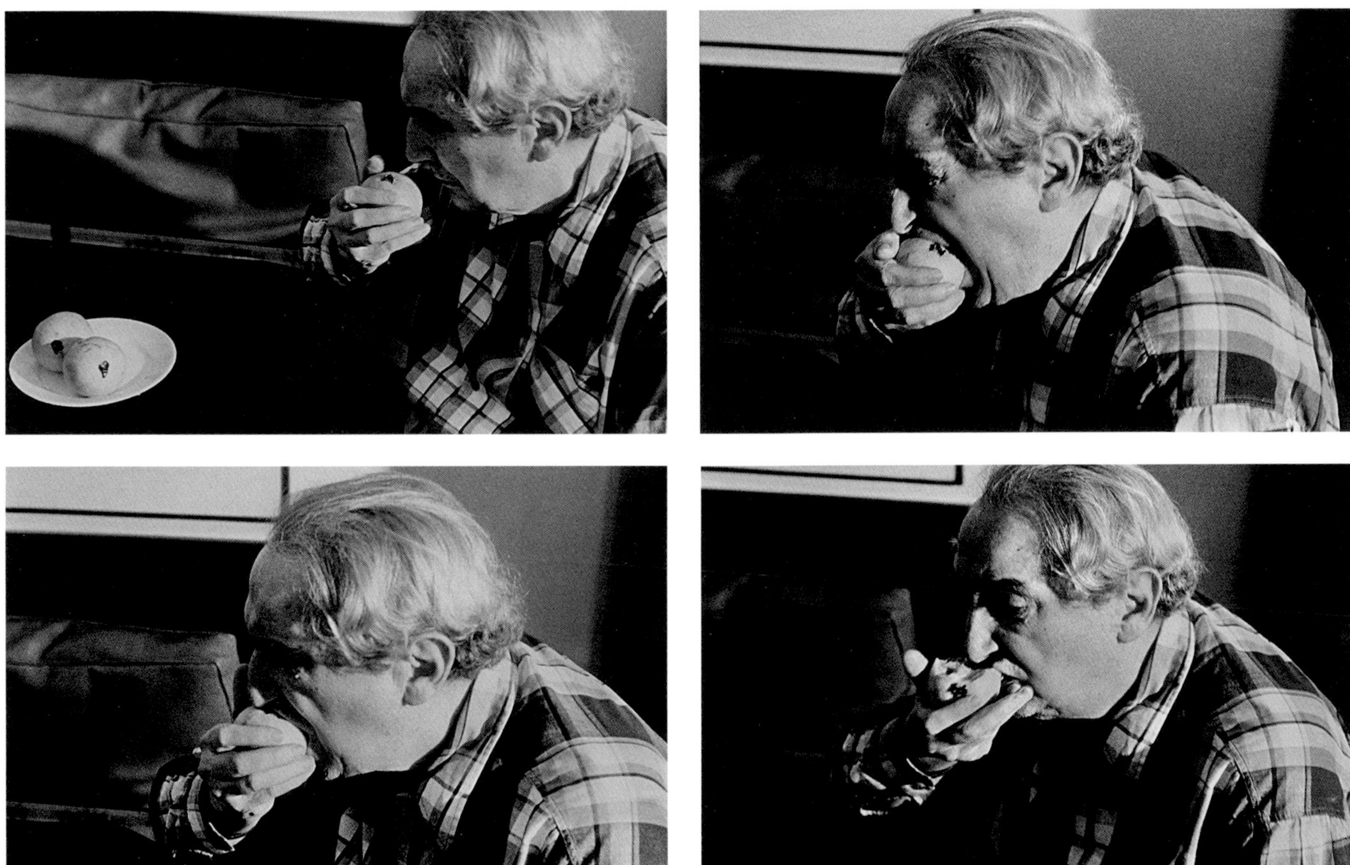

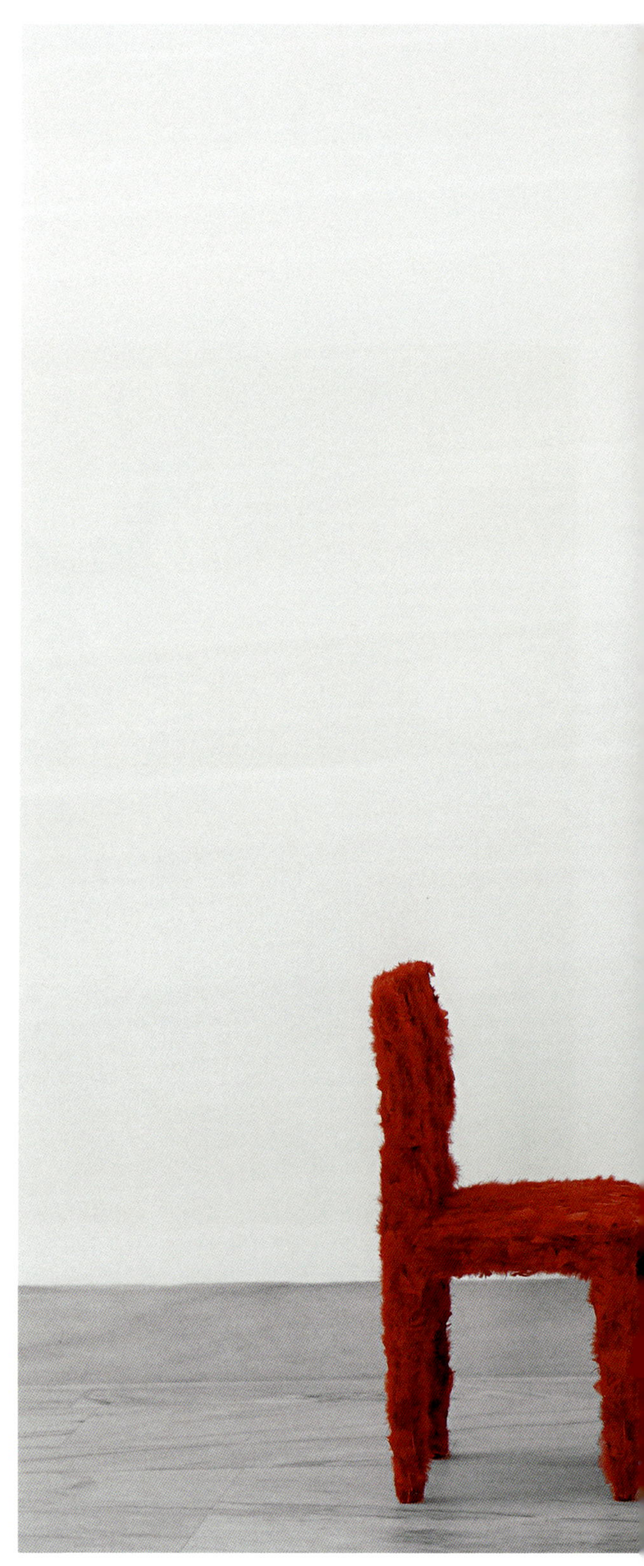

105. *Banquete Tupinambá* (*Tupinambá Banquet*), 2000

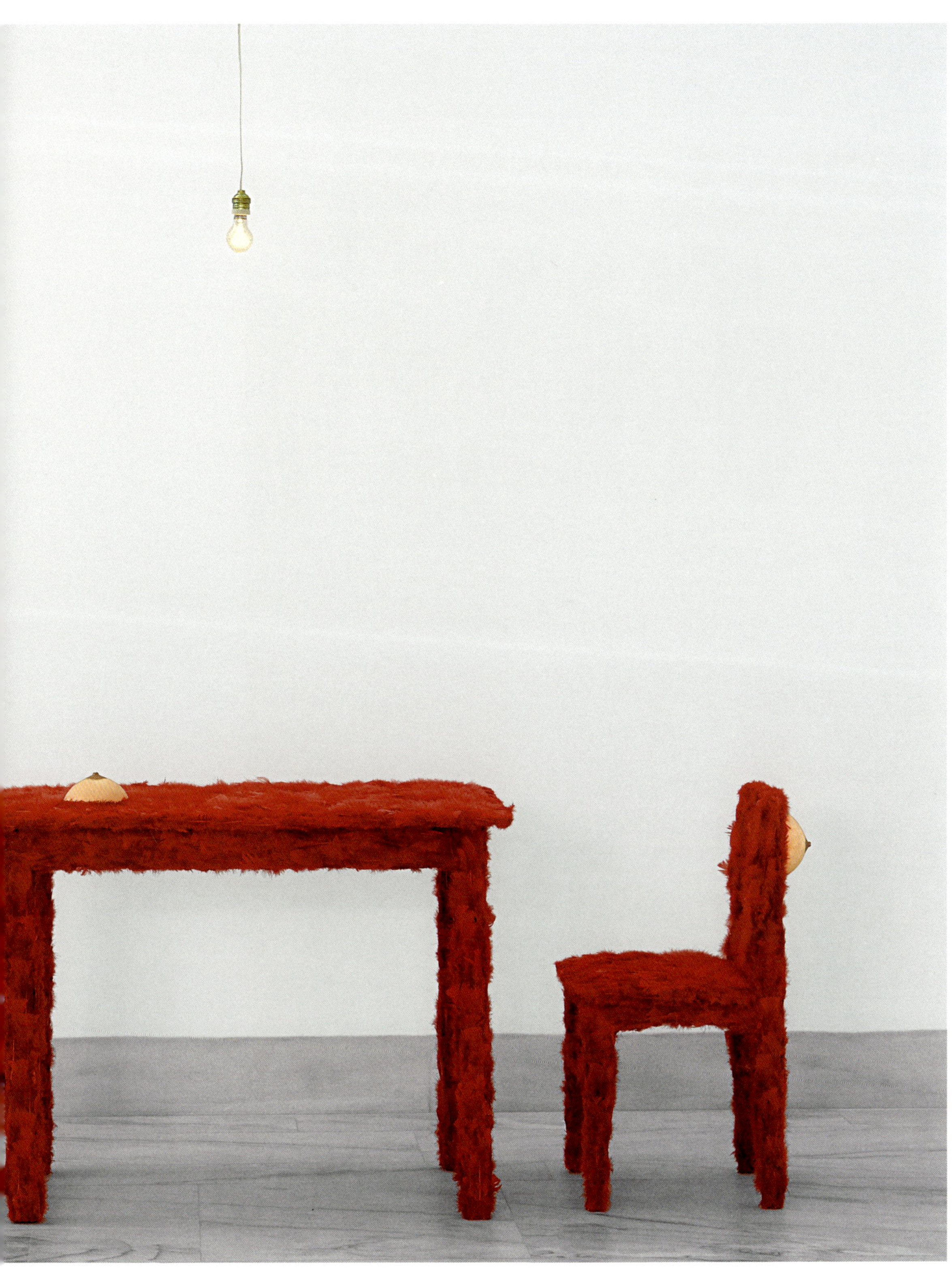

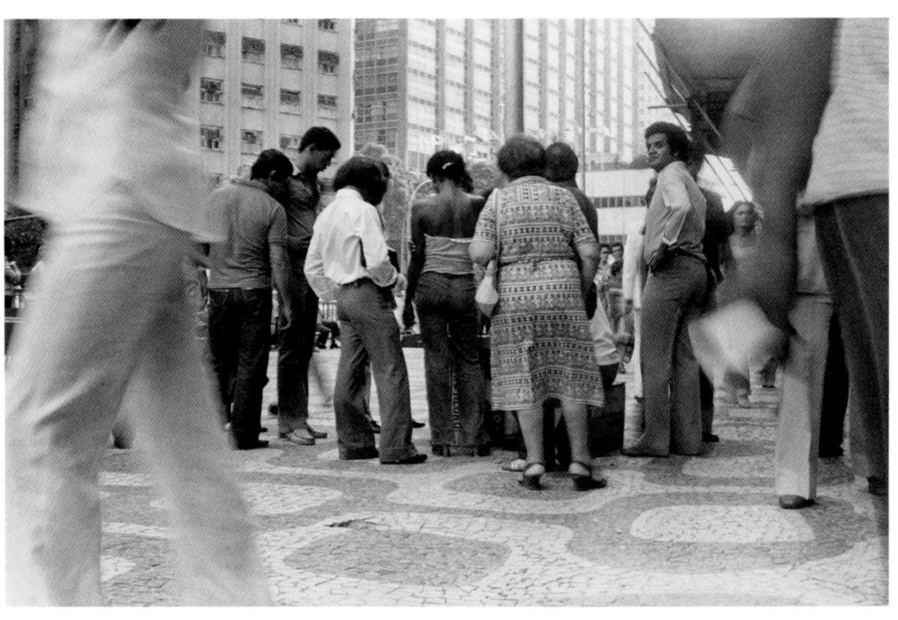

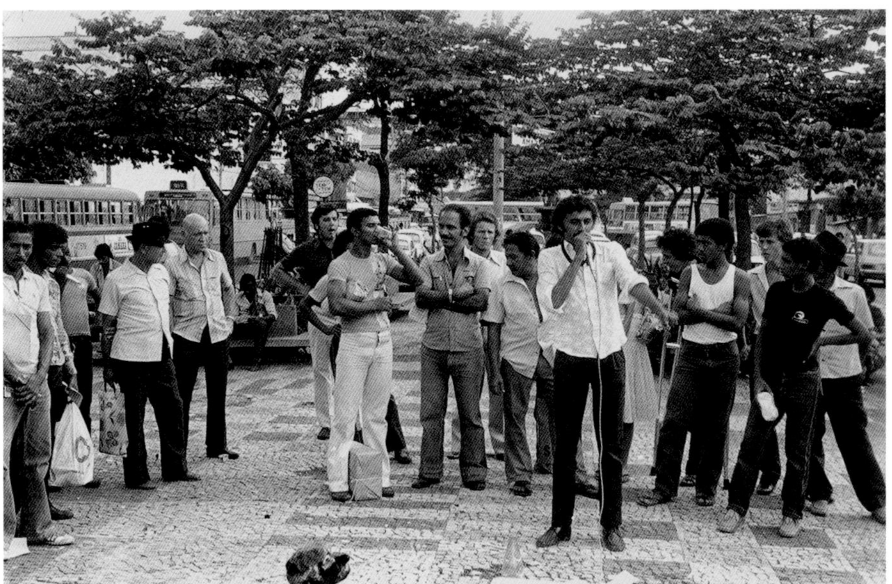

106. *Espaços imantados* (*Magnetized Spaces*), ca. 1982

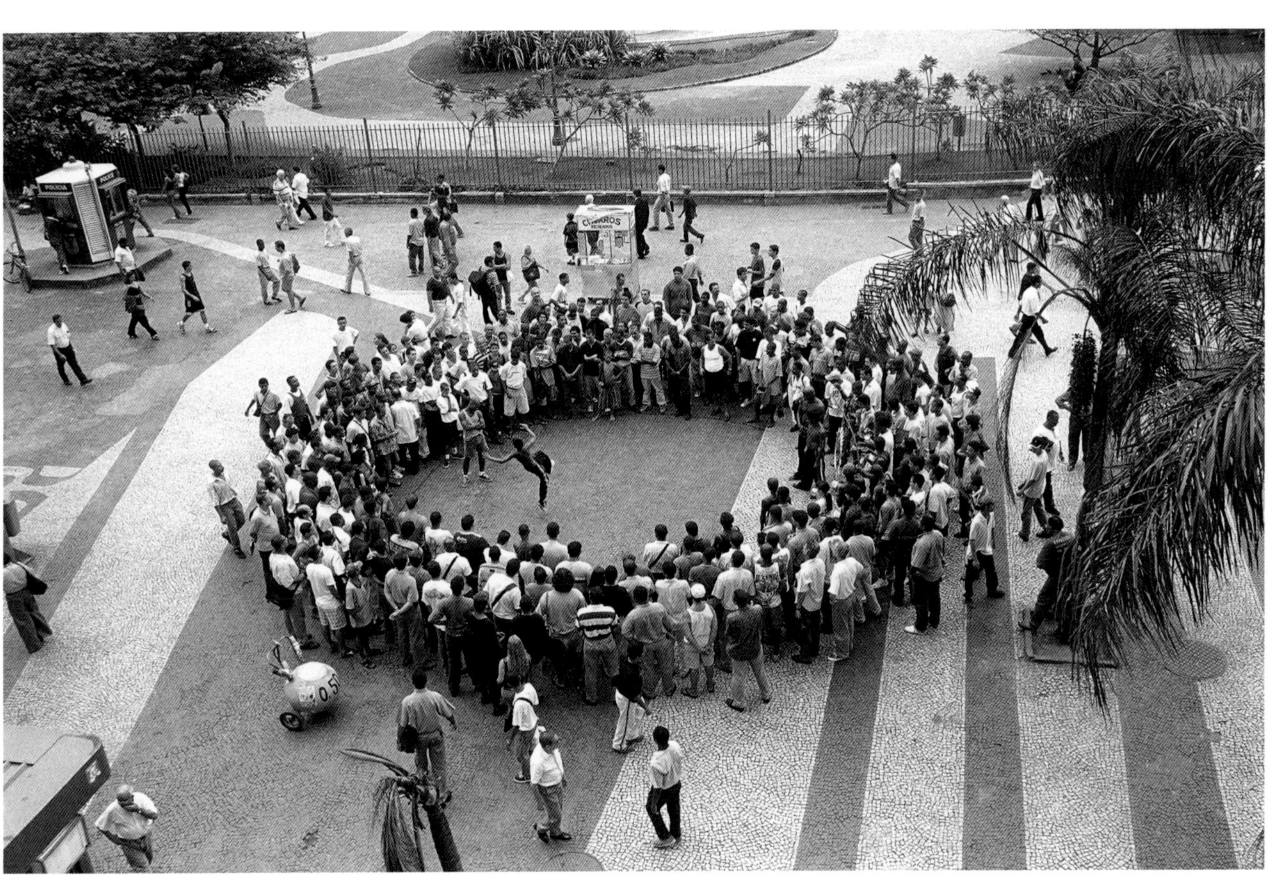

107. *Espaços imantados* (*Magnetized Spaces*), 1995

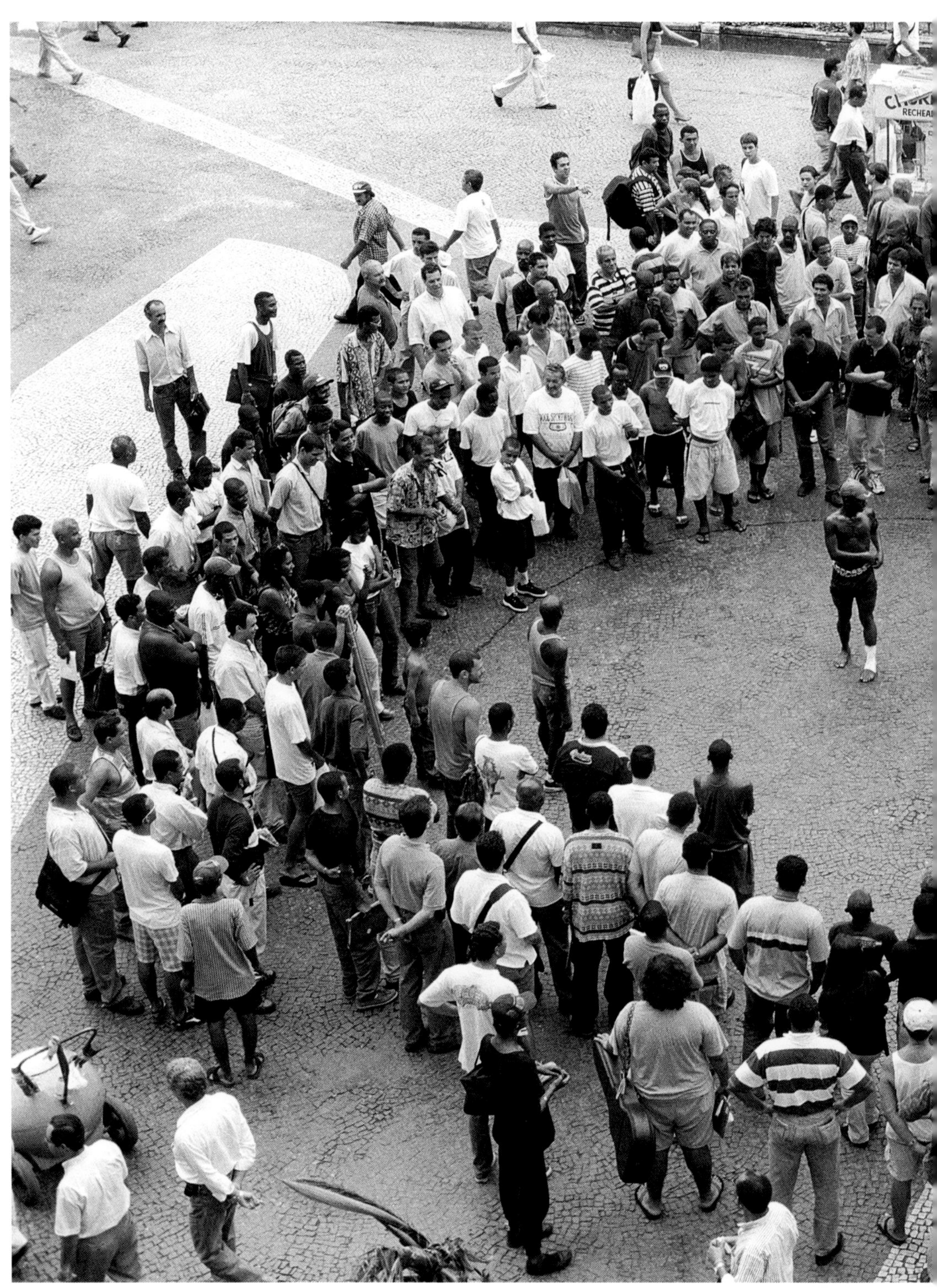

108. *Espaços imantados* (*Magnetized Spaces*), 1995

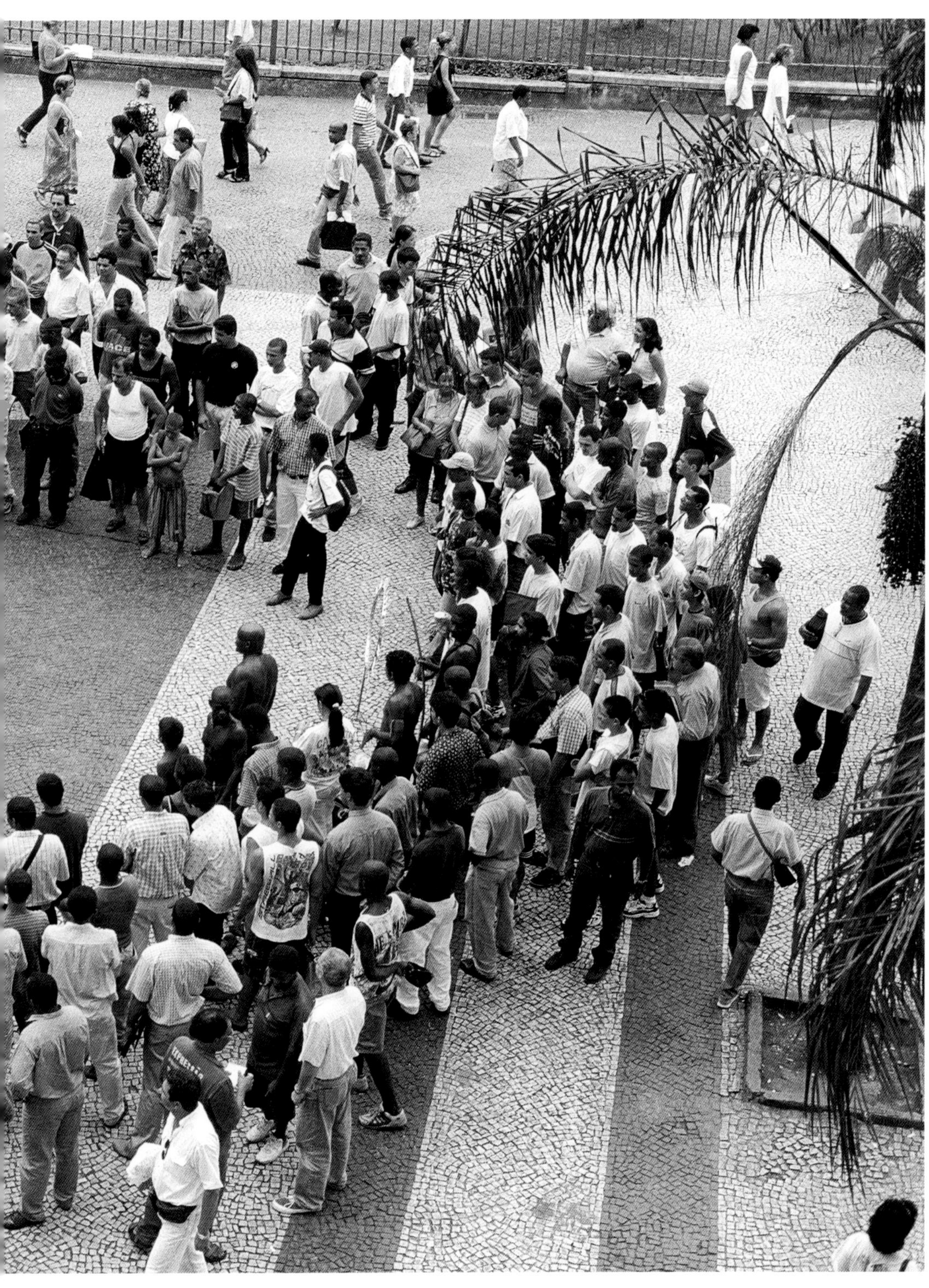

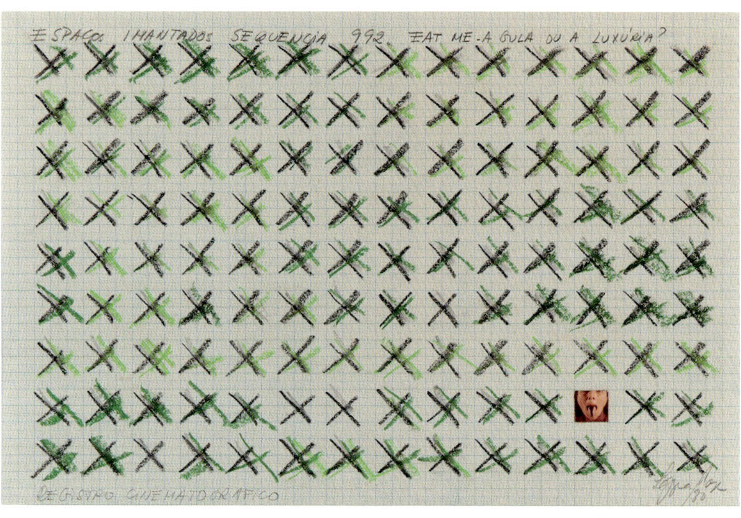

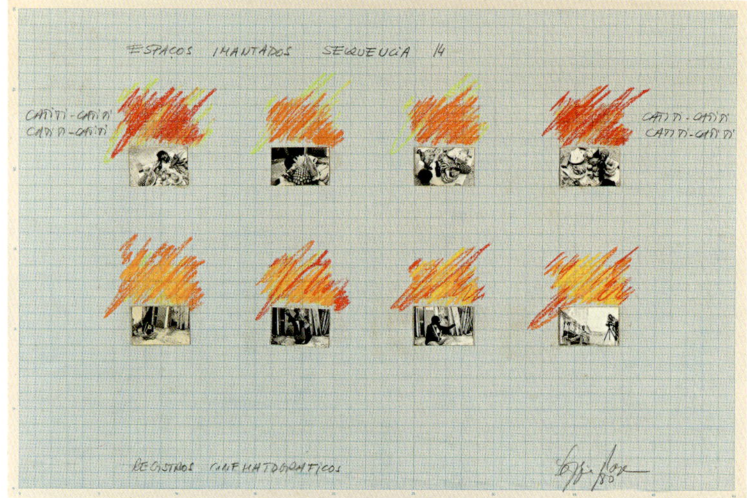

109. *Registro cinematográfico* (*Cinematic Study*), 1980

110. *Registro cinematográfico* (*Cinematic Study*), 1980

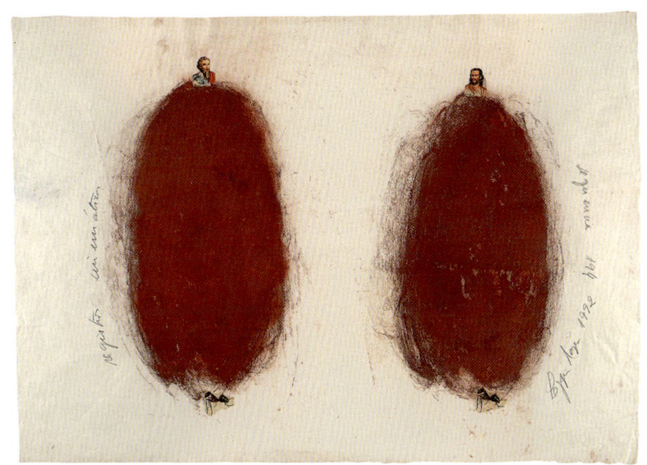

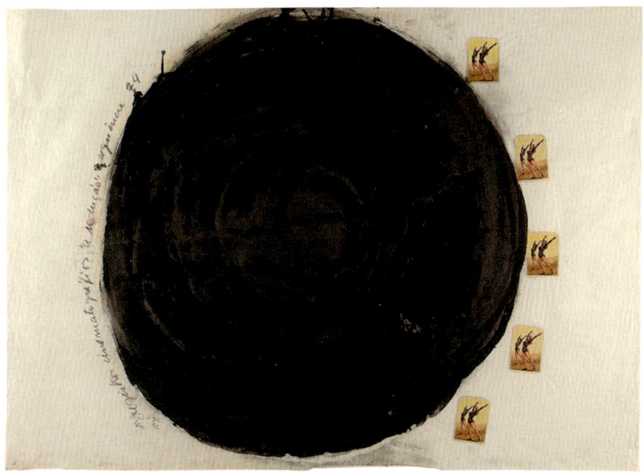

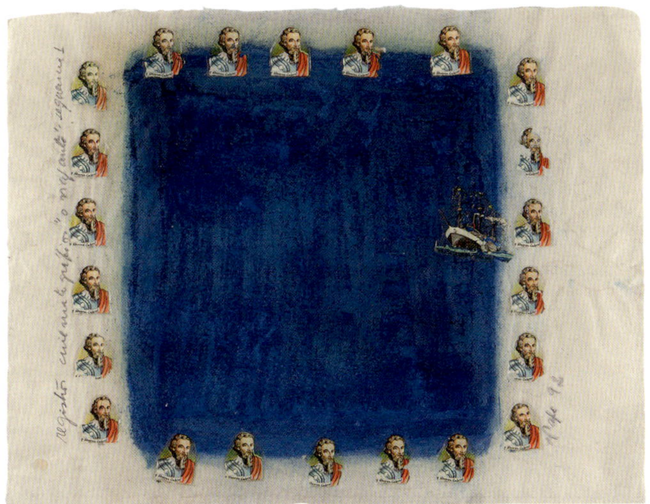

111. *Registro cinematográfico* (*Cinematic Study*), 1992

112. *Registro cinematográfico* (*Cinematic Study*), 1992

113. *Registro cinematográfico* (*Cinematic Study*), 1992

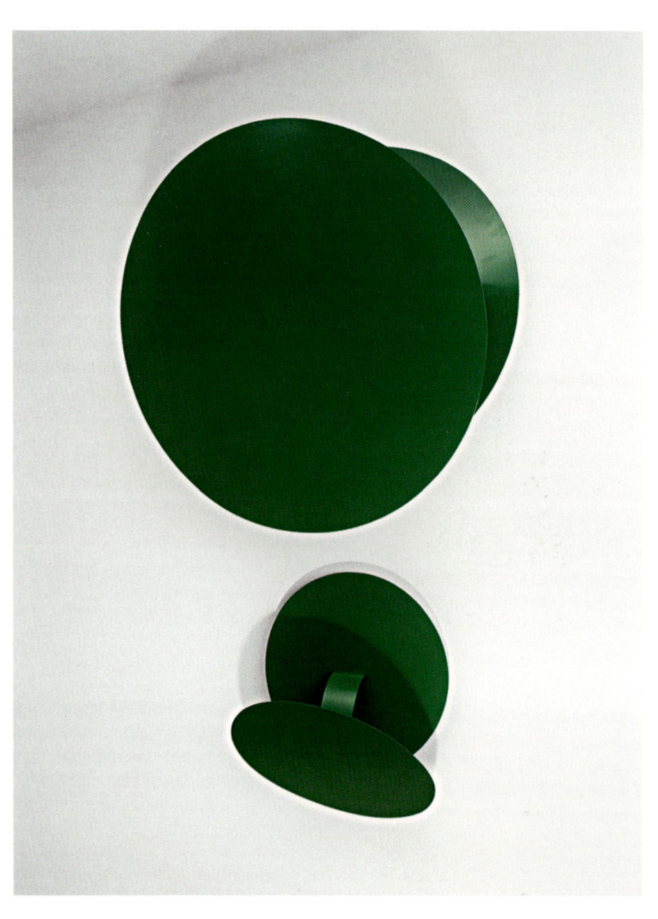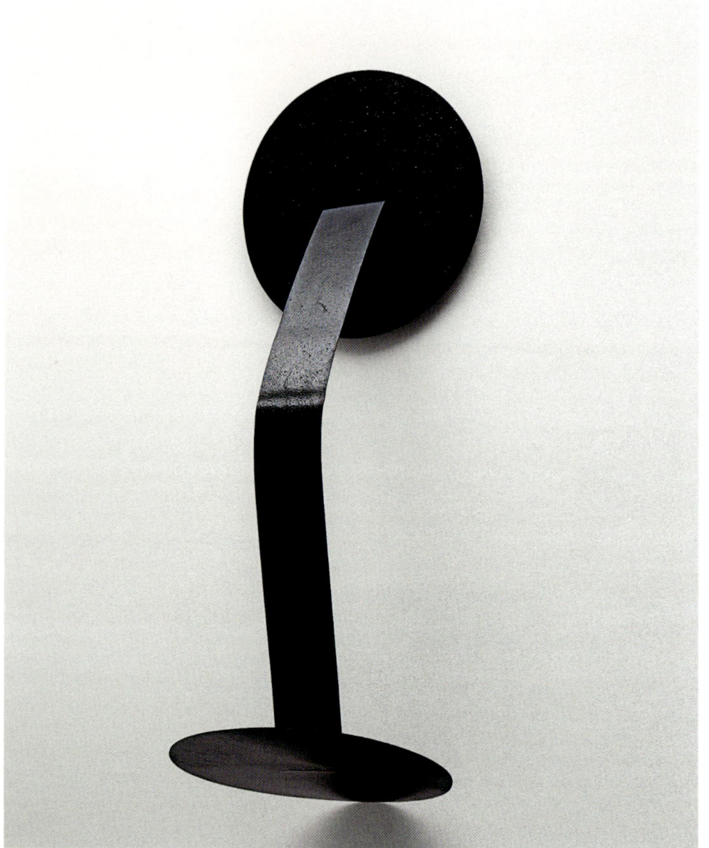

114. *Amazonino*, 1990

115. *Amazonino*, 1992

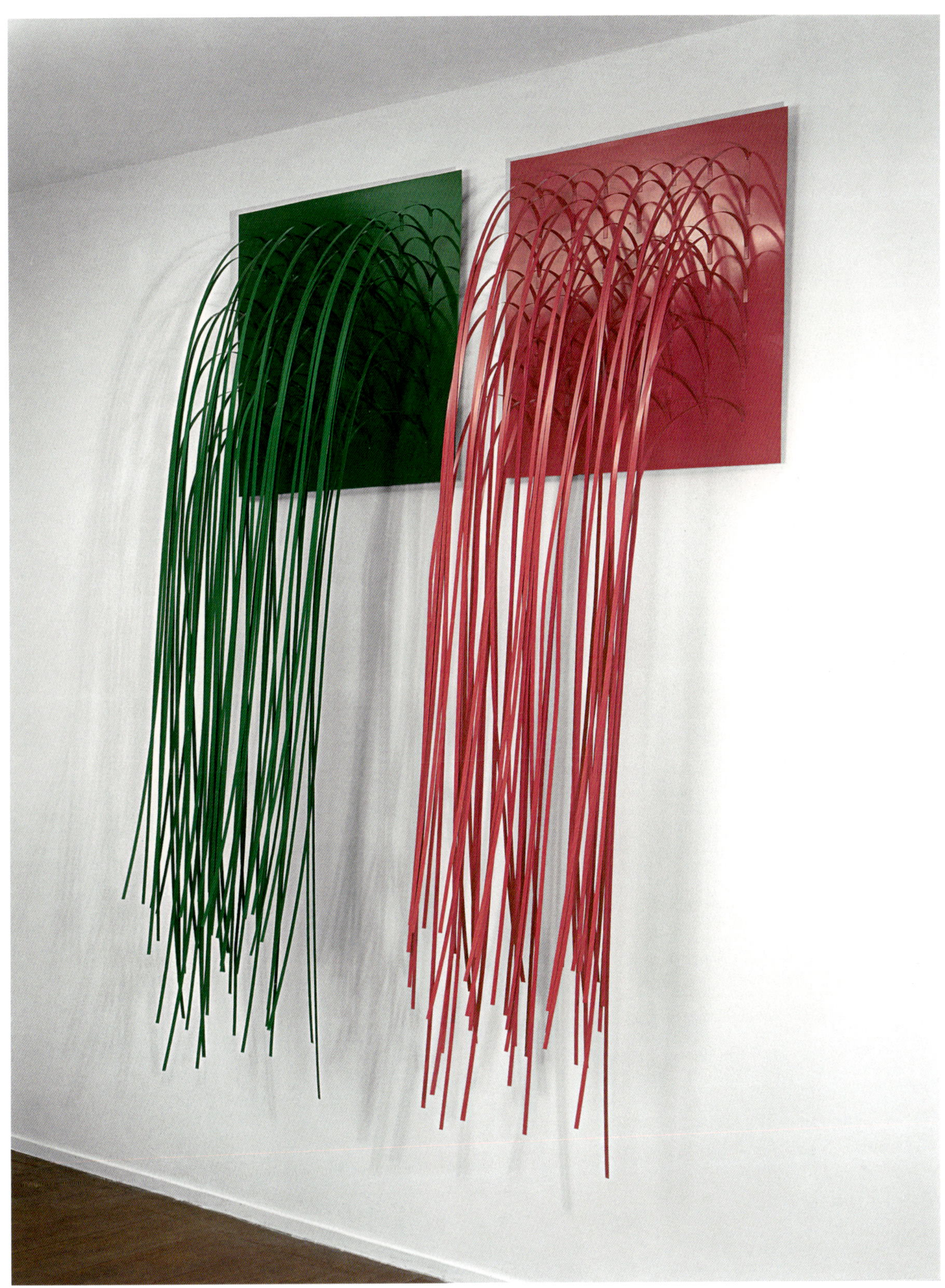

116. *Amazonino*, 1992

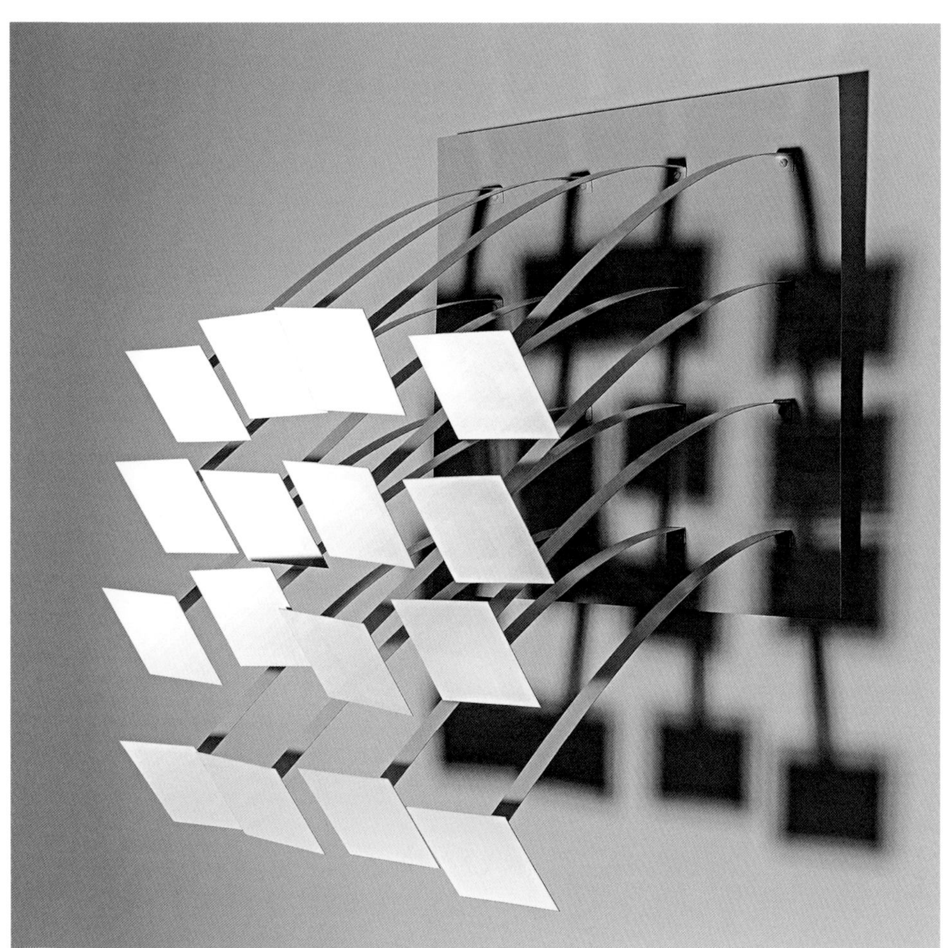

117. *Amazonino*, 1991

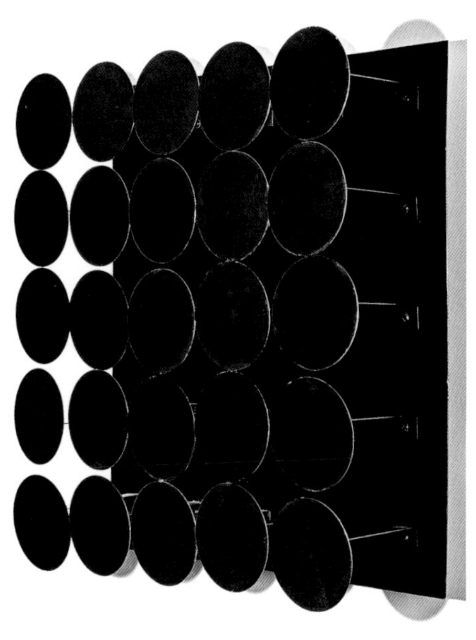 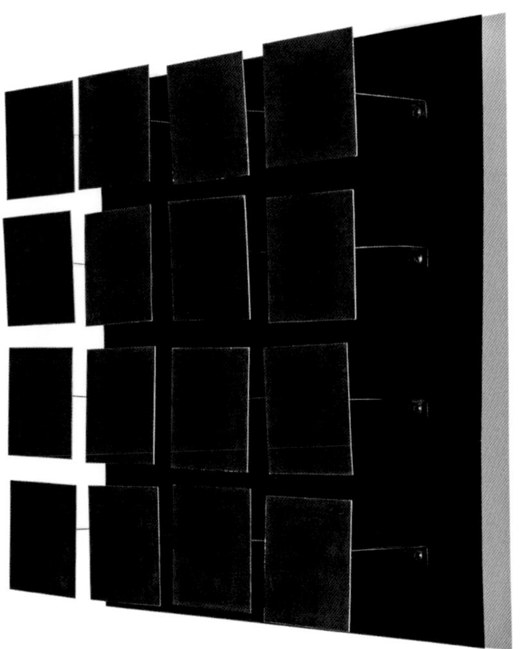

118. *Amazonino*, 1991

119. *Amazonino*, 1991

120. *Amazônia*, May 20, 1989

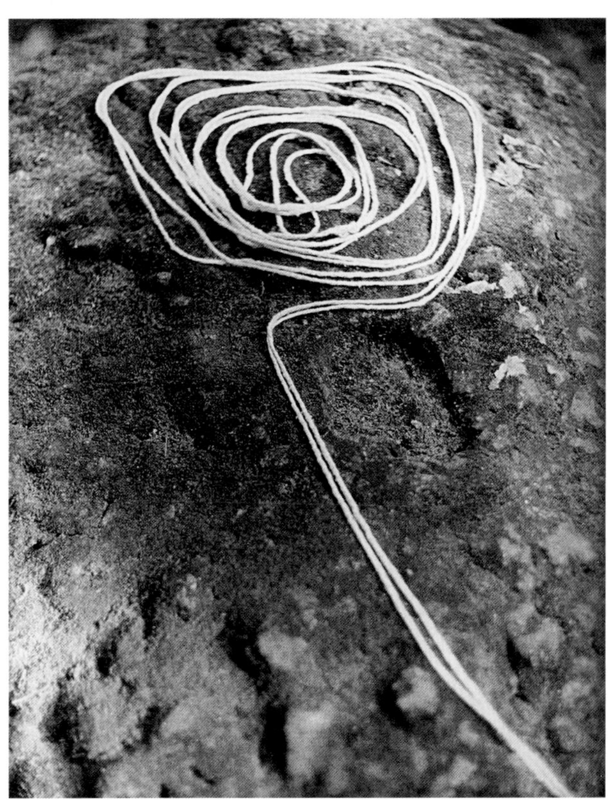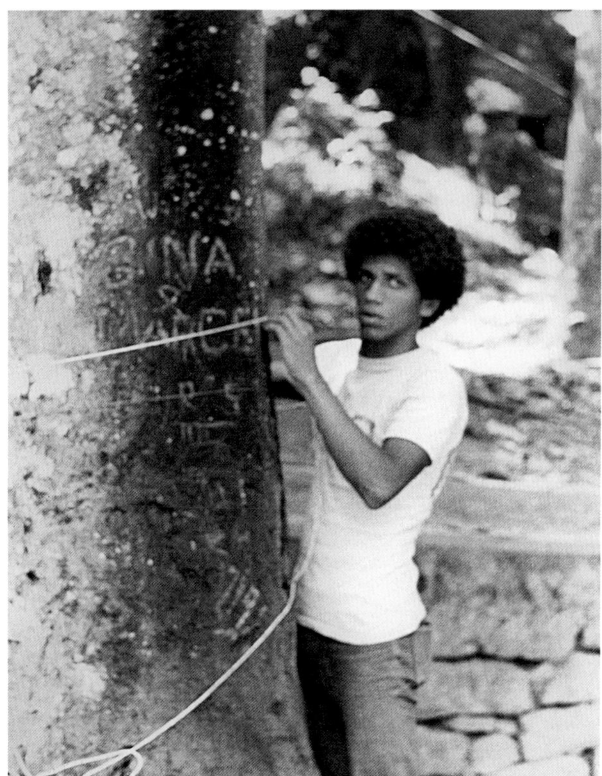

121. *Ttéia Parque Lage*, ca. 1978

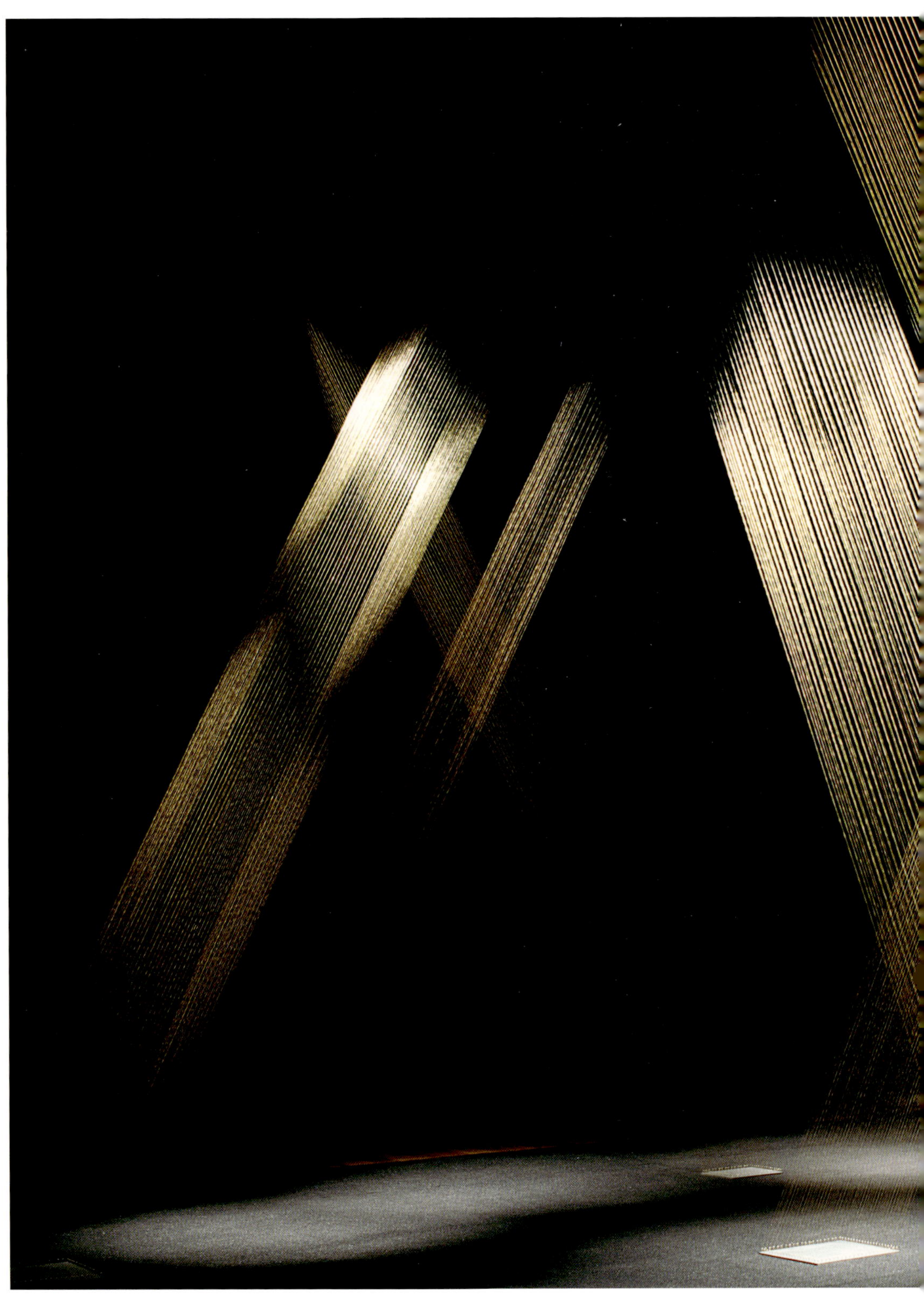

122. *Ttéia 1, C*, 1976–2004; installation view,
Pinacoteca do Estado, São Paulo, 2012

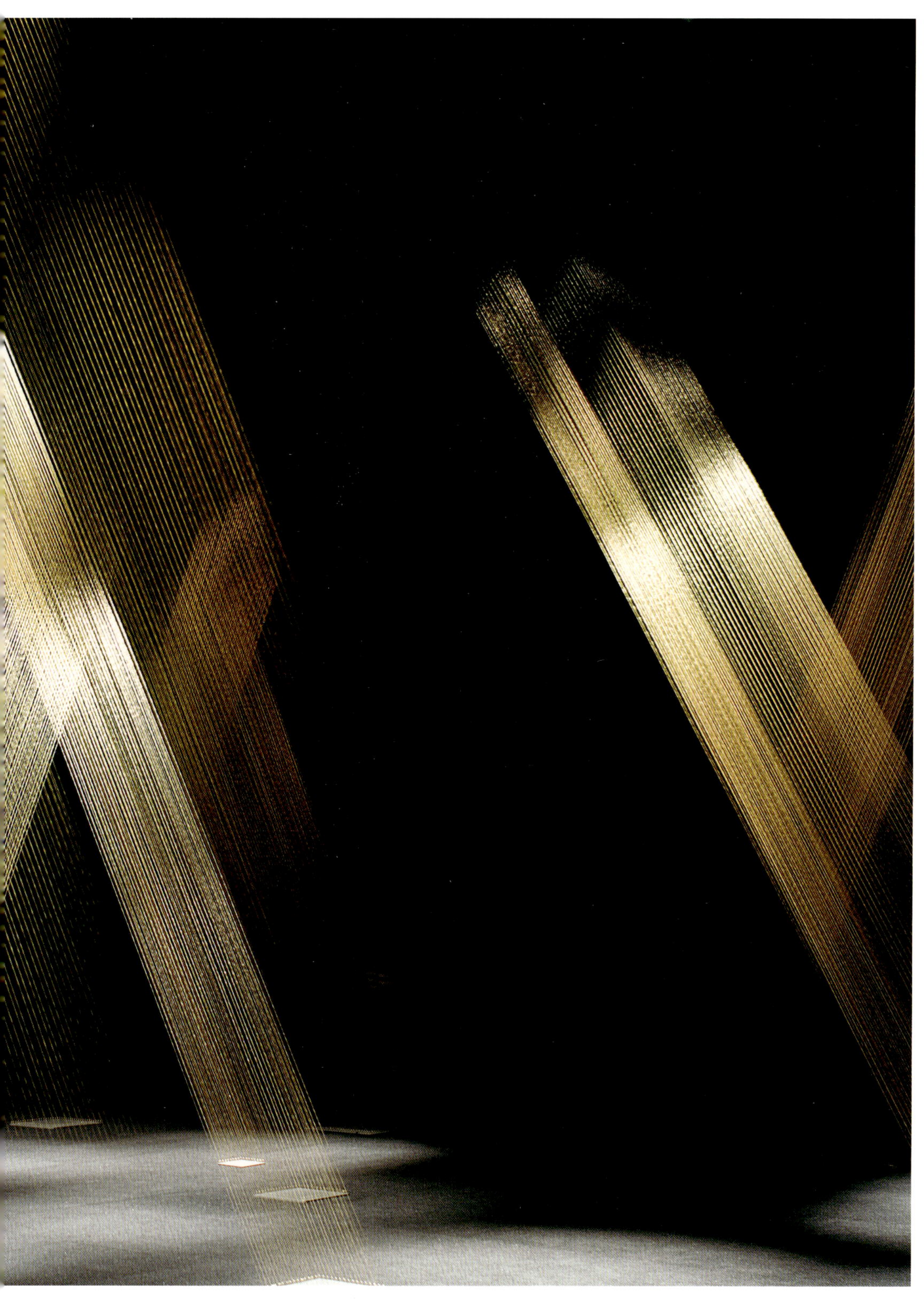

chronology

VIVIAN A. CROCKETT

This chronology features key events in Lygia Pape's artistic trajectory, along with a selection of notable moments in Brazilian political and cultural history. It is based on information provided by Projeto Lygia Pape as well as texts on Pape and additional sources acknowledged in this catalogue's selected bibliography.

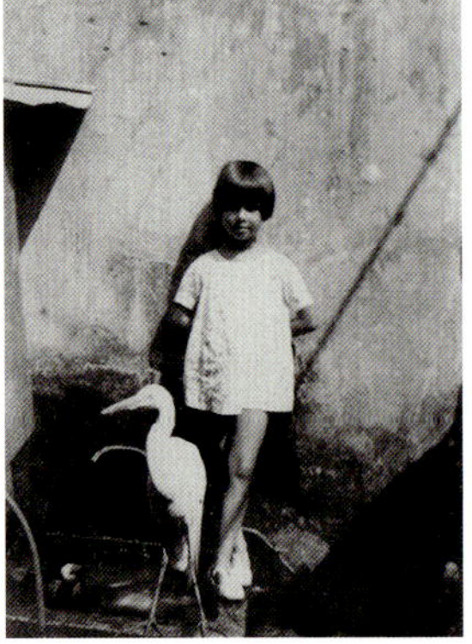

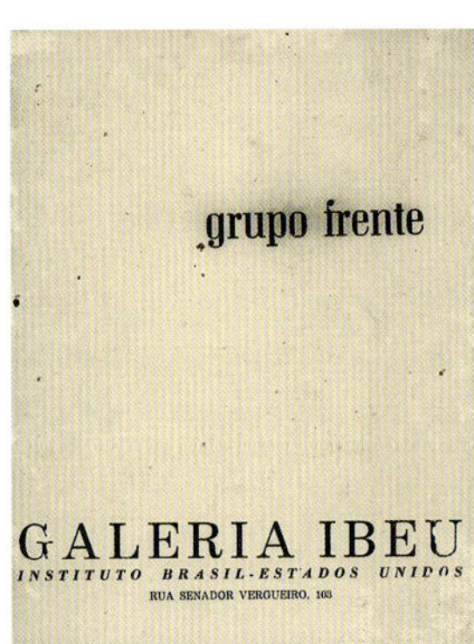

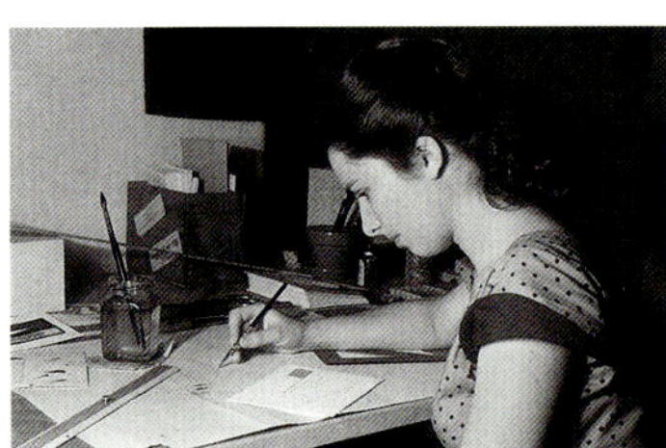

Lygia Pape at her childhood home in Rio Comprido, 1930s

Grupo Frente, Galeria IBEU (Instituto Brasil–Estados Unidos), Rio de Janeiro, 1954

Lygia Pape at work in her studio on Rua Engenheiro Alfredo Duarte, Rio de Janeiro, 1954

1927   Lygia Carvalho is born on April 7, in Nova Friburgo, in the Brazilian state of Rio de Janeiro, to parents Adhemar Carvalho and Maria José Torres de Carvalho.

1937   On November 10, Getúlio Vargas establishes the Estado Novo dictatorship, which lasts until 1945. Mário Pedrosa, among many others, goes into exile; he returns after the end of the Second World War.

1945   Brazil's first modern art gallery, Galeria Askanazy, opens in Rio de Janeiro. Galeria Domus, the first in São Paulo, opens in 1947.

1947   In October, the Museu de Arte de São Paulo (MASP) opens.

1948   Almir Mavignier, Abraham Palatnik, Ivan Serpa, and others, in dialogue with Pedrosa, form Rio de Janeiro's Concretist group.

    Museu de Arte Moderna, Rio de Janeiro (MAM-RJ) is founded. It is temporarily located at the Ministry of Education and Health (MES) building from 1952 to 1958.

    Museu de Arte Moderna, São Paulo (MAM-SP) is established with funding from Francisco "Ciccillo" Matarazzo Sobrinho.

1949   At age twenty-two, Lygia marries the chemist Günther Pape. The couple moves to Arraial do Cabo for Günther's work; there Lygia develops an interest in visual arts.

1951   Lygia and Günther move to Petrópolis, where she befriends Décio Vieira. Lygia and Vieira frequent an informal gathering of artists and regularly attend art classes at the Palácio de Cristal. She exhibits paintings and drawings at the III Exposição Anual de Pinturas in Petrópolis.

    The first Bienal de São Paulo is held at Parque Trianon from October to December.

1952   Lygia and Günther move to Rio de Janeiro. Vieira introduces Lygia to Serpa, who begins teaching art courses at MAM-RJ.

    The "Manifesto ruptura," a statement released by Grupo Ruptura, the São Paulo Concretist group, is distributed at a group show at MAM-SP in December. It is formally published in *Correio paulistano* the following month.

    Daughter Cristina is born.

1953   Begins meeting informally with a group of artists and thinkers, including Vieira, Aluísio Carvão, and João José da Silva Costa, at Serpa's residence and then regularly at the MES building.

    During this period, creates paintings and reliefs, which she calls *Jogos vetoriais* (*Vectoral Games*) and *Jogos matemáticos* (*Mathematical Games*), respectively.

    Exhibits paintings at the I Exposição Nacional de Arte Abstrata, Hotel Quitandinha, Petrópolis, and at the 3o Salão de Naturezas Mortas, where she wins the Prêmio Sul Américano.

    Participates in the II Bienal de São Paulo, inaugurated on December 12. The exhibition showcases art from the Americas, the Middle East, and Asia as well as several notable works by Alexander Calder, Paul Klee, Piet Mondrian, and Pablo Picasso.

1954   Studies printmaking with Fayga Ostrower. Around this time, she also visits with Oswaldo Goeldi at his studio at the Museu Nacional de Belas Artes, Rio de Janeiro.

    In May, the III Salão Nacional de Arte Moderna, also known as the "Salão preto e branco" ("Black-and-White Salon"), is held at MAM-RJ. Exhibiting artists are asked to submit black-and-white works in response to a new tax on imported paint. Although Pape does not exhibit work, she is among dozens of cosigners of a letter to the minister of education and culture calling for the end of restrictions on the importation of paints.

    Led by Serpa, Grupo Frente is founded in Rio de Janeiro. Early members include Pape, Carvão, Costa, and Vieira as well as Lygia Clark, Vincent Ibberson, and Carlos Val. On June 30, the 1a Exposição do Grupo Frente opens at Galeria IBEU (Instituto Brasil–Estados Unidos) in Rio de Janeiro, with accompanying catalogue text by poet and writer Ferreira Gullar.

1955   The Pape family moves to a new home in Rio de Janeiro's Jardim Botânico neighborhood, where Pape establishes an art studio.

Begins creating woodcuts, later referred to as *Tecelares*, some of which are shown at the 2a Mostra do Grupo Frente, at MAM-RJ, and at the III Bienal de São Paulo. She is awarded a Prêmio de Isenção do Juri (Jury Excellence Award) at the IV Salão Nacional de Arte Moderna, Rio de Janeiro.

In October, Juscelino Kubitschek wins the presidential election. His political platform promises "fifty years of progress in five."

1956   Attends an art course at MAM-RJ taught by Argentinian artist Tomás Maldonado.

Wins second place in the printmaking category of the Lainer Prize, MAM-SP. The title is shared with Maria Bonomi.

Exhibits works at the 3a Exposição do Grupo Frente at the Itatiaia Country Club in Resende in March and at the 4a Exposição do Grupo Frente, Companhia Siderúrgica Nacional, Volta Redonda, in June. New group members include Palatnik, Hélio Oiticica and his brother César, and Franz Weissmann. During this time, Pape and others begin gathering at Pedrosa's house.

On June 3, *Jornal do Brasil* begins publishing the *Suplemento dominical* (*Sunday Supplement*, *SDJB*) section, edited by poet Reynaldo Jardim. Gullar is the newspaper's main art critic.

On September 30, a nationwide contest is launched for the design of Brasília. Lúcio Costa's *Plano piloto* (*Pilot Plan*) is the winning design. Oscar Niemeyer leads the architectural planning for the city.

In December, members of Grupo Ruptura and Grupo Frente exhibit together at the 1a Exposição de Arte Concreta, held first at MAM-SP and later, in February of 1957, at MAM-RJ. Pape exhibits a selection of *Tecelares*.

1957   Günther and Lygia travel to Europe. They begin in England, following a *roteiro* (mapped-out trajectory) developed by Pedrosa. They then visit the Ulm School of Design in Germany before traveling through Italy, where, in Bologna, Pape meets Giorgio Morandi. She is especially influenced by the works of Paolo Uccello and Piero della Francesca. The couple also visits France, Switzerland, Belgium, Austria, Spain, and Portugal.

Wins the acquisition prize for printmaking at the VI Salão Nacional de Arte Moderna, Rio de Janeiro. In September, she exhibits *Tecelares* at the IV Bienal de São Paulo and in "Arte moderno en Brasil" ("Modern Art in Brazil"), held at the Museo Nacional de Bellas Artes, Buenos Aires. She continues work on the *Poemas-luz* (*Light-Poems*), begun in 1956, pieces of which are exhibited at the Palácio de Cristal in Petrópolis.

In December, in an article in *SDJB*, Gullar writes on Pape's *Tecelares* and includes one reproduction.

1958   On August 18, Pape's *Ballet neoconcreto I* (*Neoconcrete Ballet I*), based on Jardim's poem "Olho-Alho," premieres at the Teatro Copacabana Palace. Produced by Gilberto Motta, it is a collaboration with Jardim, with music by Gabriel Artusi and performances by professional ballet dancers from Motta's newly formed group Ballet Contemporâneo.

MAM-RJ moves to its new location at Aterro do Flamengo, in a building designed by Affonso Eduardo Reidy.

Attends courses at MAM-RJ with German graphic designer Otl Aicher, dean of the Ulm School.

Daughter Paula is born.

1959   The 1a Exposição Neoconcreta opens at MAM-RJ on March 19. On March 22, the "Manifesto neoconcreto" is published in *SDJB*. Developed by Gullar, it is signed by Gullar, Pape, Clark, Jardim, Weissmann, Amilcar de Castro, and Theon Spanúdis. In this same issue, Gullar publishes "Gravura: Depoimento de Lygia Pape" ("On Printmaking: A Statement by Lygia Pape"), in which Pape discusses the stakes of "Neoconcrete printmaking."

On April 14, Pape and Jardim present *Ballet neoconcreto II* (*Neoconcrete Ballet II*) at the Teatro da Praça (now Teatro Gláucio Gil) in Copacabana, Rio de Janeiro.

In June, seven of Pape's Concrete poems are published in *SDJB*. These, along with her *Poemas-xilogravuras* (*Poems-Woodcuts*) from 1957, are published in 1960 as the last installment of the Coleção Espaço poetry series organized by Gullar.

Works on the *Livro da criação* (*Book of Creation*), completed in 1960, which tells the story of the genesis of the world. In July, she exhibits works from the *Poema-objeto* (*Poem-Object*) series at the "Livros poemas" ("Book Poems") exhibition in the offices of the *Jornal do Brasil* in Rio de Janeiro. She also exhibits in "Brasilianische Kunst der Gegenwart" ("Brazilian Contemporary Art") at the Städtisches Museum, Leverkusen, Germany.

In December, Gullar publishes "Teoria do não-objeto" ("Theory of the Non-Object") in *SDJB*.

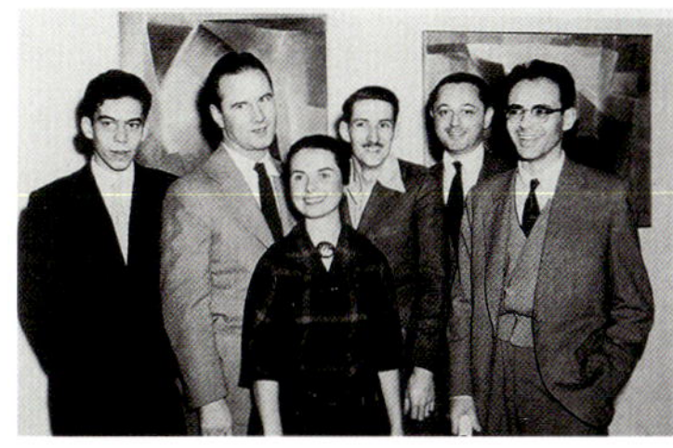

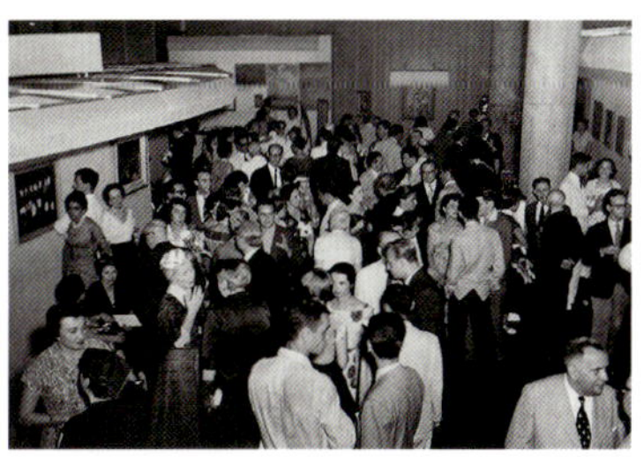

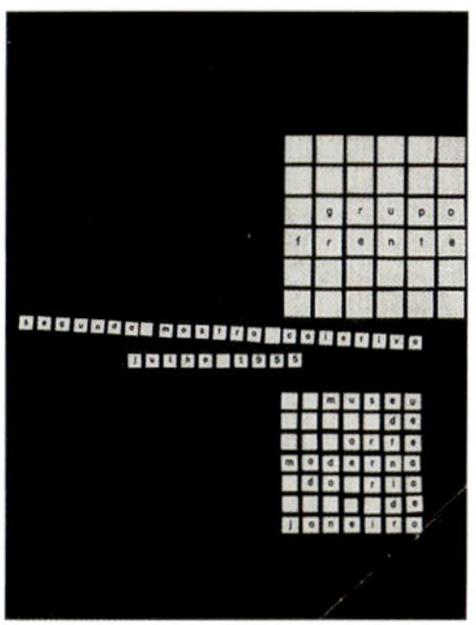

César Oiticica, Vincent Ibberson, Lygia Pape, Ivan Serpa, Eric Baruch, and Abraham Palatnik, 1954

Lygia Pape and Aluísio Carvão at the opening of "Exposição permanente" at the Museu de Arte Moderna, Rio de Janeiro, January 12, 1955. Archives of Museu de Arte Moderna, Rio de Janeiro

Grupo Frente: Segunda mostra coletiva, Museu de Arte Moderna, Rio de Janeiro, 1955

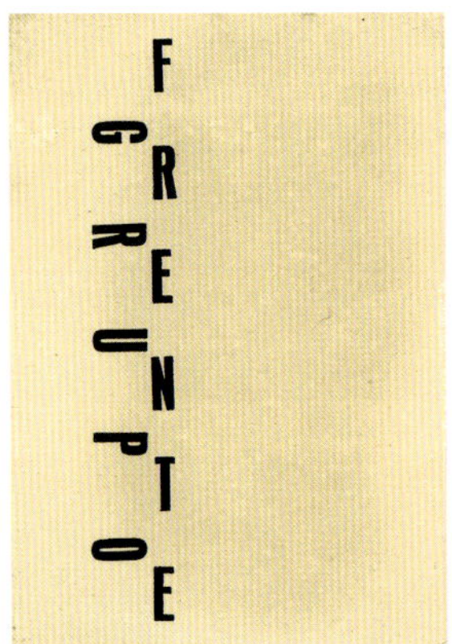

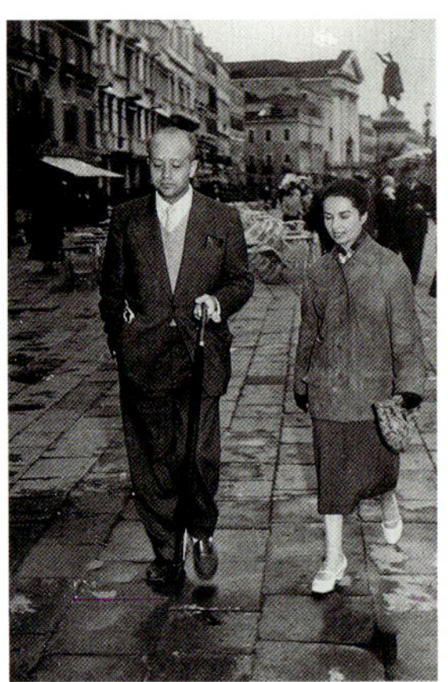

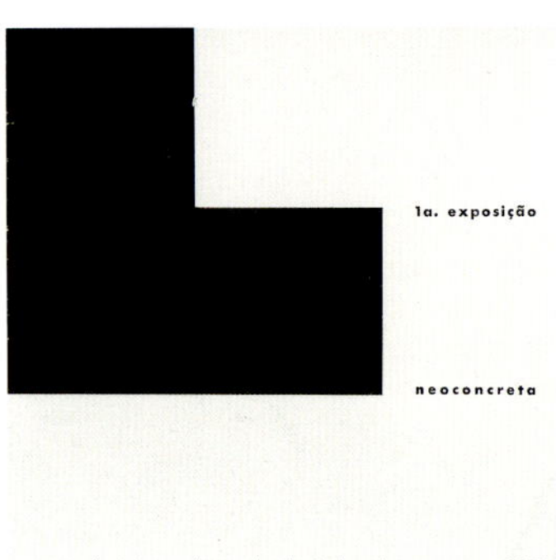

Grupo Frente, Itatiaia Country Club, Resende, Rio de Janeiro, 1956

Günther and Lygia Pape in Venice, 1957

1a Exposição neoconcreta, Museu de Arte Moderna, Rio de Janeiro, 1959

1960 Brasília is inaugurated on April 20 and 21.

In June, Pape is included in Max Bill's global survey of Concrete art, "Konkrete Kunst: 50 Jahre Entwicklung" ("Concrete Art: 50 Years of Development"), at Helmhaus Zürich, Switzerland. In November, she exhibits in the 2a Exposição Neoconcreta at the Ministry of Education, Rio de Janeiro (MEC, formerly MES).

Finishes the *Livro da arquitetura* (*Book of Architecture*).

Begins new ventures in both graphic design and experimental film, creating two shorts: *O asilo* (*The Asylum*) and *A gula* (*Greed*). She begins visual branding for Piraquê, with which she will work until 1992, creating logotypes and packaging for a range of food products.

1961 Begins work for Queen Cosmetics, creating logos, product packaging, and additional visual branding.

Creates the poster, title art, and additional graphics for Nelson Pereira dos Santos's film *Mandacaru vermelho* (*Red Mandacaru*), marking the beginning of collaborations with various Cinema Novo filmmakers throughout the 1960s, which include graphic work for Santos's *Vidas secas* (*Barren Lives*, 1963) and Glauber Rocha's *Deus e o diabo na terra do sol* (*Black God, White Devil*, 1964).

Works on the *Livro do tempo* (*Book of Time*), scheduled to be shown at the third and final Exposição Neoconcreta at MAM-SP in April. Consisting of 365 wood units, it is finally completed in 1963.

1963 Pape is commissioned to create the opening credits for MAM-RJ's Cinemateca program at Cine Paissandu.

1964 On March 31, President João Goulart is deposed by a military coup d'etat, with support from the United States. Pascoal Ranieri Mazzilli is the provisional president until General Castelo Branco establishes a dictatorial regime that rules until 1985.

1966 Begins graphic design work for film companies and, in 1967, for the International Monetary Fund and the Rio de Janeiro Stock Exchange. She works with Santos on two additional films, creating special effects for *O Rio de Machado de Assis* (*Machado de Assis's Rio*) and title art for *Cruzada ABC* (*Crusade ABC*).

Is named a jury member for the Festival de Cinema do Jornal do Brasil.

1967 In April, "Nova objetividade brasileira" ("New Brazilian Objectivity") opens at MAM-RJ. Pape is part of the assembly team, along with Oiticica (one of the event's organizers), Clark, and others. She shows *Caixa das baratas* (*Box of Cockroaches*) and *Caixa das formigas* (*Box of Ants*).

On June 1, the seminar "Declaração de princípios básicos da vanguarda" ("Declaration of Basic Principles of the Avant-Garde") is held at the Escola de Belas Artes, Universidade Federal do Rio de Janeiro (UFRJ). It is preceded by the publishing of a manifesto of the same name signed by various artists, including Pape, Clark, Oiticica, Antonio Dias, Rubens Gerchman, Anna Maria Maiolino, and Frederico Morais, in the *Jornal do comércio*.

In September, remaining construction is completed at MAM-RJ with the official inauguration of the Bloco de Exposições (Exhibition Block).

Enters a film competition during Expo 67 in Montreal, Canada, with the experimental film *La nouvelle création* (*The New Creation*) and wins the acquisition prize.

Begins work on *Divisor* (*Divider*), which she plans to show in an all-white gallery space. She cannot secure sufficient funds and instead makes a thirty-by-thirty-meter white sheet. She brings *Divisor* to a group of children in a nearby favela, Chácara do Cabeça, and realizes the work's first official activation, documented in photographs and a short Super 8 film.

Conceives the propositions *O ovo* (*The Egg*) and *Roda dos prazeres* (*Wheel of Pleasures*) with performances on Barra da Tijuca beach. Also conceived this year, *Trio do embalo maluco* (*Crazy Rocking Trio*) is performed at a quarry near Pape's home.

1968 Student protests ignite across the country following the death of sixteen-year-old student Édson Luis de Lima Souto by military police in Rio de Janeiro on March 28.

In April, exhibits in "O artista brasileiro e a iconografia de massa" ("The Brazilian Artist and Mass Iconography") at the Escola Superior de Desenho Industrial (ESDI), Rio de Janeiro.

On June 10, Rogério Duarte and Oiticica organize a roundtable "Amostragem da cultura-loucura brasileira" ("Sampling of Brazilian Culture Madness") at MAM-RJ, where Pape presents "Da loucura e da cultura" ("On Madness and On Culture"). She later appears in Antonio Manuel's film about the event, *Loucura e cultura* (*Madness and Culture*), released in 1973.

On June 26, takes part in the historic March of the One Hundred Thousand in Rio de Janeiro, mobilized in response to increasing police repression at student protests and as a general critique of the military dictatorship.

On August 4, Duarte and Oiticica organize the event "Apocalipopótese" ("Apocalypopothesis") at Aterro do Flamengo as part of Morais's "Arte no Aterro—Um mês de arte pública" ("Art at the Aterro—One Month of Public Art"). Oiticica and two Mangueira dancers, Nildo da Mangueira and Santa Teresa, emerge from Pape's red, white, and blue "eggs" and perform as the "trio do embalo maluco."

Maurício Cirne photographs Pape's housekeeper, "Mineiro," with *Roda dos prazeres* at the farm-turned-studio rented by Pape, Jackson Ribeiro, and others at Vargem Grande, Rio de Janeiro.

At different points in the year, presentations of *O ovo*, *Divisor*, and *Roda dos prazeres* are organized at the gardens of MAM-RJ.

From mid-November to December, substitutes for Morais as art critic for the visual arts column of *Diário de notícias*.

On December 13, as part of a series of Atos Institucionais (Institutional Acts, AI) that the military government started decreeing in 1965, AI-5 is enacted, eliminating all constitutional rights and resulting in increased political repression and the temporary closure of the National Congress.

1969   Begins traveling through Latin America, visiting Guatemala, Panama, El Salvador, Nicaragua, Mexico, and Peru. She is especially interested in the study of indigenous cultures.

Begins teaching courses in the Departamento de Artes Plásticas at MAM-RJ.

Works by Brazilian artists selected for the VII Biennale de Paris are first shown in an exhibition at MAM-RJ. The show is shut down by the military, and the Brazilian delegation is eventually banned from presenting in Paris.

On June 16, at an assembly held at the Musée National d'Art Moderne, Paris, a document titled "Non à la biennale" ("No to the Biennale") circulates that discusses cultural repression in Brazil. An international boycott of the X Bienal de São Paulo is organized.

In September, AI-14 calls for the death penalty or life imprisonment for government dissenters.

1970   Records a series of conversations with Pedrosa, which she edits into a nine-minute documentary, *Opção brasileira* (*The Brazilian Option*), named after Pedrosa's 1966 book.

Pedrosa and six others are indicted for slandering the military government. In July, a warrant for his arrest is ordered, and Pedrosa requests asylum from the Chilean government.

Hélio Oiticica receives notice that he has been awarded a Guggenheim Fellowship on July 20 and moves to New York in December. He returns to Brazil in 1978.

On August 23, participates in *ORGRAMURBANA*, a happening organized by Luís Otávio Pimentel and Flammarion in the gardens of MAM-RJ. She presents *Trilhas de fogo* (*Fire Trails*), in which cans of gasoline arranged in the shape of an "M" are set on fire in honor of Pedrosa.

1971   In January, participates in the first session of Morais's "Domingos da criação" ("Sundays of Creation"), which occur at MAM-RJ on the last Sunday of every month from January to July. Each iteration is led by a different artist and encourages the general public to engage a different material (paper, thread, fabric, earth, sound, and the body). For "O domingo de papel" ("Paper Sunday"), Pape creates a "swimming pool of paper."

Revives three works from 1968 at her farm-studio in Vargem Grande: *O homem e sua bainha* (*Man and His Sheath*), *Espaços imantados* (*Magnetized Spaces*), and *Linga apunhalada* (*Stabbed Tongue*).

Creates three ten-minute shorts: *A matemática e o futebol* (*Math and Soccer*), *The Super*, and *O guarda-chuva vermelho* (*The Red Umbrella*), an experimental documentary about Goeldi, with voiceovers by Oiticica and the poet Manuel Bandeira.

Artist Anna Bella Geiger invites Pape and Antonio Manuel to teach an experimental course, "Atividade-criatividade" ("Activity-Creativity"), as part of MAM-RJ's Integração Cultural (Cultural Integration) program.

1972   Receives a bachelor's degree in philosophy from the Instituto de Filosofia e Ciências Sociais, UFRJ.

Begins teaching at the Centro de Arquitetura e Artes, Universidade Santa Úrsula, Rio de Janeiro (USU), where she works until 1985. Her courses include "Metodologia Visual" ("Visual Methodology") and "Semiótica de Espaço" ("Semiotics of Space"). She employs alternative pedagogical strategies to expose students to the city's unfamiliar spaces, including the Favela da Maré.

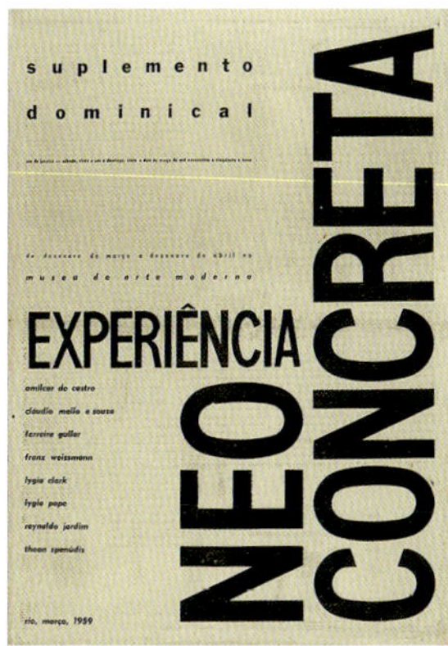

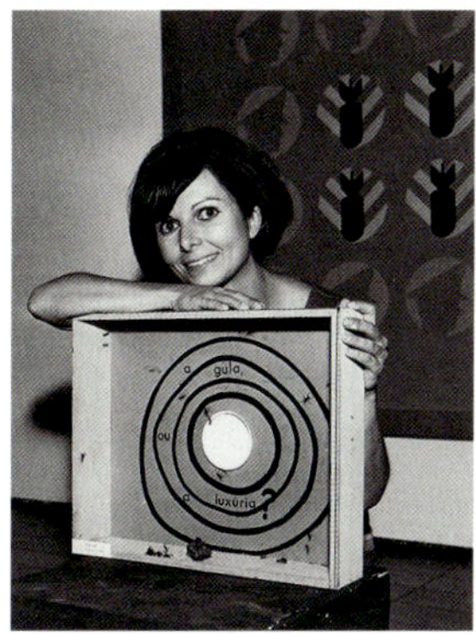

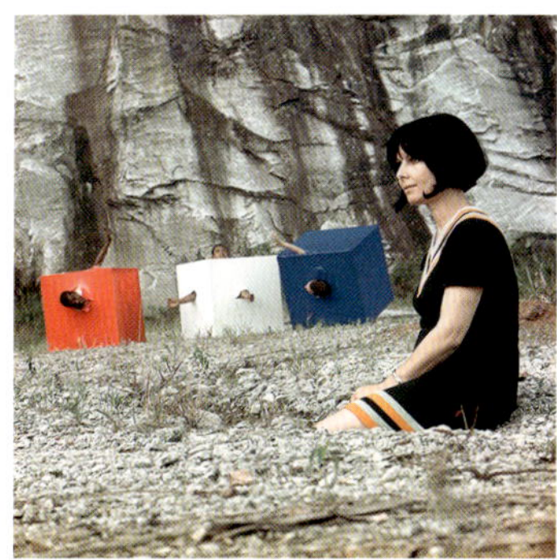

"Experiência neoconcreta," *Suplemento dominical, Jornal do Brasil*, Rio de Janeiro, March 22, 1959

Lygia Pape with *Caixa das formigas* at "Nova objetividade brasileira," Museu de Arte Moderna, Rio de Janeiro, 1967

Lygia Pape with *Trio do embalo maluco* at a quarry near the artist's home, Rio de Janeiro, 1967

Shoots *Favela da Maré*, a Super 8 film, to capture the experience of moving through the favela's shelters, boardwalks, and boats.

1973   Teaches art seminars at various universities as part of an educational initiative by the secretary of education and culture, Rio de Janeiro.

Sometime in late February, is imprisoned and disappears for more than ten days before being located by her daughter Cristina and Manuel.

According to her own later account, is first taken to the Center for Internal Defense Operations (DOI-CODI), where she spends a month in solitary confinement before being transferred to the Vila Militar, Rio de Janeiro. Under pressure from Günther, she is eventually tried and acquitted, 4–3. The government unsuccessfully tries to pressure the dean of USU, Madre Maria Beatriz Viana, to fire Pape.

In June, presents films and projections at "Expo-Projeção 73," an exhibition of experimental cinema organized by Aracy Amaral at Espaço GRIFE (Grupo de Realizadores Independentes de Filmes Experimentais), São Paulo. In addition to *I INGUageM* and *Ivan o terrível* (*Ivan the Terrible*), she shows *Wampirou*, starring Manuel as the vampire as well as herself, Clark, Ribeiro, and the poet Waly Salomão. Manuel shows his *Loucura e cultura* and *New life-geleia real* (*New Life-Royal Jelly*), starring Pape and her daughter Cristina.

1974   Exhibits the installation *WANTED* at the Centro de Arte y Comunicación, Buenos Aires.

Completes *Our Parents "Fossilis," Arenas calientes* (*Hot Sands*), *Carnival in Rio*, and *Sedução I e II* (*Seduction I and II*).

1975   Has a solo show of prints from the Neoconcrete era, "40 gravuras neoconcretas" ("40 Neoconcrete Prints"), at Galeria da Maison de France, Rio de Janeiro.

Shows a new work, *Faca de luz* (*Knife Light*), at USU.

Completes additional films, including *A mão do povo* (*The Hand of the People*) and *Eat Me*.

Wins a scholarship for her research project "Espaços poéticos: Uma arquitetura do precário" ("Poetic Spaces: An Architecture of the Precarious"). She continues her photographic documentation of the Favela da Maré during ongoing visits with students.

1976   Her multimedia installation *Eat Me: A gula ou a luxúria?* (*Eat Me: Gluttony or Lust?*) opens first at Galeria Arte Global, São Paulo, as part of the exhibition "Lygia Pape: Obras," and then at MAM-RJ as part of the exhibition "Eat Me: A gula ou a luxúria?" Along with a large exhibition space dedicated to her installation, the MAM-RJ presentation also features an adjoining exhibition titled "Espaço: Comentário" ("Space: Commentary") of works by Pape's students, in which seminars take place.

Resumes her exploration of activated public spaces with the film *Feira de campina: Espaços imantados* (*Campina Fair: Magnetized Spaces*).

1977   In July, contributes to Amaral's "Projeto construtivo brasileiro na arte (1950–1962)" ("Brazilian Constructivist Project in Art [1950–1962]") at MAM-RJ and Pinacoteca do Estado, São Paulo, curating the Neoconcrete portion of the exhibition. With assistants, she supervises the restoration of Neoconcrete works for the show.

Wins a research fellowship from the Fundação Nacional de Arte (FUNARTE) to develop the project "A mulher na iconografia de massa" ("Woman in Mass Iconography").

Pedrosa returns to Brazil in October 1977 after the revocation of his arrest orders.

Pape and Pedrosa begin planning the exhibition "Alegria de viver, alegria de criar" ("Joy of Living, Joy of Creating"), to be shown at MAM-RJ and then in São Paulo. In preparation, Pape and Pedrosa take frequent trips to the Museu Nacional da Quinta da Boa Vista, UFRJ, which houses a collection of ethnographic and indigenous art. The organization of the exhibition is canceled following a devastating fire at MAM-RJ on July 8, 1978, which destroys ninety percent of the museum's collection. No pieces for the exhibition are damaged because they have not yet arrived in the building.

1978   As part of her "Espaços poéticos" ("Poetic Spaces") course at the Escola de Artes Visuais, Parque Lage, Rio de Janeiro, taught between 1978 and 1979, creates *Ttéias-Redes* with her students, the first public manifestation of her *Ttéias*, which are first conceived in 1976.

Creates the film *Catiti-Catiti*, the content of which references Oswald de Andrade's 1928 "Manifesto antropófago" ("Cannibalist Manifesto"). Via its montage strategies, the film enacts a joining of diverse cultural references.

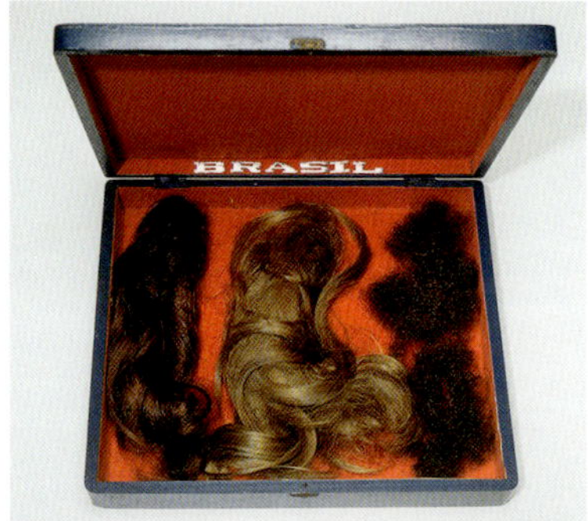

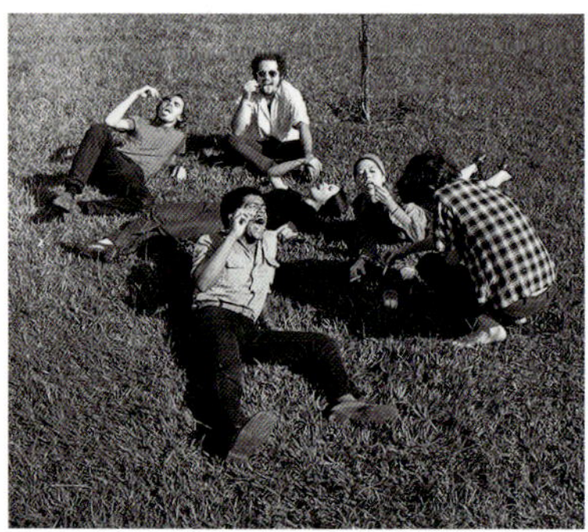

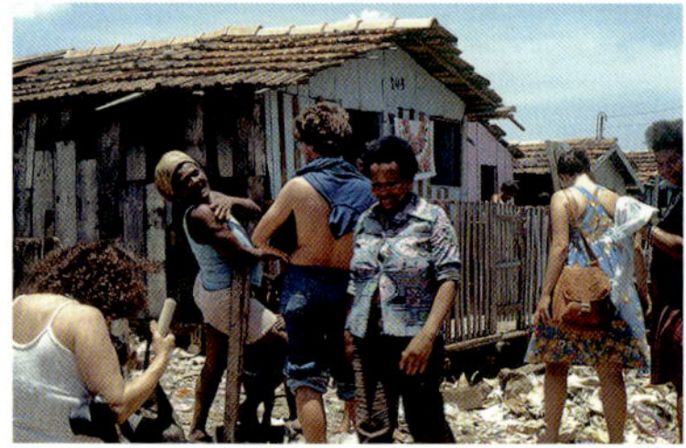

Caixa Brasil (*Brazil Box*), 1968. Projeto Lygia Pape

Lygia Pape leading *Roda dos prazeres* at Museu de Arte Moderna, Rio de Janeiro, 1968

Lygia Pape filming with students at Favela da Maré, Rio de Janeiro, 1972

Creates a thirty-minute documentary about Pedrosa's involvement with Brazil's Workers' Party, or Partido dos Trabalhadores (PT), titled *Mário Pedrosa: PT saudações* (*Mário Pedrosa: PT Greetings*).

As a challenge to the first and only Bienal Latino-Americana at Parque Ibirapuera, São Paulo, whose theme is "Mitos e magias" ("Myths and Magic"), Ivald Granato organizes the happening *Mitos vadios* (*Vagrant Myths*) on November 12 in an empty parking lot on Rua Augusta, São Paulo. Among those involved are Pape, Oiticica, Artur Barrio, Antonio Dias, Rubens Gerchman, Anna Maria Maiolino, and the collective Viajou sem Passaporte.

On December 31, AI-5 is revoked. Political exiles gradually return to Brazil.

1979   Attends a course taught by Umberto Eco, "The Problems of Visual Semiotics and the Modes of Sign Production," at USU.

At Galeria Café das Artes, Hotel Meridien, Rio de Janeiro, presents the installation *Gávea de tocaia* (*Topsail Ambushed*), where she exhibits *Ovos do vento* (*Wind Eggs*), also known as *Windbow*, alongside Oiticica's *Rijanviera PN27*.

1980   Oiticica dies on March 30, following a stroke.

In April, participates in the exhibition "Homenagem a Mário Pedrosa" ("Homage to Mário Pedrosa") at Galeria Jean Boghici, Rio de Janeiro.

Eat Me is included in "Quasi cinema: Vídeo tapes e film d'artisti in Brasile, 70/80" ("Almost Cinema: Artists' Films and Videotapes in Brazil, 70/80"), curated by the Brazilian artist Antonio Dias and the art critic Ligia Canongia, at Centro Internazionale di Brera, Milan.

In July, receives a master's degree from the Instituto de Filosofia e Ciências Sociais, UFRJ. Her master's thesis, "Catiti-Catiti, na terra dos Brasis" ("Catiti-Catiti, in the Land of the Brasis"), theorizes past and current states of art practices in Brazil and abroad.

Becomes the head of the Departamento de Análise e Representação da Forma at USU, a role she holds until 1985.

Receives a Guggenheim Fellowship for the research project "Indigenous Architecture and Favelas of Brazil."

1981   Teaches fine art courses at the Escola de Belas Artes, UFRJ.

Oiticica's brothers, César and Cláudio, establish the Projeto Hélio Oiticica in Rio de Janeiro. Pape joins the council.

Departs for New York for the Guggenheim Fellowship, returning in 1982.

Pedrosa dies on November 5.

1982   Curates the event "Arte, necessidade vital" ("The Vital Need for Art"), named after Pedrosa's 1949 book, at USU.

In May, participates in the exhibition "Contemporaneidade: Homenagem a Mário Pedrosa" ("Contemporaneity: Homage to Mário Pedrosa") at MAM-RJ.

1983   *Divisor* is staged in the gardens of MAM-RJ and at Parque Ibirapuera in celebration of the book *Lygia Pape*, released by FUNARTE (Fundação Nacional de Arte) as part of the series Arte Brasileira Contemporânea. The book features a 1979 text written by Pedrosa, along with Pape's own writings.

In honor of Pedrosa, creates *Olho do guará* (*Eye of the Guará*), shown at ARCO, Arte Contemporânea, São Paulo, and Centro Empresarial Rio the following year.

Diretas Já movement develops, demanding the return to a direct presidential election process.

1984   As part of UNESCO's World Education Congress, led by the International Society for Education through Art, organizes the conference "Arquitetura e criatividade na Favela da Maré" ("Architecture and Creativity in the Favela da Maré") at the Universidade Estadual do Rio de Janeiro (UERJ).

Restaging of *Ballet neoconcreto I* is held at Teatro Villa-Lobos, Rio de Janeiro.

Participates in retrospective exhibitions on Grupo Frente and Neoconcretism at Galeria de Arte BANERJ, Rio de Janeiro: "I Exposição Nacional de Arte Abstrata, Hotel Quitandinha, 1953," "Grupo Frente, 1954–1956," and "Neoconcretismo, 1959–1961."

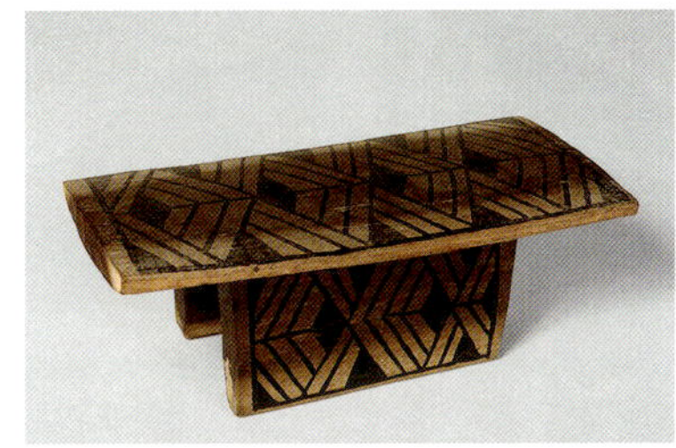

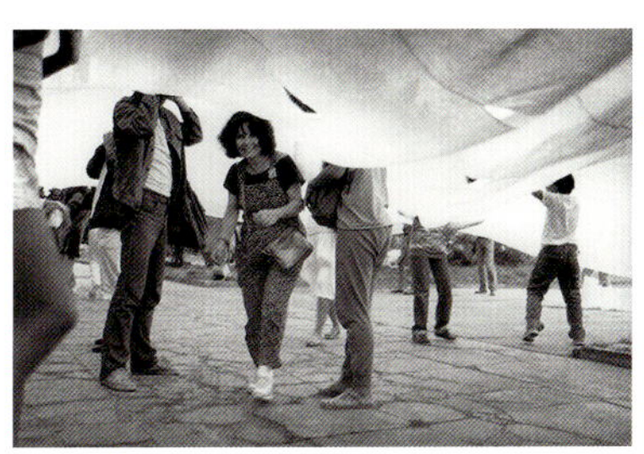

Lygia Pape: Obras, Galeria Arte Global, São Paulo, 1976

Brazilian Indian bench owned by Lygia Pape

Lygia Pape with *Divisor*, Museu de Arte Moderna, Rio de Janeiro, 1980s

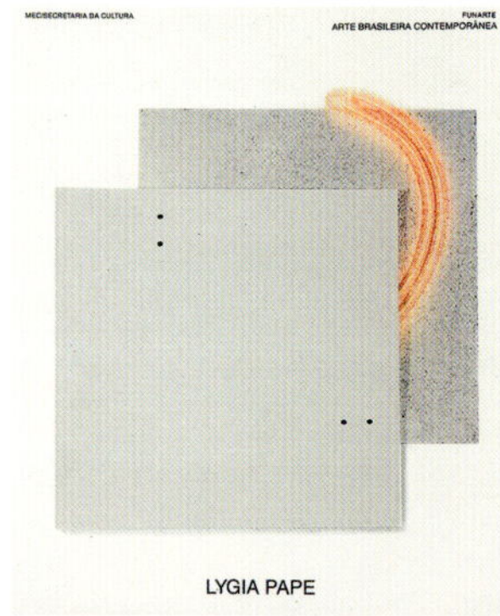

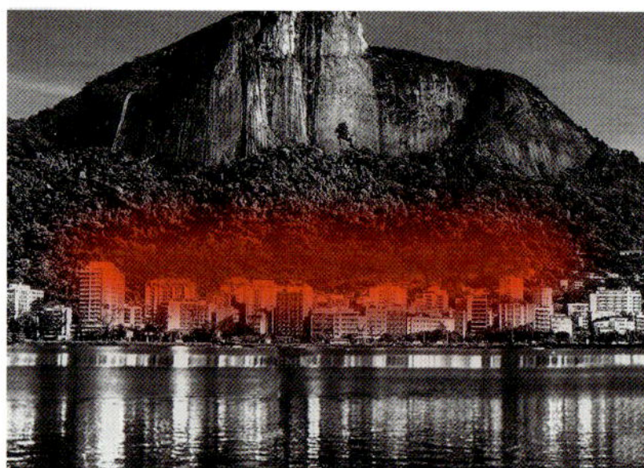

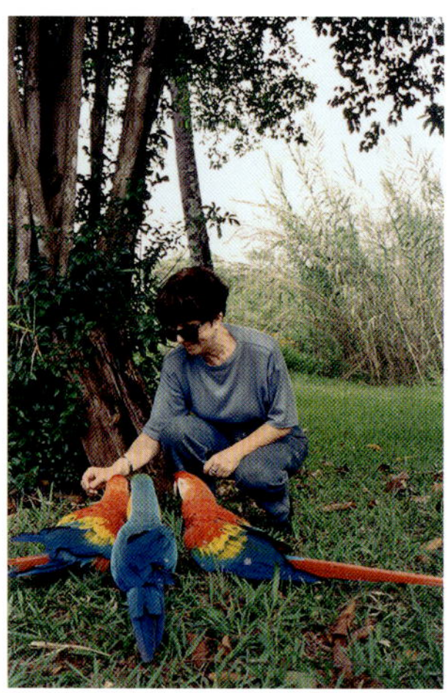

Lygia Pape, FUNARTE (Fundação Nacional de Arte), Rio de Janeiro, 1983

Manto Tupinambá (*Tupinambá Mantle*), 2000. Projeto Lygia Pape

Lygia Pape with birds, 1990s

1985   With Márcio Doctors, organizes the event "Homenagem a Mário Pedrosa" ("Homage to Mário Pedrosa") at Parque Lage.

Presents a solo show of sculptures at Galeria Arte Espaço, Rio de Janeiro.

Together with Salomão and Luciano Figueiredo, edits a selection of texts by Oiticica for the compilation *Aspiro ao grande labirinto* (*I Aspire to the Great Labyrinth*).

Military dictatorship in Brazil ends.

1986   Becomes the adviser to the director of the Escola de Belas Artes, UFRJ, a role she holds until 1990.

1988   Has a solo show at Galeria Thomas Cohn Arte Contemporânea, Rio de Janeiro, featuring Neo-concrete sculptures as well as the *Livro da criação*, *Tecelares*, and *Ttéias*.

Wins a scholarship for the research project "O ensino de arquitetura no Rio de Janeiro" ("Architectural Education in Rio de Janeiro") from the Conselho Nacional de Desenvolvimento Científico e Tecnológico (CNPq).

1989   Becomes a professor in the master's program of the Escola de Belas Artes, UFRJ. She teaches here until 1999.

With Figueiredo, curates "Mundo abrigo" ("World Haven"), an exhibition of Oiticica's work at Galeria 110 Arte Contemporânea, Rio de Janeiro.

Begins the *Amazoninos* series, shown in the exhibition "Rio hoje" ("Rio Today") at MAM-RJ.

Participates in the traveling exhibition "Art in Latin America: The Modern Era, 1820–1980," shown in London, Stockholm, and Madrid.

Curates an auction in support of the indigenous people of Roraima at the Centro Empresarial Rio.

1990   Exhibits works from *Amazoninos* in a solo show at Galeria Thomas Cohn Arte Contemporânea. The show wins the 1991 Prêmio Mário Pedrosa for the best exhibition of 1990, an award established by Associação Internacional de Críticos de Arte (ABCA–AICA).

Receives the Prêmio Brasília de Artes Plásticas from the Museu de Arte de Brasília.

Profiled in Paula Gaitan's film *Lygia Pape*.

1991   Participates in the roundtable "Mário Pedrosa: Crítico de arte" ("Mário Pedrosa: Art Critic") with Amaral, Gullar, and Otília Arantes for the event "Mário Pedrosa: Arte e política" ("Mário Pedrosa: Art and Politics"), organized by the Secretaria Municipal de Cultura de São Paulo in honor of Pedrosa on the tenth anniversary of his death.

The installation *Ttéia nº 7* is exhibited at Galeria IBEU, Rio de Janeiro. In 1992, the show wins the Prêmio IBEU das Artes Plásticas for the best exhibition of 1991.

1992   Travels to New York with funds from Prêmio IBEU.

Becomes the technical director of Projeto Hélio Oiticica and is part of the curatorial team for the Oiticica retrospective that travels to Rotterdam, Paris, Barcelona, Lisbon, and Minneapolis.

1994   Completes carnival decorations for Avenida Rio Branco in a project titled *Branco sobre branco* (*White on White*). Approximately 140 white banners with geometric abstractions in silver, red, and black are made during a residency at the Museu Nacional de Belas Artes, Rio de Janeiro.

Eat Me: A gula ou a luxúria? is reinstalled at the Bienal Brasil Século XX at the Fundação Bienal de São Paulo, shown alongside *Amazoninos* and works from the 1950s and 1960s.

1995   Produces the *Poemas visuais* (*Visual Poems*) series with works such as *Das Haus* (*The House*) and *Luar do sertão* (*Hinterlands Moonlight*).

1996   Stages *Divisor* in the streets of New York's SoHo district as part of the exhibition "Walk on the SoHo Side."

Narizes e línguas (*Noses and Tongues*) is first shown at her retrospective at the Centro Cultural São Paulo. For the exhibition "Transparências" ("Transparencies") at MAM-RJ, the work *Cortina de maçãs* (*Curtain of Apples*) is shown for the first time.

1997   Participates as an exhibitor and member of the art commission for the "Lygia Clark and Hélio Oiticica" room at "II Colóquio Latino-Americano de estética: Estética em questão" ("II Latin-American Colloquium on Aesthetics: Aesthetics in Question"), UERJ.

Exhibits *Alva de prata* (*Silver Alb*) at Fundação Joaquim Nabuco, Recife.

Featured in a dedicated room at the XXV Salão Nacional de Arte Moderna de Belo Horizonte, held at Museu de Arte da Pampulha.

Begins work on her *Tupinambá* series, which she continues to produce until 2003.

1998 Participates in the selection and prize committee of the XVI Salão Nacional de Artes Plásticas, held at the MAM-RJ and Centro de Artes FUNARTE, where she exhibits *Ttéia 1, A*.

Has a solo show at Museo de Arte Carrillo Gil, Mexico City.

Receives a special tribute at the 10a Mostra Internacional do Filme, Rio de Janeiro, and designs the event's catalogue cover and poster.

Lúcia Carneiro and Ileana Pradilla publish the artist interview book *Lygia Pape*.

1999 Begins her doctorate in *linguagens visuais* (visual languages) at the Centro de Letras e Artes, UFRJ.

Wins first place in the III Prêmio Johnnie Walker das Artes Plásticas.

Has solo shows in Rio de Janeiro at Paço Imperial, Galeria Casa Amarela, and Museu da Chácara do Céu. Exhibits *Ttéia/Fios dourados* (*Ttéia/Golden Strings*, 1996–99) in a solo show at Galeria Canvas, Porto, Portugal.

In September, is featured in "LHL—Lygia Clark, Hélio Oiticica e Lygia Pape: Universo dos sentidos" ("LHL—Lygia Clark, Hélio Oiticica and Lygia Pape: Universe of the Senses") at Conjunto Cultural da Caixa Econômica Federal, Brasília.

Produces two new film works: *Maiakóvski, a viagem* (*Mayakovsky, the Journey*) and *Sedução III* (*Seduction III*).

2000 A book on Pape, *Gávea de tocaia* (*Topsail Ambushed*), is published.

Manto Tupinambá (*Tupinambá Mantle*) is exhibited as part of "Brasil +500: Mostra do redescobrimento" ("Brazil +500: Rediscovery Exhibition") at Parque Ibirapuera, held on the occasion of Brazil's five-hundredth year.

Ballet neoconcreto I and *II* are restaged during Pape's solo exhibition at Fundação de Serralves —Museu de Arte Contemporânea, Porto, Portugal. *Divisor* is presented with one of its sides attached to a wall.

2001 Completes the short film *But I Fly*.

Presents new works at the Centro de Arte Hélio Oiticica, Rio de Janeiro: *New House*, *Jogo de tênis* (*Tennis Match*), *Livros* (*Books*), and *Carandiru*.

2002 Exhibits *Ttéia 1, C*, also known as *Ttéia quadrada* (*Ttéia Squared*), at Paço Imperial, Rio de Janeiro. A later iteration of the work presented at the 53rd Venice Biennale in 2009 earns a Special Mention.

Participates in the panel "Lygia Pape: Artista gráfica do Cinema Novo" ("Lygia Pape: Cinema Novo's Graphic Artist") as part of a lecture series at the Centro Cultural Banco do Brasil (CCBB), Rio de Janeiro.

Her more recent films *Sedução III* and *Maiakóvski, a viagem* are screened alongside *La nouvelle création*, *Catiti-Catiti*, *Eat Me*, and *Cinemateca MAM-Rio* at "Cinema marginal e suas fronteiras" ("Marginal Cinema and Its Borders"), CCBB, Rio de Janeiro.

Banquete Tupinambá (*Tupinambá Banquet*) is acquired by and exhibited at Galeria Caixa Geral de Depósitos, Lisbon.

New House is permanently installed at Museu do Açude, located in the Parque Nacional da Tijuca, Rio de Janeiro.

Wins the Prêmio O Globo "Personalidade do ano" ("Personality of the Year") award.

2003 Exhibits *Love* at the 50th Venice Biennale: "La dittatura dello spettatore" ("The Dictatorship of the Spectator").

Denise Mattar publishes *Lygia Pape: Intrinsecamente anarquista* (*Lygia Pape: Intrinsically Anarchist*), which features Pape's autobiographical account of her life and art.

2004 Organizes an exhibition at Galeria Graça Brandão, Porto, Portugal, where she presents *Ttéia I, C*.

On May 3, dies at Hospital São Lucas, Copacabana, Rio de Janeiro, from complications related to long-term myelodysplasia.

In November, Associação Cultural Lygia Pape, now Projeto Lygia Pape, is founded by Pape's daughter Paula Pape.

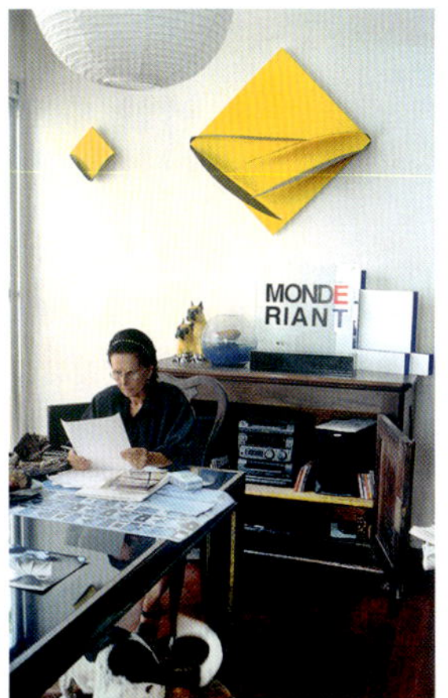

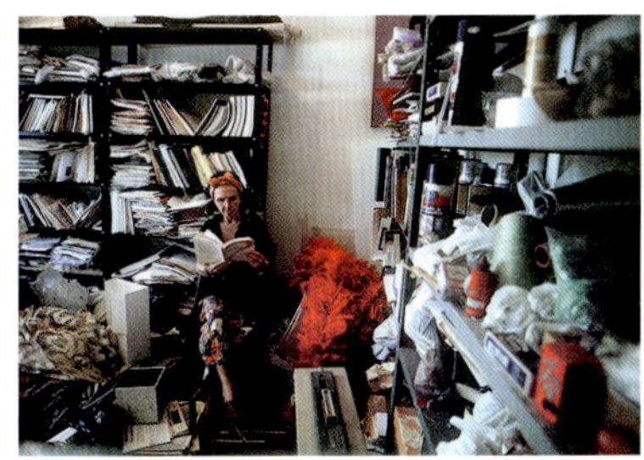

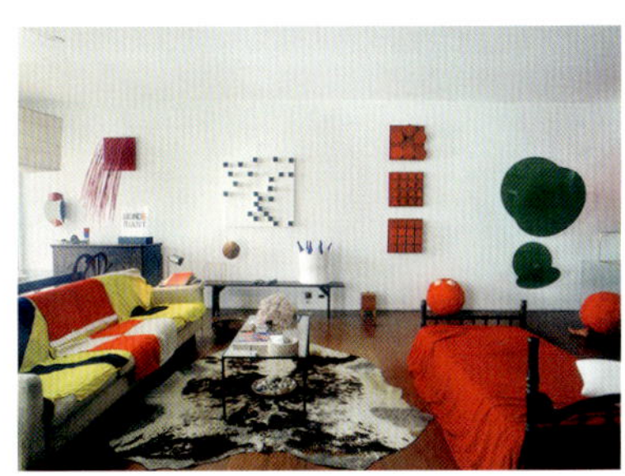

Lygia Pape in her studio on Rua Inglês de Souza, Jardim Botânico, Rio de Janeiro, 2000

Lygia Pape reading at home, Jardim Botânico, Rio de Janeiro, 2000s

Lygia Pape's home, Jardim Botânico, Rio de Janeiro, 2004

checklist

Unless otherwise noted, all works are from Projeto Lygia Pape, Rio de Janeiro.

Painting
1953
Oil on canvas
27⅝ × 39⅜ in. (70 × 100 cm)
Pl. 1

Painting
1953
Oil on canvas
29⅝ × 39⅜ in. (75 × 100 cm)
Pl. 2

Painting
1954
Gouache on fiberboard
15¾ × 15¾ × 1¼ in.
(40 × 40 × 3 cm)
Colección Patricia Phelps de Cisneros (1997.63)
Pl. 4

Relevo
1954
Tempera and industrial paint on fiberboard on wood
15¾ × 15¾ × 1⅞ in.
(40 × 40 × 4.7 cm)
Private collection, New York
Pl. 22

Tarugo
1954
Industrial paint on wood
15¾ × 16 × 3¾ in.
(39.8 × 40.5 × 9.5 cm)
Luisa Malzoni Strina
Pl. 17

Painting
1954–56
Gouache on fiberboard
15¾ × 15¾ × 1¼ in.
(40 × 40 × 3 cm)
Pl. 9

Painting
1954–56
Gouache on fiberboard
15¾ × 15¾ × 1¼ in.
(40 × 40 × 3 cm)
Courtesy Projeto Lygia Pape and Hauser & Wirth
Pl. 3

Painting
1954–56
Gouache on fiberboard
15¾ × 15¾ × 1¼ in.
(40 × 40 × 3 cm)
Pl. 5

Painting
1954–56
Gouache and tempera on fiberboard
15¾ × 15¾ × 1¼ in.
(40 × 40 × 3 cm)
Pl. 8

Painting
1954–56
Gouache on paper and fiberboard
15¾ × 15¾ × 1¼ in.
(40 × 40 × 3 cm)
Andréa and José Olympio Pereira
Pl. 7

Painting
1954–56
Gouache on paper and fiberboard
15¾ × 15¾ × 1¼ in.
(40 × 40 × 3 cm)
Andréa and José Olympio Pereira
Pl. 6

Relevo
1954–56
Tempera and industrial paint on fiberboard on wood
15¾ × 15¾ × 2 in.
(40 × 40 × 5 cm)
Pl. 15

Relevo
1954–56
Tempera and industrial paint on fiberboard on wood
15¾ × 15¾ × 2 in.
(40 × 40 × 5 cm)
Pl. 19

Relevo
1954–56
Tempera and industrial paint on fiberboard on wood
15¾ × 15¾ × 2¼ in.
(40 × 40 × 5.5 cm)
Harald Orneberg Collection
Pl. 20

Relevo
1954–56
Tempera and industrial paint on fiberboard on wood
15¾ × 15¾ × 2 in.
(40 × 40 × 5 cm)
Pl. 23

Relevo
1954–56
Tempera and industrial paint on fiberboard on wood
15¾ × 15¾ × 2 in. (40 × 40 × 5 cm)
Pl. 16

Relevo
1954–56
Gouache and tempera on fiberboard on wood
15¾ × 15¾ × 2 in.
(40 × 40 × 5 cm)
Pl. 10

Tarugo
1954–56
Industrial paint, oil, and gouache on wood
15¾ × 15¾ × 3⅜ in.
(40 × 40 × 8.5 cm)
Pl. 24

Tarugo
1954–56
Industrial paint, oil, and gouache on wood
15¾ × 15¾ × 3⅜ in.
(40 × 40 × 8.5 cm)
Pl. 26

Tarugo
1954–56
Industrial paint, oil, and gouache on wood
15¾ × 15¾ × 3⅜ in.
(40 × 40 × 8.5 cm)
Pl. 25

Drawing
1955
Ink on paper
9⅞ × 13⅞ in. (25 × 35 cm)
Pl. 36

Relevo
1955
Gouache and industrial paint on fiberboard on wood
15¾ × 15¾ × 2⅛ in.
(40 × 40 × 5.4 cm)
Collection of Diane and Bruce Halle
Pl. 21

Relevo
1955
Gouache and industrial paint on fiberboard on wood
15¾ × 15¾ × 2⅛ in.
(40 × 40 × 5.4 cm)
Collection of Diane and Bruce Halle
Pl. 18

Study for a Painting
1955
Collage on cardboard
11 × 11 in. (27.7 × 27.7 cm)
Pl. 13

Study for a Relief
1955
Collage on cardboard
9⅞ × 9 ⅞ in. (24.9 × 24.9 cm)
Pl. 12

Study for a Relief
1955
Collage on cardboard
7½ × 7½ in. (19.1 × 19.1 cm)
Pl. 11

Tecelar
1955
Woodcut on Japanese paper
18⅜ × 23⅝ in. (46.5 × 60 cm)
Pl. 30

Tecelar
1955
Woodcut on Japanese paper
19½ × 24 in. (49.5 × 61 cm)
Pl. 29

Tecelar
1955
Woodcut on Japanese paper
15⅝ × 19⅞ in. (39.7 × 50.5 cm)
Pl. 31

Drawing
1956
Ink on Japanese paper
21¼ × 16⅜ in. (54 × 41.5 cm)
Pl. 39

Drawing
1956
Ink on Japanese paper
21¼ × 16⅝ in. (54 × 42 cm)
Pl. 40

Tecelar
1956
Woodcut on Japanese paper
19¾ × 19¾ in. (50 × 50 cm)
Pl. 37

Tecelar
1956
Woodcut on Japanese paper
17⅝ × 12⅞ in. (44.7 × 32.7 cm)
Pl. 28

Tecelar
1956
Woodcut on Japanese paper
17⅝ × 12⅞ in. (44.6 × 32.7 cm)
Pl. 27

Poema-luz (*Light-Poem*)
1956–57
Tempera on acrylic
15¾ × 28 in. (40 × 71 cm)
Pl. 72

Drawing
1957
Ink on Japanese paper
35⅛ × 26 in. (89 × 66 cm)
Pl. 34

Drawing
1957
Ink on Japanese paper
35⅛ × 26 in. (89 × 66 cm)
Pl. 35

Drawing
1957
Ink on Japanese paper
35¼ × 25⅝ in. (89.5 × 65 cm)
Pl. 32

Drawing
1957
Ink on Japanese paper
36½ × 24¼ in. (92.6 × 61.6 cm)
Museo Nacional Centro de Arte Reina Sofía, Madrid (DE01860)
Pl. 33

Em vão (In Vain)
Poema-objeto (Poem-Object) series
1957
Tempera on paper
8½ × 8½ in. (21.5 × 21.5 cm)
Pl. 61

Rompe (Burst)
Poema-objeto (Poem-Object) series
1957
Tempera on paper
8¼ × 8¼ in. (21 × 21 cm)
Pl. 58

Tecelar
1957
Woodcut on Japanese paper
17⅝ × 12⅞ in. (44.6 × 32.5 cm)
Pl. 43

Tecelar
1957
Woodcut on Japanese paper
17⅝ × 12⅞ in. (44.6 × 32.5 cm)
Pl. 42

Tecelar
1957
Woodcut on Japanese paper
15⅞ × 11⅞ in. (40.1 × 30.2 cm)
Pl. 52

Tecelar
1957
Woodcut on Japanese paper
12 × 17½ in. (30.5 × 44.5 cm)
Pl. 53

Tecelar
1957
Woodcut on Japanese paper
19⅝ × 19⅝ in. (49.9 × 49.9 cm)
Museu de Arte Moderna, São Paulo,
patrocínio Petrobrás (2001.088)
Pl. 38

Traço (Line)
Poema-objeto (Poem-Object) series
1957
Tempera on paper
8½ × 8½ in. (21.5 × 21.5 cm)
Pl. 62

Vazio (Void)
Poema-objeto (Poem-Object) series
1957
Tempera on paper
8¼ × 12⅝ in. (21 × 32 cm)
Pl. 60

Vem (Come)
Poema-objeto (Poem-Object) series
1957
Tempera on cardboard
8½ × 8½ in. (21.5 × 21.5 cm)
Pl. 63

Verde (Green)
Poema-objeto (Poem-Object) series
1957
Tempera on paper
8½ × 8½ in. (21.5 × 21.5 cm)
Pl. 64

Ballet neoconcreto I
(Neoconcrete Ballet I)
1958
Performance at Fundação de
Serralves—Museu de Arte
Contemporânea, Porto, Portugal,
2000
Digital video
19 min. 35 sec.
Pl. 70

Tecelar
1958
Woodcut on Japanese paper
11¾ × 17 in. (29.8 × 43.2 cm)
Ella Fontanals-Cisneros Collection
Pl. 49

Ballet neoconcreto II
(Neoconcrete Ballet II)
1959
Performance at Fundação de
Serralves—Museu de Arte
Contemporânea, Porto, Portugal,
2000
Digital video
5 min.
Pl. 71

Drawing
1959
Ink on Japanese paper
21⅞ × 16⅝ in. (54.5 × 42 cm)
Pl. 44

Drawing
1959
Ink on Japanese paper
21¾ × 17⅜ in. (55 × 44 cm)
B.A.F. Collection
Pl. 45

Study for Ballet no. 3
1959
Collage on cardboard
5⅞ × 24⅞ in. (14.7 × 63.1 cm)
Pl. 14

Tecelar
1959
Woodcut on Japanese paper
11¼ × 14 in. (28.5 × 35.5 cm)
Colección Patricia Phelps de
Cisneros, on long-term loan to the
Museo Nacional Centro de Arte
Reina Sofía, Madrid (DO01969)
Pl. 48

Tecelar
1959
Woodcut on Japanese paper
11⅞ × 21¼ in. (30 × 54 cm)
Pl. 46

Tecelar
1959
Woodcut on Japanese paper
9¾ × 11⅝ in. (24.6 × 29.5 cm)
Pl. 47

Tecelar
1959
Woodcut on Japanese paper
13⅛ × 16¾ in. (33.1 × 42.5 cm)
Pl. 41

Tecelar
1959
Woodcut on Japanese paper
19½ × 19½ in. (49.5 × 49.5 cm)
Colección Patricia Phelps de
Cisneros (1998.146)
Pl. 55

Tecelar
1959
Woodcut on Japanese paper
9 × 21¾ in. (22.7 × 55.1 cm)
Museu de Arte Moderna, São Paulo,
patrocínio Petrobrás (2001.061)
Pl. 50

Livro da arquitetura
(Book of Architecture)
1959–60
Tempera on cardboard,
twelve pieces
Each piece: 11⅞ × 11⅞ in.
(30 × 30 cm)
Pl. 74

Livro da criação
(Book of Creation)
1959–60
Gouache on board, sixteen pieces
Each piece: 12 × 12 in.
(30.5 × 30.5 cm)
Museum of Modern Art, New York,
Gift of Patricia Phelps de Cisneros,
2001 (1349.2001.a–r)
Pl. 73a, b

Coleção espaço #5
(Spatial Collection #5)
Livro-poema (Book-Poem)
1960
Woodcut on cardboard
8¼ × 8¼ in. (21 × 21 cm)
Pl. 59

Drawing
1960
Ink on Japanese paper
24 × 19⅛ in. (61 × 48.5 cm)
Pl. 57

Tecelar
1960
Woodcut on Japanese paper
8¾ × 11 in. (22.2 × 27.9 cm)
Colección Patricia Phelps de
Cisneros (1993.45)
Pl. 51

Tecelar
1960
Woodcut on Japanese paper
12⅝ × 21¼ in. (32 × 54 cm)
Estrellita and Daniel Brodsky
Collection
Pl. 54

Aranha (Spider)
ca. 1960s
Poem
Pl. 66

Balão (Balloon)
ca. 1960s
Poem
Pl. 69

Eco (Echo)
ca. 1960s
Poem
Pl. 65

Lembrança (Memory)
ca. 1960s
Poem
Pl. 67

Simples (Simple)
ca. 1960s
Poem
Pl. 68

Title credits for Cinema Novo films
1960s
35mm film transferred to digital
video in black and white with sound
17 min. 51 sec.
Pl. 92

Drawing
1961
Ink on Japanese paper
25 × 17½ in. (63.4 × 44.5 cm)
Pl. 56

Livro do tempo (Book of Time)
1961–63
Tempera on wood, 365 pieces
Each piece: 6⅜ × 6⅜ × 1¼ in.
(16 × 16 × 3.2 cm)
Pl. 75

Film title design for *Cinemateca
MAM-Rio*
1963
Collage on paper
9¾ × 13⅜ in. (24.5 × 34 cm)
Fig. 34

Livro dos caminhos
(Book of Paths)
1963–76
Oil and latex on wood
39⅜ × 39⅜ × 7⅞ in.
(100 × 100 × 20 cm)
Pl. 78

Livro dos caminhos
(Book of Paths)
1963–76
Oil and latex on wood
39⅜ × 39⅜ × 7⅞ in.
(100 × 100 × 20 cm)
Pl. 79

Livro dos caminhos
(Book of Paths)
1963–76
Oil and latex on wood
39⅜ × 39⅜ × 7⅞ in.
(100 × 100 × 20 cm)
Not illustrated

Livro dos caminhos
(Book of Paths)
1963–76
Oil and tempera on wood
39⅜ × 39⅜ × 7⅞ in.
(100 × 100 × 20 cm)
Not illustrated

Livro noite e dia
(Book Night and Day)
1963–76
Tempera and acrylic on wood
Each piece: 6⅜ × 6⅜ × 1¼ in.
(16 × 16 × 3 cm)
Private collection, courtesy
Hauser & Wirth
Pl. 76

Livro do tempo (médio)
(Book of Time [medium])
1965
Tempera and acrylic on wood
19¾ × 19¾ × 4⅛ in.
(50 × 50 × 10.5 cm)
Collection of Clarissa and Edgar
Bronfman, Jr.
Pl. 77

Caixa das baratas
(Box of Cockroaches)
1967
Acrylic, mirror, mummified
cockroaches
10⅛ × 14 × 4 in.
(25.5 × 35.5 × 10 cm)
Coll. Fundação de Serralves—
Museu de Arte Contemporânea,
Porto, Portugal, Acquisition 2006
Pl. 81

Caixa das formigas (*Box of Ants*)
1967
Color photograph of original work
Original: 13⅞ × 13⅞ × 4 in.
(35 × 35 × 10 cm)
Pl. 80

Divisor (*Divider*)
1967
Performance at Favela da Cabeça,
Rio de Janeiro, 1967
Super 8 film transferred to digital
video in color
3 min. 36 sec.
Pl. 84

La nouvelle création
(*The New Creation*)
1967
35mm film transferred to digital
video in color with sound
50 sec.
Pl. 93

Livro da criação (*Book of Creation*)
1967
Super 8 film transferred to digital
video in color
4 min. 5 sec.
Not illustrated

O ovo (*The Egg*)
1967
Performance at Barra da Tijuca
beach, Rio de Janeiro, 1967
Vintage black-and-white
photographs
Pl. 86 (two illustrated)

O ovo (*The Egg*)
1967
Performance at Barra da Tijuca
beach, Rio de Janeiro, 1967
Super 8 film transferred to digital
video in color with sound
1 min. 20 sec.
Pl. 87

Roda dos prazeres
(*Wheel of Pleasures*)
1967
Performance at Barra da Tijuca
beach, Rio de Janeiro, 1967
Vintage color photograph
Not illustrated

Roda dos prazeres
(*Wheel of Pleasures*)
1967
Porcelain vessels, droppers, water,
flavorings, food dyes
Dimensions variable
Pl. 91

Roda dos prazeres
(*Wheel of Pleasures*)
1967
Performance at Barra da Tijuca
beach, Rio de Janeiro, 1967
Super 8 film transferred to digital
video in color
1 min. 50 sec.
Pl. 90

Trio do embalo maluco
(*Crazy Rocking Trio*)
1967
Performance at a quarry near the
artist's home, Rio de Janeiro, 1967
Betacam transferred to digital video
in color with sound
1 min.
Pl. 88

Trio do embalo maluco
(*Crazy Rocking Trio*)
1967
Performance at a quarry near the
artist's home, Rio de Janeiro, 1967
Vintage black-and-white photograph
Pl. 89

Trio do embalo maluco
(*Crazy Rocking Trio*)
1967
Performance at "Apocalipopótese,"
Aterro do Flamengo, Rio de Janeiro,
1968
Vintage black-and-white photograph
Not illustrated

Divisor (*Divider*)
1968
Performance at Museu de Arte
Moderna, Rio de Janeiro, 1990
Black-and-white photographs
Pls. 82, 85

Divisor (*Divider*)
1968
Performance at Museu de Arte
Moderna, Rio de Janeiro, 2010
Black-and-white photographs
Pl. 83

Divisor (*Divider*)
1968
Performance at Museu de Arte
Moderna, Rio de Janeiro, 2010
Digital video in color
4 min. 52 sec.
Not illustrated

Lingua apunhalada
(*Stabbed Tongue*)
1968
Lightbox and newspapers
Dimensions variable
Pl. 102

Product packaging for Piraquê
ca. 1970
Printed scrolls
Dimensions variable
Pages 185, 188

Favela da Maré
1972
Super 8 film transferred to digital
video in color
5 min. 11 sec.
Pl. 100

Carnival in Rio
1974
Super 8 film transferred to digital
video in color with sound
9 min. 20 sec.
Pl. 94

Film title design for *Carnival in Rio*
1974
Collage on paper
8⅛ × 10⅝ in. (20.5 × 27 cm)
Not illustrated

Our Parents "Fossilis"
1974
Super 8 film transferred to digital
video in color with sound
10 min.
Pl. 98

Poster for the film *Poluttio planet*
(*Pollution Planet*)
Print from "Carpeta 22"
("Portfolio 22")
1974
Printed poster
12¼ × 13 in. (31 × 33 cm)
Not illustrated

Favela da Maré
1974–76
Series of color photographs
Pl. 101 (four illustrated)

A mão do povo
(*The Hand of the People*)
1975
16mm film transferred to digital
video in black and white with sound
10 min.
Pl. 95

Objetos de sedução
(*Objects of Seduction*)
1976
Installation view,
"Eat Me: A gula ou a luxúria?",
Museu de Arte Moderna,
Rio de Janeiro, 1976
Collection of paper bags containing
cosmetic items, such as dentures,
false eyelashes, mirrors, and
perfumes
Dimensions variable
Pl. 103

Ttéia 1, C
1976–2004
Installation view, Pinacoteca do
Estado, São Paulo, 2012
Golden thread
Dimensions variable
Pl. 122

Aula sedução (*Seduction Class*)
1977
Vintage black-and-white
photographs
Not illustrated

Catiti-Catiti
1978
16mm film transferred to digital
video in black and white with sound
10 min.
Pl. 96

Mário Pedrosa Eating Fruit
1978
Eight vintage black-and-white
photographs
Pl. 104

Mitos vadios (*Vagrant Myths*)
1978
Vintage black-and-white
photographs
Not illustrated

Ttéia Parque Lage
ca. 1978
Vintage black-and-white
photographs
Pl. 121 (two illustrated)

Casa Sapé
1979
Series of black-and-white and color
photographs
Pl. 99 (four illustrated)

Registro cinematográfico
(*Cinematic Study*)
1980
Collage on graph paper
12½ × 18⅜ in. (31.5 × 46.7 cm)
Pl. 109

Registro cinematográfico
(*Cinematic Study*)
1980
Collage on graph paper
12½ × 18⅜ in. (31.5 × 46.7 cm)
Pl. 110

Espaços imantados
(*Magnetized Spaces*)
ca. 1982
Series of black-and-white
photographs
Pl. 106 (two illustrated)

Amazônia
Published in *Suplemento sábado,
Jornal da tarde*, São Paulo,
May 20, 1989
Typewritten text on paper
Pl. 120

Amazonino
1990
Automotive paint on iron
70⅞ × 39⅜ × 27⅝ in.
(180 × 100 × 70 cm)
Pl. 114

Amazonino
1991
Automotive paint on iron
19¾ × 19¾ × 6⅜ in.
(50 × 50 × 16 cm)
Pl. 119

Amazonino
1991
Automotive paint on iron
19¾ × 19¾ × 6⅜ in.
(50 × 50 × 16 cm)
Pl. 118

Amazonino
1991
Automotive paint on iron
19¾ × 19¾ × 19¾ in.
(50 × 50 × 50 cm)
Pl. 117

Amazonino
1992
Automotive paint on iron
70⅞ × 78¾ × 15¾ in.
(180 × 200 × 40 cm)
Pl. 116

Amazonino
1992
Automotive paint on iron
50⅞ × 19¾ × 19¾ in.
(129 × 50 × 50 cm)
Colección Patricia Phelps de
Cisneros (1993.33)
Pl. 115

Registro cinematográfico
(*Cinematic Study*)
1992
Collage on Japanese paper
24 × 32¾ in. (61 × 83 cm)
Pl. 111

Registro cinematográfico
(*Cinematic Study*)
1992
Collage on Japanese paper
16¾ × 21 in. (42.5 × 53.5 cm)
Pl. 113

Registro cinematográfico
(*Cinematic Study*)
1992
Collage on Japanese paper
25⅝ × 35⅛ in. (65 × 89 cm)
Pl. 112

Espaços imantados
(*Magnetized Spaces*)
1995
Series of black-and-white
photographs
Pls. 107, 108

Banquete Tupinambá
(*Tupinambá Banquet*)
2000
Wood table and two chairs, covered
in red feathers; two polyurethane
breasts; lightbulb
Overall dimensions (not including
bulb): 30⅜ × 55⅛ × 36¼ in. (77 ×
140 × 92 cm)
Coleção Caixa Geral de Depósitos,
Lisbon, Portugal (533756)
Pl. 105

Archival Material

Grupo Frente
1954
Galeria IBEU (Instituto Brasil–
Estados Unidos), Rio de Janeiro
Exhibition catalogue
Page 168

Lygia Pape at work in her studio on
Rua Engenheiro Alfredo Duarte,
Rio de Janeiro
1954
Vintage black-and-white photograph
Page 168

Grupo Frente
1956
Itatiaia Country Club, Resende,
Rio de Janeiro
Exhibition catalogue
Page 170

Lygia Pape working on a *Tecelar* in
her studio, Jardim Botânico,
Rio de Janeiro
1958
Vintage black-and-white photograph
Fig. 3

1a Exposição neoconcreta
1959
Museu de Arte Moderna,
Rio de Janeiro
Exhibition catalogue
Page 170

"Experiência neoconcreta,"
*Suplemento dominical,
Jornal do Brasil*, Rio de Janeiro,
March 22, 1959
Page 171

Lygia Pape
Script for *Brasília*
1959
Typewritten text in Portuguese,
three pages
Not illustrated

II Exposição neoconcreta
1960
Ministry of Education,
Rio de Janeiro
Exhibition catalogue
Not illustrated

Nova objetividade brasileira
(*New Brazilian Objectivity*)
1967
Museu de Arte Moderna,
Rio de Janeiro
Exhibition catalogue
The Metropolitan Museum of Art,
New York, Thomas J. Watson Library
Not illustrated

Students at one of Lygia Pape's free
workshops, Museu de Arte Moderna,
Rio de Janeiro
1970s
Series of color photographs
Fig. 12 (one illustrated)

Commercial postcards of Indians
used in *Our Parents "Fossilis"* (1974)
Pl. 97 (four illustrated)

Lygia Pape: Obras
(*Lygia Pape: Works*)
1976
Galeria Arte Global, São Paolo
Exhibition catalogue
The Metropolitan Museum of Art,
New York, Thomas J. Watson Library
Page 173

*Projeto construtivo brasileiro na arte
(1950–1962)*
(*Brazilian Constructivist Project in Art
[1950–1962]*)
Edited by Aracy Amaral
1977
Museu de Arte Moderna, Rio de
Janeiro, and Pinacoteca do Estado,
São Paulo
Exhibition catalogue
Museum of Modern Art, New York
Not illustrated

Lygia Pape
"Catiti-Catiti, na terra dos Brasis"
("Catiti-Catiti, in the Land of the
Brasis")
1980
Master's thesis, Instituto de
Filosofia e Ciências Sociais,
Universidade Federal do Rio de
Janeiro
Fig. 26

Lygia Pape
1983
FUNARTE (Fundação Nacional de
Arte), Rio de Janeiro
Page 174

notes

The Risk of Invention Iria Candela

1 For an introduction to Neoconcretism and its importance in the history of Brazilian art, see Ronaldo Brito, *Neoconcretismo: Vértice e ruptura do projeto construtivo brasileiro,* [2nd ed.] (São Paulo: Cosac & Naify, 1999).

2 *Lygia Pape: Entrevista a Lúcia Carneiro e Ileana Pradilla* (Rio de Janeiro: Lacerda Editores and Centro de Arte Hélio Oiticica, Secretaria Municipal de Cultura do Rio de Janeiro, 1998), p. 23.

3 Lygia Pape, "Lygia por Lygia," in Denise Mattar, *Lygia Pape: Intrinsecamente anarquista* (Rio de Janeiro: Relume Dumará, 2003), p. 59.

4 Designed in 1936 after an original design by Le Corbusier, the Ministry of Education, inaugurated in 1945, was regarded as the first building in the Americas to respond to modern architecture. Paulo Venancio Filho, "Modernity in a Tropical Metropolis by the Sea," in Paulo Venancio Filho and Annika Gunnarsson, *Time and Place: Rio de Janeiro, 1956–1964,* exh. cat. (Stockholm: Moderna Museet; Göttingen: Steidl, 2008), p. 18.

5 Theo van Doesburg, "Base de la peinture concrète," *Art concret* (Paris), no. 1 (April 1930), p. 1.

6 Grupo Ruptura was formed by Lothar Charoux, Waldemar Cordeiro, Geraldo de Barros, Kazmer Féjer, Leopold Haar, Luís Sacilotto, and Anatol Wladyslaw.

7 Lothar Charoux et al., *Ruptura* (1952), in *Projeto construtivo brasileiro na arte (1950–1962),* ed. Aracy Amaral, exh. cat. (Rio de Janeiro: Museu de Arte Moderna; São Paulo: Pinacoteca do Estado, 1977; reprint, São Paulo: Pinacoteca do Estado, 2015), p. 69.

8 Mário Pedrosa, "Grupo Frente," in *Mário Pedrosa: Primary Documents,* ed. Glória Ferreira and Paulo Herkenhoff, trans. Stephen Berg (New York: Museum of Modern Art, 2015), pp. 269–70; originally published in *Grupo Frente: Segunda mostra coletiva,* exh. cat. (Rio de Janeiro: Museu de Arte Moderna, 1955).

9 See Kazimir Malevich, "From Cubism and Futurism to Suprematism: The New Painterly Realism" (1915), in *Russian Art of the Avant-Garde: Theory and Criticism, 1902–1934,* ed. and trans. John E. Bowlt (New York: Viking Press, 1976), pp. 116–35.

10 The *Tarugos* have a depth of approximately 3⅜ in. (8.5 cm).

11 See Gyula Kosice et al., "Madí" (June 1946), in Mari Carmen Ramírez and Héctor Olea, *Inverted Utopias: Avant-Garde Art in Latin America,* exh. cat. (New Haven, Conn.: Yale University Press, in association with the Museum of Fine Arts, Houston, 2004), p. 493, no. 45; published in *Arte Madí* (Buenos Aires), nos. 0–1 (1947).

12 Lygia Pape, "Statement" (Oct. 2, 1979), in *Lygia Pape: Magnetized Space,* exh. cat. (2011; Madrid: Museo Nacional Centro de Arte Reina Sofía; Zurich: JRP Ringier, 2014), p. 91.

13 Adele Nelson, "Sensitive and Nondiscursive Things: Lygia Pape and the Reconception of Printmaking," *Art Journal* 71, no. 3 (Fall 2012), p. 30.

14 For a comparison with the prints of Josef Albers, see Sérgio B. Martins's essay in this volume.

15 Lygia Pape, "Forty Neo-Concrete Woodcuts" (July 17, 1975), in *Lygia Pape: Magnetized Space,* p. 89.

16 "The only printmaker I knew of who also made the most of the weight of his hand and the technique of sanding was Goeldi," Pape said. Lygia Pape, interview in Fernando Cocchiarale and Anna Bella Geiger, *Abstracionismo, geométrico e informal: A vanguarda brasileira nos anos cinqüenta* (Rio de Janeiro: FUNARTE and Instituto Nacional de Artes Plásticas, 1987; reprint, 2004), p. 160.

17 Pape, "Statement," p. 91.

18 Pape, "Forty Neo-Concrete Woodcuts," p. 88.

19 Mário Pedrosa, "Paulistas and Cariocas," in Ferreira and Herkenhoff, *Mário Pedrosa: Primary Documents,* p. 274; originally published as "Paulistas e Cariocas," *Jornal do Brasil* (Rio de Janeiro), Feb. 19, 1957.

20 Willys de Castro and Hércules Barsotti joined the movement later.

21 Ferreira Gullar, "Manifesto neoconcreto"/"Neo-Concrete Manifesto," in *Arte construtiva no Brasil: Coleção Adolpho Leirner/Constructive Art in Brazil: Adolpho Leirner Collection,* ed. Aracy Amaral (São Paulo: Dórea Books and Art and Melhoramentos, 1998), pp. 270, 271; published in *Suplemento dominical, Jornal do Brasil* (Rio de Janeiro), Mar. 22, 1959.

22 Gullar, "Manifesto neoconcreto"/"Neo-Concrete Manifesto," pp. 272–74.

23 Pape, interview in Cocchiarale and Geiger, *Abstracionismo, geométrico e informal,* p. 161.

24 Fernand Léger, "The Ballet Spectacle, the Object-Spectacle" (1925), in Fernand Léger, *Functions of Painting,* trans. Alexandra Anderson (New York: Viking Press, 1973), p. 71.

25 Lygia Pape, "Ballet: A Visual Experience," in *Lygia Pape: Magnetized Space,* p. 162; originally published as "Ballet: Experiência visual," *Suplemento dominical, Jornal do Brasil,* Mar. 22, 1959.

26 Pape, "Ballet: A Visual Experience," p. 162.

27 *Lygia Pape: Entrevista a Lúcia Carneiro e Ileana Pradilla,* p. 33.

28 See Pedro Corrêa do Lago, *Brasiliana Itaú: Uma grande coleção dedicada ao Brasil,* new ed. (São Paulo: Capivara, 2014), pp. 244–45. In the second half of the nineteenth century, advances in printing techniques in Germany made it possible to produce delicate lithographic prints, such as these "roses" with views of major cities, which catered particularly to women.

29 Lygia Pape, "Poems-Invention," in *Lygia Pape: Magnetized Space,* p. 178; originally published as "Poemas-invenção," in *Suplemento dominical, Jornal do Brasil,* Nov. 26, 1960.

30 Ferreira Gullar, "Teoria do não-objeto," *Suplemento dominical, Jornal do Brasil,* Dec. 19–20, 1959. Gullar's theory is further elaborated in "Diálogo sobre o não-objeto," *Suplemento dominical, Jornal do Brasil,* Mar. 26, 1960. Both essays appeared in a brochure published by the *Suplemento dominical* to accompany the 2a Exposição Neoconcreta. The texts published in the brochure are reprinted in Ferreira Gullar, "Teoria do não-objeto," in Amaral, *Projeto construtivo brasileiro na arte,* pp. 85–94.

31 Gullar, "Teoria do não-objeto," in Amaral, *Projeto construtivo brasileiro na arte,* p. 94.

32 Ibid., p. 93.

33 For her first cinematic experiences and her collaboration with the Cinema Novo directors, see Angélica de Moraes's interview with Lygia Pape in this volume.

34 Hélio Oiticica, "Esquema geral da nova objetividade," in *Nova objetividade brasileira,* exh. cat. (Rio de Janeiro: Museu de Arte Moderna, 1967), n.p.

35 Lygia Pape, "*Caixa das baratas* and *Caixa das formigas*" (n.d.), in *Lygia Pape: Magnetized Space,* p. 243.

36 See Pape, "Lygia por Lygia," pp. 75–78.

37 Lygia Clark left for Paris in 1968 and returned to Brazil in 1976. Pedrosa went into exile in Chile in 1970, later moving to Paris, before returning to Brazil in 1977. In 1970, Oiticica went to New York on a Guggenheim Fellowship; he returned to Brazil in 1978.

38 Lygia Pape to Hélio Oiticica, Jan. 3, 1969, Archives, Projeto Lygia Pape, Rio de Janeiro. "Things out there," she continued, "are lacking so much perspective and are so sick of dullness, like a steamroller."

39 On this episode, see Pape, "Lygia por Lygia," pp. 79–82.

40 "Lygia Pape and Lauro Cavalcanti: A Conversation" (Paço Imperial, Rio de Janeiro, 2003), in *Lygia Pape: Magnetized Space*, p. 305.

41 Ibid., p. 307 (English translation modified by the author).

42 Lygia Pape, "Favela da Maré or Miracle on Stilts" (1972), in *Lygia Pape: Magnetized Space*, pp. 287, 288.

43 Ibid., p. 288.

44 Ibid. "There was no hint of any urban-planning concept, far from it, but there was a strong aesthetic and poetic conception, of temporary duration: it was precisely this non-duration that constantly prompted us to return."

45 Hélio Oiticica, "Tropicália" (Mar. 4, 1968), originally published in *Folha de São Paulo, Folhetim*, Jan. 8, 1984; quoted in Ariane Figueiredo, María C. Gaztambide, and Daniela Matera Lins, "Chronology (1937–1980)," in Mari Carmen Ramírez, with Luciano Figueiredo et al., *Hélio Oiticica: The Body of Colour*, exh. cat. (London: Tate Publishing, in association with the Museum of Fine Arts, Houston, 2007), p. 382.

46 Lygia Pape, "Brasília," 1959, Archives, Projeto Lygia Pape. The Palácio da Alvorada is the official residence of the president of Brazil.

47 Mário Pedrosa, "Exposição de arte indígena: 'Alegria de viver, alegria de criar,'" n.d. (ca. 1978), Archives, Projeto Lygia Pape.

48 Mário Pedrosa to Heloisa Lustosa (director, Museu de Arte Moderna, Rio de Janeiro), Dec. 19, 1977, Archives, Projeto Lygia Pape.

49 Mário Pedrosa to Luiz Emygdio de Mello Filho, June 20, 1978, Archives, Projeto Lygia Pape. Professor Luiz Emygdio de Mello Filho was the director of the Museu Nacional da Universidade Federal do Rio de Janeiro. The letter includes the complete organization chart for the project. The committee was formed by Maria Conceição Beltrão of the Museu Nacional, Odylo Costa Filho of the Conselho Federal de Cultura, and Mário Pedrosa, appointed by Heloisa Lustosa, director of the MAM-RJ. The working team was composed of Mário Pedrosa, curatorial general director; Lygia Pape, adjunct curator; Heloisa Fenelon, Berta Ribeiro, Eduardo Viveiros de Castro, and Tereza Bauman, anthropologists; Maria Conceição Beltrão, archaeologist; Cláudia Andujar and Maureen Bisilliat, photographers; and Darcy Ribeiro, general consultant.

50 Mário Pedrosa to Heloisa Lustosa, Rio de Janeiro, Dec. 19, 1977, Archives, Projeto Lygia Pape. Mário Pedrosa and "fellow committee member" Lygia Pape express gratitude for the "unreservedly enthusiastic" reception given to the project by the MAM-RJ.

51 See Lygia Pape, "Sinopse: 'Alegria de viver, alegria de criar,'" proposal for a film addressed to Leandro Tocantins (director, Operações Não Comerciais da Embrafilme, Rio de Janeiro), Mar. 9, 1978, Archives, Projeto Lygia Pape. Pape describes a project for a film to document the exhibition and field trips to such cities as Rio Claro in São Paulo and Itaboraí in the state of Rio de Janeiro, the states Paraíba and Piauí, and the rivers Xingu and Uaupés.

52 Lygia Pape, "Catiti-Catiti, na terra dos Brasis" (master's thesis, Instituto de Filosofia e Ciências Sociais, Universidade Federal do Rio de Janeiro, 1980).

53 Ibid., p. 9.

54 Ibid., p. 4.

55 The title *Ttéia* is a play on the Portuguese word *teia* (web), a reference to the artist's interest in wandering through the city and connecting different points of its urban morphology, and the colloquial Portuguese word *teteia* (a funny person or thing).

56 See Lygia Pape, "Ttéia: Open Area" (June 2, 1979), in *Lygia Pape: Magnetized Space*, pp. 369–70.

Birds of Marvelous Colors Lúcia Carneiro and Ileana Pradilla

1 The complete interview was published in *Lygia Pape: Entrevista a Lúcia Carneiro e Ileana Pradilla* (Rio de Janeiro: Lacerda Editores and Centro de Arte Hélio Oiticica, Secretaria Municipal de Cultura do Rio de Janeiro, 1998).

2 The Museu de Arte Moderna, Rio de Janeiro, was founded in 1948. In 1958, the museum moved to its new location at Aterro do Flamengo.

3 Mário Pedrosa, "Discurso aos Tupiniquins ou Nambás" (written in Paris, October 1975); published in *Versus* (São Paulo), no. 4 (1976), p. 40.

4 On July 8, 1978, a fire destroyed most of the Museu de Arte Moderna's building and permanent collection, including all of the work on display for an exhibition dedicated to the work of Joaquín Torres-García.

5 The term Pape uses here is *parto*, which literally translates as "childbirth."

6 Rodrigo Naves, *A forma difícil: Ensaios sobre arte brasileira* (São Paulo: Editora Atica, 1996).

7 The Coleção Espaço was a limited series, or collection, of art books published by *Suplemento dominical, Jornal do Brasil* (Rio de Janeiro).

8 Frederico Morais, "Neoconcretismo: Cavar novas linguagens" (interview with Lygia Pape), *O globo* (Rio de Janeiro), July 22, 1975.

9 Tarsila's *A negra* is in the collection of the Museu de Arte Contemporânea, Universidade de São Paulo.

An Anticlass in Avant-Gardism Sérgio B. Martins

I would like to thank Luiz Camillo Osorio for our conversations on Pape's work and for granting me access to his research material, and also Kaira Cabañas for her helpful comments on this essay.

1 Antonio Salomone, conversation with the author, Apr. 16, 2016. English translations in this essay are mine, unless otherwise stated.

2 *Lygia Pape: Entrevista a Lúcia Carneiro e Ileana Pradilla* (Rio de Janeiro: Lacerda Editores and Centro de Arte Hélio Oiticica, Secretaria Municipal de Cultura do Rio de Janeiro, 1998), p. 75.

3 Artistic training at UFRJ was deeply anachronistic and remains so, at least in part. In fact, the university absorbed ENBA as its own fine-arts department in 1971.

4 *Lygia Pape: Entrevista a Lúcia Carneiro e Ileana Pradilla*, p. 75.

5 Oiticica insisted on the need to counter cultural and social "conditioning" in various texts from the mid-1960s onward. For a discussion in relation to Pape's work, see Hélio Oiticica, "Appearance of the Supra-Sensorial"/ "Aparecimento do suprasensorial" (Nov.–Dec. 1967), in *Hélio Oiticica*, exh. cat. (1992; Rio de Janeiro: Centro de Arte Hélio Oiticica, 1997), p. 128; originally published as "O aparecimento do suprasensorial na arte brasileira," *GAM* (Rio de Janeiro), no. 13 (1968).

6 See "Gravura: Depoimento de Lygia Pape," in *Lygia Pape: Espaço imantado*, exh. cat. (São Paulo: Pinacoteca do Estado, 2012), p. 85; originally published in *Suplemento dominical, Jornal do Brasil* (Rio de Janeiro; hereafter *SDJB*), Mar. 22, 1959, p. 8.

7 Indeed, the title *Tecelar* was added to the woodcuts only as the 1970s turn to the 1980s and, as Adele Nelson argues, signaled the artist's willingness to project her later exploration of Brazilian Amerindian visual culture onto her previous Concretist production. Adele Nelson, "Sensitive and Nondiscursive Things: Lygia Pape and the Reconception of Printmaking," *Art Journal* 71, no. 3 (Fall 2012), pp. 26–45.

8 Cordel literature is a popular cultural expression of the Brazilian northeast consisting of cheaply printed booklets containing rhymes and stories, which are illustrated by woodcut prints. "Cordel" means "string" and refers to the usual way the booklets are displayed in stalls, hanging from strings.

9 The "Unidade experimental" was jointly created by artists Cildo Meireles, Guilherme Vaz, Luiz Alphonsus, and critic Frederico Morais, and was later institutionalized as the "Sala Experimental" ("Experimental Room"), which

held numerous exhibitions by young artists in the early 1970s. Conceived by Morais, the "Domingos da criação" invited artists and visitors to experiment with a chosen material, such as paper, thread, earth, sound, or the body.

10 Ferreira Gullar authored several articles and short notices for the *SDJB*, especially in 1957. In one notice, Gullar even mentions that Albers corresponded with Lygia and Günther Pape. Ferreira Gullar, "Albers e as bicicletas," *SDJB*, Nov. 3, 1957, p. 9.

11 Rosalind E. Krauss, "Perpetual Inventory," *October* 88 (Spring 1999), p. 88.

12 For Gullar's explanation of Albers's position, see Ferreira Gullar, "A natureza e a arte de Josef Albers," *SDJB*, Nov. 17, 1957, p. 9. For the material emphasis and experimental quality of Albers's woodcutting, see Ferreira Gullar, "Albers e outros," in *Etapas da arte contemporânea: Do cubismo à arte neoconcreta*, 3rd ed. (Rio de Janeiro: Revan, 1999), pp. 227–28; originally published in *SDJB*, July 7, 1960.

13 Susanne K. Langer, *Feeling and Form: A Theory of Art* (New York: Charles Scribner's Sons, 1953), p. 14. Langer was introduced to Gullar by Pedrosa and became, alongside Maurice Merleau-Ponty, one of the theoretical pillars of Neoconcretism. Critic Ronaldo Brito would later use the same laboratory metaphor in his seminal study of the movement. See Ronaldo Brito, *Neoconcretismo: Vértice e ruptura do projeto construtivo brasileiro* (Rio de Janeiro: FUNARTE and Instituto Nacional de Artes Plásticas, 1985), p. 107.

14 Gullar would privilege the breakdown of frame and base as guarantors of the transcendental space of painting and sculpture, but even Clark would question his view and insist instead on the death of the plane as the major historical rupture in this regard. I discuss this topic in Sérgio B. Martins, *Constructing an Avant-Garde: Art in Brazil, 1949–1979* (Cambridge, Mass.: MIT Press, 2013), chap. 1, "(Non-)Objects," pp. 17–48, 200–206.

15 Apropos of the artificial pattern Albers constructed in *Weisser Kreis/White Circle* (1933), see Brenda Danilowitz, *The Prints of Josef Albers: A Catalogue Raisonné, 1915–1976*, rev. ed. (Manchester, Vt.: Hudson Hills Press, 2010), pp. 63–64, no. 60. I thank Paloma Carvalho dos Santos for bringing this particular example to my attention.

16 Lygia Pape, "Debate sobre a gravura: Afirma Lygia Pape, 'Os jovens devem abrir seu próprio caminho,'" *SDJB*, Dec. 15, 1957, p. 3.

17 Pape often discussed the *Tecelares* in terms of light and darkness. See, for example, Lygia Pape, "40 gravuras neoconcretas" (July 17, 1975), in *Lygia Pape: Espaço imantado*, p. 88.

18 Nuno Ramos, "Agouro e libertação," in *Ensaio geral: Projetos, roteiros, ensaios, memória* (São Paulo: Globo, 2007), p. 186; originally published in *O estado de São Paulo*, Oct. 15, 1994.

19 Pape restricted her editions in order to retain strict control of the intensity and contrast of the resulting prints. On her handling of editions, see Nelson, "Sensitive and Nondiscursive Things."

20 See Lygia Pape, "Lygia por Lygia," in Denise Mattar, *Lygia Pape: Intrinsecamente anarquista* (Rio de Janeiro: Relume Dumará, 2003), p. 65.

21 Clark, for one, explicitly equates the square with the metaphysical primacy of the picture plane. See Lygia Clark, "A morte do plano" (1960), in *Lygia Clark* (Rio de Janeiro: FUNARTE, 1980), p. 13.

22 *Ballet neoconcreto I* was initially called *Ballet concreto* and was performed by choreographer Gilberto Motta's newly formed group Ballet Contemporâneo. It was part of a series proposed by Motta based on various artistic movements (there was also a Realist, a Surrealist, and a Neoclassical ballet). To the best of my knowledge, it was first announced in *SDJB* on July 6, 1958. On August 3, the front page of *SDJB* fully disclosed the program and discussed Motta's trajectory next to an article by Reynaldo Jardim on the *Ballet concreto*. After the cancellation of the August 11 event, the ballet was finally staged on August 18.

23 For a suggestive comparative analysis of the antitheatrical strategies of Pape's and Robert Morris's sculptures from the 1960s, see critic Luiz Camillo Osorio's essay "Lygia Pape: Experimentation and Resistance," *Third Text* 20, no. 5 (Sept. 2006), pp. 571–83.

24 Reynaldo Jardim, "Ballet concreto," in *Lygia Pape: Espaço imantado*, p. 165; originally published in *SDJB*, Aug. 3, 1958. A 1954 talk by Schöffer on his

key notion of spatiodynamism was published in *SDJB*. The Neoconcrete ballets clearly share Schöffer's declared aim of promoting "a constructive and dynamic integration of space in the visual artwork," but Pape nevertheless viewed his attempt to integrate cybernetic sculptures with dancers as a failed solution, with the former ultimately remaining a "moving scenery." See Nicolas Schöffer, "O espaciodinamismo," *SDJB*, Oct. 7, 1956, p. 5. See also Lygia Pape, "Ballet: Experiência visual," in *Lygia Pape: Espaço imantado*, p. 162; originally published in *SDJB*, Mar. 22, 1959.

25 The notion of expressive form that informed Neoconcrete discussions is heavily indebted to Mário Pedrosa's work on perception, which privileged, as Kaira Cabañas has demonstrated, a physiognomic rather than formal take on Gestalt theory. See Kaira M. Cabañas, "Learning from Madness: Mário Pedrosa and the Physiognomic Gestalt," *October* 153 (Summer 2015), pp. 42–64.

26 Ferreira Gullar, "Ballet concreto: Arte nova," in *Lygia Pape: Espaço imantado*, pp. 166–67; originally published in *SDJB*, Aug. 31, 1958.

27 Pape, "Ballet: Experiência visual," p. 162. Once again, the similarity with Pape's take on the *Tecelares* is striking: "There should be no void, no background in woodcutting—everything is form"; Lygia Pape, "Novos depoimentos sobre a gravura," *SDJB*, Feb. 2, 1958, p. 2. Indeed, this view of form as an organic whole is typical of Neoconcretism's anti-Gestaltian stance.

28 Hélio Oiticica, "Pape: Ovo"/"Pape: Egg" (Sept. 8, 1973), in *Lygia Pape: Gávea de Tocaia* (São Paulo: Cosac & Naify, 2000), pp. 300–303.

29 For an account in English on art and architecture that addresses the problems of public space in 1960s Brazil, see Guilherme Wisnik, "Public Space on the Run: Brazilian Art and Architecture at the End of the 1960s," *Third Text* 26, no. 1 (Jan. 2012), pp. 117–29. Unlike Clark and Oiticica, Pape remained in Brazil throughout the dictatorship (1964–85). In the 1970s, she was imprisoned and tortured for hiding a young clandestine militant from police persecution. On this topic, see Pape, "Lygia por Lygia," pp. 79–82.

30 Oiticica, "Pape: Ovo"/"Pape: Egg," pp. 300–303. The Portuguese word for "shelter" (*abrigo*) is already used by Oiticica in his 1964 essay "Anotações sobre o 'Parangolé'" (see Hélio Oiticica, "Notes on the Parangolé"/"Anotações sobre o Parangolé," in *Hélio Oiticica*, pp. 93, 96; Oiticica distributed copies of this essay at the exhibition "Opinião 65," held at the MAM-RJ in 1965), but it gains a more forceful valence after his encounter with "Gimme Shelter," when he starts to use the word in English while considering the song's tragic content. I discuss his relationship with rock extensively in Sérgio B. Martins, "Hendrix Unbound: Hélio Oiticica's Tragic Take on Rock," in *Hélio Oiticica: To Organize Delirium*, exh. cat. (Pittsburgh: Carnegie Museum of Art; Munich: DelMonico Books/Prestel, 2016), pp. 211–22.

31 On this introspective tendency, especially in Oiticica and Clark, see Nuno Ramos, "À espera de um sol interno," in *Ensaio geral*, pp. 119–44; originally published in *Jornal do Brasil*, July 28, 2001.

32 See Herbert Marcuse, *Eros and Civilization: A Philosophical Inquiry into Freud* (Boston: Beacon Press, 1955), especially pp. 11–19. Pape began her intervention at the roundtable "Amostragem da cultura-loucura brasileira," organized by Oiticica and Rogério Duarte and held on June 10, 1968, at MAM-RJ, by drawing from *Eros and Civilization*. See Lygia Pape, "Da loucura e da cultura" (June 10, 1968), in *Lygia Pape: Espaço imantado*, p. 241.

33 Former members of the Neoconcrete group, especially Hélio Oiticica and Lygia Clark, often referred to their participatory works as propositions rather than performances. In his essay "Pape: Ovo"/"Pape: Egg" (see note 28), Oiticica equally refers to *O ovo* as a proposition, although he also uses the term "performance" in various moments; the latter is meant not so much as an artistic genre as in the sense it appears in his discussions of rock performances, which he admired for their cathartic power and tragic ethos.

34 Marcuse, *Eros and Civilization*, p. 16.

35 For Ronaldo Brito, the very existence of a largely apolitical constructive movement in Neoconcretism was contradictory from the outset; see Brito, *Neoconcretismo*. Indeed, Oiticica's inclusion of collectivity and politics as major concerns of the "Nova objetividade brasileira" exhibition in 1967, at MAM-RJ, is, to a great extent, a response to Gullar's (self-)criticism of avant-gardist alienation in his book *Cultura posta em questão* (1965). My point is that Marcuse seemed to offer a way out of this historical shortcoming.

36 For my full discussion of this topic, see Martins, *Constructing an Avant-Garde*, chap. 2, "The Constructive," pp. 51–78, 206–13.

37 For a feminist reading of Pape, see Roberta Barros, *Elogio ao toque; ou, Como falar de arte feminista à brasileira* (Rio de Janeiro: Relacionarte, 2016), chap. 2, "Dieta de imagens," pp. 102–70, especially pp. 121–25.

38 Film would subsequently remain an integral part of Pape's work even after she resumed her artistic career; in the late 1960s and 1970s, she would engage in Super 8 filming, which allowed for a great degree of mobility and individual control over the final results. Indeed, she would take part in some of the events that marked the reception of the Super 8 format in Brazil, such as "Expo-Projeção 73," in 1973.

39 Take, for example, the film and photographs Pape made at Favela da Maré, where she took her architecture students. Today such excursions risk registering either as a cliché or worse, as primitivistic forays, but Pape's interest rested on probing the clash of different spatial orders, in order to wrest her students from the formalist strictness of their discipline. Further, the peculiar relationship between the *palafita* (stilt house) constructions and the tides at Favela da Maré pointed precisely to the kind of organic spatiality that Pape pursued throughout her career and would further elaborate in her citywide *Ttéia: Área aberta* proposition. See Lygia Pape, "Favela da Maré ou milagre das palafitas" (1972) and "Ttéia: Área aberta" (June 2, 1979), in *Lygia Pape: Espaço imantado*, pp. 287–89 and 369–70.

Lygia Pape's Vital Ideas John Rajchman

1 Mário Pedrosa, "Lygia Pape" (1979), in *Mário Pedrosa: Primary Documents*, ed. Glória Ferreira and Paulo Herkenhoff, trans. Stephen Berg (New York: Museum of Modern Art, 2015), pp. 335–36; published in *Lygia Pape* (Rio de Janeiro: FUNARTE, 1983).

2 See Hélio Oiticica, "Tropicália Time Series 2: Lygia Pape" (London and Paris, May 1969), in *Lygia Pape: Magnetized Space*, exh. cat. (2011; Madrid: Museo Nacional Centro de Arte Reina Sofía; Zurich: JRP Ringier, 2014), pp. 245–47; see also Guy Brett, "A Permanently Open Seed," in *Lygia Pape: Magnetized Space*, pp. 255–67.

3 Lygia Pape, "Catiti-Catiti, na terra dos Brasis" (master's thesis, Instituto de Filosofia e Ciências Sociais, Universidade Federal do Rio de Janeiro, 1980). "Catiti Catiti" means "new moon" in Tupinambá. I would like to thank Lexie Cook, Columbia University, for her help in translating and discussing the thesis.

4 Lygia Pape, "What I Do Not Know," in *Lygia Pape: Magnetized Space*, pp. 190–92; originally published as "O que eu não sei," *Item* (Rio de Janeiro), no. 1 (June 1995), pp. 17–19.

5 Pedrosa, "Lygia Pape," pp. 335–36.

6 Pape, "What I Do Not Know," p. 191.

7 Mário Pedrosa, "Klee and the Present," in Ferreira and Herkenhoff, *Mário Pedrosa: Primary Documents*, pp. 310–11; originally published as "Klee e a atualidade," *Jornal do Brasil* (Rio de Janeiro), Mar. 5, 1961. In 1902, Klee wrote in his diary: "I want to be as though new-born, knowing nothing, absolutely nothing about Europe . . . to know nothing, to be completely without sophistication, virtually at the origin." In this Pedrosa found the formula for "every true artist of our time." In particular, in the way "Klee's signs function as a team, dancing about like elements of a ballet," Pedrosa realized something akin to "Sino-Japanese calligraphy," rather as did Henri Michaux at the time. See Pedrosa, "Klee and the Present," pp. 310–11. On the key role Klee played in Pedrosa's revised history of art, see Adele Nelson, "Radical and Inclusive: Mário Pedrosa's Modernism," in Ferreira and Herkenhoff, *Mário Pedrosa: Primary Documents*, pp. 35–43.

8 Pedrosa's pessimism is captured in the series of interviews, including one with Pape, that he gave upon his return from exile, first in Chile then in Paris, collected in the section "A Singular Socialist" in Ferreira and Herkenhoff, *Mário Pedrosa: Primary Documents*, pp. 375–402. Pedrosa had already used the term "postmodernism" in relation to the new challenge Pop Art posed to modernist painting. But his pessimistic essays in Rio de Janeiro came at the same time the category of postmodernism took off up North and may now be read as diagnosing some of the same forces.

9 See Maurice Merleau-Ponty, *The Visible and the Invisible; Followed by Working Notes*, ed. Claude Lefort, trans. Alphonso Lingis (1964; Evanston, Ill.: Northwestern University Press, 1968).

10 "Experimental exercise of freedom" is perhaps now the best-known epithet for the Neoconcretist artists. The striking phrase comes from a conversation Pedrosa had with Antonio Manuel, whose scandalous nude performance *O corpo é a obra* (*The Body Is the Work*) at the Museu de Arte Moderna, Rio de Janeiro, in 1970 led the artist to repair to Pedrosa's house, where he carried on a conversation later published, transcribed, and edited by Lygia Pape. See "Antonio Manuel: On Antonio Manuel's Presentation at the Opening of the Salão Nacional de Arte Moderna, as a Work of Art," in Ferreira and Herkenhoff, *Mário Pedrosa: Primary Documents*, pp. 325–27 (with accompanying photograph of the piece); originally published as "Antonio Manuel: Sobre a apresentação de Antonio Manuel na abertura do Salão Nacional de Arte Moderna, coma obra de arte; conversa entre Mário Pedrosa, Antonio Manuel, Alex Varela e Hugo Denizart, 1970," in "Exposição de Antonio Manuel (de zero às 24 horas nas bancas de jornais)," *O jornal*, suppl., *Tema* (Rio de Janeiro), July 15, 1973.

11 Pierre Boulez, *Boulez on Music Today*, trans. Susan Bradshaw and Richard Rodney Bennett (1963; Cambridge, Mass.: Harvard University Press, 1971), pp. 83–98. For a study of visual implications of the idea, remarkably close to Pape's own preoccupations at the time, see Henri Maldiney, "Esthétique des rythmes" (1967), in *Regard, parole, espace* (1973; Lausanne: L'Âge d'Homme, 1994), pp. 142–72. Boulez develops this idea further in a beautiful series of lectures on Klee, brought together in *Le pays fertile: Paul Klee* (Paris: Gallimard, 1989).

12 See Gilles Deleuze, "Occupy without Counting: Boulez, Proust and Time" (1986), in *Two Regimes of Madness: Texts and Interviews, 1975–1995*, ed. David Lapoujade, trans. Ames Hodges and Mike Taormina (Los Angeles: Semiotext(e), 2006), pp. 292–99. The contrast is with "counting in order to occupy," as, for example, with the "machine eye" of the Grupo Ruptura.

13 See Pape's own description in "Favela da Maré or Miracle on Stilts" (1972), in *Lygia Pape: Magnetized Space*, p. 287: "Maré differs from other shantytowns because it looks like a living organism, possibly because it merges with the ocean." See also Gilles Deleuze and Félix Guattari, *A Thousand Plateaus: Capitalism and Schizophrenia*, trans. Brian Massumi (1980; Minneapolis: University of Minnesota Press, 1987), pp. 474–500. The maritime model of the two spaces includes a striking reference to shantytowns that is very close in many ways to Pape's documentary work on Favela da Maré; see pp. 480–82.

14 On the role of print in Pape's work, see Adele Nelson, "Sensitive and Nondiscursive Things: Lygia Pape and the Reconception of Printmaking," *Art Journal* 71, no. 3 (Fall 2012), pp. 26–45; and Sérgio B. Martins's essay in this volume.

15 Paulo Herkenhoff evokes this larger international context of woodcuts in "Lygia Pape: The Art of Passage," in *Lygia Pape: Magnetized Space*, pp. 26–36. An important source for woodcuts in Asia was the collection and influence of Lu Xun. The medium was later taken up in Korea and other Asian countries, as well as in China, where it would assume new forms. For an account of this influence in contemporary Chinese art, see *Woodcuts in Modern China, 1937–2008: Towards a Universal Pictorial Language*, ed. Joachim Homann, with an interview with Xu Bing, exh. cat. (Hamilton, N.Y.: Picker Art Gallery, Colgate University, 2009). For Pedrosa's essay on Kollwitz, see Mário Pedrosa, "The Social Tendencies of Art and Käthe Kollwitz," in Ferreira and Herkenhoff, *Mário Pedrosa: Primary Documents*, pp. 233–40; excerpted from the work originally published as "As tendências sociais da arte e Käthe Kollwitz," *O homem livre* (São Paulo), nos. 6–9 (July 2, 8, 17, and 14, 1933).

16 Mário Pedrosa, "Crisis of Poetry: Art and Communication," in Ferreira and Herkenhoff, *Mário Pedrosa: Primary Documents*, p. 124; originally published as "Crise de arte-poesia e comunicação," *Correio da manhã* (Rio de Janeiro), Feb. 26, 1967. See Pape's own telling early account in "Poems-Invention," in *Lygia Pape: Magnetized Space*, pp. 178–79; originally published as "Poemas-invenção," *Suplemento dominical, Jornal do Brasil* (Rio de Janeiro), Nov. 26, 1960.

17 "Verbivocovisual" is a term taken from James Joyce, adopted and developed by the de Campos brothers Augusto and Haroldo within the Concrete poetry movement in Brazil, pursued in Rio by Gullar in the manner described by Pedrosa in "Crisis of Poetry," pp. 123–24. See also the 1958 Concrete poetry manifesto written by Augusto de Campos, Décio Pignatari, and Haroldo de Campos, "Plano-pilôto para poesia concreta"/"Pilot Plan for Concrete Poetry,"

in *Concrete Poetry: A World View*, ed. Mary Ellen Solt (Bloomington: Indiana University Press, 1969), pp. 70–72; originally published in *Noigrandes* 4 (1958). In Canada, Marshall McLuhan also used the phrase as a title for a book of essays around the same time. We can now see the idea as part of the larger international legacy of Mallarmé in the visual arts surrounding the questions of text, image, and book. See, for example, Rosalind E. Krauss, "The Motivation of the Sign" (1992), in *Perpetual Inventory* (Cambridge, Mass.: MIT Press, 2010), pp. 229–56.

18   *Aberto fechado: Caixa e livro na arte brasileira / The Enclosed Openness: Box and Book in Brazilian Art*, ed. Guy Brett, exh. cat. (São Paulo: Pinacoteca do Estado, 2012).

19   For a suggestive recent discussion of Pape's relation to Malevich, see Briony Fer, "Abstraction at War with Itself," in *Adventures of the Black Square: Abstract Art and Society, 1915–2015*, ed. Iwona Blazwick, exh. cat. (Munich: Prestel; London: Whitechapel Gallery, 2015), p. 230.

20   In 1959, citing Peking opera and Oskar Schlemmer as predecessors, Pape talks of a "cybernetic monster that was able to move but was still in need of the aid of a human figure." In contrast, the dancers in a "Neo-Concrete ballet" were meant to figure as invisible activating agents within a singular technical assemblage, which, in contrast with any robotic or mechanical operation, would introduce a vital rhythm. In such a "Concrete ballet," Reynaldo Jardim saw the possibility of a new "leftist position" in art, beyond "the lyrical and outmoded leftism of Socialist Realism." See Lygia Pape, "Ballet: A Visual Experience," in *Lygia Pape: Magnetized Space*, pp. 162–63 (originally published as "Ballet: Experiência visual," *Suplemento dominical, Jornal do Brasil*, Mar. 22, 1959); Reynaldo Jardim, "Concrete Ballet," in *Lygia Pape: Magnetized Space*, p. 164 (originally published as "Ballet concreto," *Suplemento dominical, Jornal do Brasil*, Aug. 3, 1958).

21   See *Tropicália: A Revolution in Brazilian Culture (1967–1972)*, ed. Carlos Basualdo, exh. cat., Museum of Contemporary Art, Chicago, and other institutions (São Paulo: Cosac & Naify, 2005).

22   Lygia Pape, "Cinema Marginal" (n.d.), in *Lygia Pape: Magnetized Space*, pp. 326–29.

23   Gilles Deleuze, *Cinema*, vol. 2, *The Time-Image*, trans. Hugh Tomlinson and Robert Galeta (1985; Minneapolis: University of Minnesota, 1989), pp. 215–24. Deleuze was interested in the role of the Third World and minorities in postwar cinema; see Deleuze, *Time-Image*, p. 217. The Revolutionary film of Eisenstein, with its dialectical editing and striking close-ups, was instead an attempt to make the masses conscious, supposing their movement to be already given, or, in other words, that the people are already there. After Stalinism, after Hitlerism, the presupposition of such a mass subject was no longer possible. In Kafka's remark in the Bauhaus that the people are missing, or in Kafka's appeal in Prague to a creative minority within German literature, Deleuze found another model, prior to the stable divisions between private/public, which would be developed in postwar cinema and in one way by Glauber Rocha; see Deleuze, *Time-Image*, p. 218. For an elaboration of the idea that the people are missing in Rocha's cinema, see James Phillips, "Glauber Rocha: Hunger and Garbage," in *Cinematic Thinking: Philosophical Approaches to the New Cinema*, ed. James Phillips (Stanford, Calif.: Stanford University Press, 2008), pp. 90–108, 181–83.

24   Oswald de Andrade, "Manifesto antropófago," *Revista de antropofagia* (São Paulo), no. 1 (May 1928), pp. 3, 7. In Márcio Doctors, "The Art of Seeing through the Cracks," Pape insists that there is "no tinge of folklore or nationalism" in her attitude, and Doctors asserts that she "does not hide behind the mask of exoticism, and she refuses to play the world's subtle cultural-policy games of domination." Quoted in *Lygia Pape: Magnetized Space*, p. 373; originally published as "A arte de ver pelas frestas," *O globo* (Rio de Janeiro), Feb. 7, 1988, p. 3.

25   See Lygia Pape, "Magnetized Spaces" (n.d.), in *Lygia Pape: Magnetized Space*, p. 285: "It was as if we now enjoyed an aerial view of the city that was like an enormous cobweb, a huge entanglement." The idea of spider webbing leading to magnetized space is also discussed in 1979 in terms of those "threshold situations in which special poetic things are happening." Pape continued, "TEIAR [to web or weave] is the new principle of moving upward or downward, to and fro, not restricted to a single point of view. . . . This new appreciation of space and objects . . . has so far been the privilege of birds alone." Lygia Pape, "Ttéia: Open Area" (June 2, 1979), in *Lygia Pape: Magnetized Space*, pp. 369–70.

26   For further discussion of the *Ttéias* and an explanation of the term, see Iria Candela's essay in this volume.

Irreverence and Marginality Glória Ferreira

1   Lygia Pape, "Lygia por Lygia," in Denise Mattar, *Lygia Pape: Intrinsecamente anarquista* (Rio de Janeiro: Relume Dumará, 2003), p. 100; statement originally made during an interview with Lygia Pape by Adolfo Montejo Navas published in the electronic journal *no.com*, Nov. 20, 2000.

2   Lygia Pape, "Cinema marginal" (n.d.), in *Lygia Pape: Espaço imantado*, exh. cat. (São Paulo: Pinacoteca do Estado, 2012), p. 326.

3   Lygia Pape, "Depoimento: Da 'Expo-Projeção 73,'" in *Som, audio-visual, Super 8, 16mm*, ed. Aracy Amaral, exh. cat., Espaço GRIFE, São Paulo (São Paulo: Centro de Artes Novo Mundo, 1973), n.p.

4   Lygia Pape, "Superoito" (June 2, 1975), in *Lygia Pape: Espaço imantado*, p. 319.

5   Roberto Schwarz, "Cultura e política, 1964–1969" (Oct. 1969–Feb. 1970), in *O pai de família e outros estudos* (Rio de Janeiro: Paz e Terra, 1978), pp. 61–92 (quotation on p. 62); originally published as "Remarques sur la culture et la politique de Brésil, 1964–1969," *Les temps modernes* 27, no. 288 (July 1970), pp. 37–73, when the author was living in exile.

6   *Lygia Pape: Entrevista a Lúcia Carneiro e Ileana Pradilla* (Rio de Janeiro: Lacerda Editores and Centro de Arte Hélio Oiticica, Secretaria Municipal de Cultura do Rio de Janeiro, 1998), p. 48.

7   Lygia Pape, "Morar na cor," *Arquitetura revista* (Faculdade de Arquitetura e Urbanismo, Universidade Federal do Rio de Janeiro) 6 (1986), p. 29. See also Roberto Conduru, *Arte afro-brasileira* (Belo Horizonte: C/Arte, 2007), pp. 82–83.

8   Lygia Pape, in Márcio Doctors, "A arte de ver pelas frestas," in *Lygia Pape: Espaço imantado*, p. 373; originally published in *O globo* (Rio de Janeiro), Feb. 7, 1988, p. 3.

9   Ivana Bentes, "Caos-construção: O formal e o sensorial no cinema de Lygia Pape," in *Lygia Pape: Espaço imantado*, p. 335.

10   Oswald de Andrade, "Manifesto antropófago," *Revista de antropofagia* (São Paulo), no. 1 (May 1928), p. 3.

11   See Gilberto Freyre, *Casa-grande & senzala* (1933; Rio de Janeiro: Record, 2000).

12   Mário Pedrosa, "Arte dos Caduceus, arte negra, artistas de hoje," in *Mundo, homem, arte em crise*, ed. Aracy Amaral (São Paulo: Perspectiva, 1975), p. 225; originally published in *Correio da manhã* (Rio de Janeiro), Jan. 14, 1968.

13   Lygia Pape, in Mattar, *Lygia Pape: Intrinsecamente anarquista*, pp. 43–44.

14   *Lygia Pape: Entrevista a Lúcia Carneiro e Ileana Pradilla*, p. 19.

15   Paula Pape, in conversation with the author.

16   Pape, "Cinema marginal," p. 329.

17   Bentes, "Caos-construção," p. 341.

18   Regina Cornwell, "Le cinéma structural: Dix ans plus tard," *Parachute*, no. 19 (Summer 1980), p. 42.

19   Pape, "Cinema marginal," p. 328; English translation in *Lygia Pape: Magnetized Space*, exh. cat. (2011; Madrid: Museo Nacional Centro de Arte Reina Sofía; Zurich: JRP Ringier, 2014), p. 328.

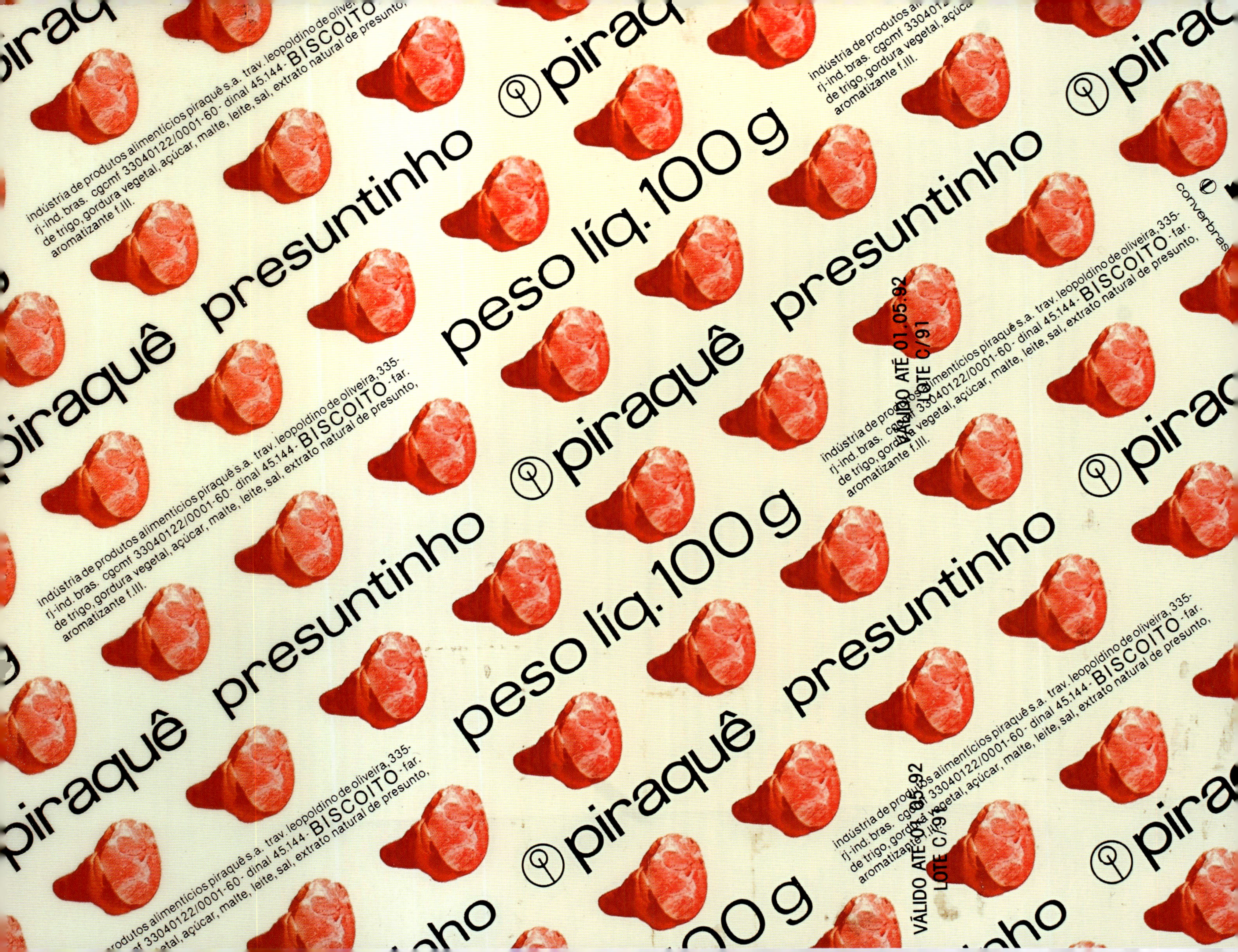

piraquê
presuntinho
peso líq. 100 g
piraquê
BISCOITO
indústria de produtos alimentícios piraquê s.a. trav. leopoldino de oliveira, 335· rj·ind. bras. cgcmf 33040122/0001·60· dinal 45.144· far· de trigo, gordura vegetal, açúcar, malte, leite, sal, extrato natural de presunto, aromatizante f.lll.
VÁLIDO ATÉ 01.05.92
LOTE C/91
convérbras

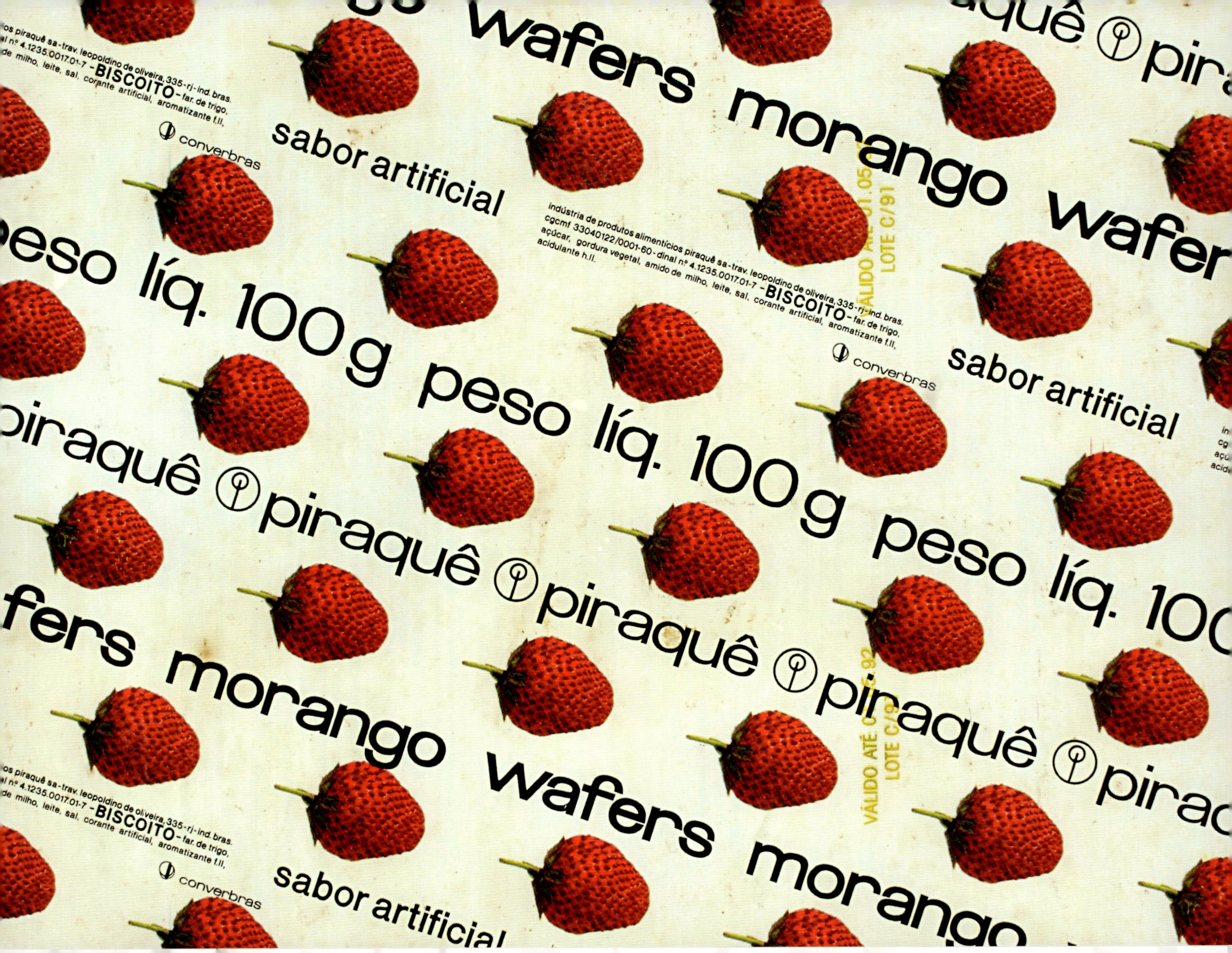
wafers morango
piraquê
peso líq. 100 g
sabor artificial
BISCOITO
converbras
VÁLIDO ATÉ 01.05.92
LOTE C/91
indústria de produtos alimentícios piraquê sa-trav. leopoldino de oliveira 335-ri-ind bras
cgcmf 33.04.027/0001-60 - cimaf, n° 4.1235.00170-7 - BISCOITO - far. de trigo,
açúcar, gordura vegetal, amido de milho, leite, sal, corante artificial, aromatizante t.il.

This catalogue is published in conjunction with "Lygia Pape: A Multitude of Forms," on view at The Metropolitan Museum of Art, New York, from March 21 through July 23, 2017.

The exhibition is made possible by The Daniel and Estrellita Brodsky Foundation and The Garcia Family Foundation.

It is organized by The Metropolitan Museum of Art in collaboration with Projeto Lygia Pape.

Published by The Metropolitan Museum of Art, New York
Mark Polizzotti, Publisher and Editor in Chief
Gwen Roginsky, Associate Publisher and General Manager of Publications
Peter Antony, Chief Production Manager
Michael Sittenfeld, Senior Managing Editor

Edited by Anne Rebecca Blood with Frances Malcolm
Designed by Catherine Mills
Production by Peter Antony and Lauren Knighton
Bibliography edited by Jayne Kuchna
Image acquisitions and permissions by Elizabeth De Mase and Crystal Dombrow
Translations from Portuguese by Stephen Anthony Berg;
from Spanish by Philip Sutton

Photographs of works in The Metropolitan Museum of Art's collection are by the Imaging Department, The Metropolitan Museum of Art, unless otherwise noted.

Additional photography credits appear on page 193.

"Birds of Marvelous Colors" is excerpted and translated from the original Portuguese *Lygia Pape: Entrevista a Lúcia Carneiro e Ileana Pradilla*
Copyright © 1998 by Ileana Pradilla Cerón and Maria Lúcia Boardman Carneiro

Typeset in Benton Gothic and Interstate Bold
Printed on 150 gsm Perigord
Separations by Professional Graphics, Inc., Rockford, Illinois
Printed by Brizzolis, Madrid
Bound by Ramos, Madrid
Printing and binding coordinated by Ediciones El Viso, S.A., Madrid

Jacket illustration: Detail of *Livro do tempo* (*Book of Time*), 1961–63, pl. 75
Cover illustration: *Drawing*, 1960, pl. 57
Frontispiece, page II: Lygia Pape with *Divisor*, 1980s
Frontispiece, page IV: Detail of *Roda dos prazeres*, 1967, pl. 91
Page 25: Detail of *Ttéia 1, C*, 1976–2004, pl. 122
Page 33: Detail of *Tecelar*, 1960, pl. 51
Page 41: Detail of *Drawing*, 1961, pl. 56
Pages 185, 188: Product packaging for Piraquê, ca. 1970

The Metropolitan Museum of Art endeavors to respect copyright in a manner consistent with its nonprofit educational mission. If you believe any material has been included in this publication improperly, please contact the Publications and Editorial Department.

The Metropolitan Museum of Art
1000 Fifth Avenue
New York, New York 10028
metmuseum.org

Distributed by
Yale University Press, New Haven and London
yalebooks.com/art
yalebooks.co.uk

Cataloguing-in-Publication Data is available from the Library of Congress.
ISBN 978-1-58839-616-7